YOTSUBA&!

3

KIYOHIKO AZUMA

CONTENTS

YOTSUBA&!
KIYOHIKO AZUMA

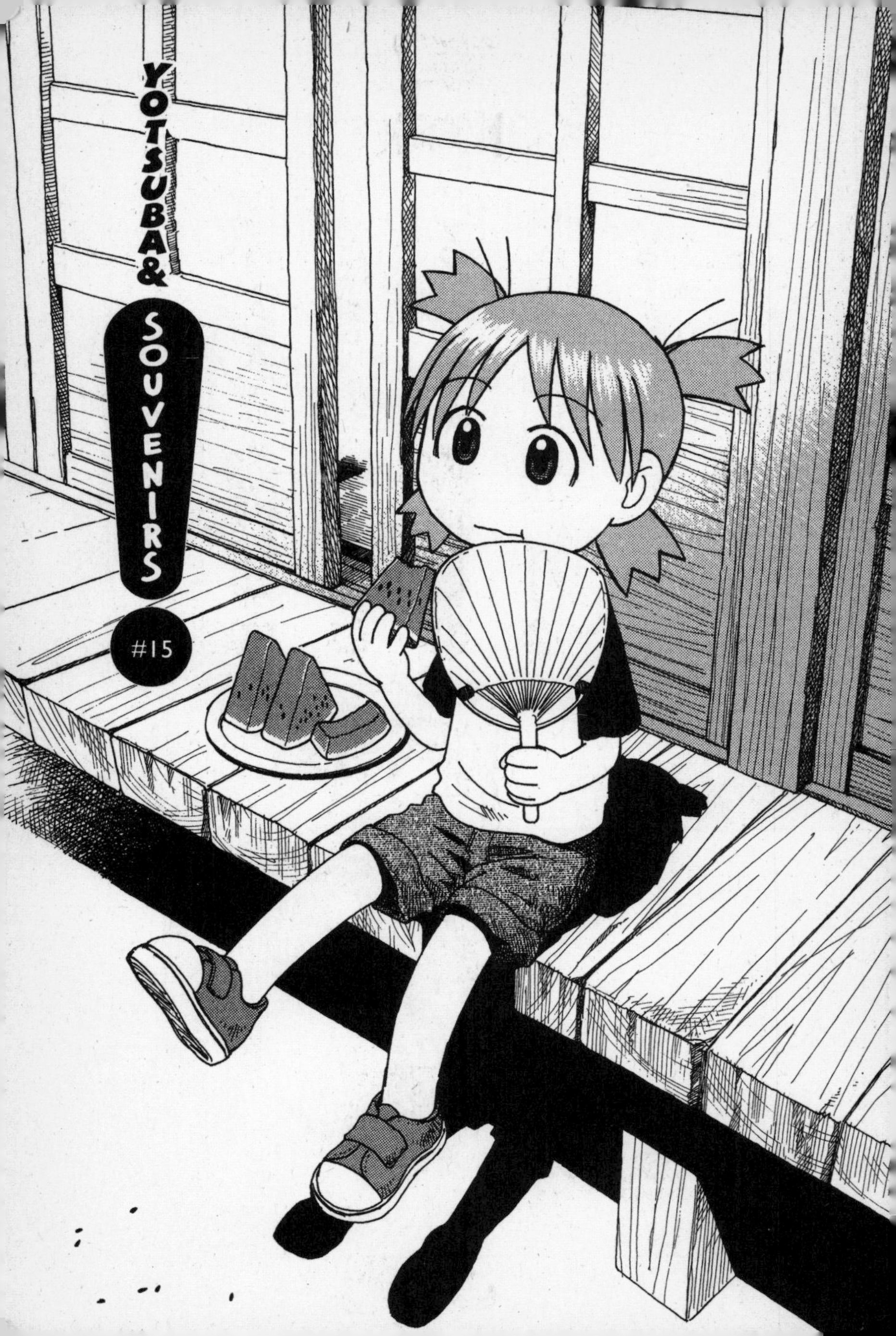
YOTSUBA&
SOUVENIRS
#15

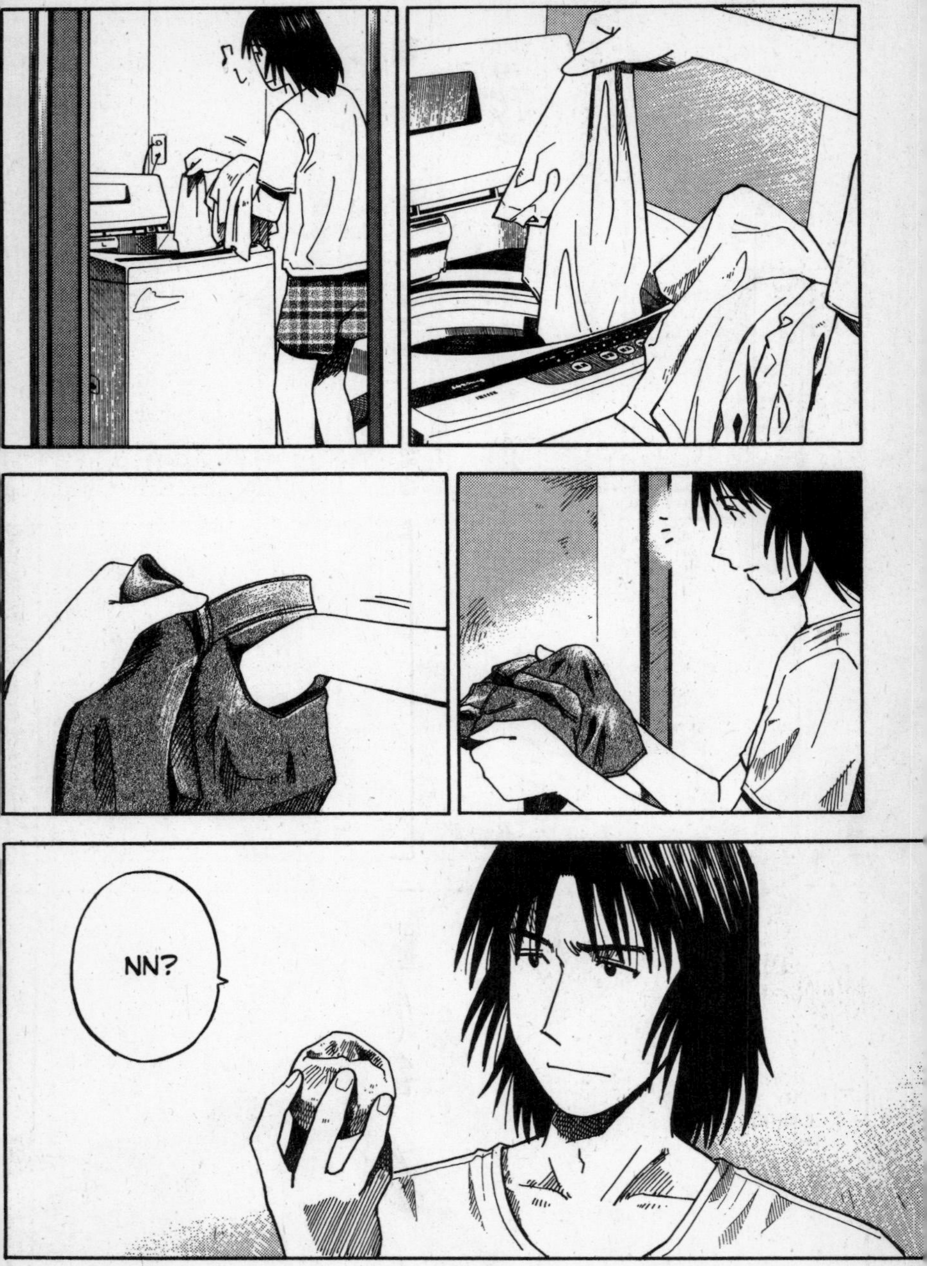
NN?

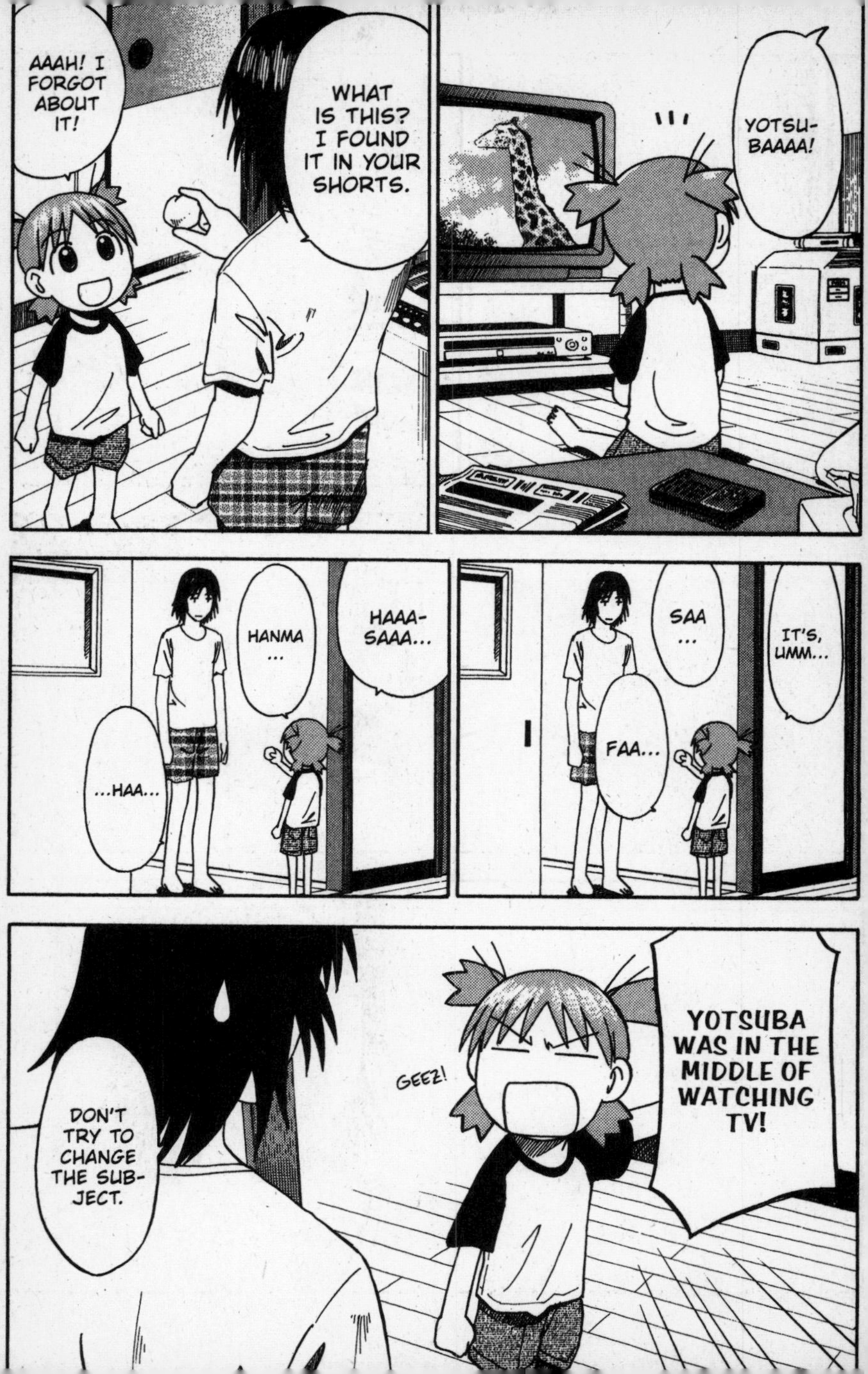
YOTSU-BAAAA!
WHAT IS THIS? I FOUND IT IN YOUR SHORTS.
AAAH! I FORGOT ABOUT IT!
IT'S, UMM...
SAA ...
FAA...
HAAA-SAAA...
HANMA ...
...HAA...
YOTSUBA WAS IN THE MIDDLE OF WATCHING TV!
GEEZ!
DON'T TRY TO CHANGE THE SUBJECT.

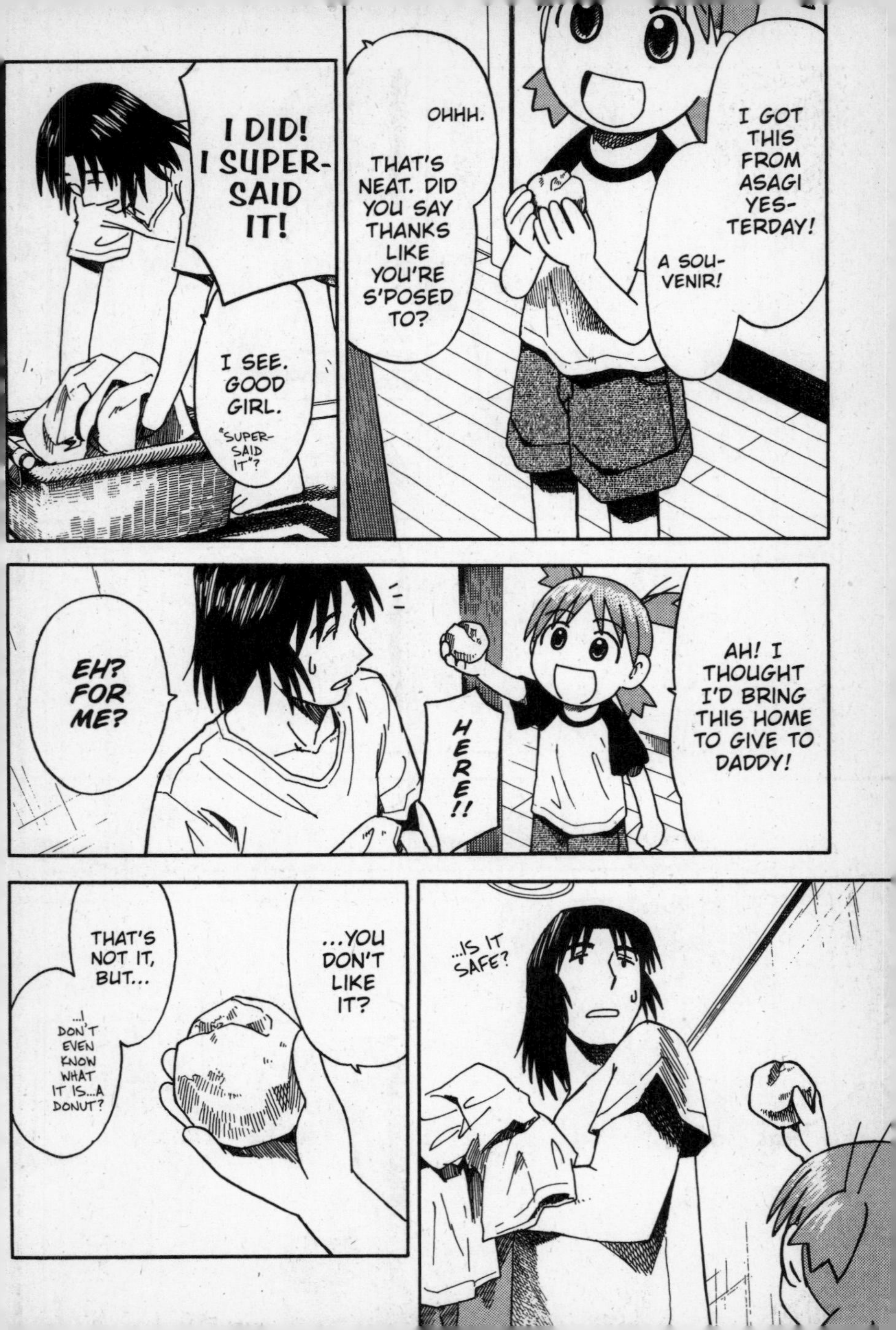
I GOT THIS FROM ASAGI YESTERDAY!
A SOUVENIR!
OHHH.
THAT'S NEAT. DID YOU SAY THANKS LIKE YOU'RE S'POSED TO?
I DID! I SUPER-SAID IT!
I SEE. GOOD GIRL.
"SUPER-SAID IT"?
AH! I THOUGHT I'D BRING THIS HOME TO GIVE TO DADDY!
HERE!!
EH? FOR ME?
...IS IT SAFE?
...YOU DON'T LIKE IT?
THAT'S NOT IT, BUT...
...I DON'T EVEN KNOW WHAT IT IS...A DONUT?

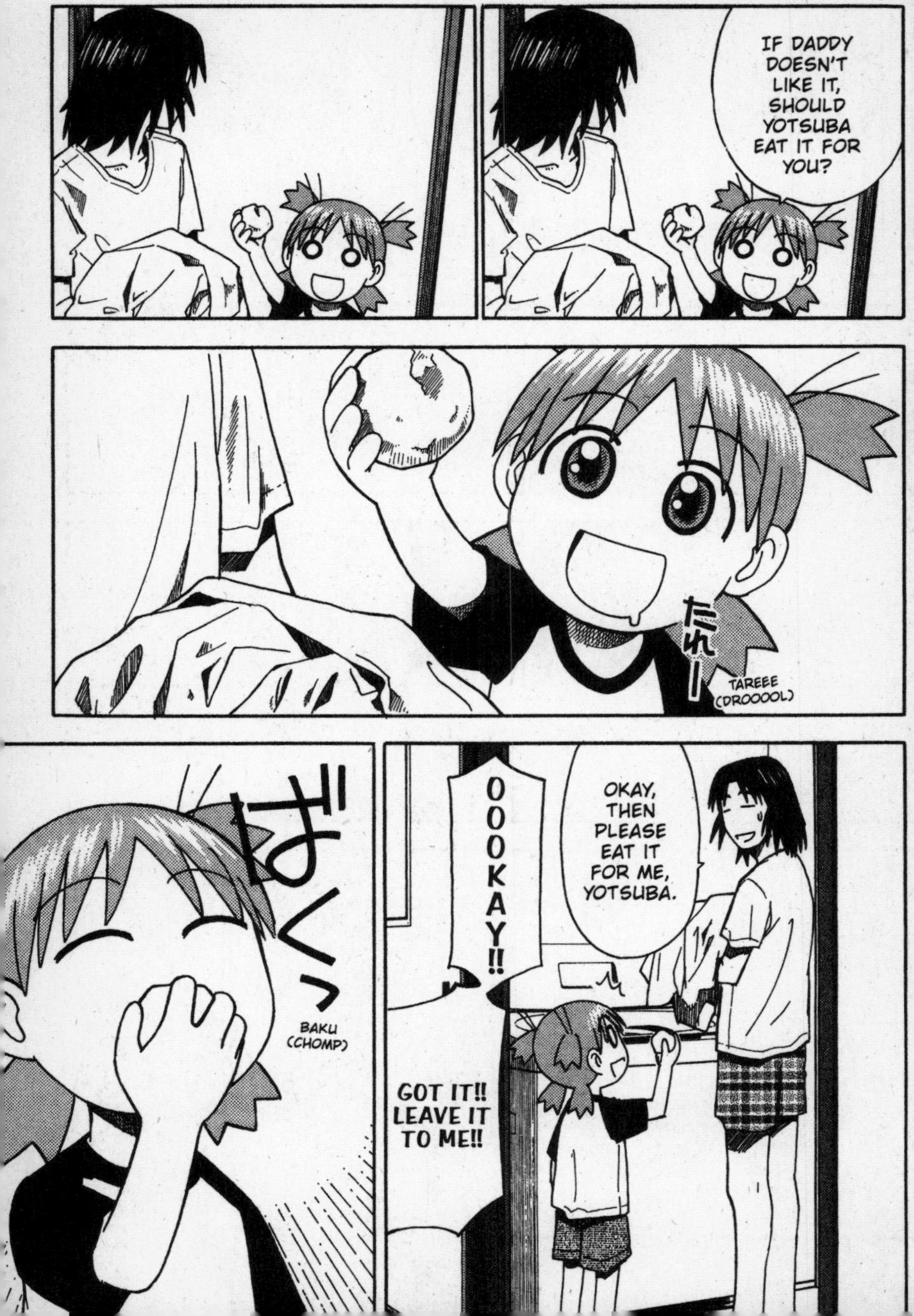
IF DADDY DOESN'T LIKE IT, SHOULD YOTSUBA EAT IT FOR YOU?
たれー
TAREEE (DROOOOL)
OKAY, THEN PLEASE EAT IT FOR ME, YOTSUBA.
OOOOKAY!!
GOT IT!! LEAVE IT TO ME!!
ばくっ
BAKU (CHOMP)

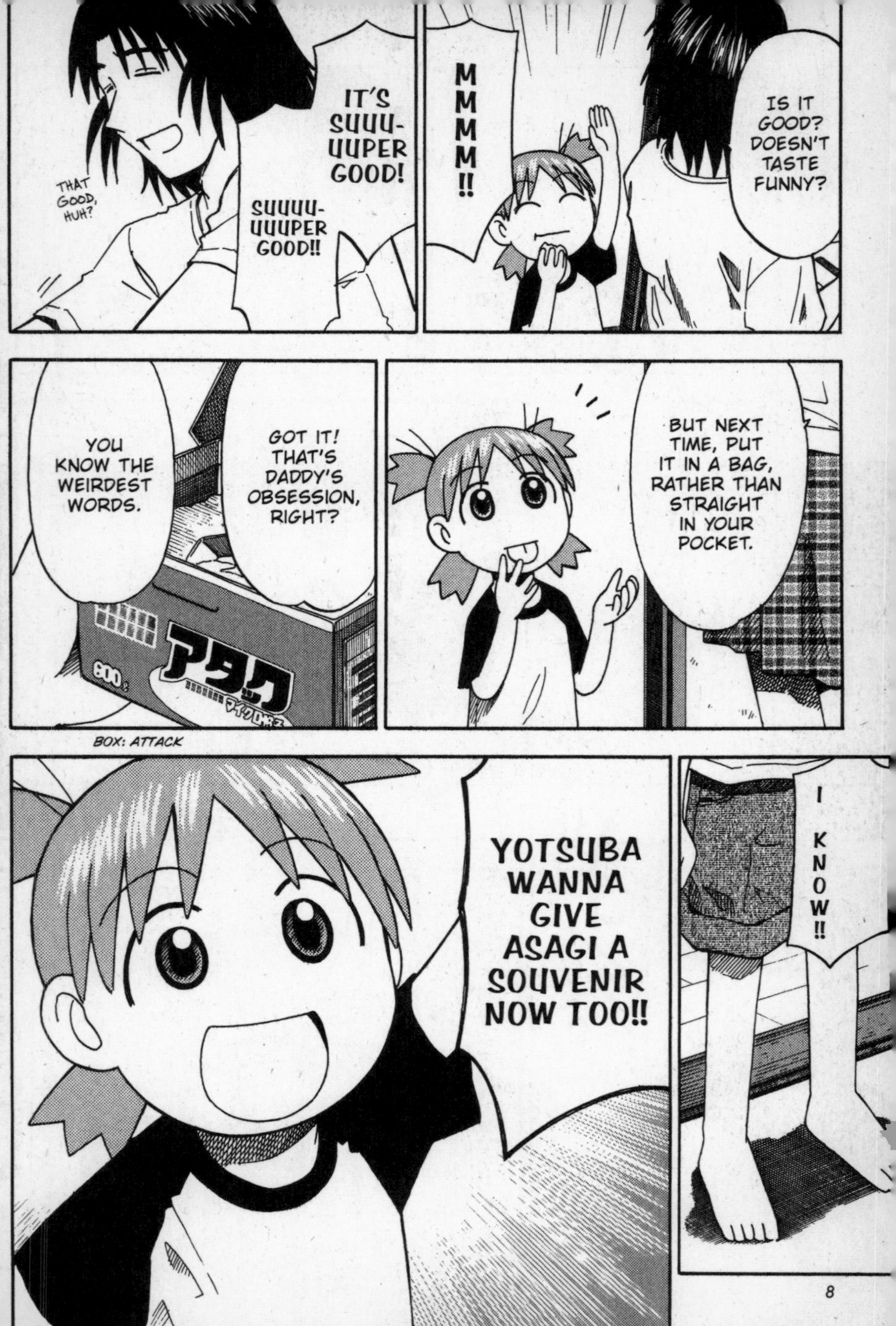
IS IT GOOD? DOESN'T TASTE FUNNY?
MMMM!!
IT'S SUUU-UUPER GOOD!
SUUUU-UUUPER GOOD!!
THAT GOOD, HUH?
BUT NEXT TIME, PUT IT IN A BAG, RATHER THAN STRAIGHT IN YOUR POCKET.
GOT IT! THAT'S DADDY'S OBSESSION, RIGHT?
YOU KNOW THE WEIRDEST WORDS.
アタック
BOX: ATTACK
I KNOW!!
YOTSUBA WANNA GIVE ASAGI A SOUVENIR NOW TOO!!

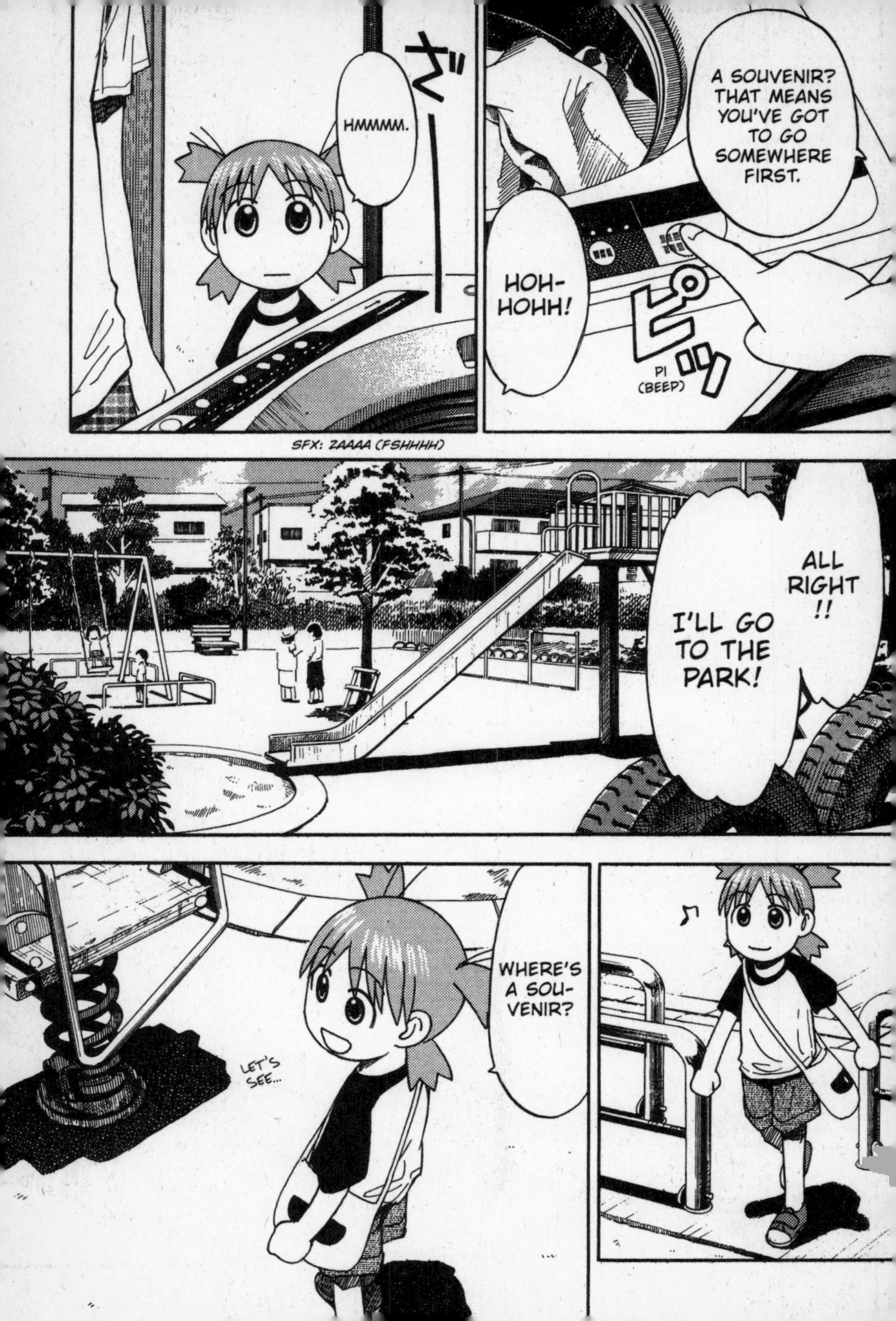
A SOUVENIR? THAT MEANS YOU'VE GOT TO GO SOMEWHERE FIRST.
HOH-HOHH!
PI (BEEP)
HMMMM.
SFX: ZAAAA (FSHHHH)
ALL RIGHT!!
I'LL GO TO THE PARK!
WHERE'S A SOU-VENIR?
LET'S SEE...

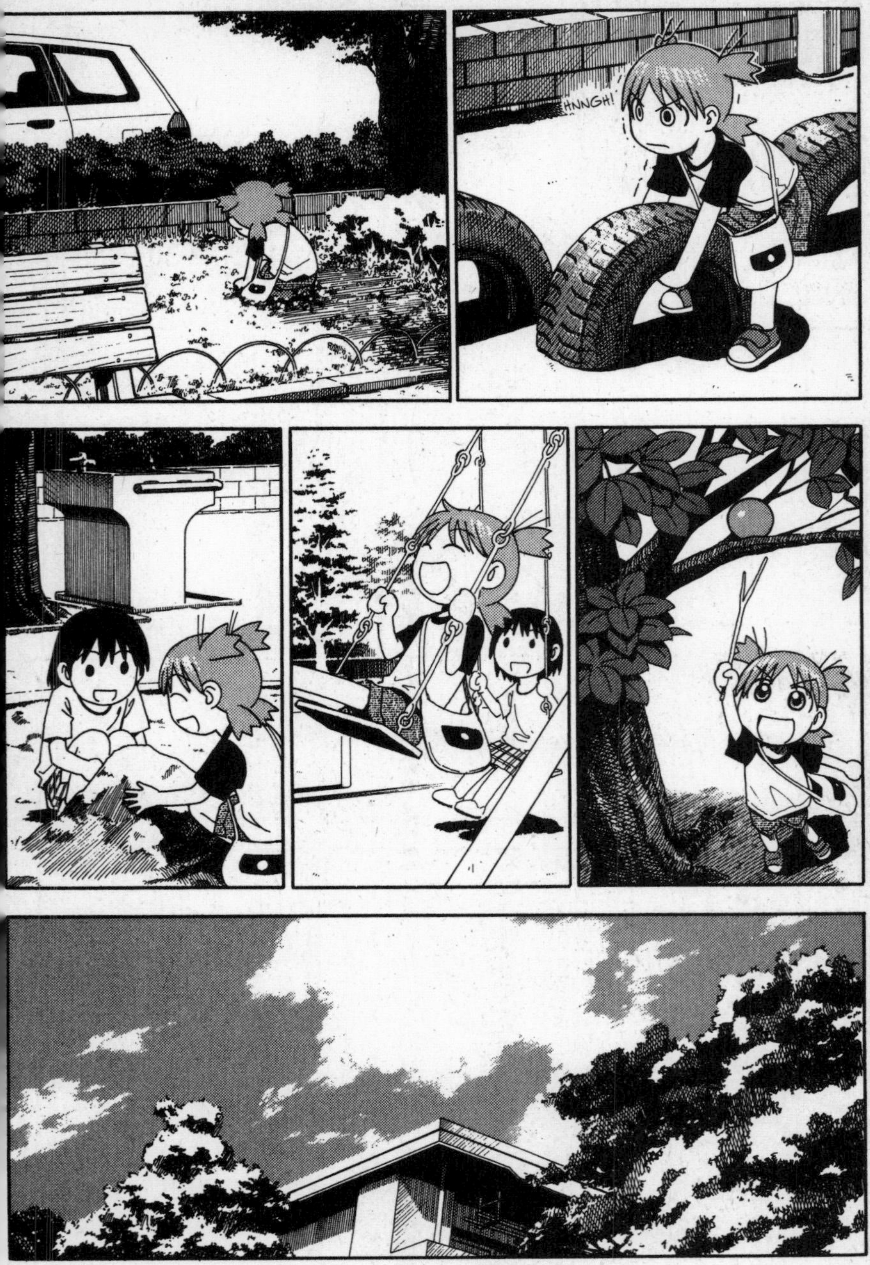
HNNGH!

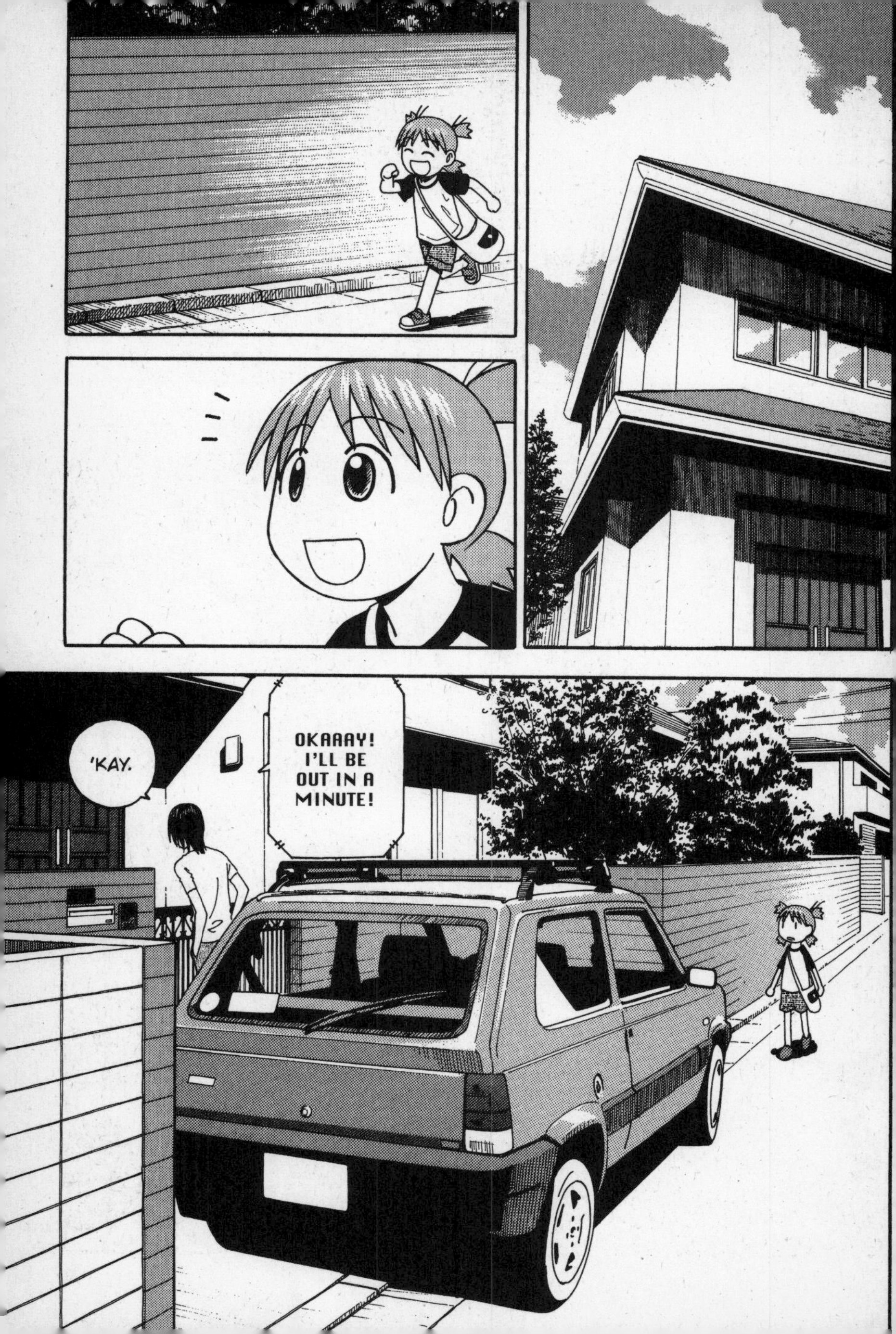
OKAAAY! I'LL BE OUT IN A MINUTE!
'KAY.

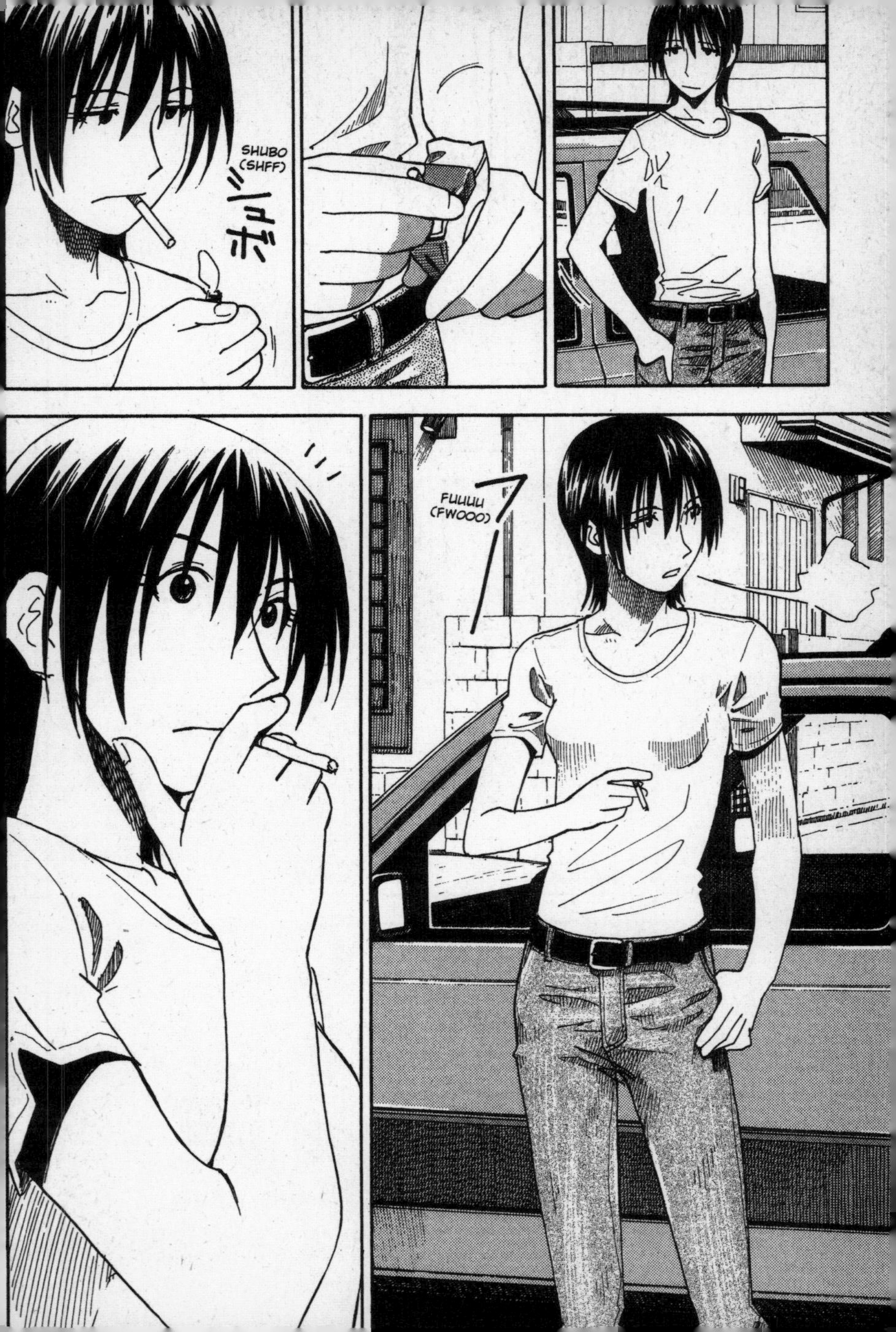
SHUBO (SHFF)
シュボ
FUUUU (FWOOO)

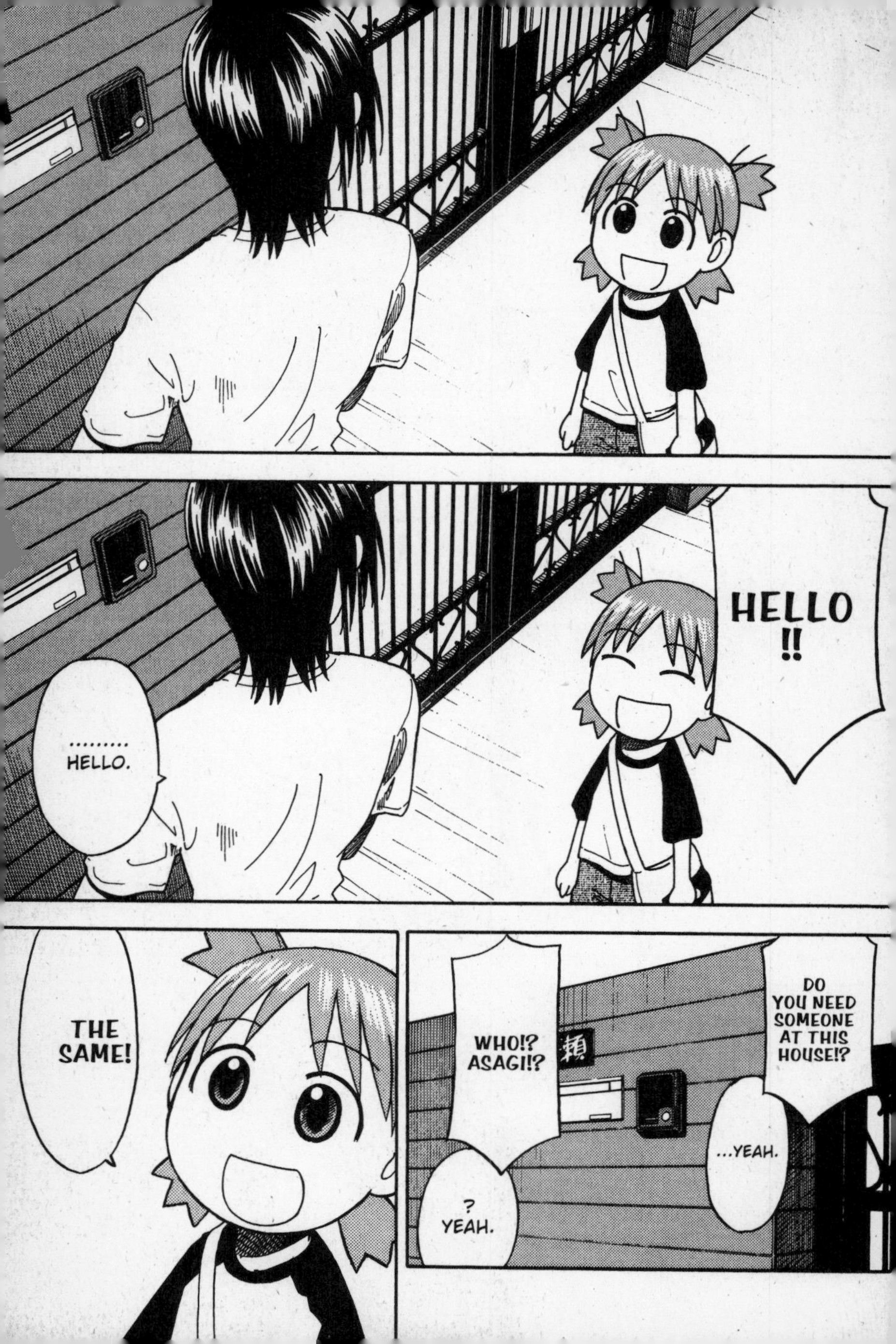
HELLO!!
....
HELLO.
DO YOU NEED SOMEONE AT THIS HOUSE!?
...YEAH.
WHO!? ASAGI!?
? YEAH.
THE SAME!

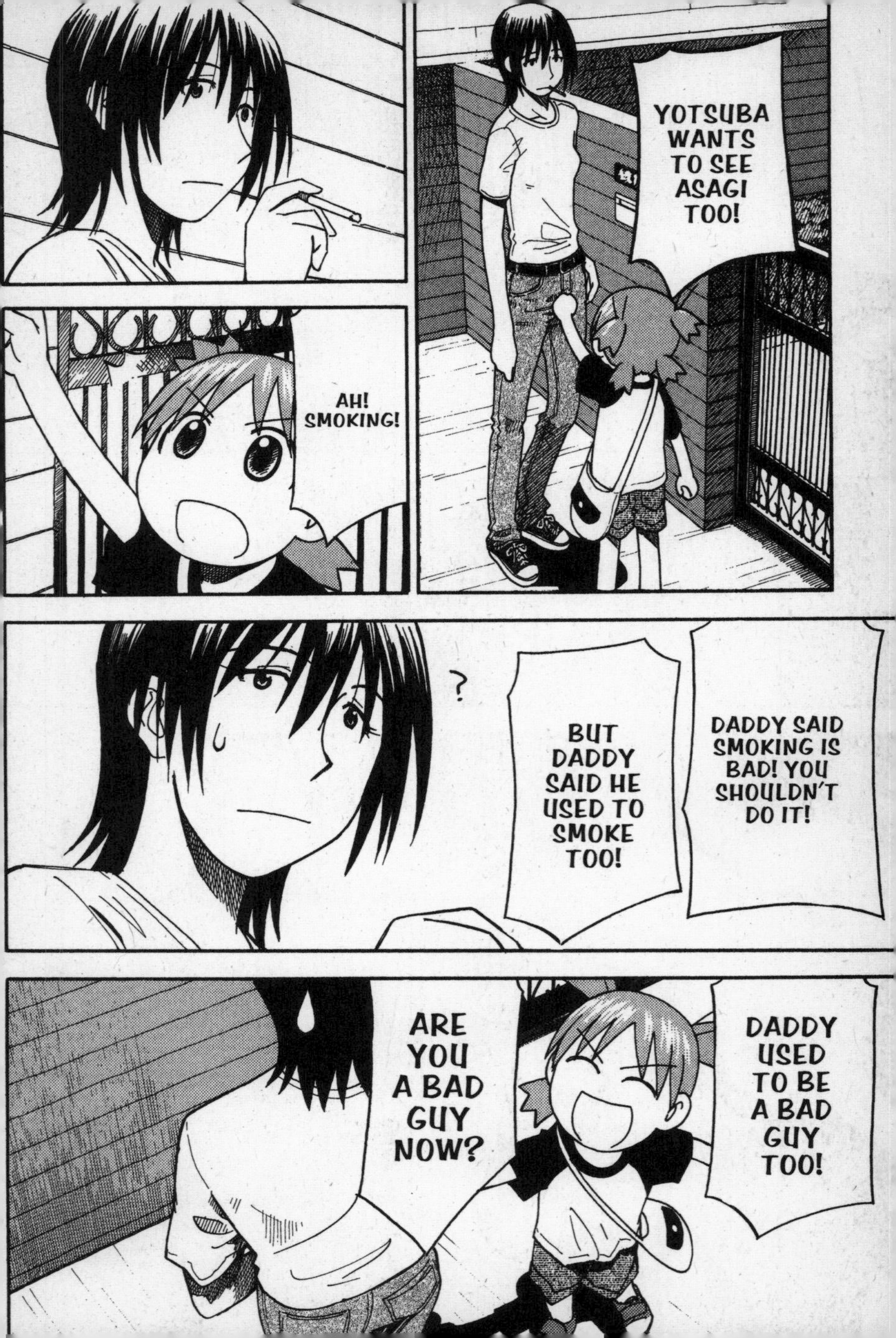
YOTSUBA WANTS TO SEE ASAGI TOO!
AH! SMOKING!
DADDY SAID SMOKING IS BAD! YOU SHOULDN'T DO IT!
BUT DADDY SAID HE USED TO SMOKE TOO!
?
DADDY USED TO BE A BAD GUY TOO!
ARE YOU A BAD GUY NOW?

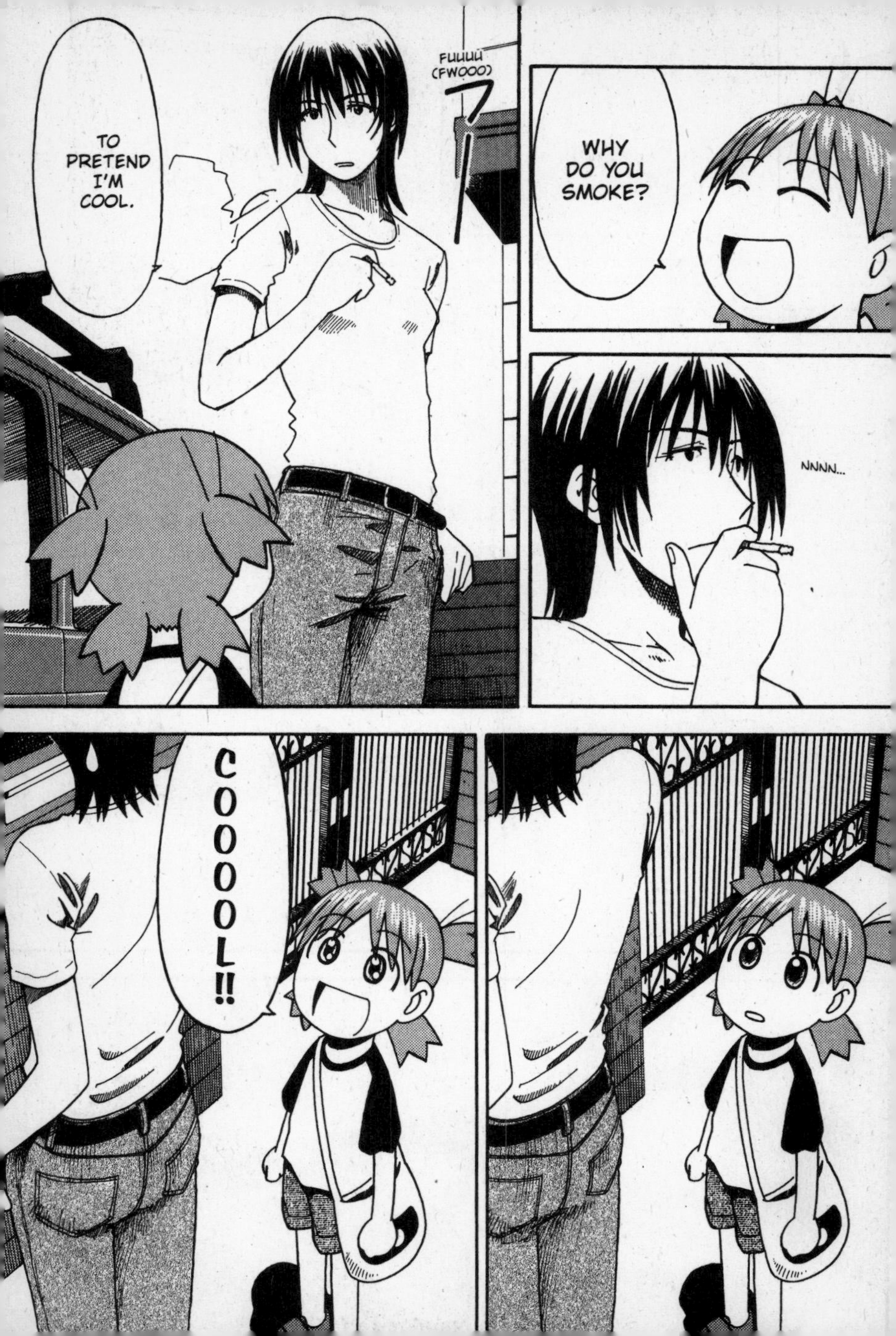
WHY DO YOU SMOKE?
NNNN...
FUUUU (FWOOO)
TO PRETEND I'M COOL.
COOOOOL!!

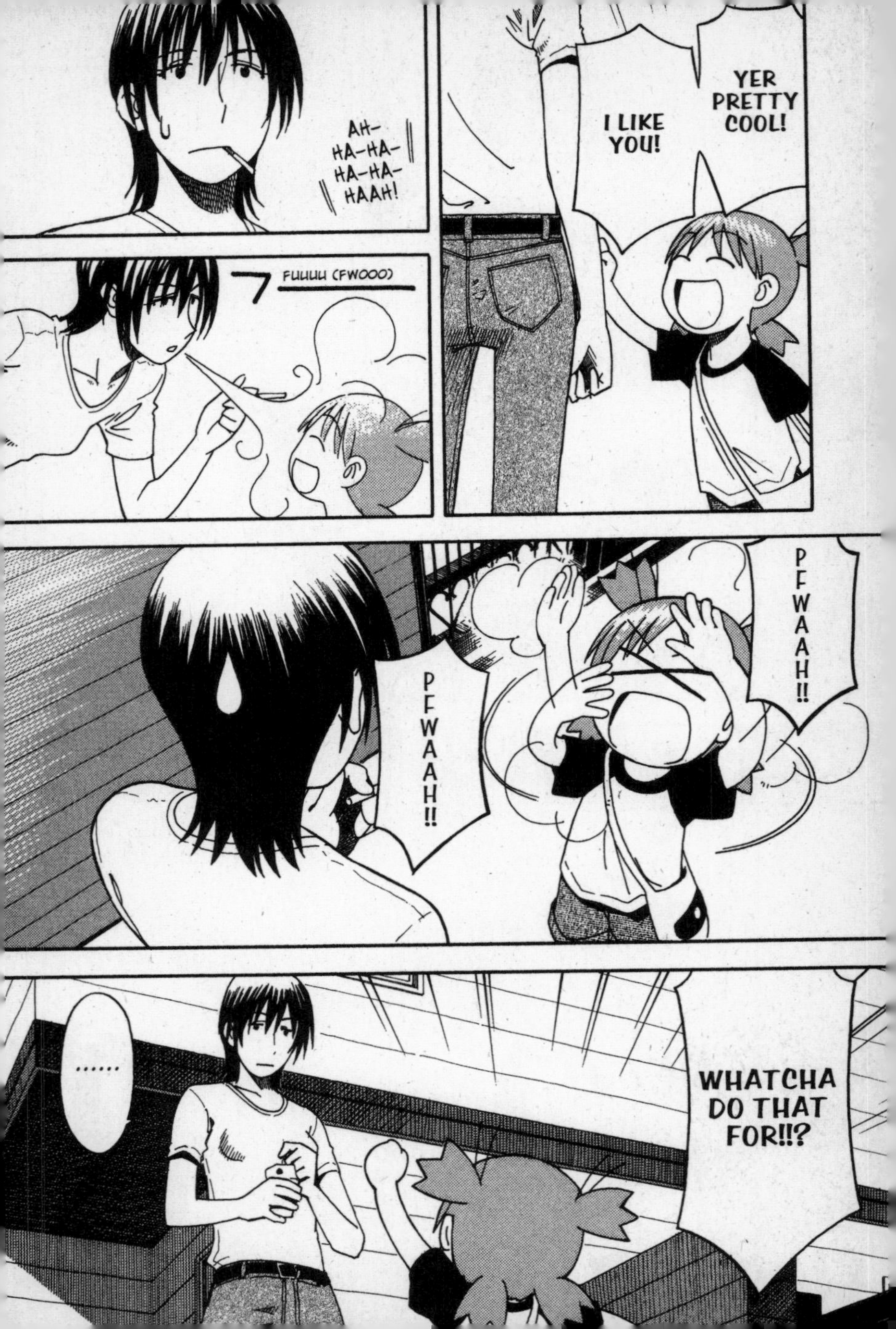
YER PRETTY COOL!
I LIKE YOU!
AH-HA-HA-HA-HA-HAAH!
FUUUU (FWOOO)
PFWAAH!!
PFWAAH!!
WHATCHA DO THAT FOR!!?
......

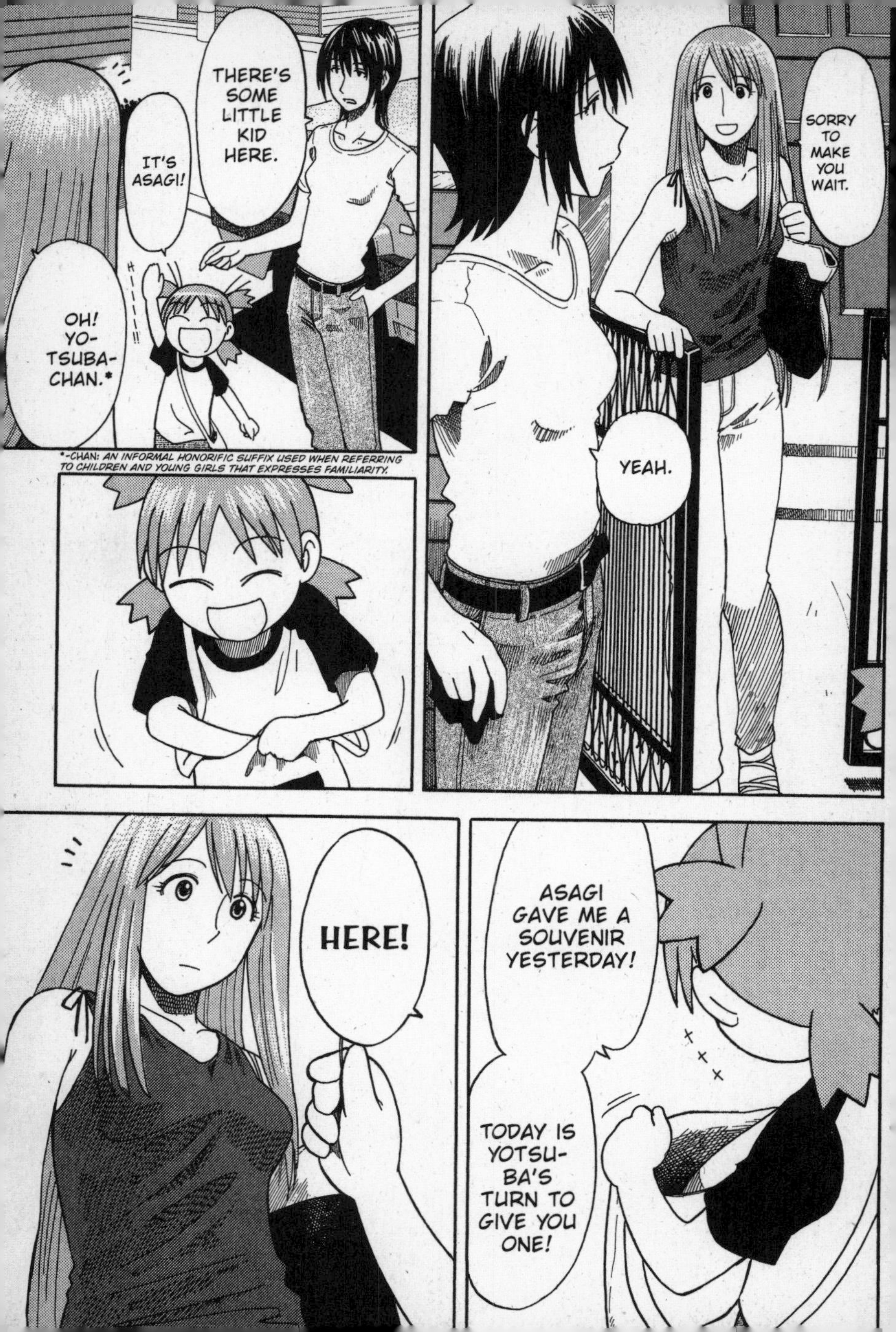
SORRY TO MAKE YOU WAIT.
YEAH.
THERE'S SOME LITTLE KID HERE.
IT'S ASAGI!
OH! YO-TSUBA-CHAN.*
*-CHAN: AN INFORMAL HONORIFIC SUFFIX USED WHEN REFERRING TO CHILDREN AND YOUNG GIRLS THAT EXPRESSES FAMILIARITY.
ASAGI GAVE ME A SOUVENIR YESTERDAY!
TODAY IS YOTSU-BA'S TURN TO GIVE YOU ONE!
HERE!

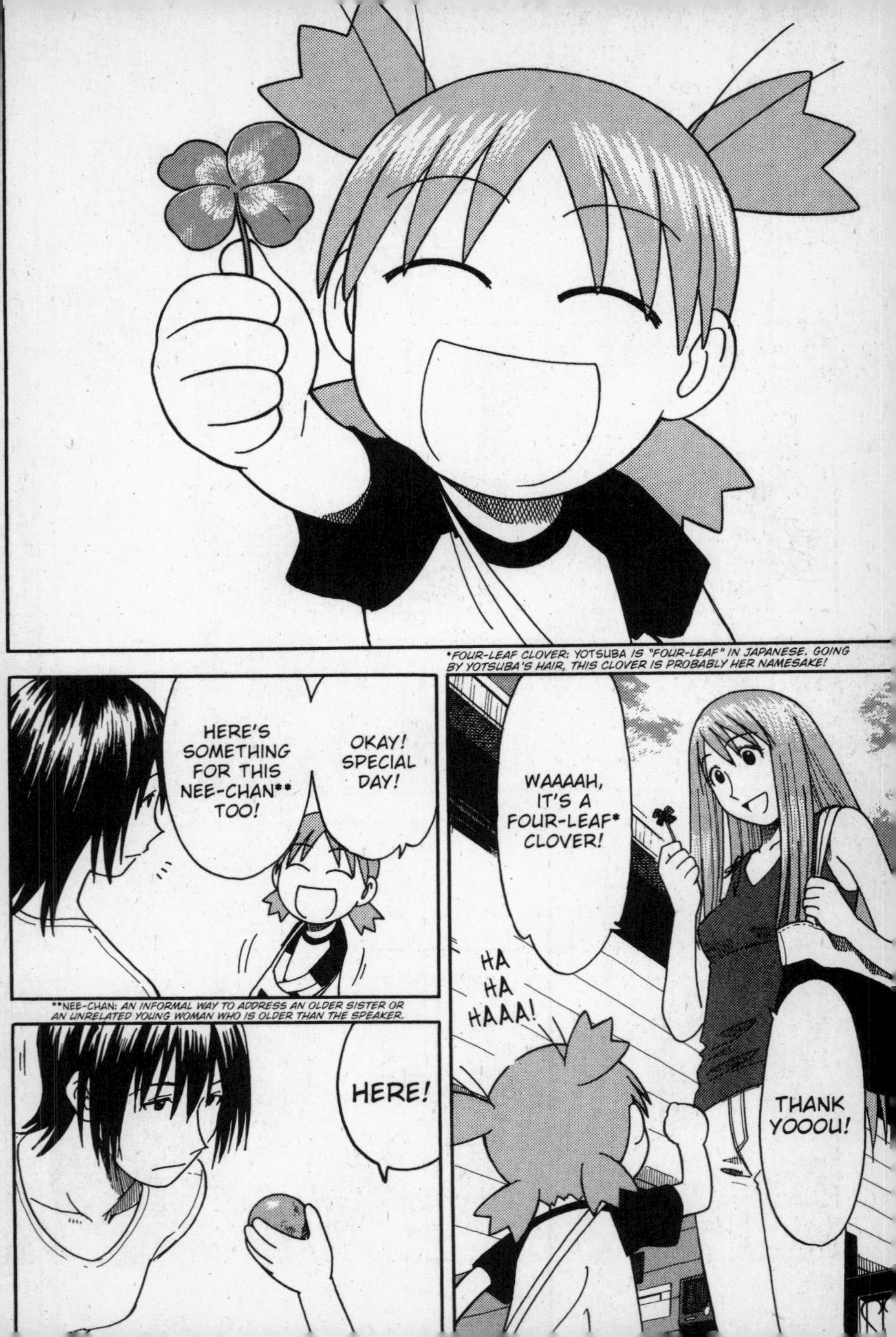
WAAAAH, IT'S A FOUR-LEAF* CLOVER!
HA HA HAAA!
THANK YOOOU!
OKAY! SPECIAL DAY!
HERE'S SOMETHING FOR THIS NEE-CHAN** TOO!
HERE!

*FOUR-LEAF CLOVER: YOTSUBA IS "FOUR-LEAF" IN JAPANESE. GOING BY YOTSUBA'S HAIR, THIS CLOVER IS PROBABLY HER NAMESAKE!

**NEE-CHAN: AN INFORMAL WAY TO ADDRESS AN OLDER SISTER OR AN UNRELATED YOUNG WOMAN WHO IS OLDER THAN THE SPEAKER.

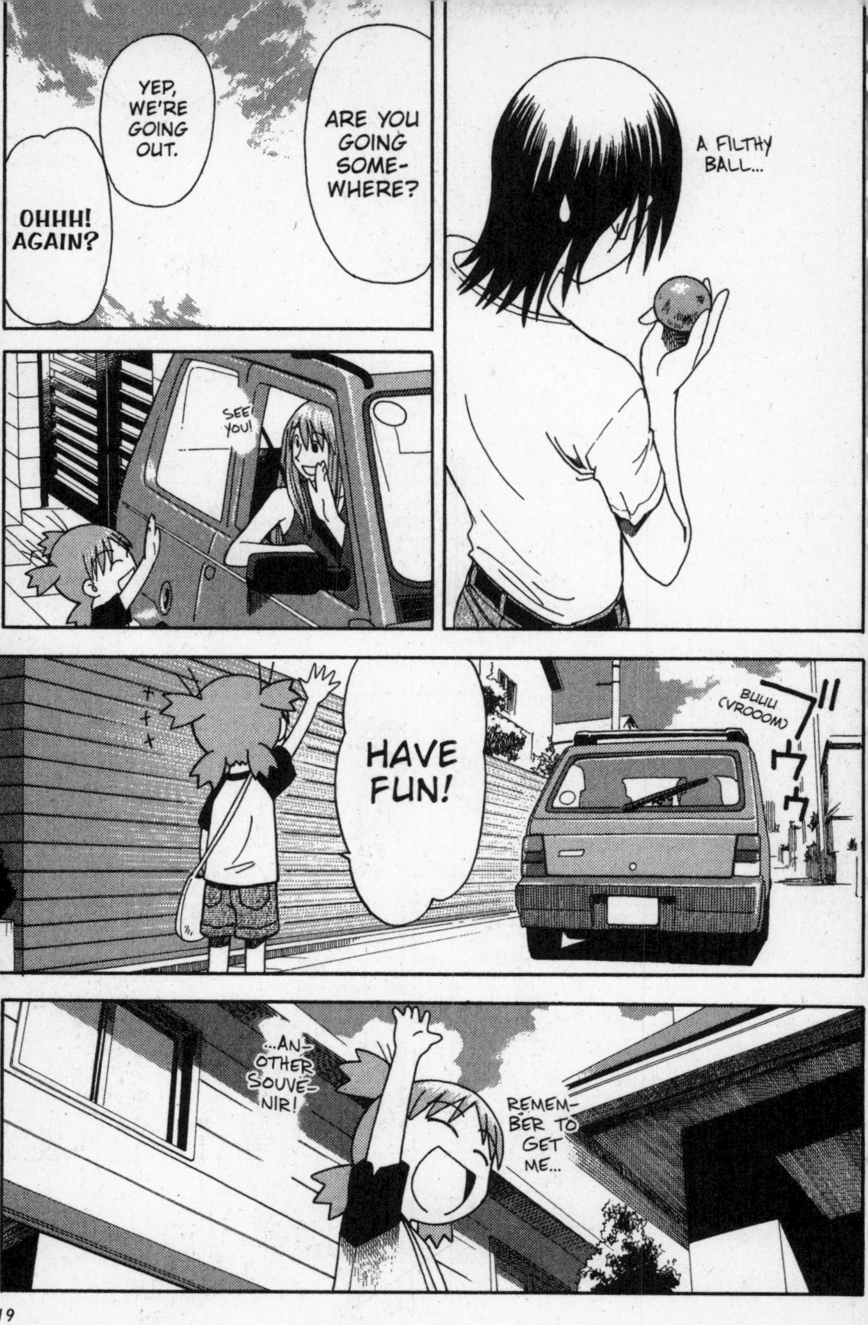
A FILTHY BALL...
ARE YOU GOING SOME-WHERE?
YEP, WE'RE GOING OUT.
OHHH! AGAIN?
SEE YOU!
ブウウ
BUUU (VROOOM)
HAVE FUN!
REMEM-BER TO GET ME...
...AN-OTHER SOUVE-NIR!

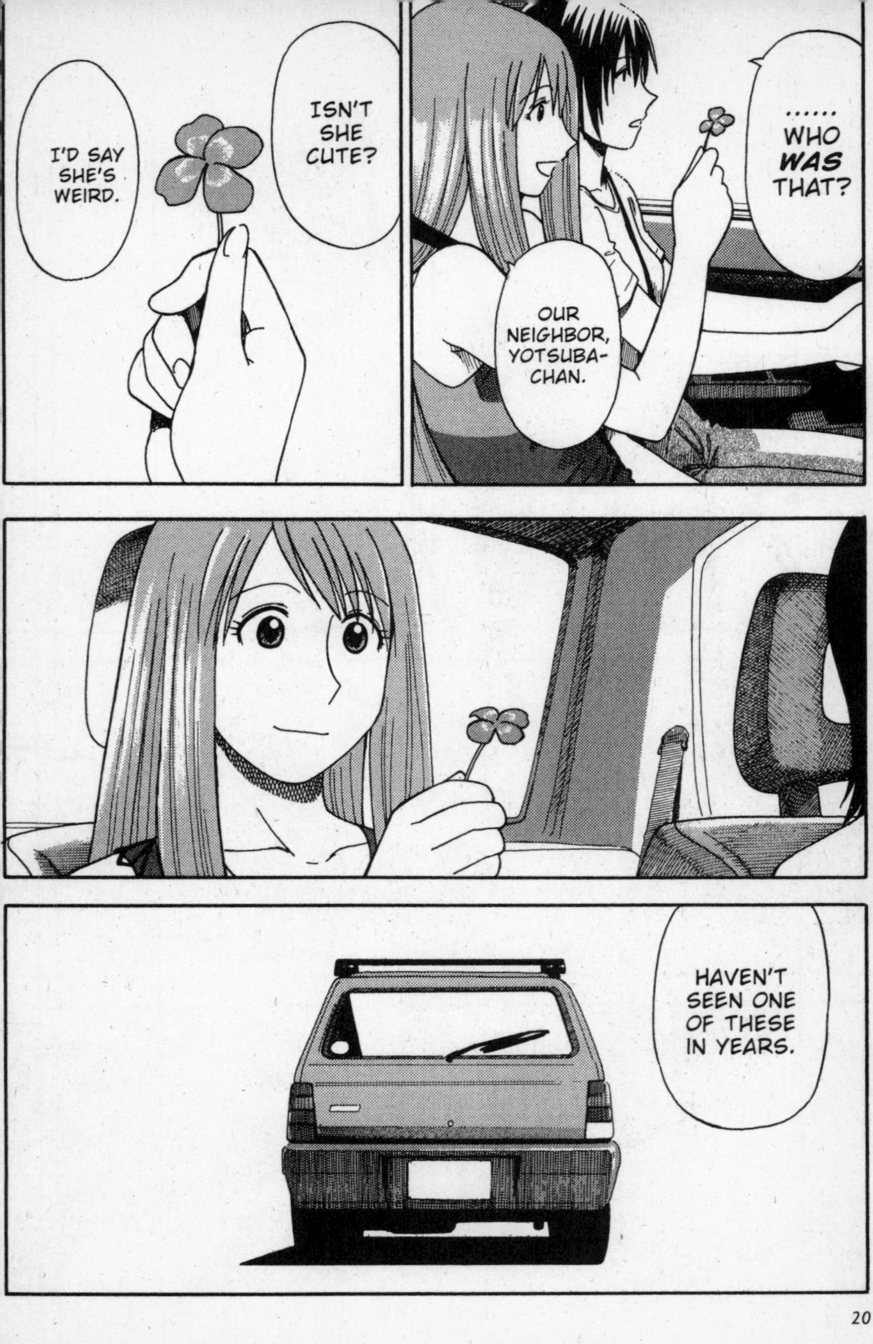

...... WHO WAS THAT?
OUR NEIGHBOR, YOTSUBA-CHAN.
ISN'T SHE CUTE?
I'D SAY SHE'S WEIRD.
HAVEN'T SEEN ONE OF THESE IN YEARS.

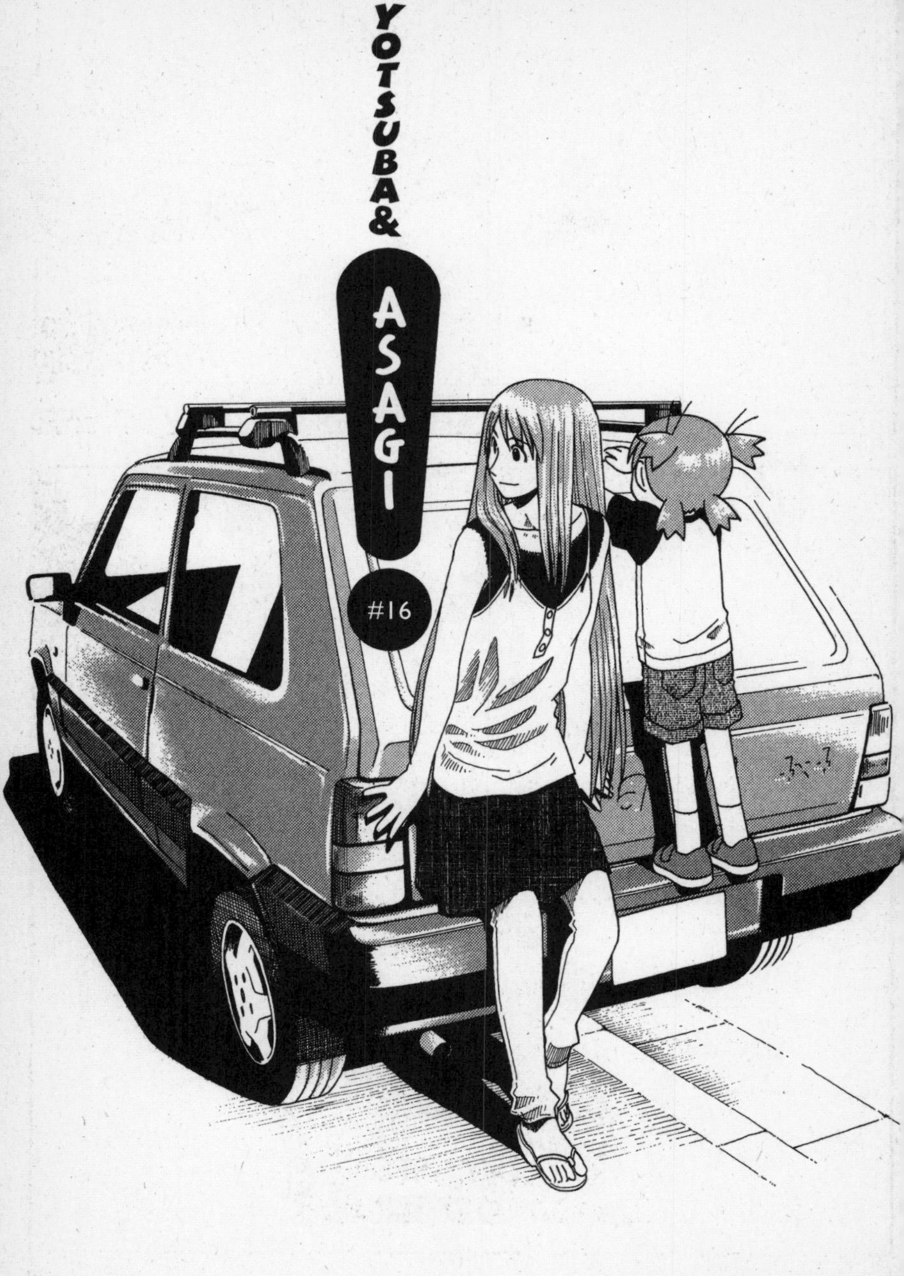
YOTSUBA&
ASAGI
!
#16

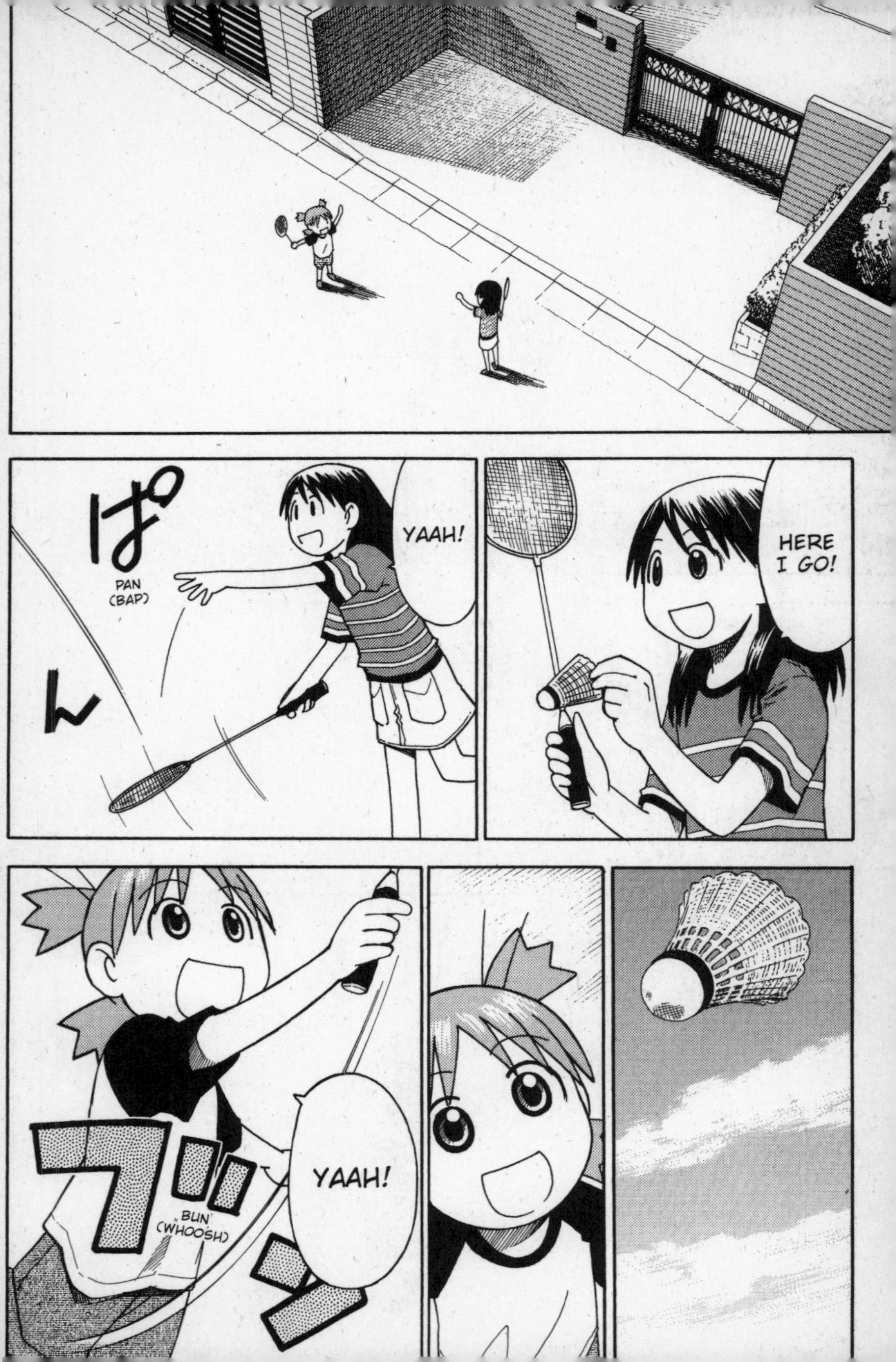
HERE I GO!
YAAH!
ぱん
PAN (BAP)
YAAH!
BUN (WHOOSH)

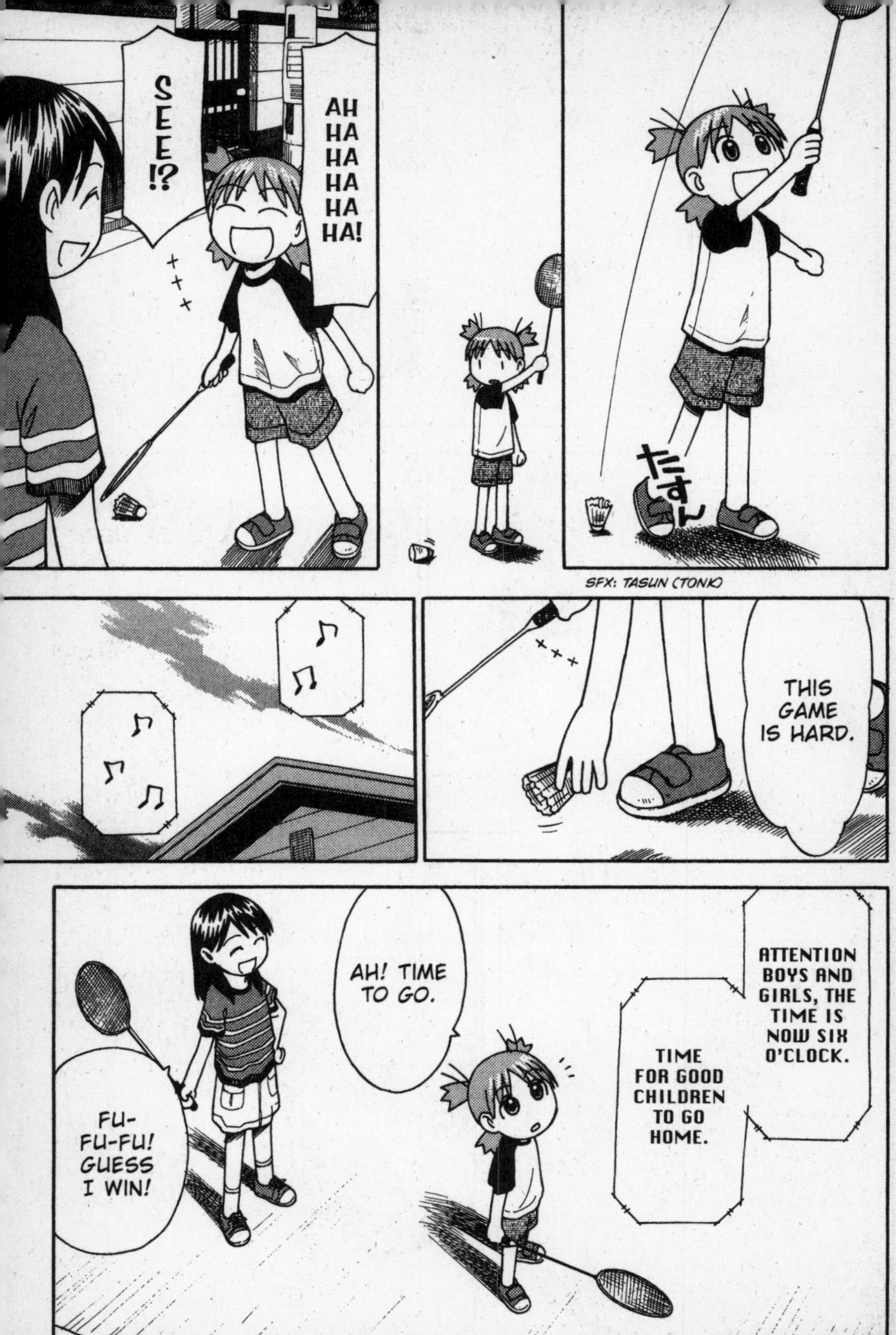
たすん
SFX: TASUN (TONK)
AH HA HA HA HA HA!
SEE!?
THIS GAME IS HARD.
ATTENTION BOYS AND GIRLS, THE TIME IS NOW SIX O'CLOCK.
TIME FOR GOOD CHILDREN TO GO HOME.
AH! TIME TO GO.
FU-FU-FU! GUESS I WIN!

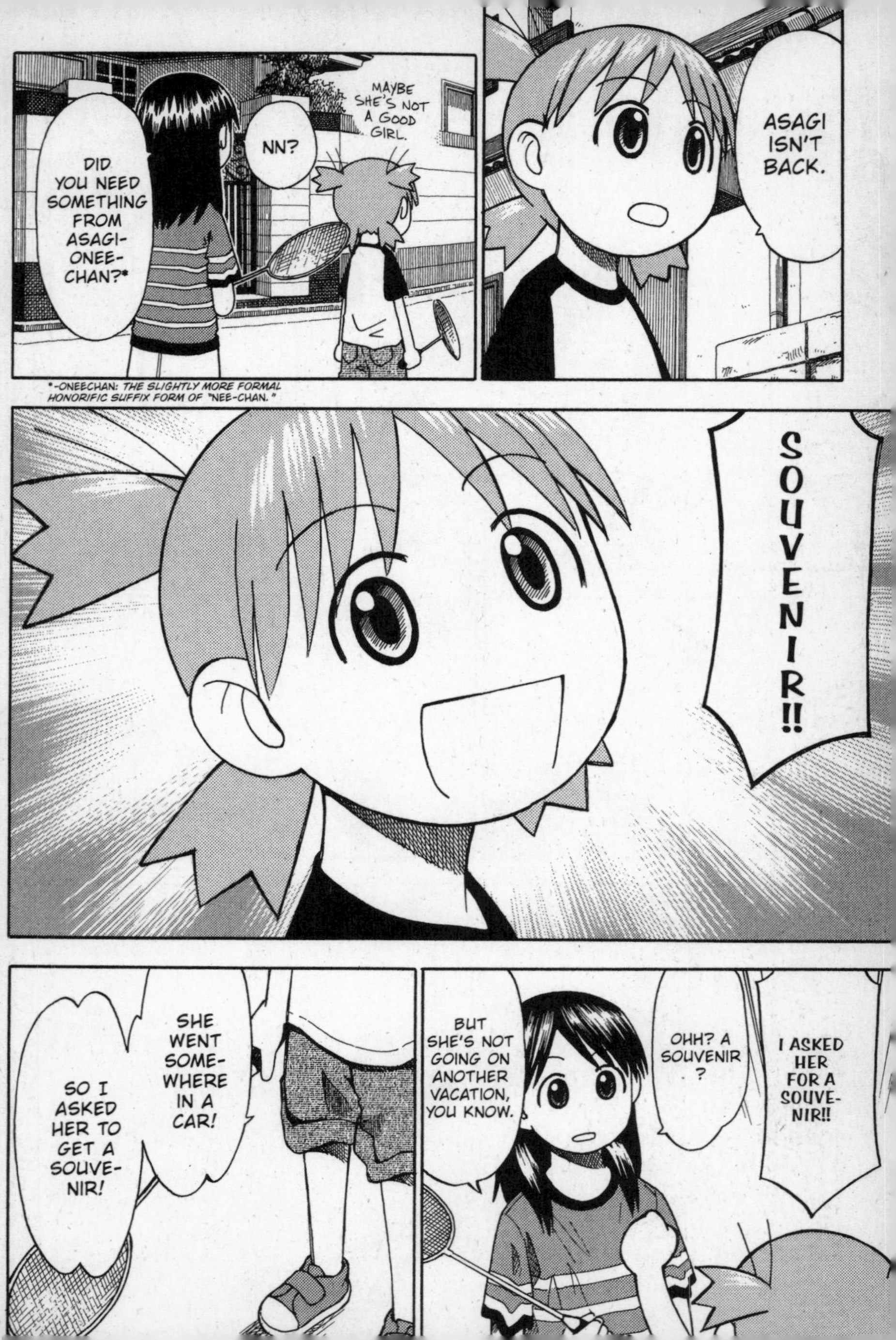
ASAGI ISN'T BACK.
MAYBE SHE'S NOT A GOOD GIRL.
NN?
DID YOU NEED SOMETHING FROM ASAGI-ONEE-CHAN?*
SOUVENIR!!
I ASKED HER FOR A SOUVENIR!!
OHH? A SOUVENIR?
BUT SHE'S NOT GOING ON ANOTHER VACATION, YOU KNOW.
SHE WENT SOMEWHERE IN A CAR!
SO I ASKED HER TO GET A SOUVENIR!

*-ONEECHAN: THE SLIGHTLY MORE FORMAL HONORIFIC SUFFIX FORM OF "NEE-CHAN."

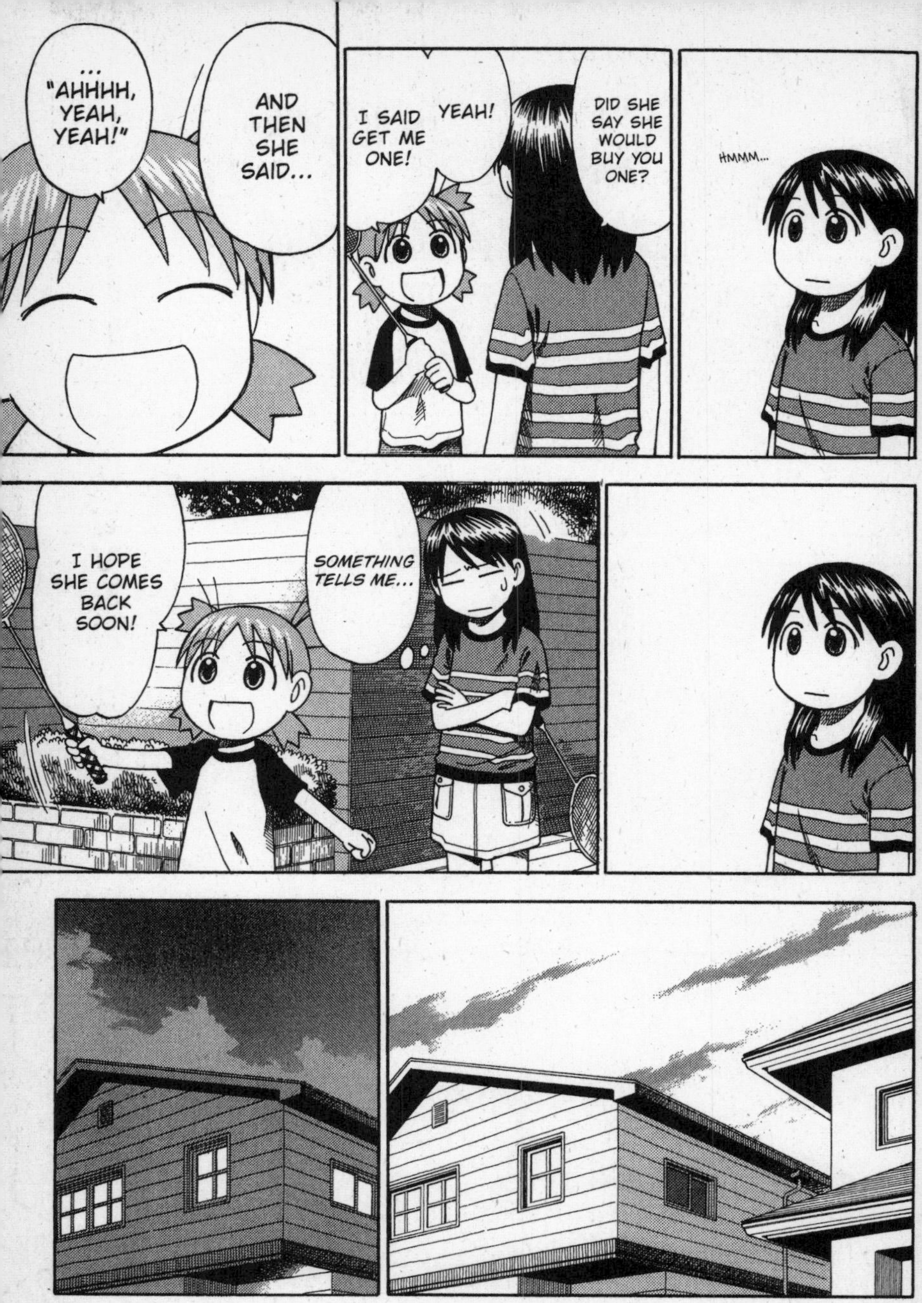
HMMM...
DID SHE SAY SHE WOULD BUY YOU ONE?
YEAH!
I SAID GET ME ONE!
AND THEN SHE SAID...
... "AHHHH, YEAH, YEAH!"
SOMETHING TELLS ME...
I HOPE SHE COMES BACK SOON!

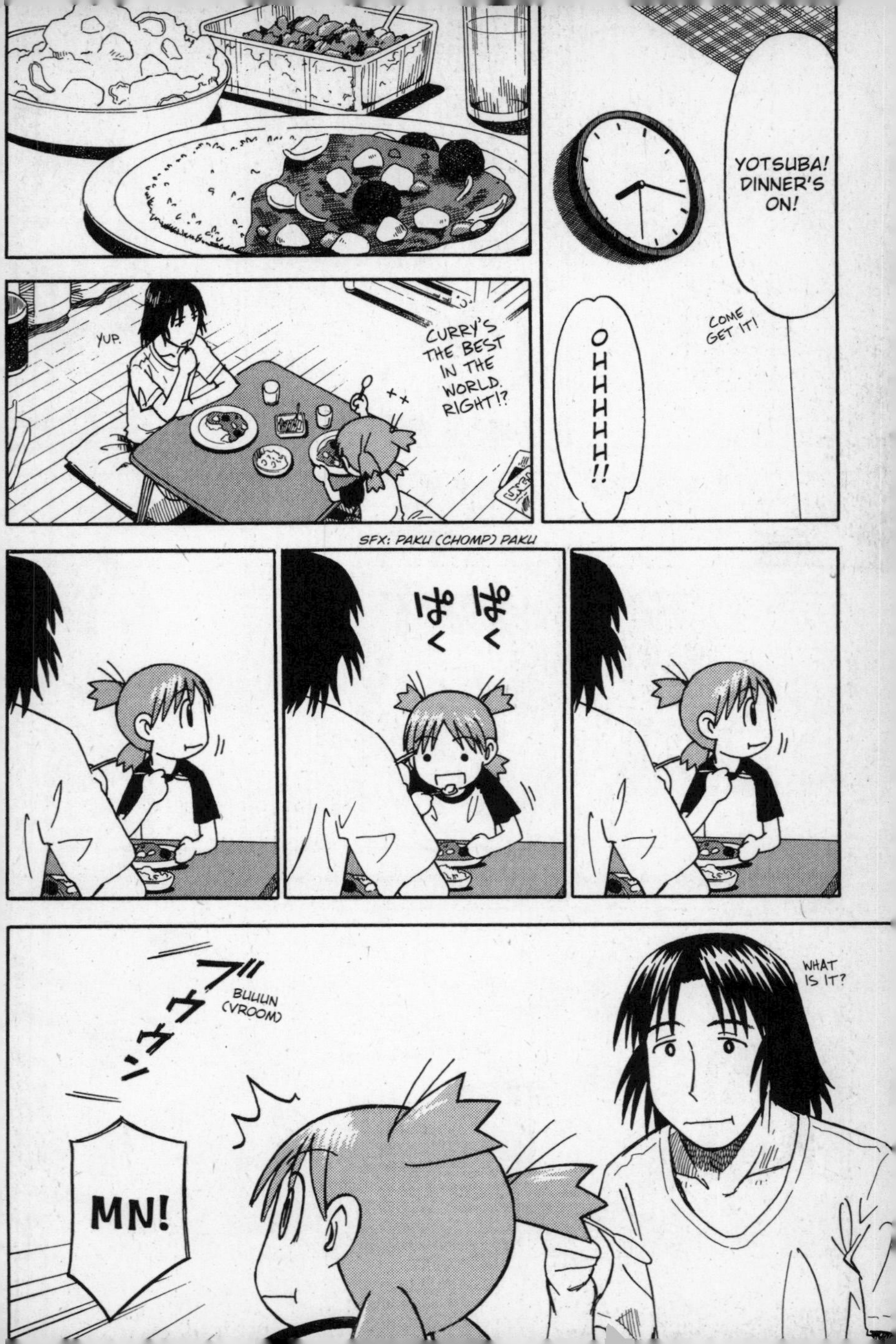

YOTSUBA! DINNER'S ON!
COME GET IT!
OHHHHH!!
CURRY'S THE BEST IN THE WORLD. RIGHT!?
YUP.
SFX: PAKU (CHOMP) PAKU
ぱく ぱく
WHAT IS IT?
ブウウン
BUUUN (VROOM)
MN!

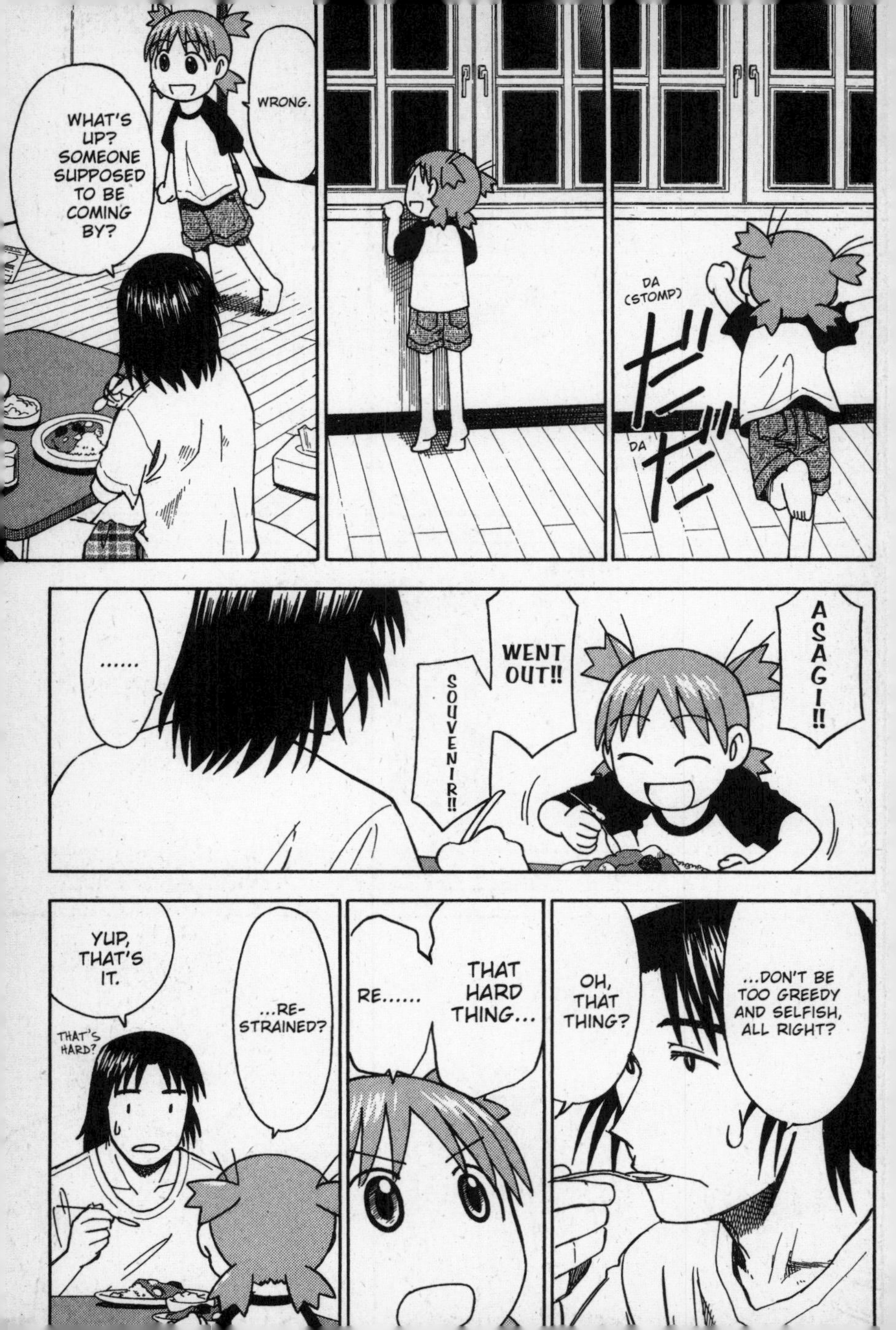
DA (STOMP)
DA
WRONG.
WHAT'S UP? SOMEONE SUPPOSED TO BE COMING BY?
ASAGI!!
WENT OUT!!
SOUVENIR!!
......
...DON'T BE TOO GREEDY AND SELFISH, ALL RIGHT?
OH, THAT THING?
THAT HARD THING...
RE......
...RE-STRAINED?
YUP, THAT'S IT.
THAT'S HARD?

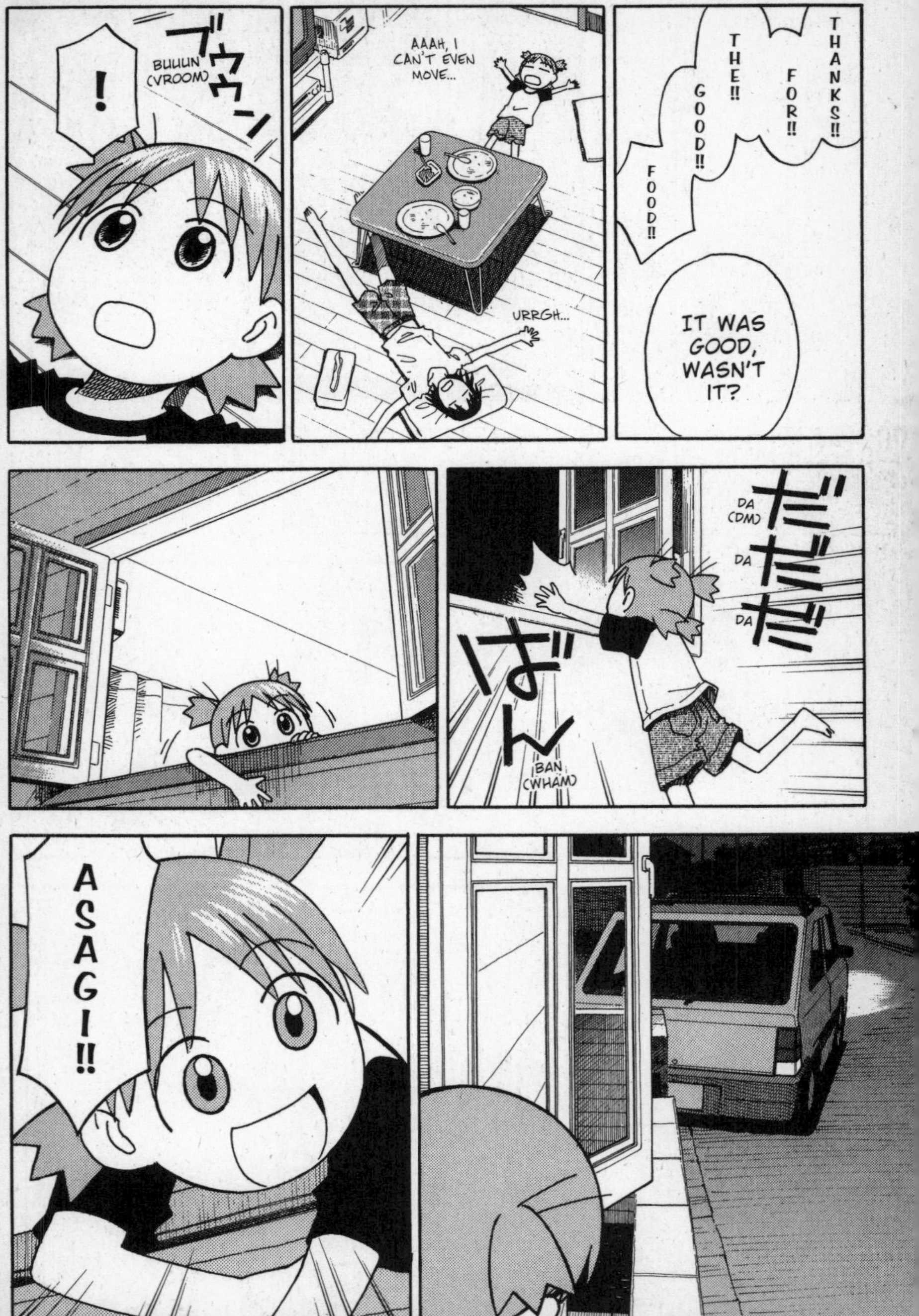
THANKS!! FOR!! THE!! GOOD!! FOOD!!
IT WAS GOOD, WASN'T IT?
AAAH, I CAN'T EVEN MOVE...
URRGH...
!
ブウーン
BUUUN (VROOM)
だだだ
DA (DM)
DA
DA
ばん
BAN (WHAM)
ASAGI!!

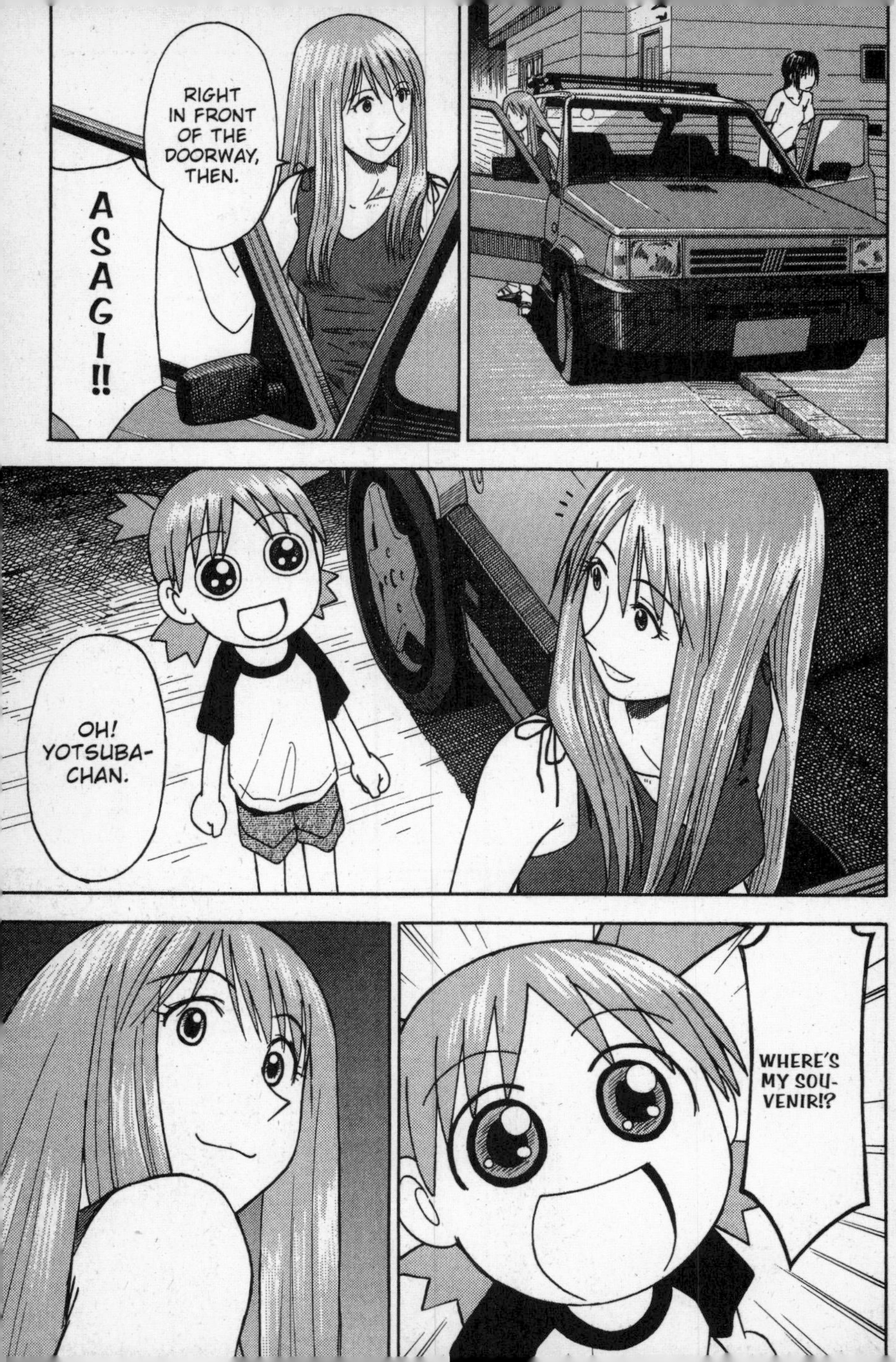
RIGHT IN FRONT OF THE DOORWAY, THEN.
ASAGI!!
OH! YOTSUBA-CHAN.
WHERE'S MY SOU-VENIR!?

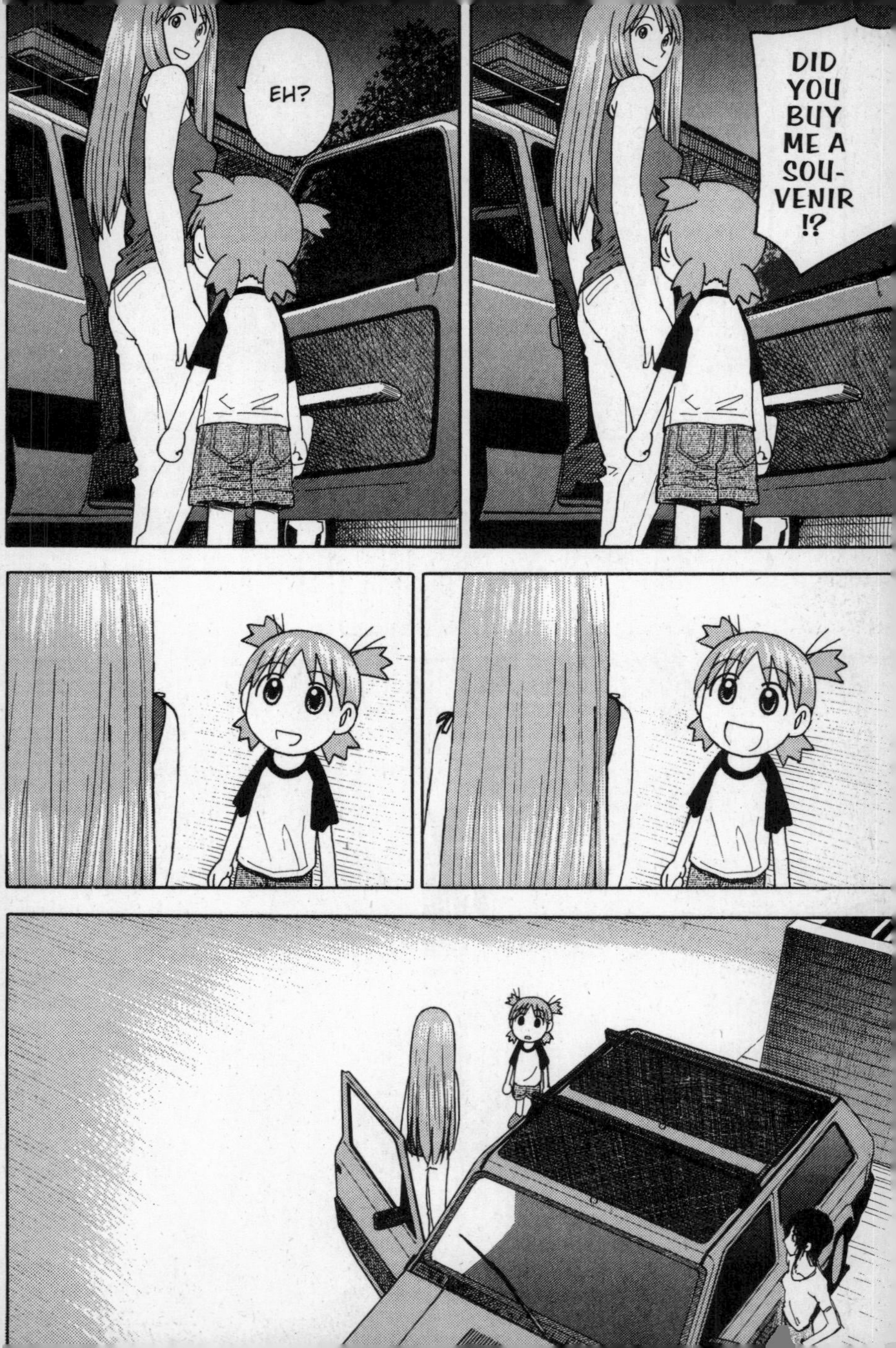
DID YOU BUY ME A SOU-VENIR !?
EH?

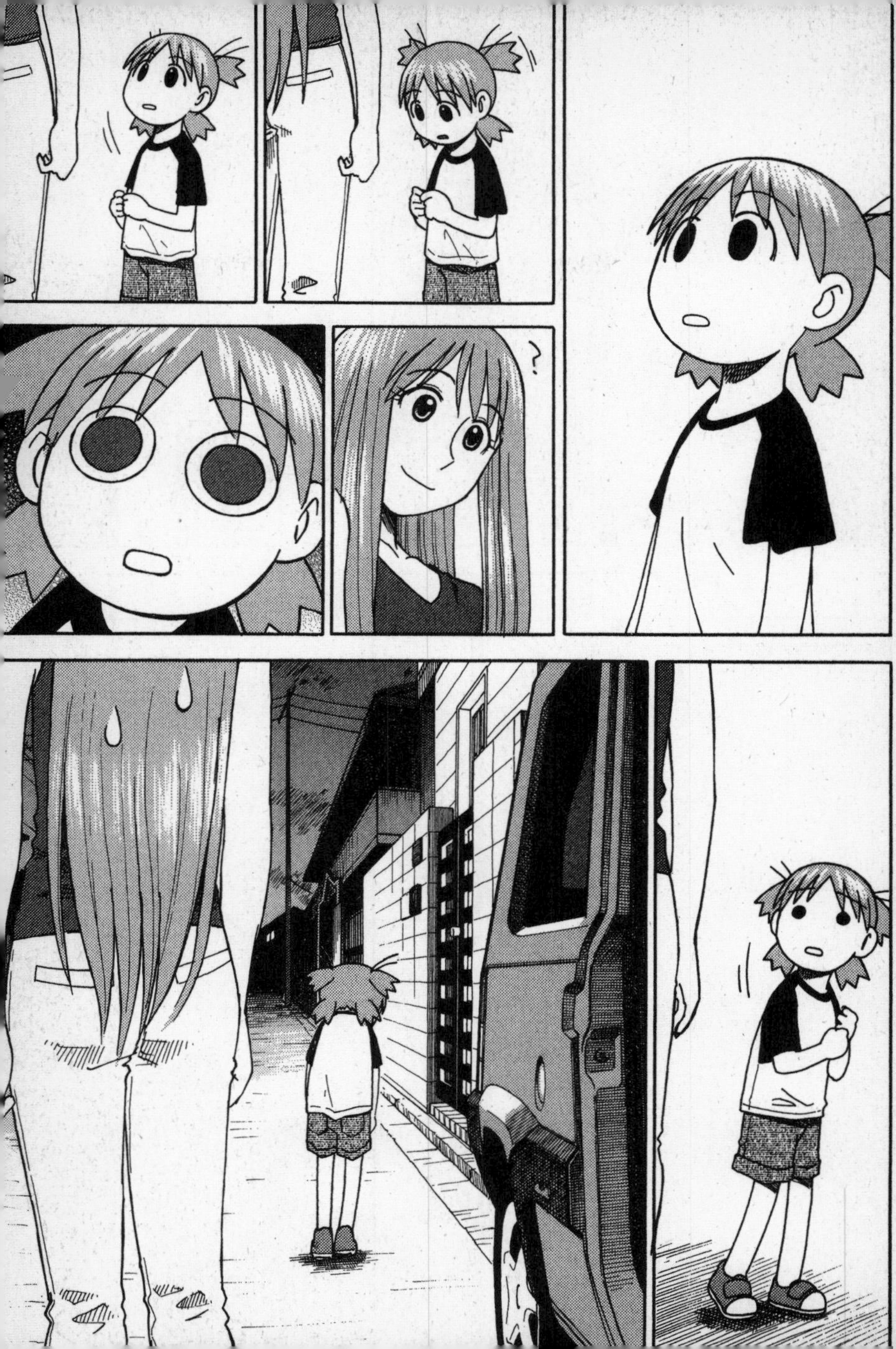
?

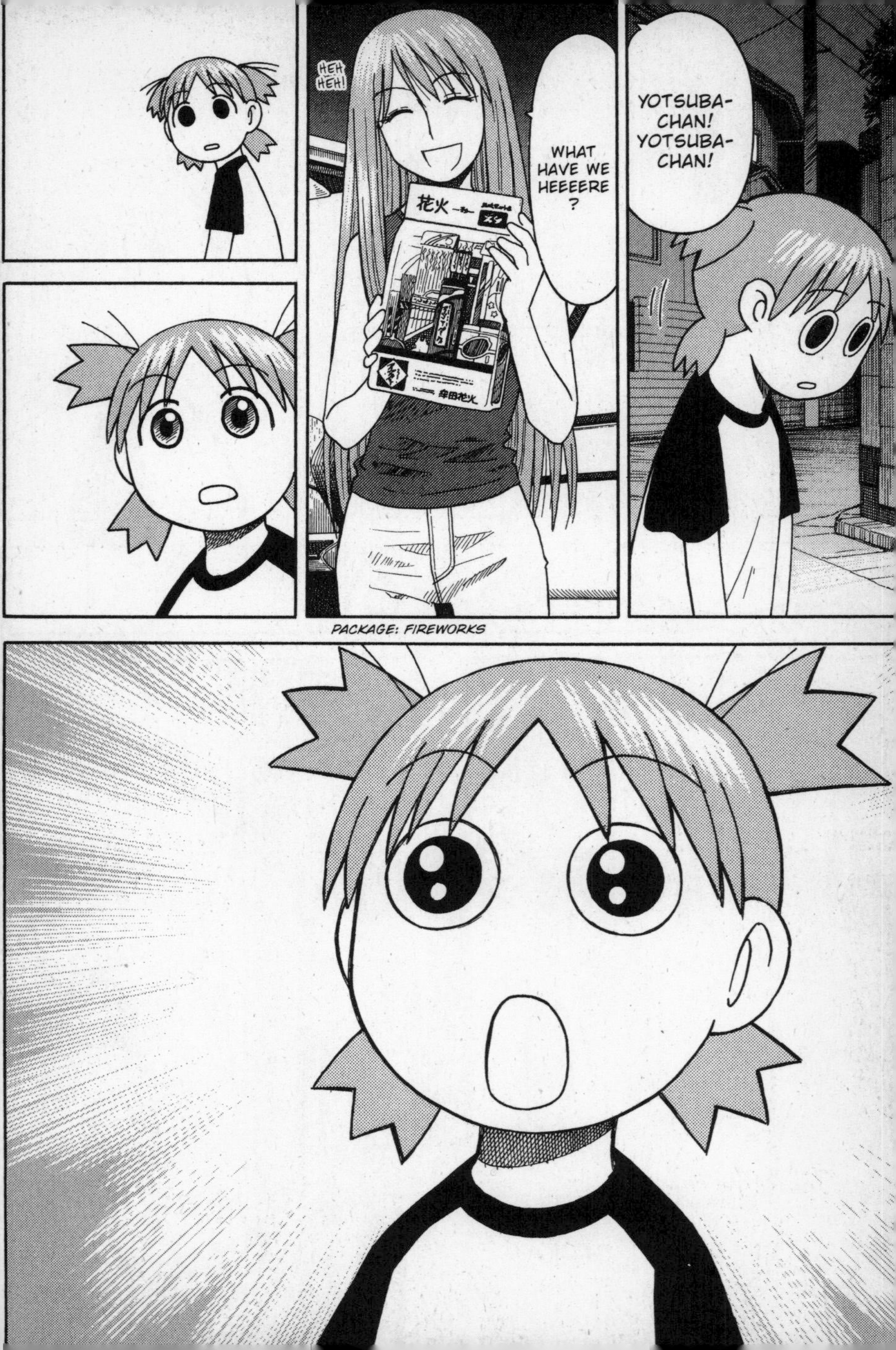
YOTSUBA-CHAN! YOTSUBA-CHAN!
WHAT HAVE WE HEEEERE?
HEH HEH!
PACKAGE: FIREWORKS

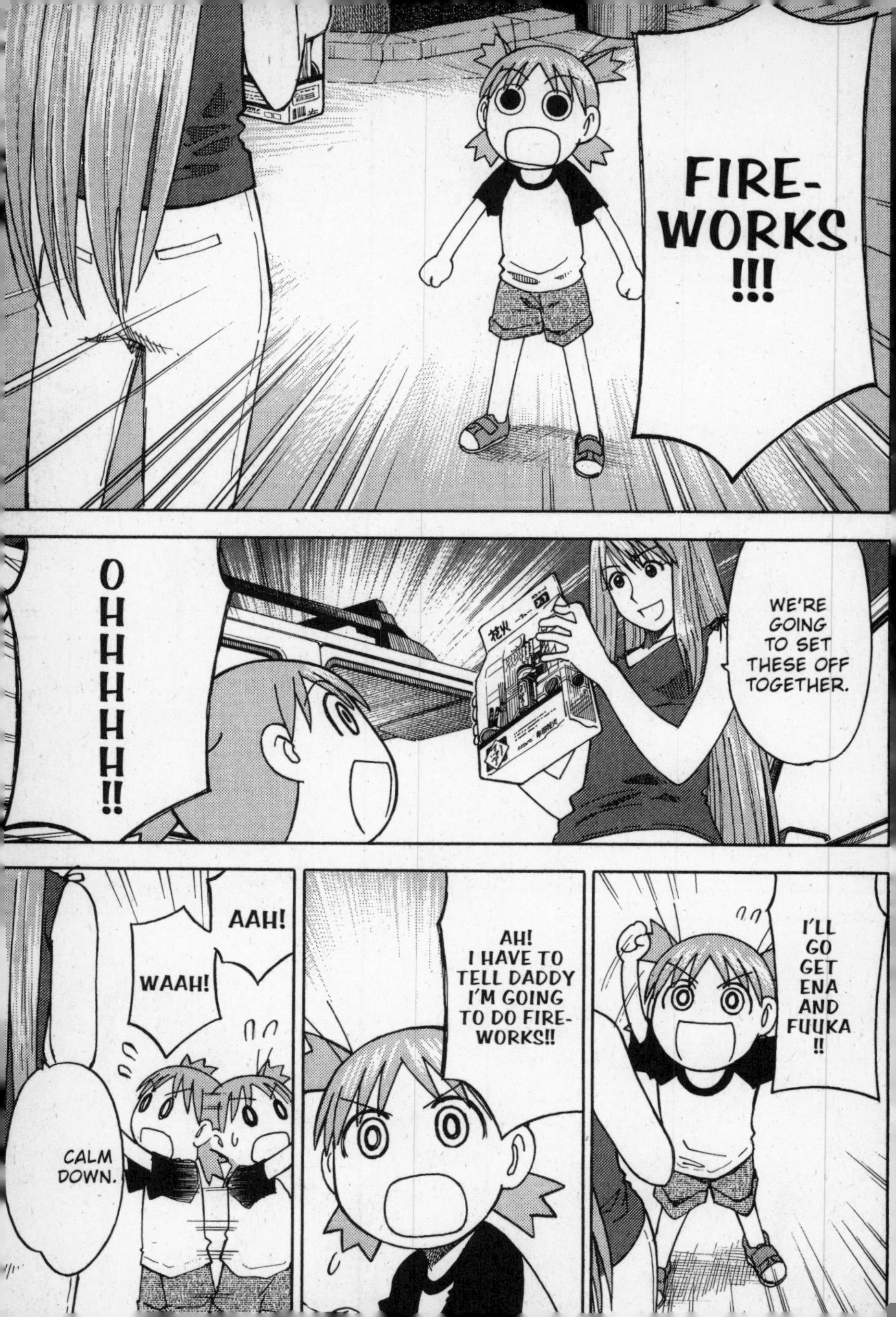
FIRE-WORKS!!!
WE'RE GOING TO SET THESE OFF TOGETHER.
OHHHHH!!
I'LL GO GET ENA AND FUUKA!!
AH! I HAVE TO TELL DADDY I'M GOING TO DO FIRE-WORKS!!
AAH!
WAAH!
CALM DOWN.

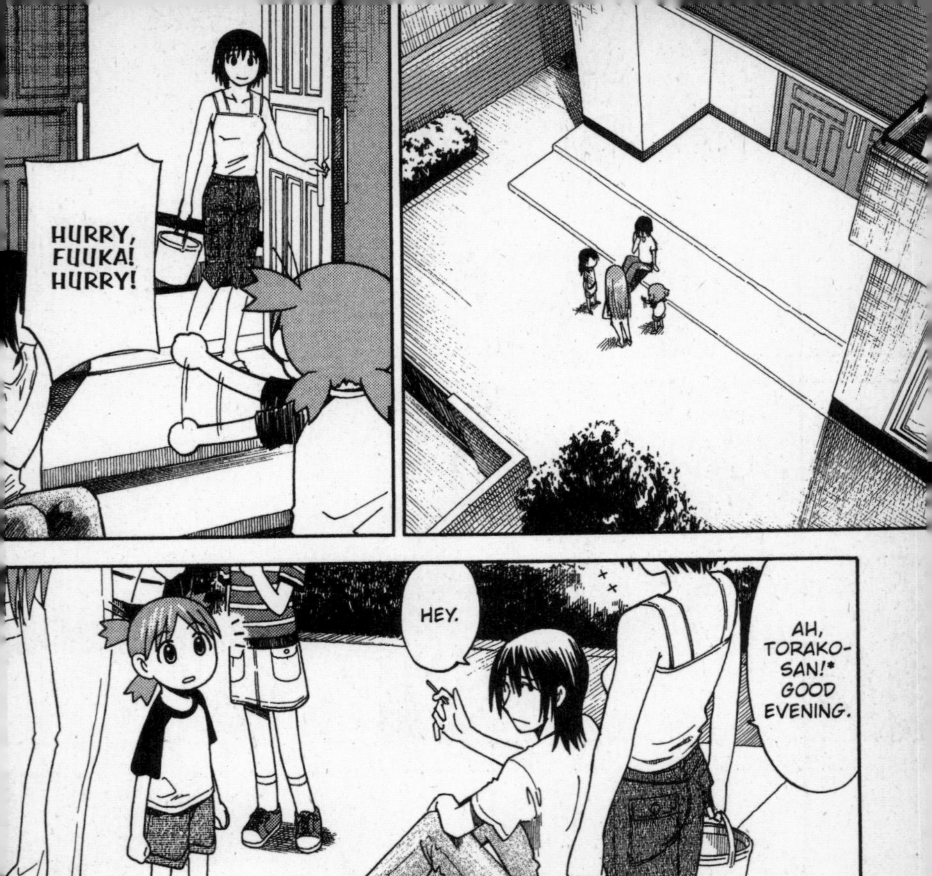
HURRY, FUUKA! HURRY!
AH, TORAKO-SAN!* GOOD EVENING.
HEY.

*TORAKO: HER NAME IS WRITTEN WITH THE CHARACTERS FOR "TIGER" AND "BABY."
-SAN: AN HONORIFIC SUFFIX THAT IS THE EQUIVALENT OF "MR.," "MRS.," OR "MISS."

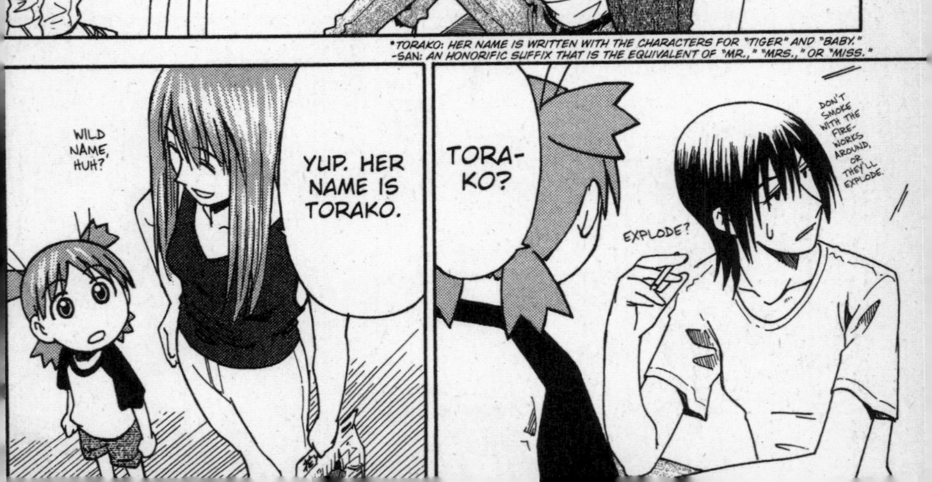
DON'T SMOKE WITH THE FIREWORKS AROUND, OR THEY'LL EXPLODE.
TORA-KO?
EXPLODE?
YUP. HER NAME IS TORAKO.
WILD NAME, HUH?

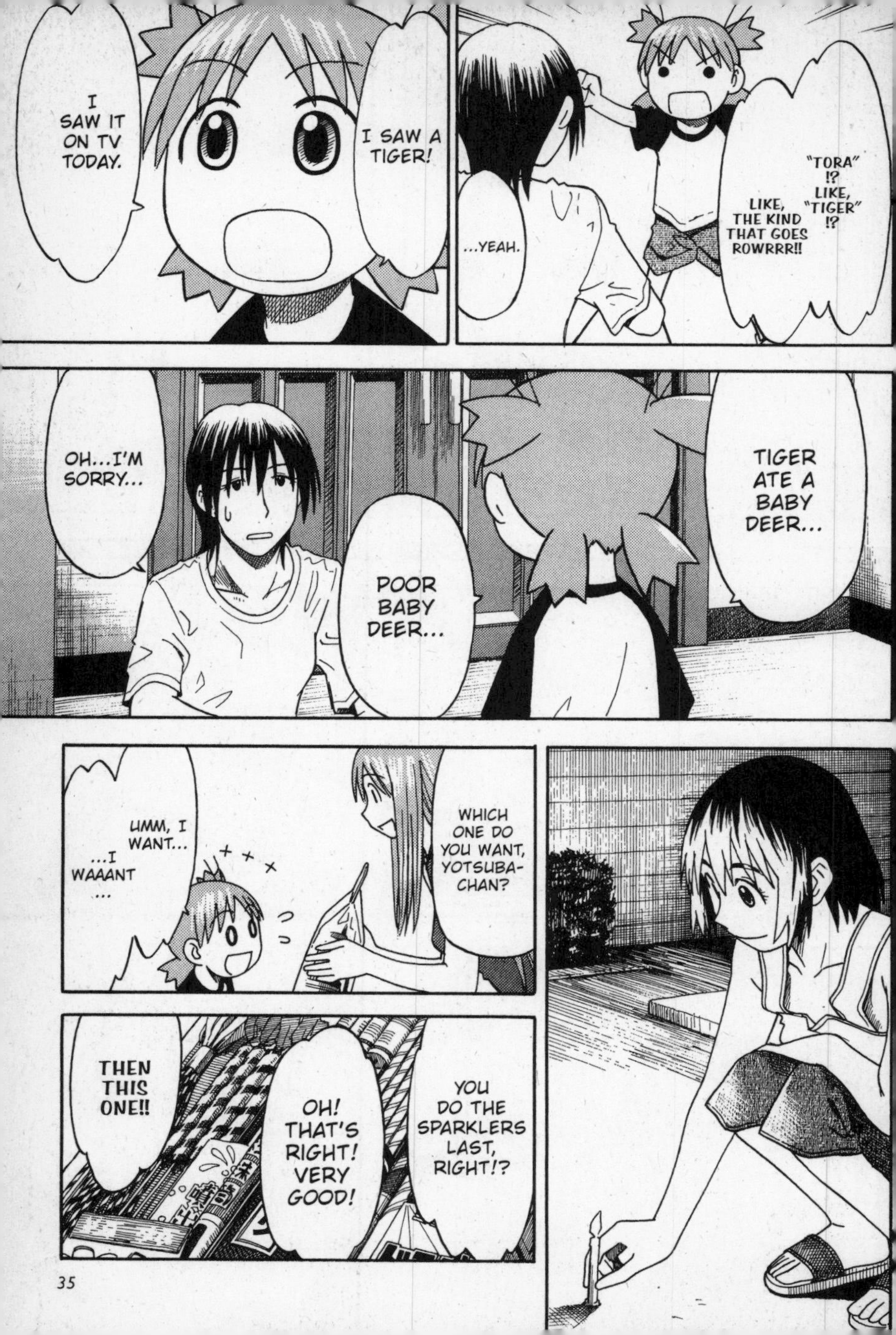
"TORA"!? LIKE, "TIGER"!?
LIKE, THE KIND THAT GOES ROWRRR!!
...YEAH.
I SAW A TIGER!
I SAW IT ON TV TODAY.
TIGER ATE A BABY DEER...
POOR BABY DEER...
OH...I'M SORRY...
WHICH ONE DO YOU WANT, YOTSUBA-CHAN?
UMM, I WANT...
...I WAAANT ...
YOU DO THE SPARKLERS LAST, RIGHT!?
OH! THAT'S RIGHT! VERY GOOD!
THEN THIS ONE!!

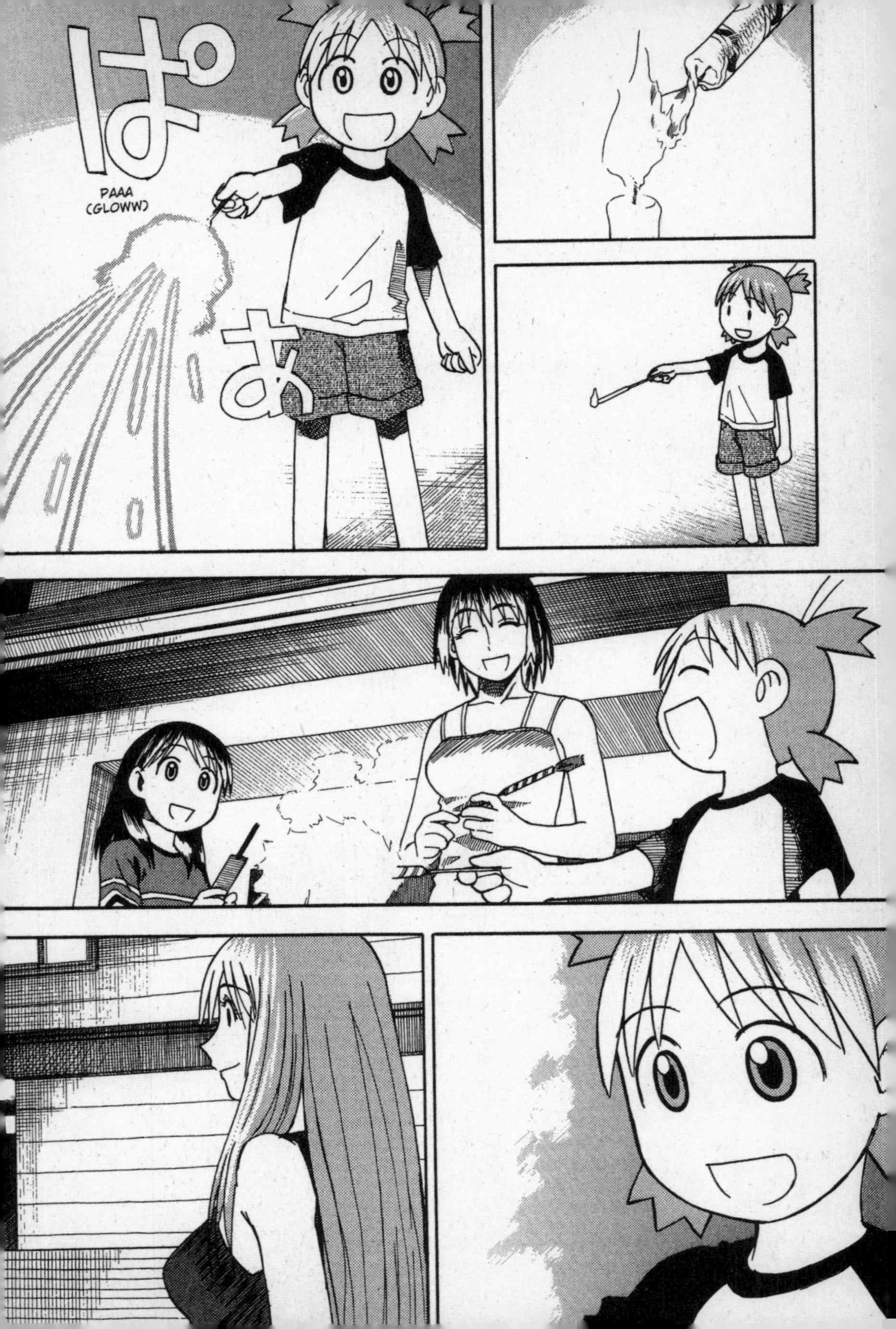
ぱあ
PAAA
(GLOWW)

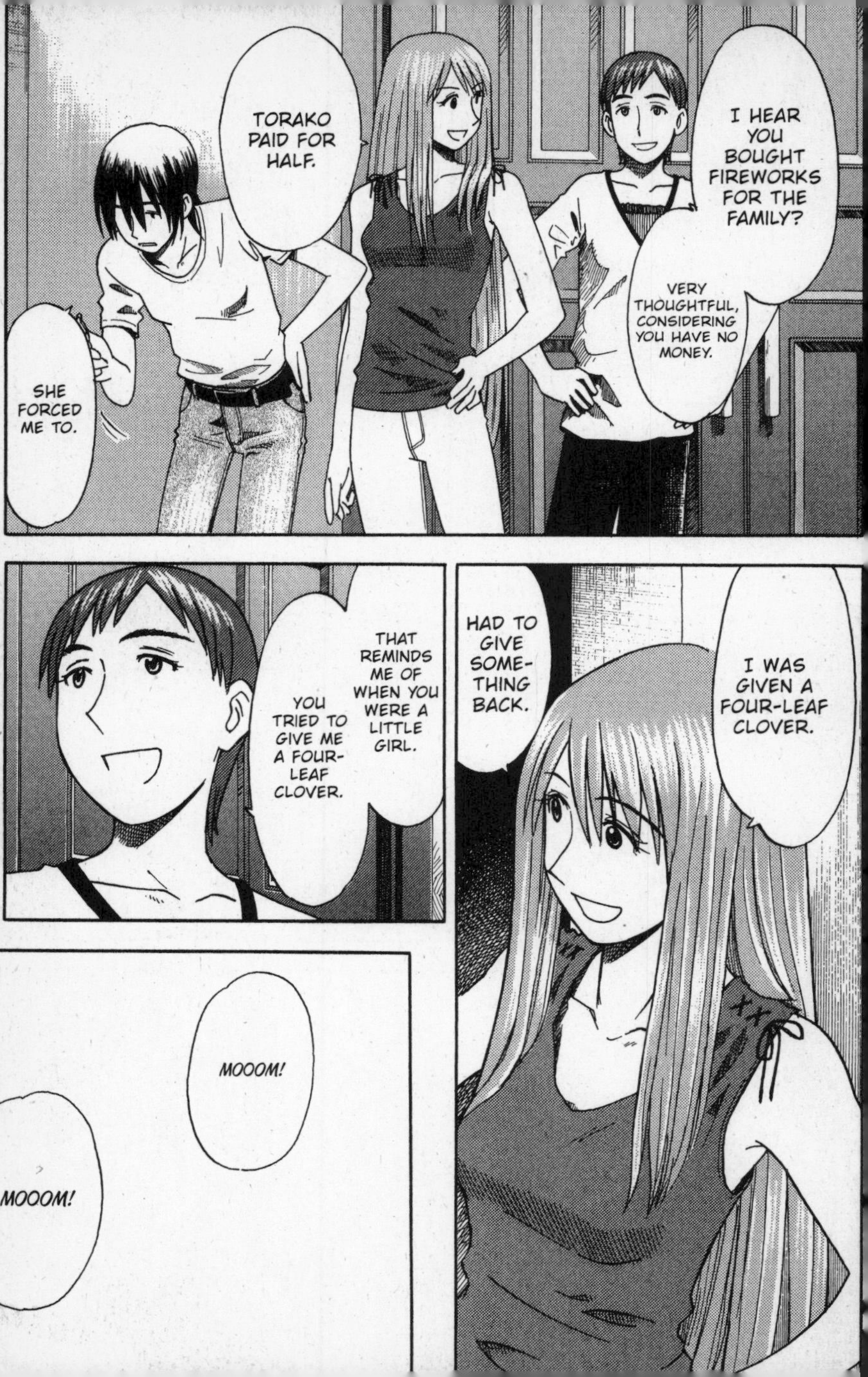
I HEAR YOU BOUGHT FIREWORKS FOR THE FAMILY?
VERY THOUGHTFUL, CONSIDERING YOU HAVE NO MONEY.
TORAKO PAID FOR HALF.
SHE FORCED ME TO.
I WAS GIVEN A FOUR-LEAF CLOVER.
HAD TO GIVE SOME-THING BACK.
THAT REMINDS ME OF WHEN YOU WERE A LITTLE GIRL.
YOU TRIED TO GIVE ME A FOUR-LEAF CLOVER.
MOOOM!
MOOOM!

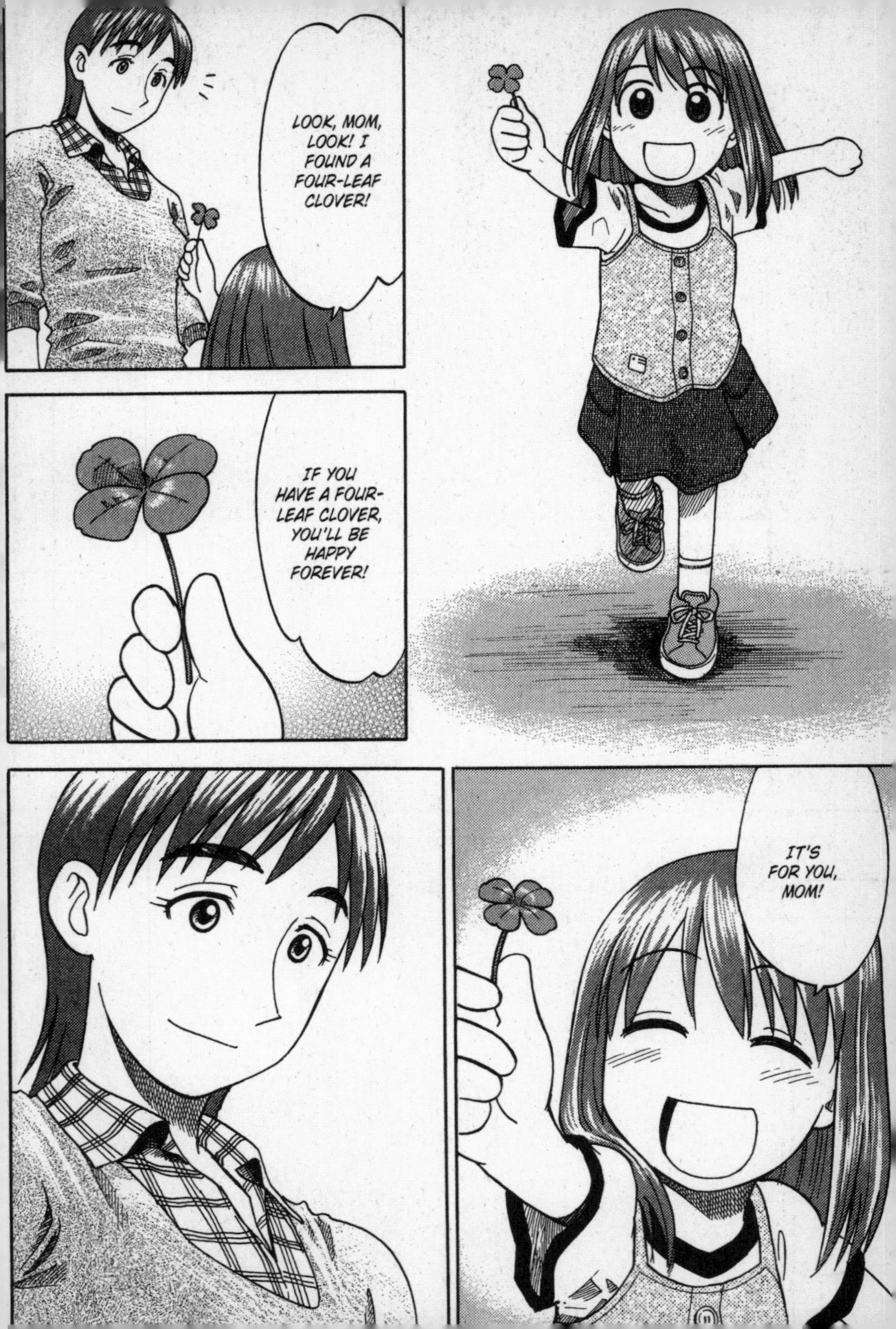
LOOK, MOM, LOOK! I FOUND A FOUR-LEAF CLOVER!
IF YOU HAVE A FOUR-LEAF CLOVER, YOU'LL BE HAPPY FOREVER!
IT'S FOR YOU, MOM!

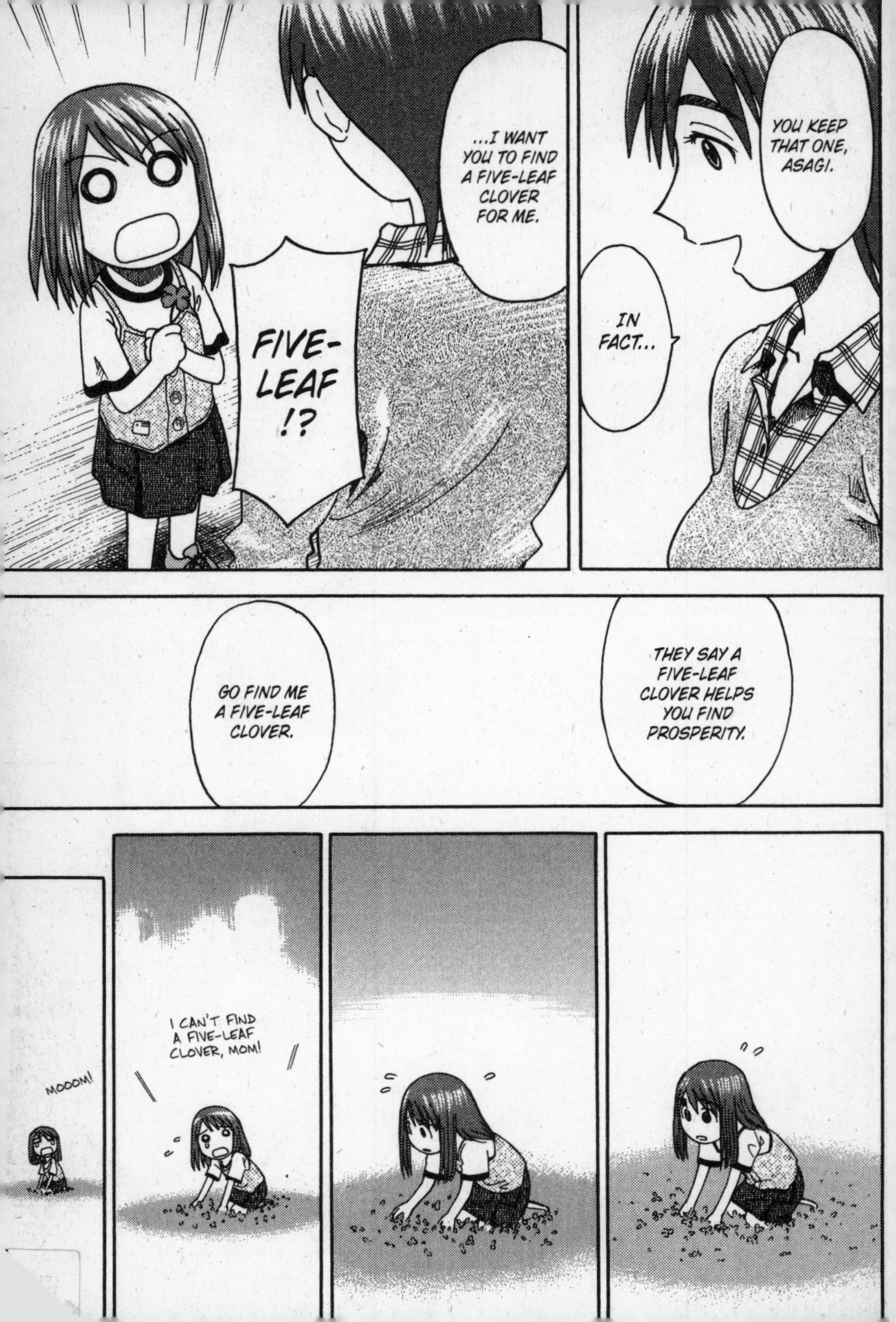
YOU KEEP THAT ONE, ASAGI.
IN FACT...
...I WANT YOU TO FIND A FIVE-LEAF CLOVER FOR ME.
FIVE-LEAF!?
THEY SAY A FIVE-LEAF CLOVER HELPS YOU FIND PROSPERITY.
GO FIND ME A FIVE-LEAF CLOVER.
I CAN'T FIND A FIVE-LEAF CLOVER, MOM!
MOOOM!

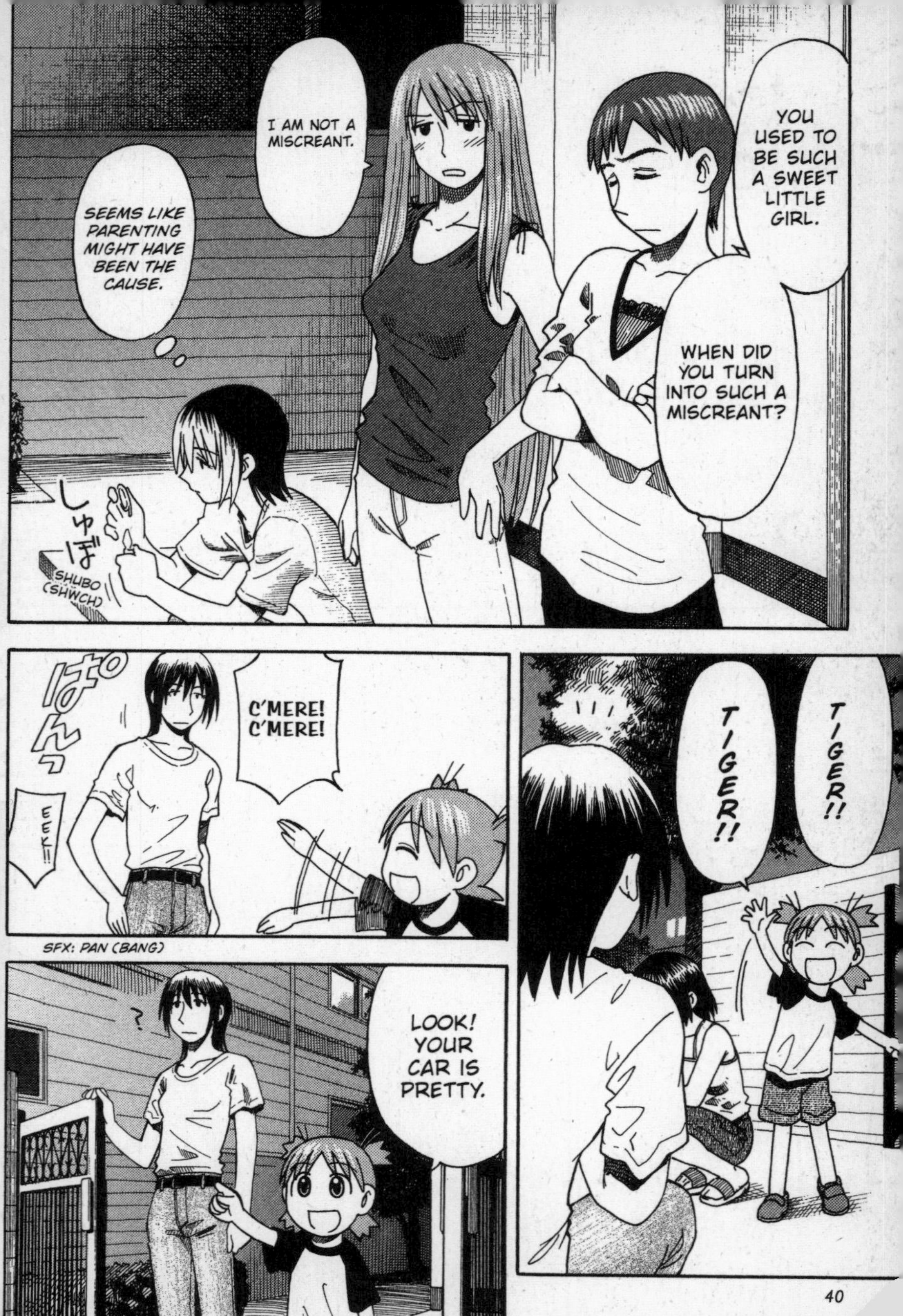
YOU USED TO BE SUCH A SWEET LITTLE GIRL.
WHEN DID YOU TURN INTO SUCH A MISCREANT?
I AM NOT A MISCREANT.
SEEMS LIKE PARENTING MIGHT HAVE BEEN THE CAUSE.
しゅぼ
SHUBO (SHWCH)
TIGER!!
TIGER!!
C'MERE! C'MERE!
ぱんっ
EEK!!
SFX: PAN (BANG)
?
LOOK! YOUR CAR IS PRETTY.

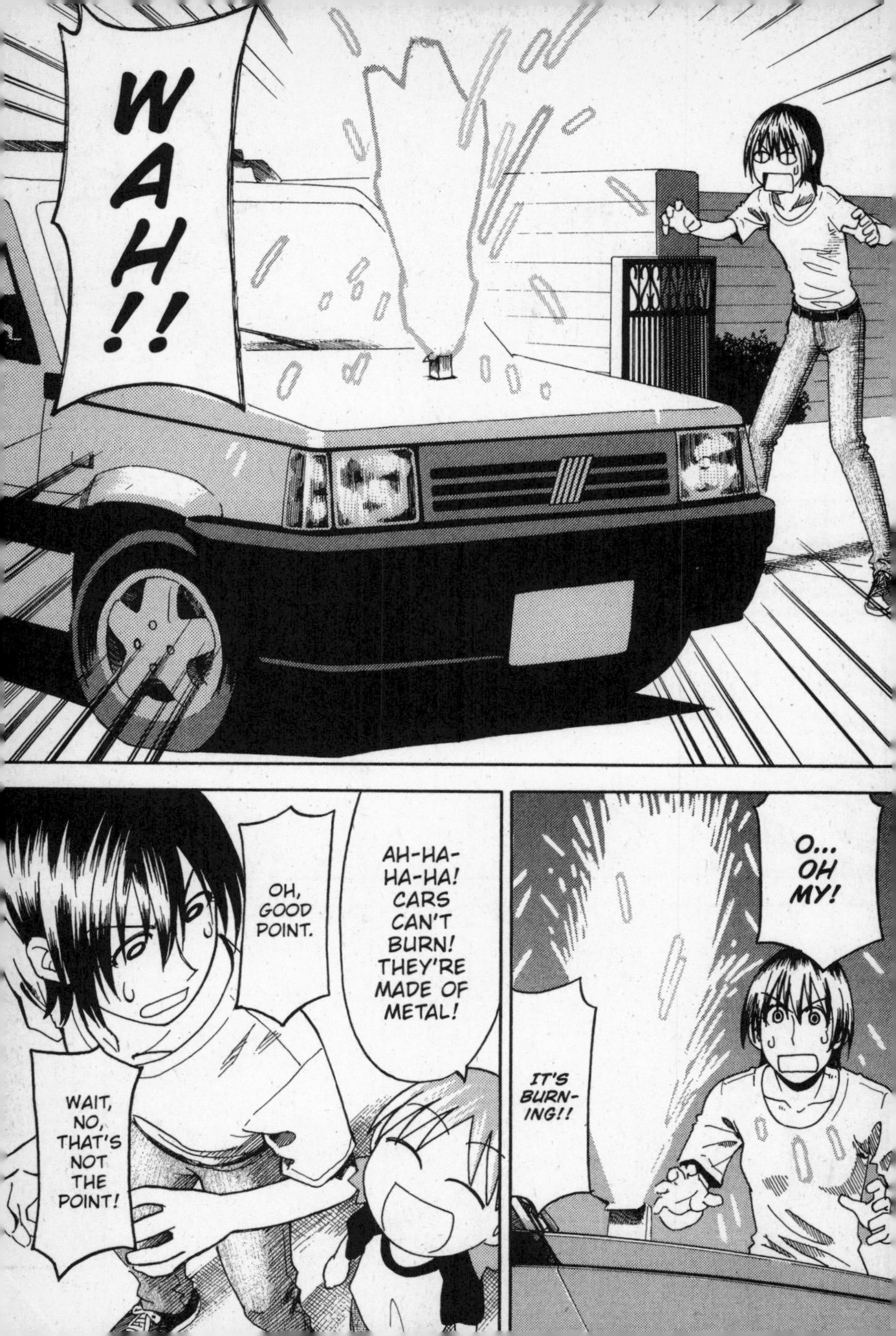
WAH!!
O... OH MY!
IT'S BURNING!!
AH-HA-HA-HA! CARS CAN'T BURN! THEY'RE MADE OF METAL!
OH, GOOD POINT.
WAIT, NO, THAT'S NOT THE POINT!

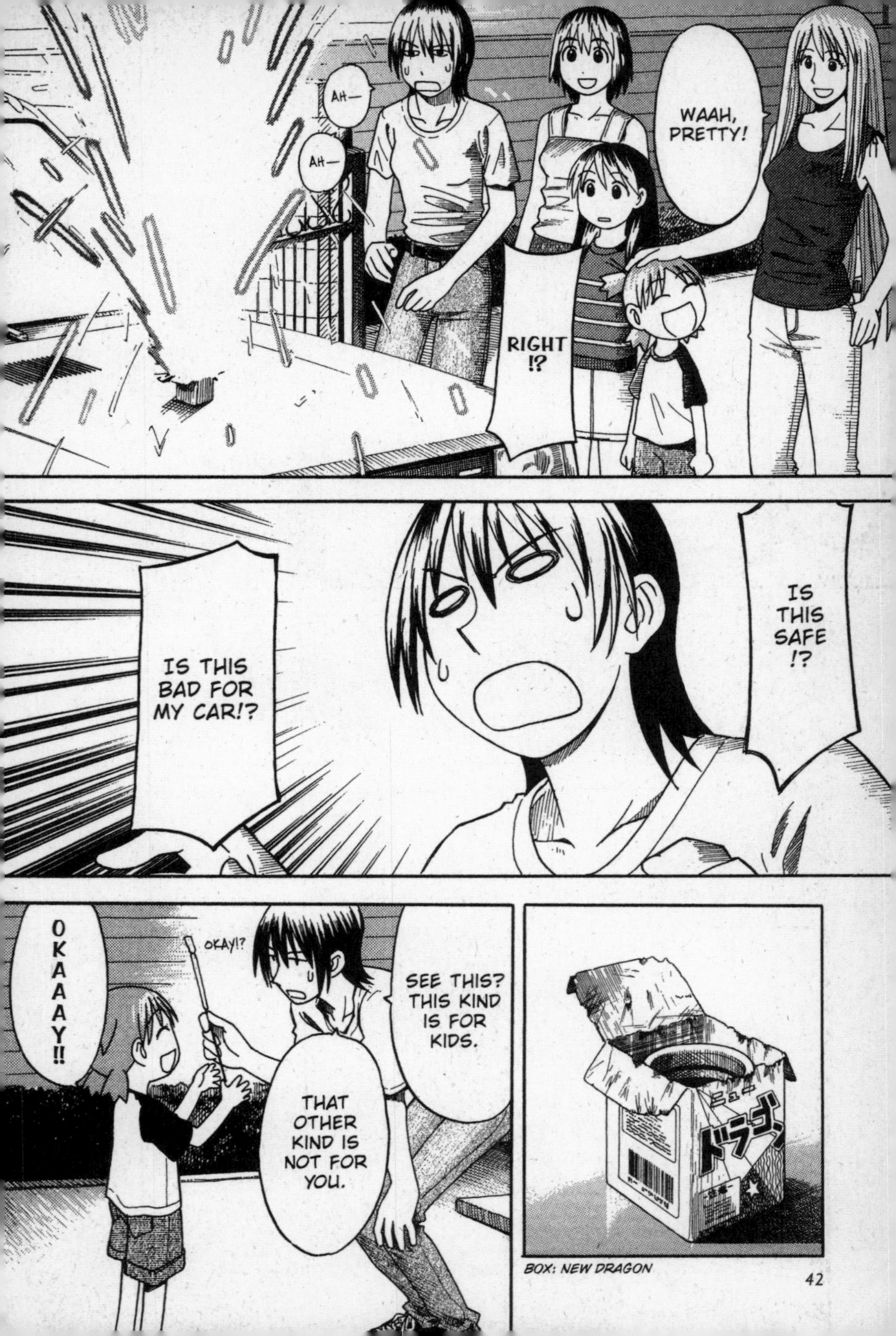
WAAH, PRETTY!
RIGHT!?
AH—
AH—
IS THIS SAFE!?
IS THIS BAD FOR MY CAR!?
SEE THIS? THIS KIND IS FOR KIDS.
THAT OTHER KIND IS NOT FOR YOU.
OKAY!?
OKAAAAY!!

BOX: NEW DRAGON

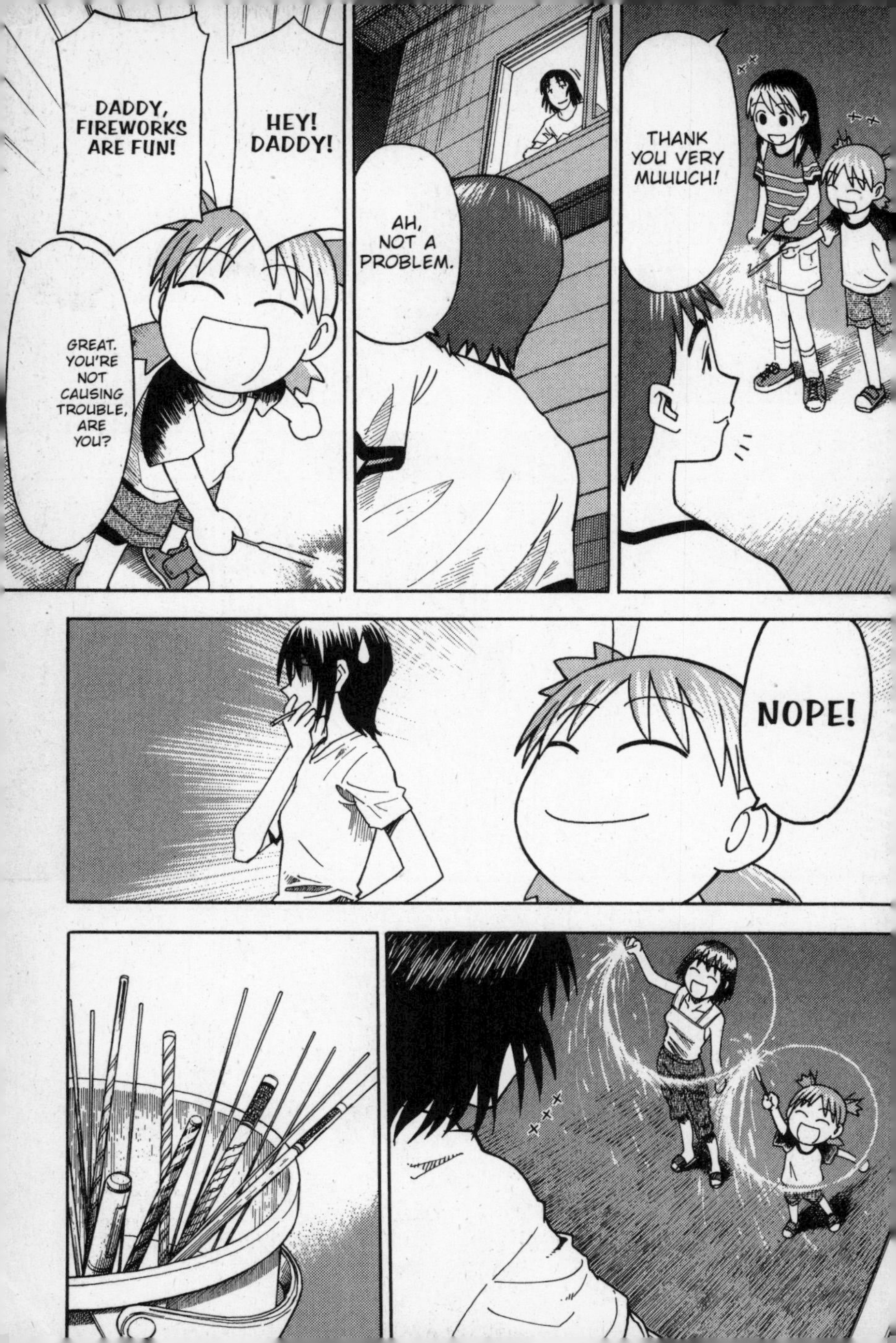
THANK YOU VERY MUUUCH!
AH, NOT A PROBLEM.
HEY! DADDY!
DADDY, FIREWORKS ARE FUN!
GREAT. YOU'RE NOT CAUSING TROUBLE, ARE YOU?
NOPE!

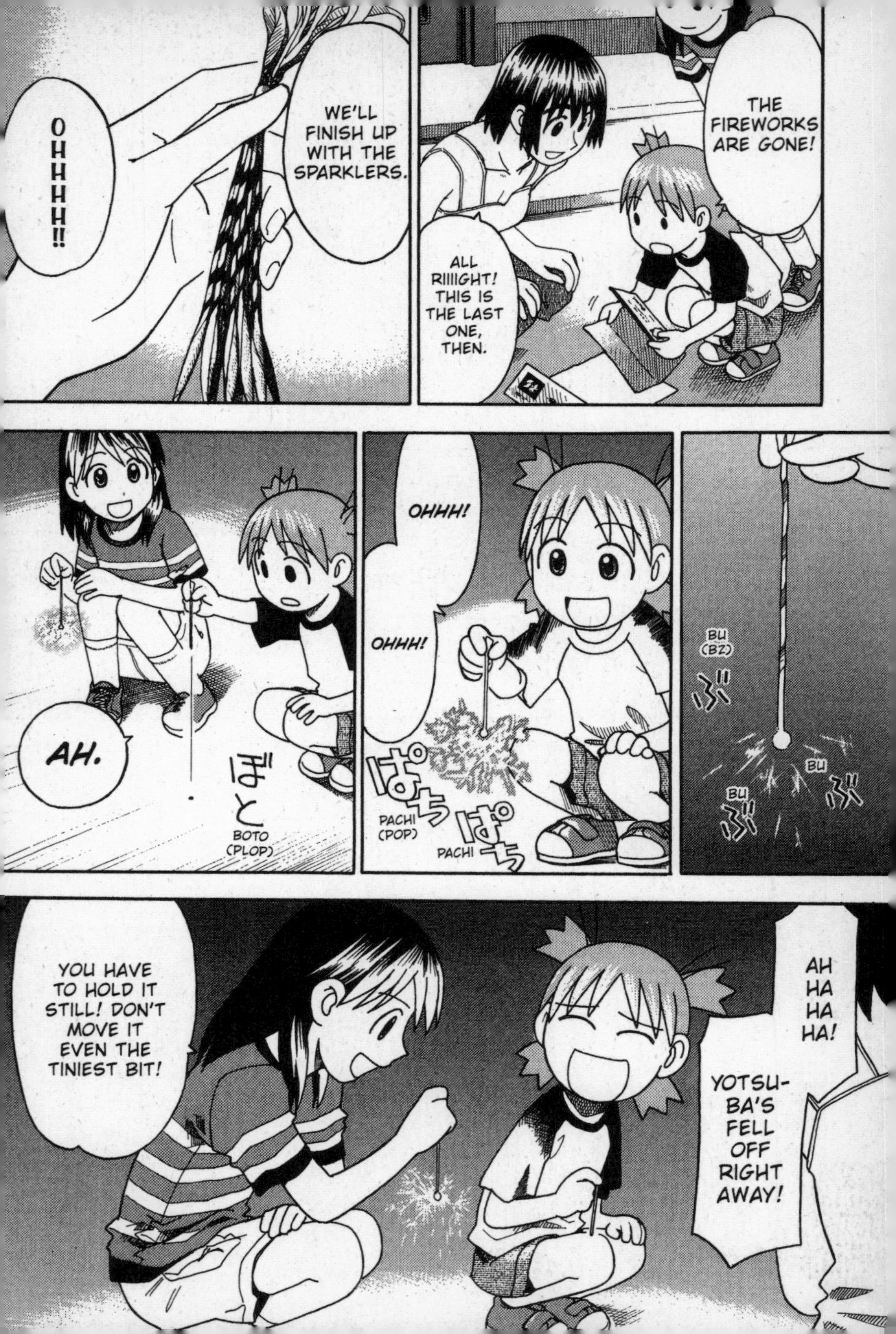
THE FIREWORKS ARE GONE!
ALL RIIIIGHT! THIS IS THE LAST ONE, THEN.
WE'LL FINISH UP WITH THE SPARKLERS.
OHHHHH!!
BU (BZ)
ぶ
BU
ぶ
BU
ぶ
OHHH!
OHHH!
ぱち
PACHI (POP)
ぱち
PACHI
AH.
ぼと
BOTO (PLOP)
AH HA HA HA!
YOTSU-BA'S FELL OFF RIGHT AWAY!
YOU HAVE TO HOLD IT STILL! DON'T MOVE IT EVEN THE TINIEST BIT!

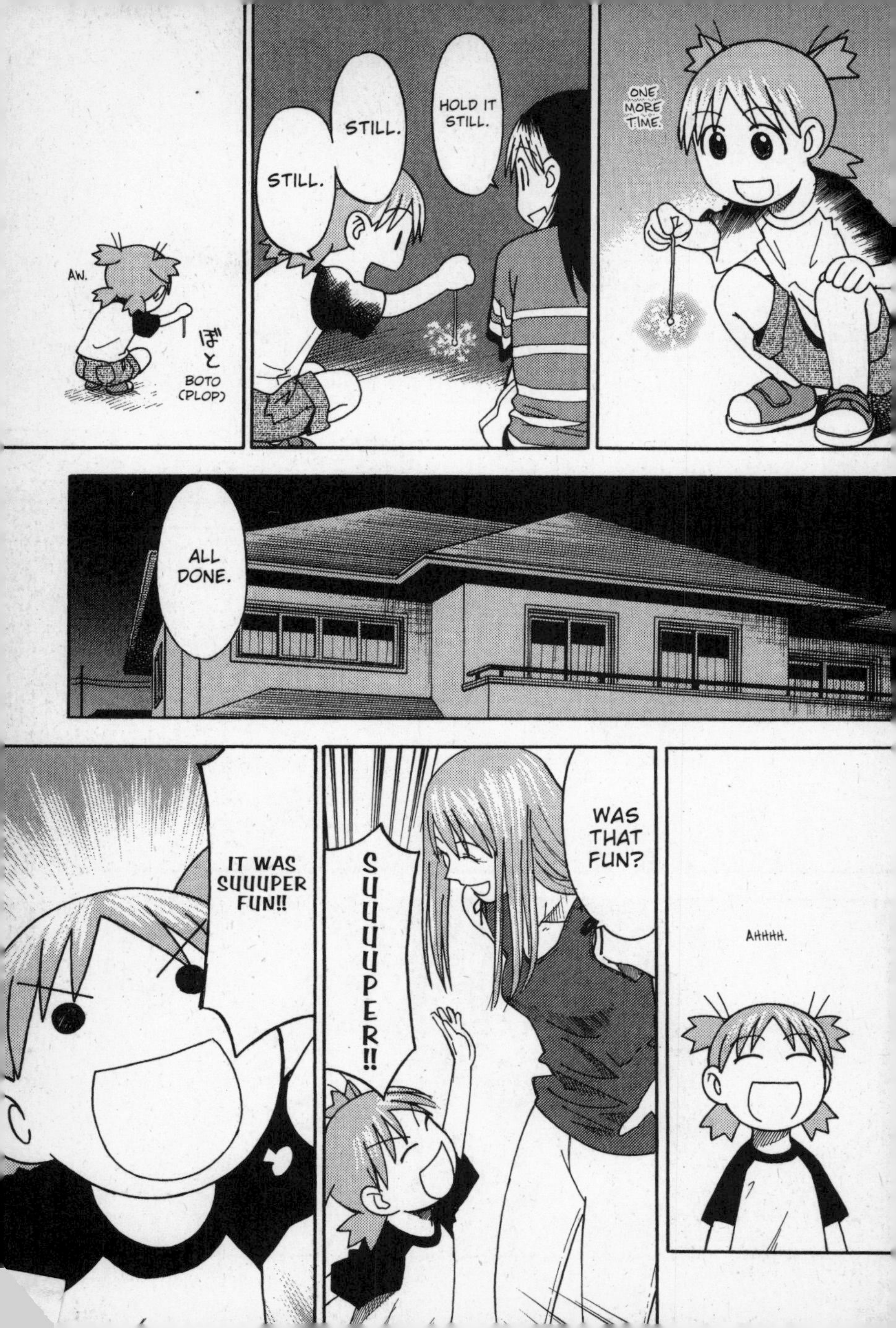
ONE MORE TIME.
HOLD IT STILL.
STILL.
STILL.
AW.
ぼと
BOTO (PLOP)
ALL DONE.
AHHHH.
WAS THAT FUN?
SUUUUPER!!
IT WAS SUUUPER FUN!!

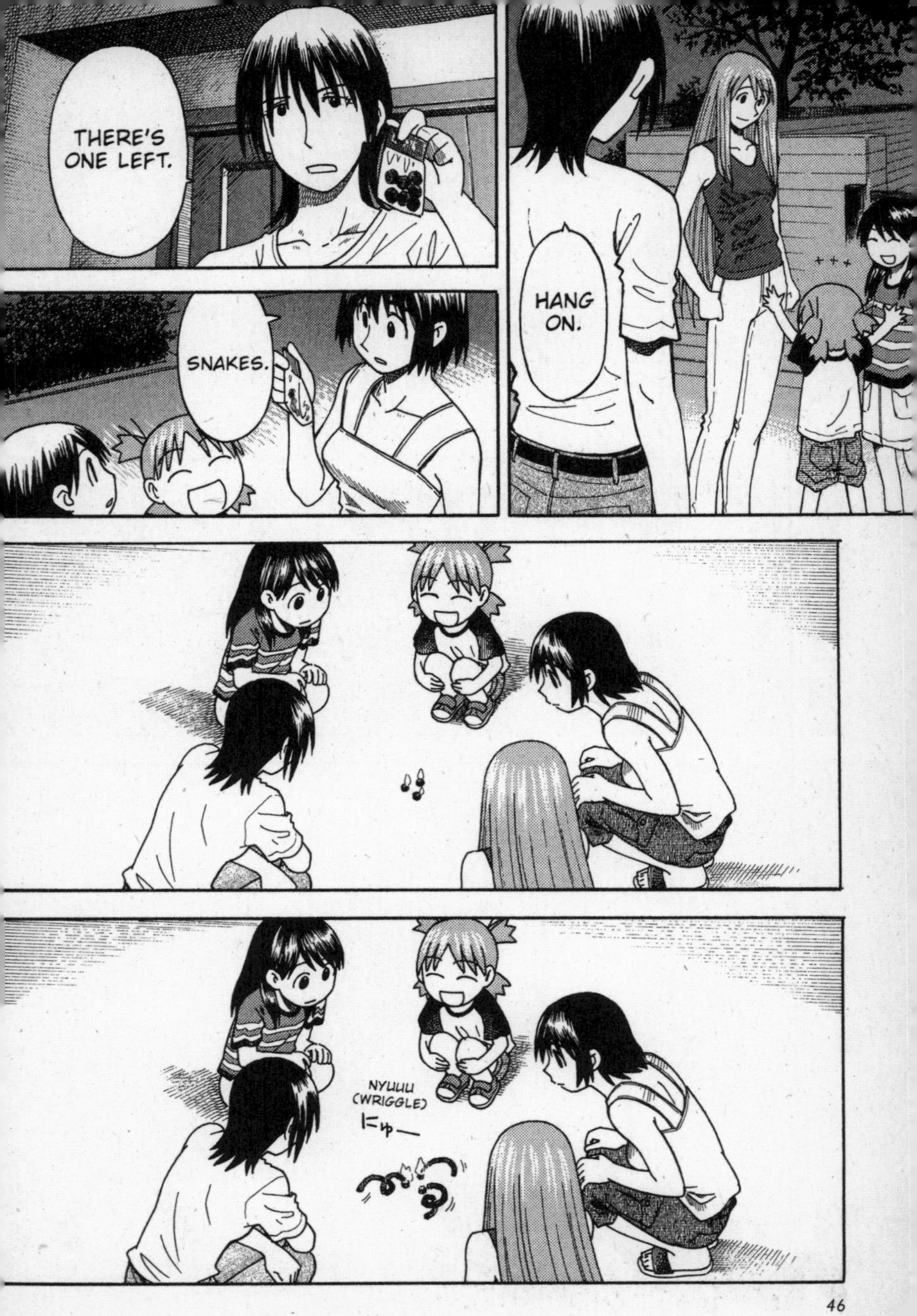
HANG ON.
THERE'S ONE LEFT.
SNAKES.
NYUUU (WRIGGLE)
にゅー

YOTSUBA&!

TREASURE!!

BOX: DRAGON

YOTSUBA&FLOWERS!

#17

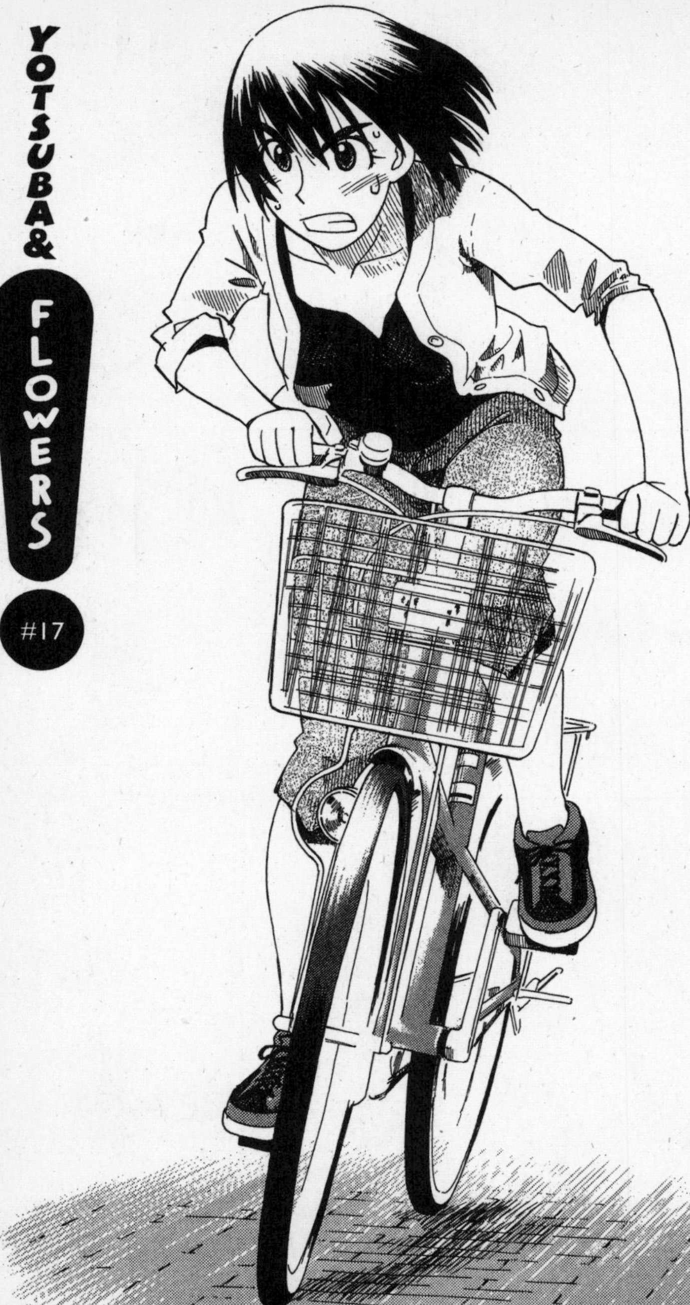

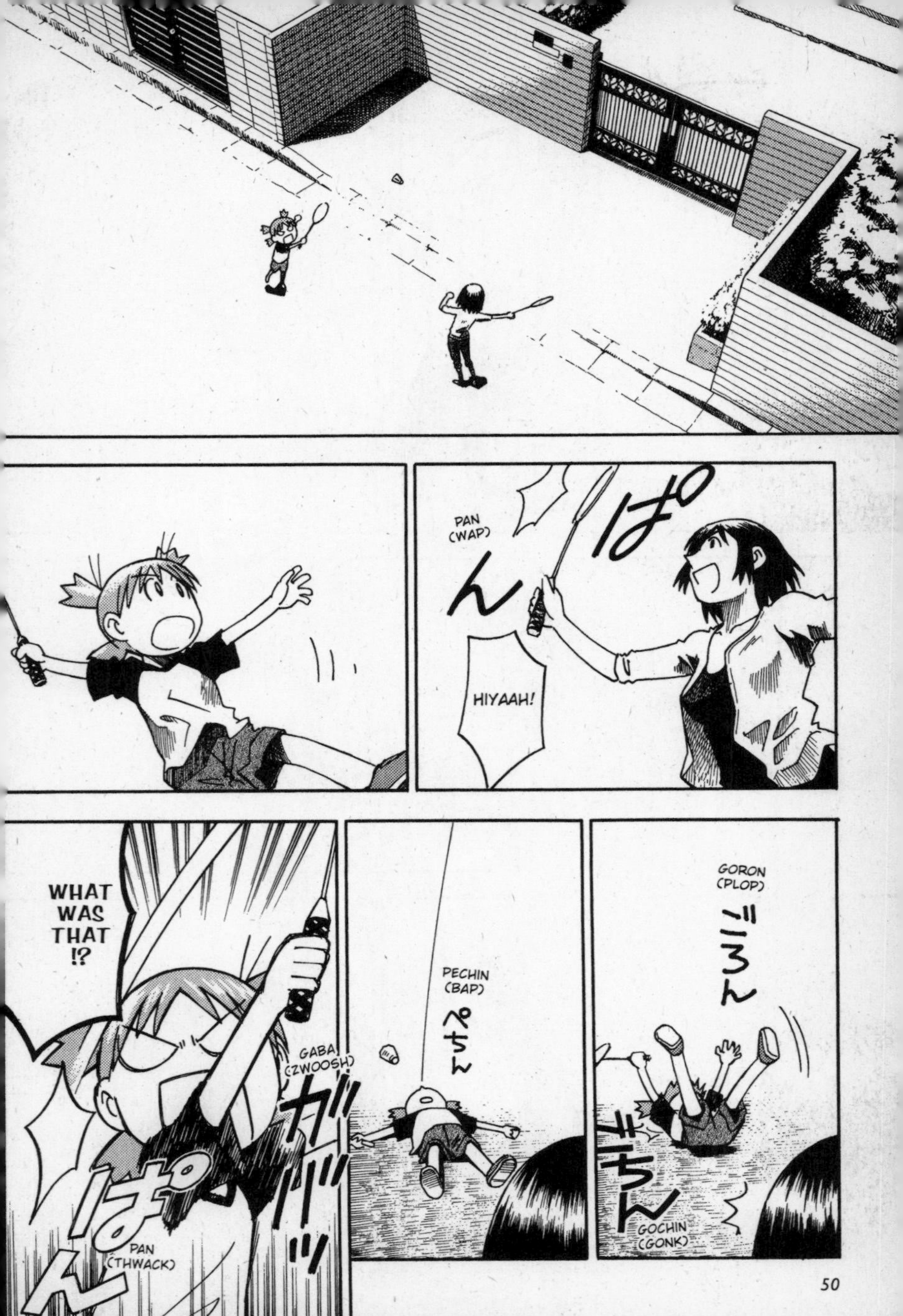
PAN (WAP)
ぱん
HIYAAH!
GORON (PLOP)
ごろん
GOCHIN (GONK)
ごちん
PECHIN (BAP)
ぺちん
WHAT WAS THAT!?
GABA (ZWOOSH)
ガバッ
PAN (THWACK)
ぱん

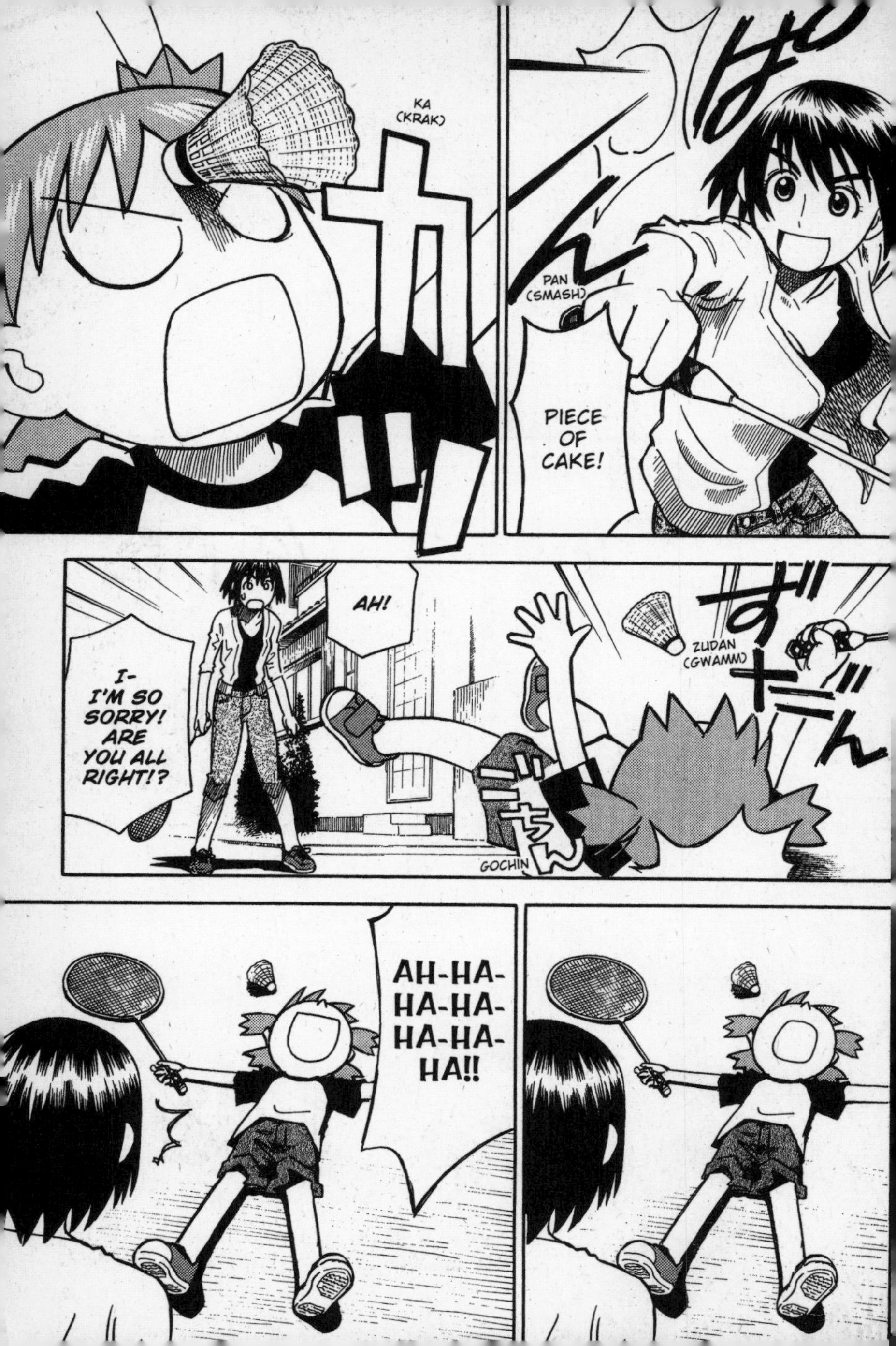

ぱん
PAN (SMASH)
PIECE OF CAKE!
カッ
KA (KRAK)
ずだーん
ZUDAN (GWAMM)
AH!
I- I'M SO SORRY! ARE YOU ALL RIGHT!?
ごちん
GOCHIN
AH-HA-HA-HA-HA-HA-HA!!

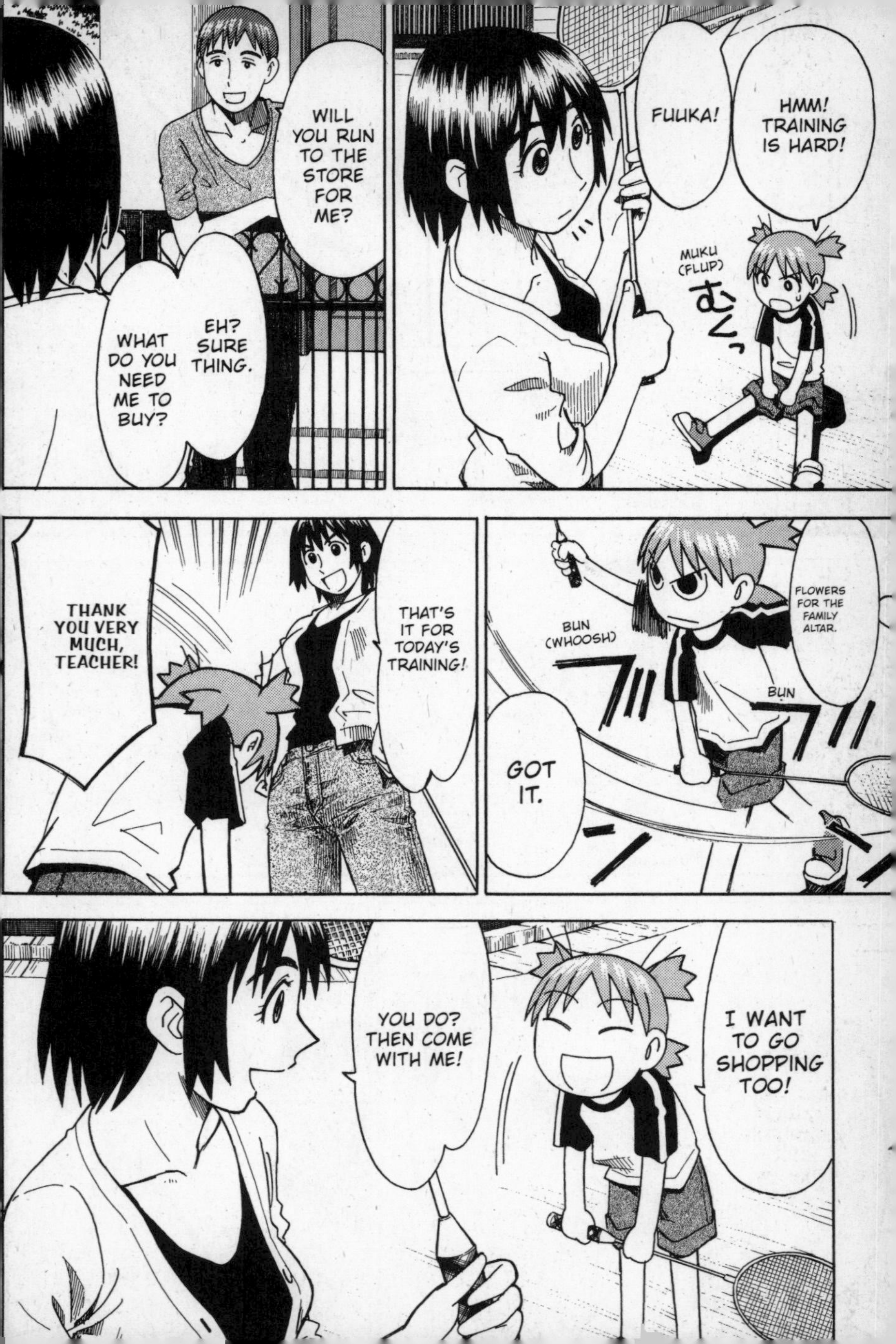
HMM! TRAINING IS HARD!
FUUKA!
MUKU (FLUP)
むくっ
WILL YOU RUN TO THE STORE FOR ME?
EH? SURE THING.
WHAT DO YOU NEED ME TO BUY?
FLOWERS FOR THE FAMILY ALTAR.
BUN
BUN (WHOOSH)
GOT IT.
THAT'S IT FOR TODAY'S TRAINING!
THANK YOU VERY MUCH, TEACHER!
I WANT TO GO SHOPPING TOO!
YOU DO? THEN COME WITH ME!

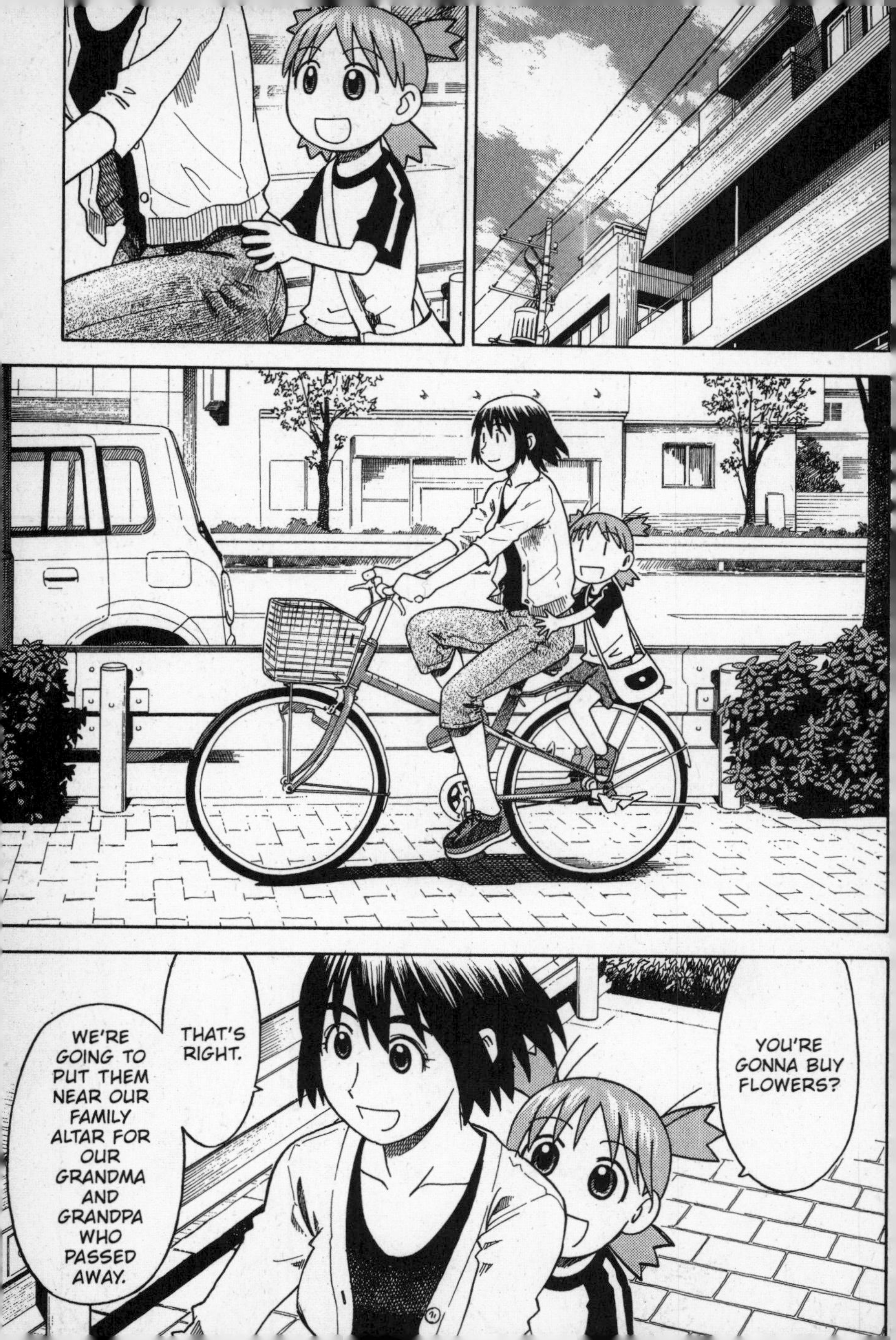
YOU'RE GONNA BUY FLOWERS?
THAT'S RIGHT.
WE'RE GOING TO PUT THEM NEAR OUR FAMILY ALTAR FOR OUR GRANDMA AND GRANDPA WHO PASSED AWAY.

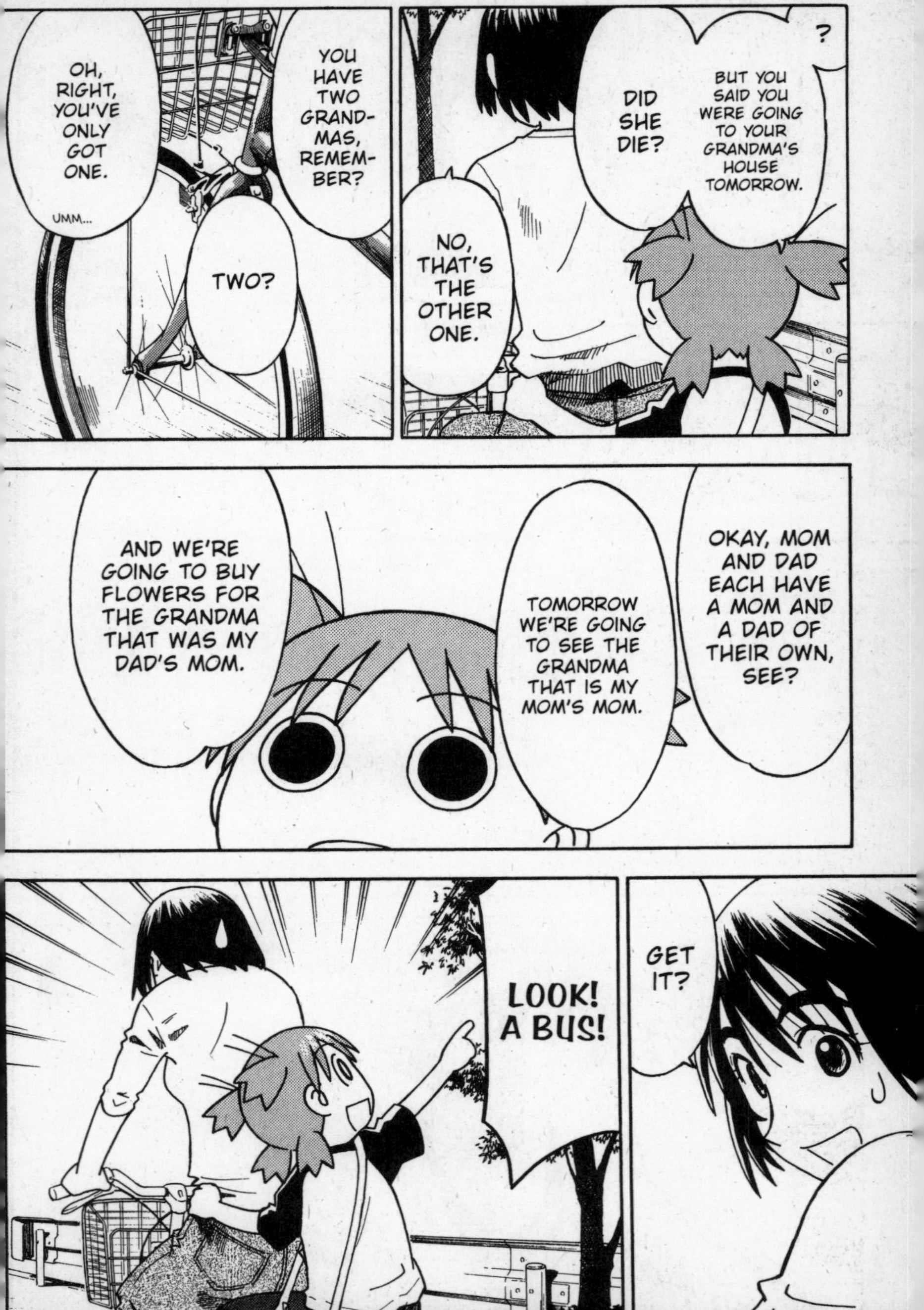
?
BUT YOU SAID YOU WERE GOING TO YOUR GRANDMA'S HOUSE TOMORROW.
DID SHE DIE?
NO, THAT'S THE OTHER ONE.
YOU HAVE TWO GRAND-MAS, REMEM-BER?
OH, RIGHT, YOU'VE ONLY GOT ONE.
UMM...
TWO?
OKAY, MOM AND DAD EACH HAVE A MOM AND A DAD OF THEIR OWN, SEE?
TOMORROW WE'RE GOING TO SEE THE GRANDMA THAT IS MY MOM'S MOM.
AND WE'RE GOING TO BUY FLOWERS FOR THE GRANDMA THAT WAS MY DAD'S MOM.
GET IT?
LOOK! A BUS!

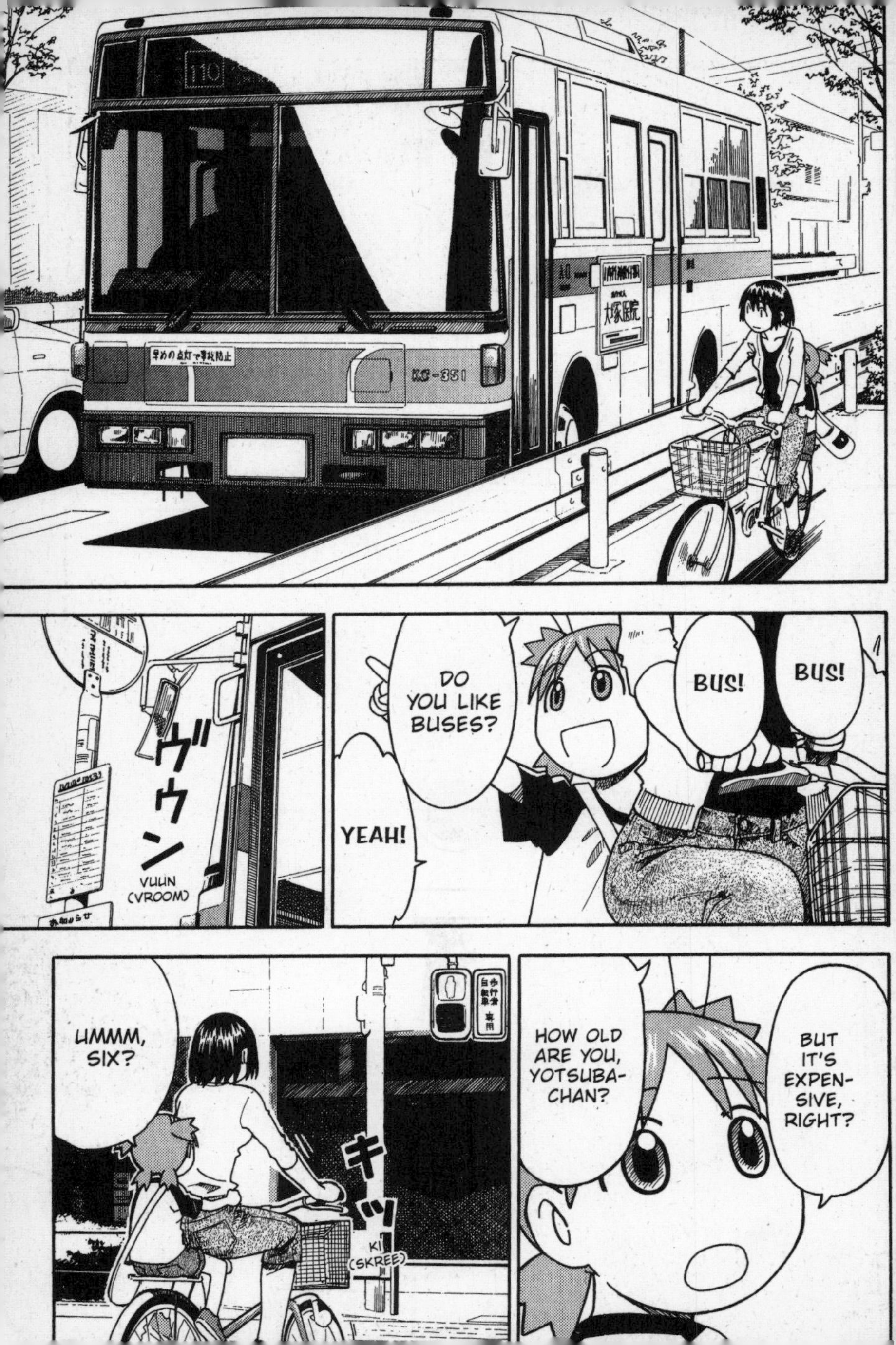
110
大塚医院
早めの点灯で事故防止
KS-351
BUS!
BUS!
DO YOU LIKE BUSES?
YEAH!
ヴゥン
VUUN (VROOM)
BUT IT'S EXPEN-SIVE, RIGHT?
HOW OLD ARE YOU, YOTSUBA-CHAN?
歩行者 自転車 専用
UMMM, SIX?
キッ
KI (SKREE)

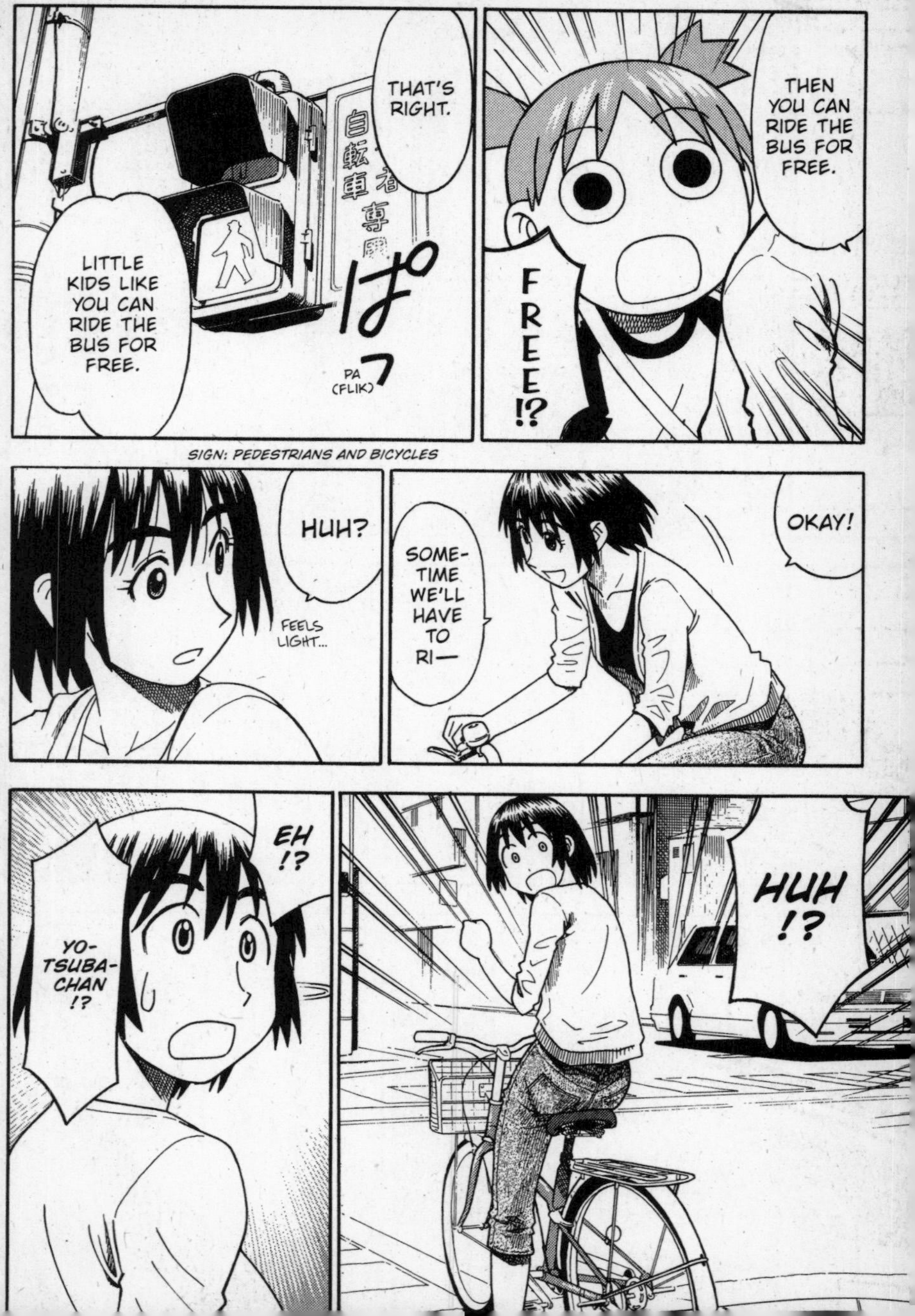
THEN YOU CAN RIDE THE BUS FOR FREE.
FREE!?
THAT'S RIGHT.
LITTLE KIDS LIKE YOU CAN RIDE THE BUS FOR FREE.
ぱっ
PA (FLIK)
SIGN: PEDESTRIANS AND BICYCLES
OKAY!
SOMETIME WE'LL HAVE TO RI—
HUH?
FEELS LIGHT...
HUH!?
EH!?
YO-TSUBA-CHAN!?

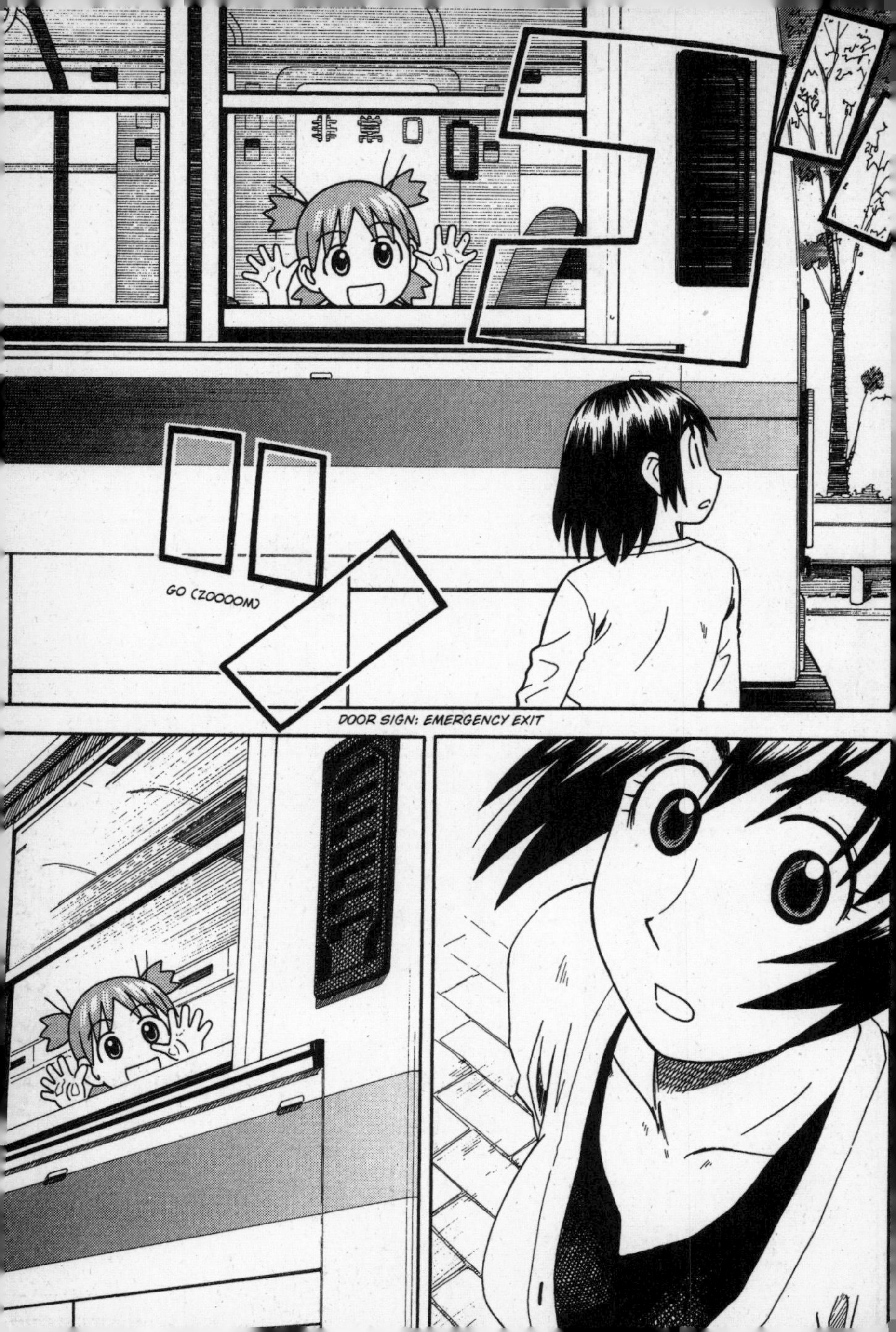
非常口
GO (ZOOOOM)
DOOR SIGN: EMERGENCY EXIT

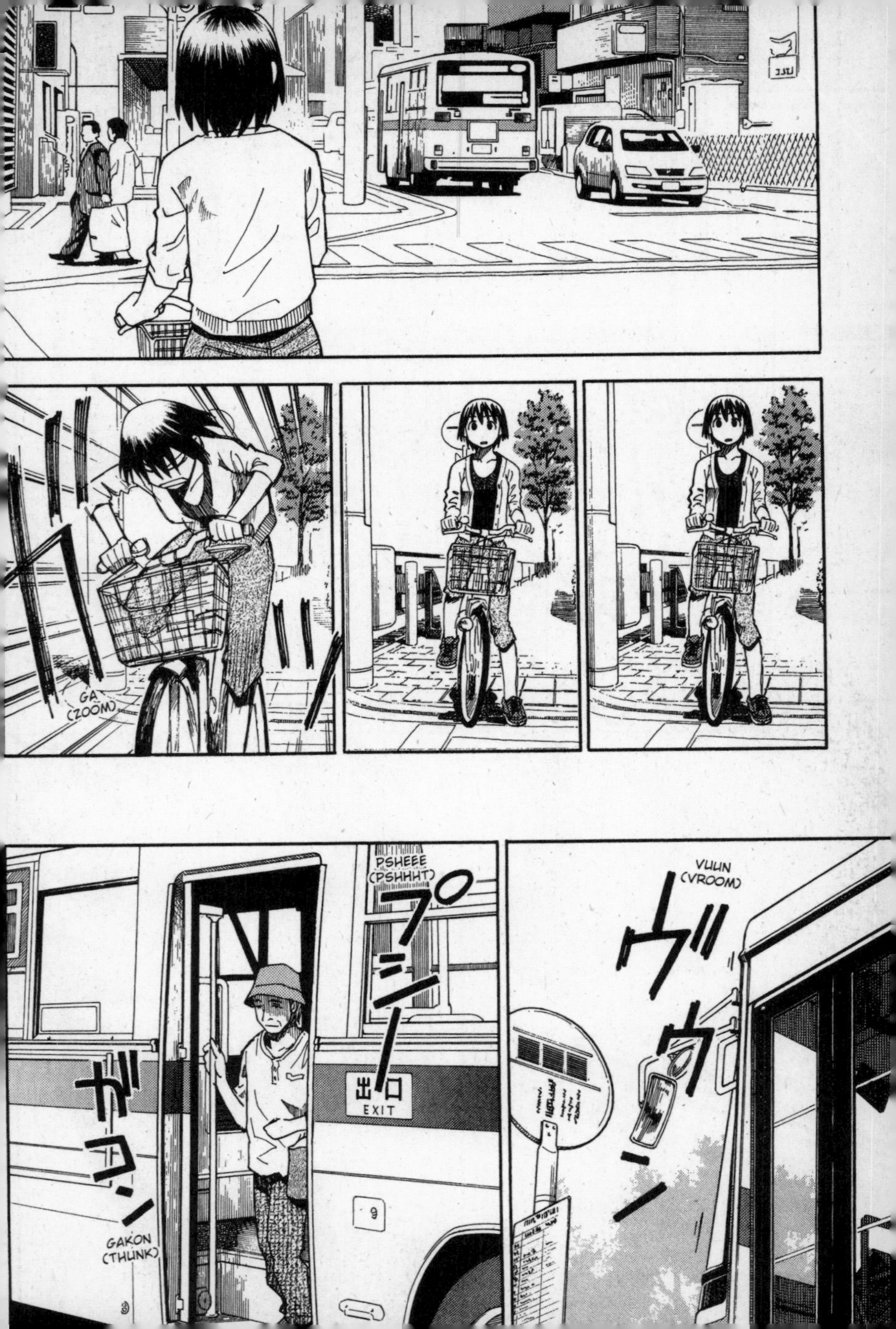
GA
(ZOOM)
ヴゥー
VUUN
(VROOM)
プシー
PSHEEE
(PSHHHT)
出口
EXIT
ガコン
GAKON
(THUNK)

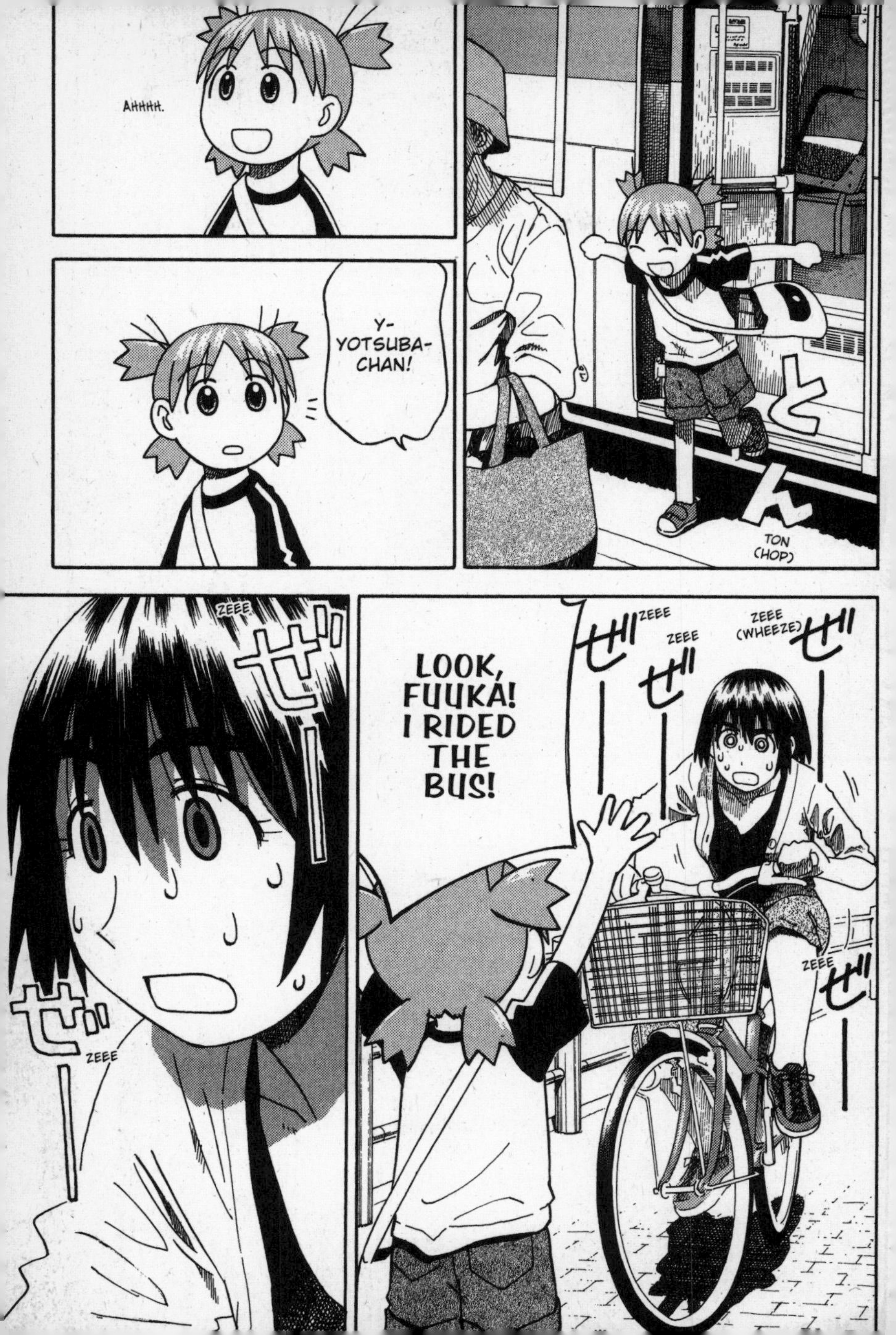

とん
TON (HOP)
AHHHH.
Y-YOTSUBA-CHAN!
LOOK, FUUKA! I RIDED THE BUS!
ZEEE (WHEEZE)
ZEEE
ZEEE
ZEEE
ZEEE
ZEEE

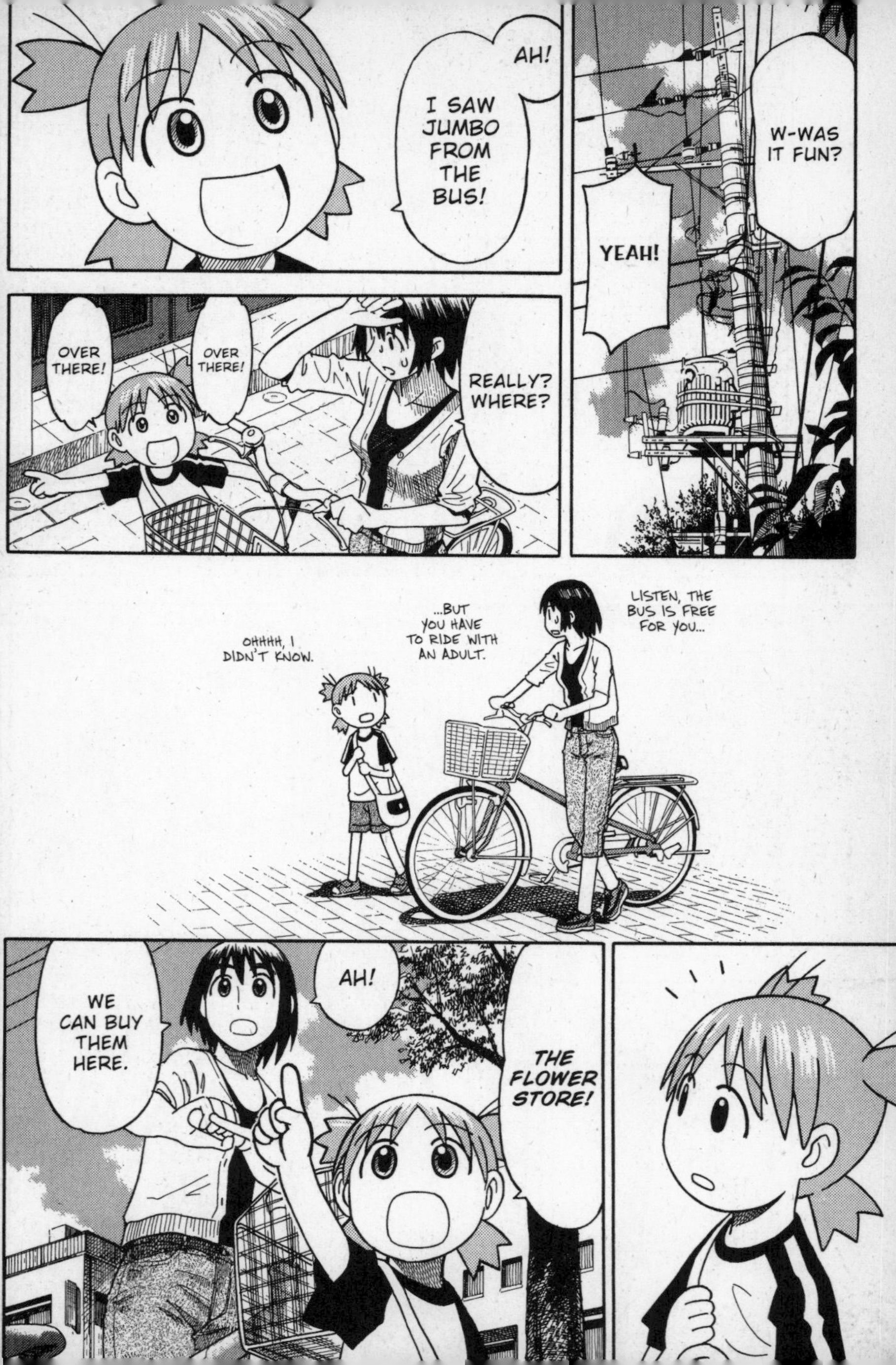
W-WAS IT FUN?
YEAH!
AH!
I SAW JUMBO FROM THE BUS!
REALLY? WHERE?
OVER THERE!
OVER THERE!
LISTEN, THE BUS IS FREE FOR YOU...
...BUT YOU HAVE TO RIDE WITH AN ADULT.
OHHHH, I DIDN'T KNOW.
THE FLOWER STORE!
AH!
WE CAN BUY THEM HERE.

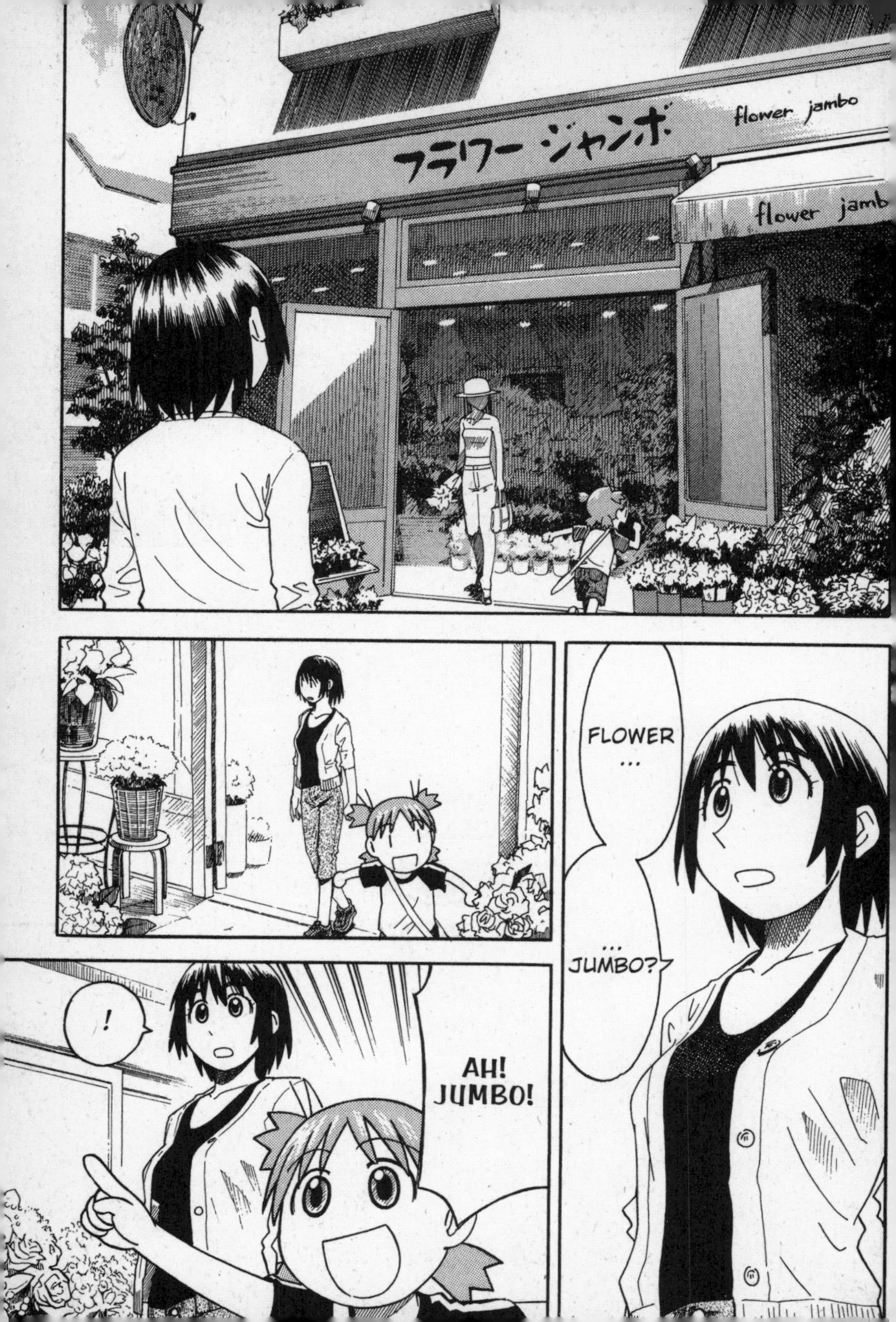
フラワー ジャンボ
flower jambo
flower jamb
FLOWER ...
... JUMBO?
AH! JUMBO!
!

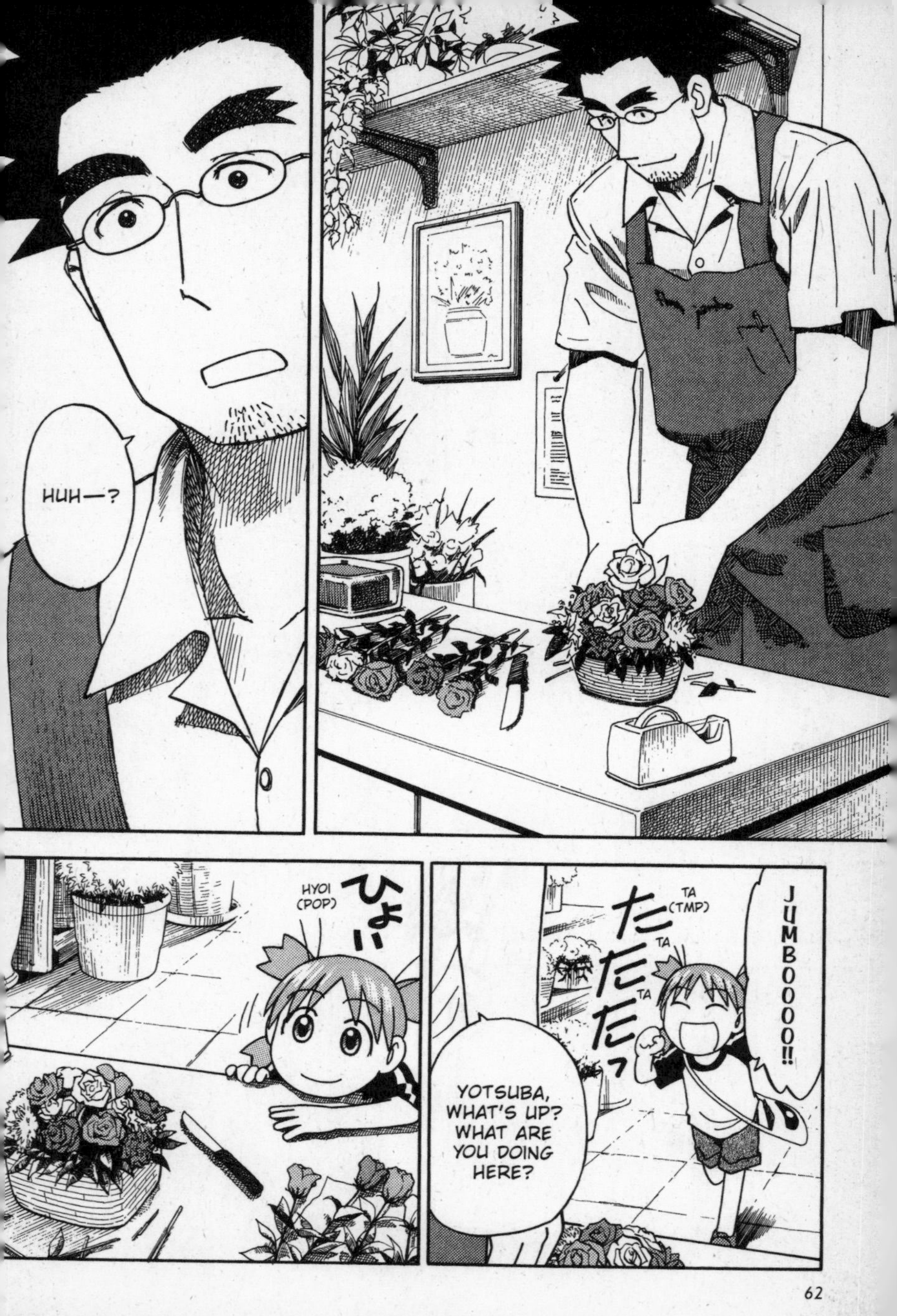
HUH—?
JUMBOOOOO!!
たたたっ
TA (TMP)
TA
TA
YOTSUBA, WHAT'S UP? WHAT ARE YOU DOING HERE?
ひょい
HYOI (POP)

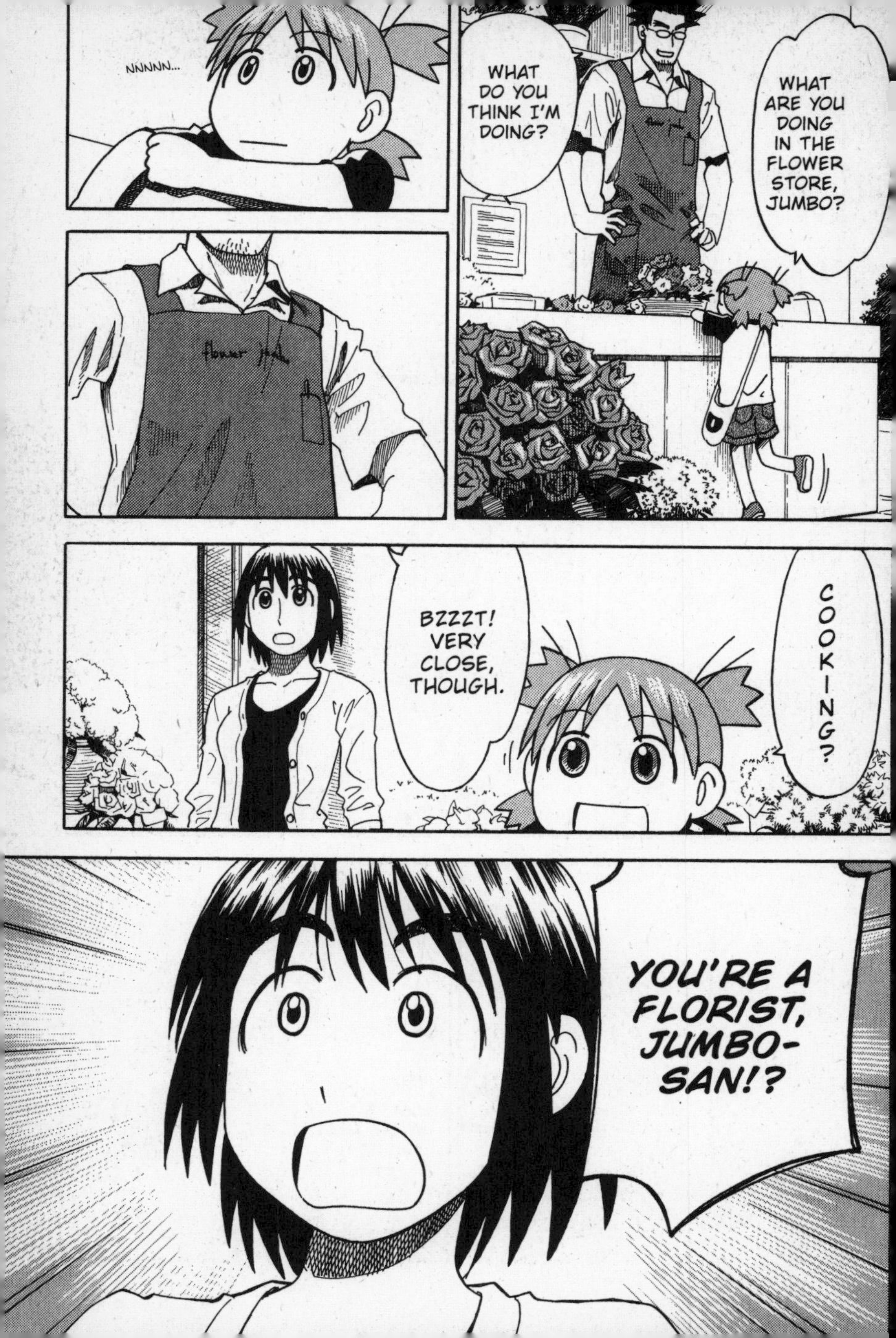
WHAT ARE YOU DOING IN THE FLOWER STORE, JUMBO?
WHAT DO YOU THINK I'M DOING?
NNNNN...
flower jumbo
COOKING?
BZZZT! VERY CLOSE, THOUGH.
YOU'RE A FLORIST, JUMBO-SAN!?

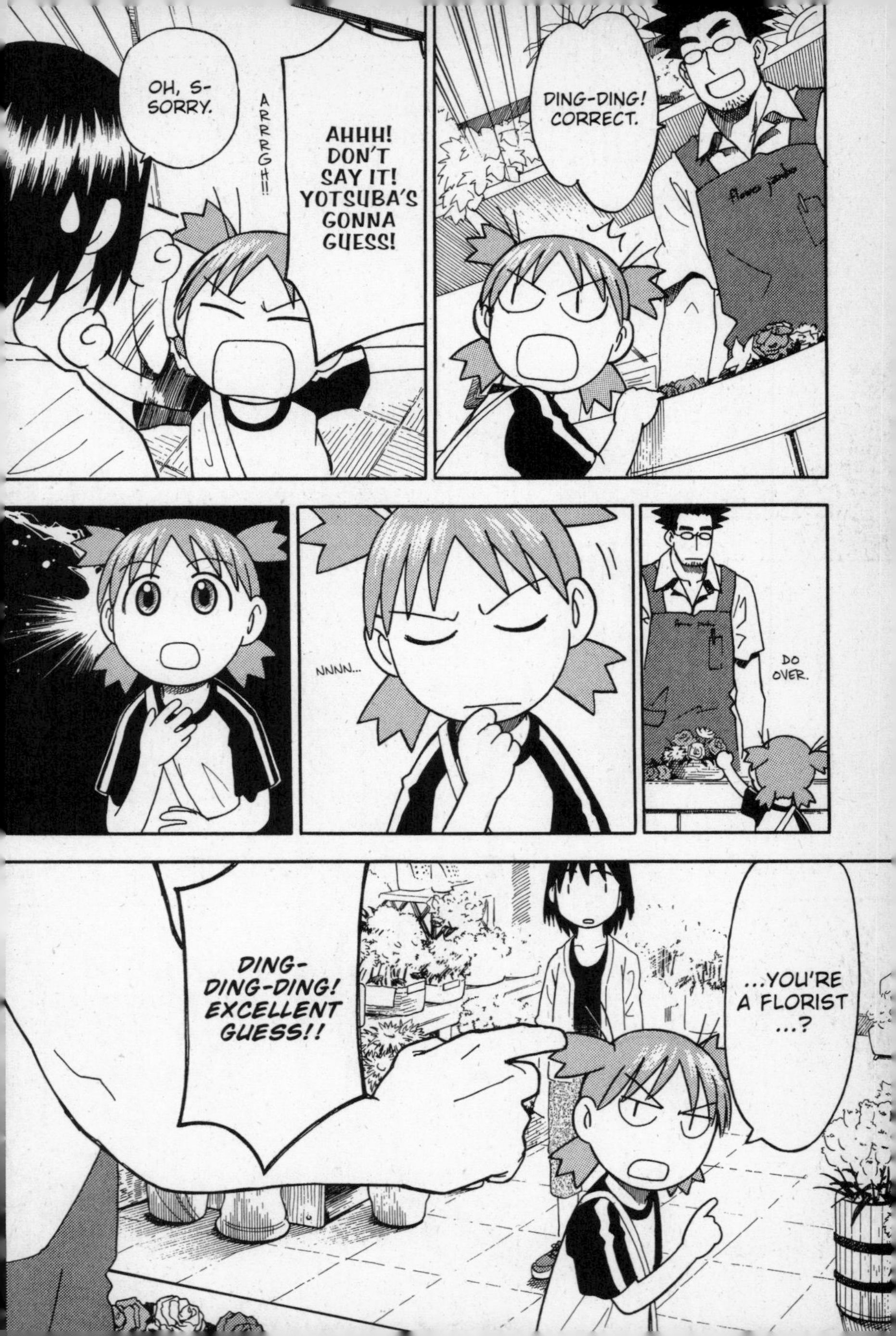
DING-DING! CORRECT.
AHHH! DON'T SAY IT! YOTSUBA'S GONNA GUESS!
ARRRGH!!
OH, S-SORRY.
DO OVER.
NNNN...
...YOU'RE A FLORIST ...?
DING-DING-DING! EXCELLENT GUESS!!

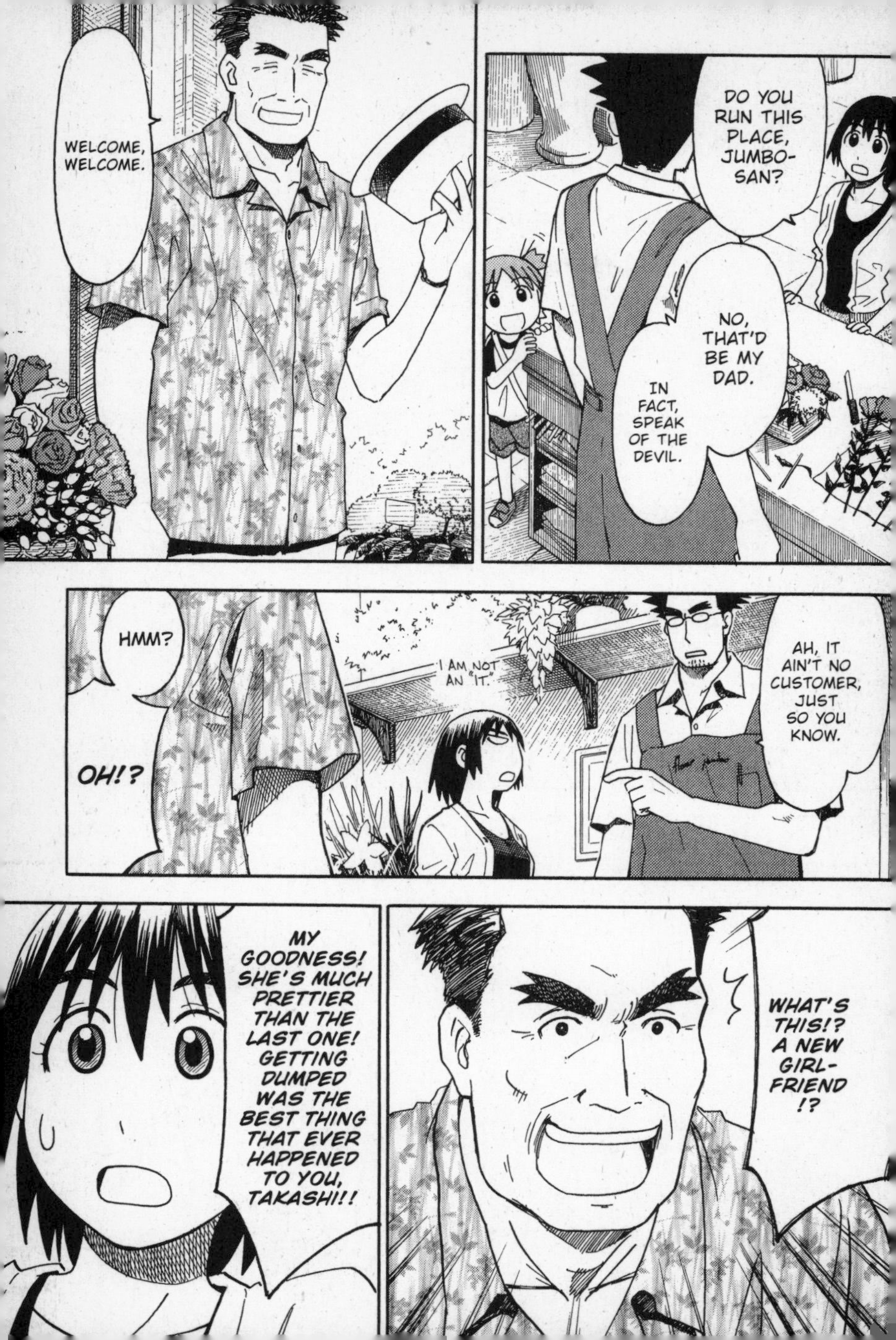
DO YOU RUN THIS PLACE, JUMBO-SAN?
NO, THAT'D BE MY DAD.
IN FACT, SPEAK OF THE DEVIL.
WELCOME, WELCOME.
AH, IT AIN'T NO CUSTOMER, JUST SO YOU KNOW.
I AM NOT AN "IT."
HMM?
OH!?
WHAT'S THIS!? A NEW GIRL-FRIEND!?
MY GOODNESS! SHE'S MUCH PRETTIER THAN THE LAST ONE! GETTING DUMPED WAS THE BEST THING THAT EVER HAPPENED TO YOU, TAKASHI!!

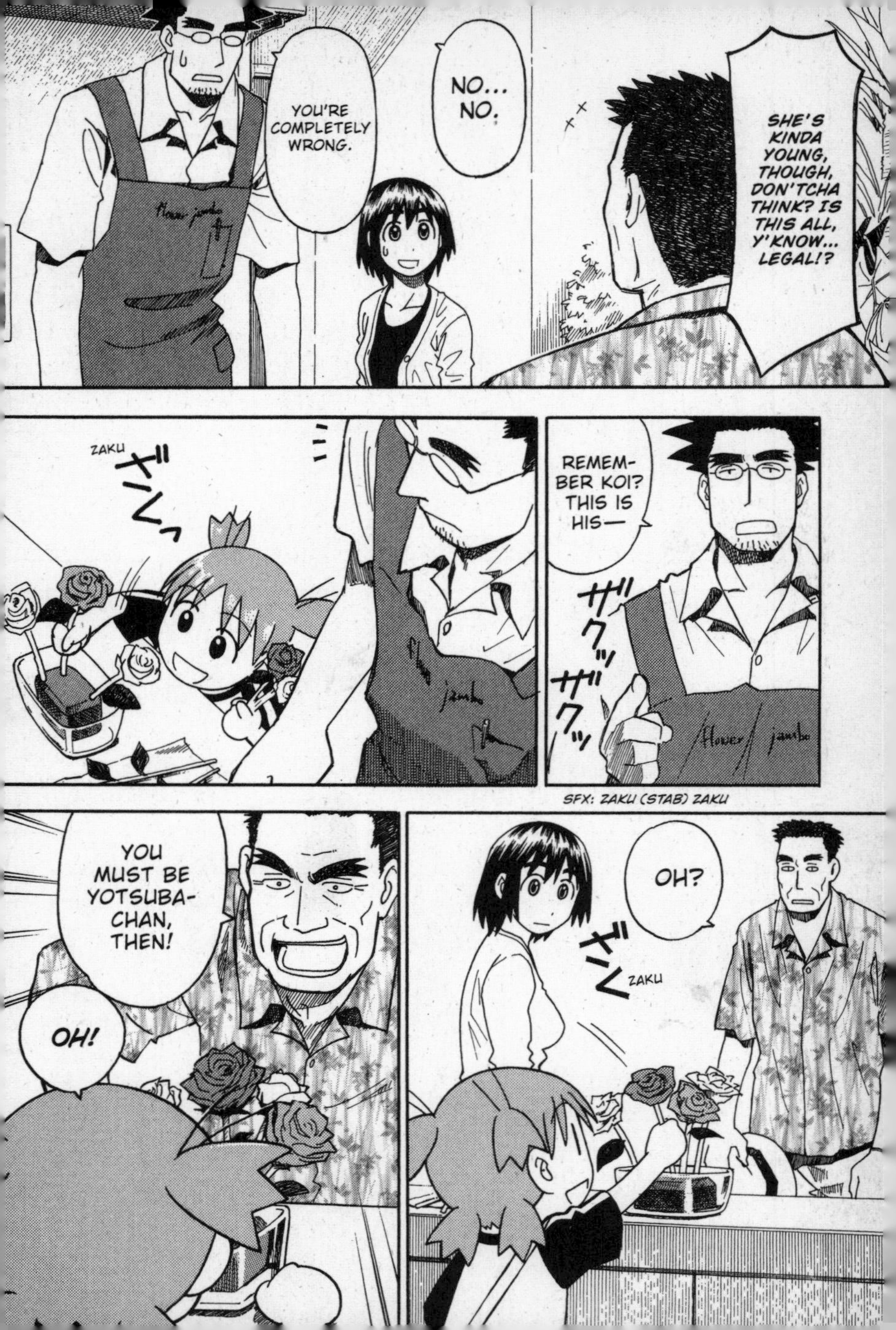
SHE'S KINDA YOUNG, THOUGH, DON'TCHA THINK? IS THIS ALL, Y'KNOW... LEGAL!?
NO... NO.
YOU'RE COMPLETELY WRONG.
REMEM-BER KOI? THIS IS HIS—
ZAKU
SFX: ZAKU (STAB) ZAKU
OH?
ZAKU
YOU MUST BE YOTSUBA-CHAN, THEN!
OH!

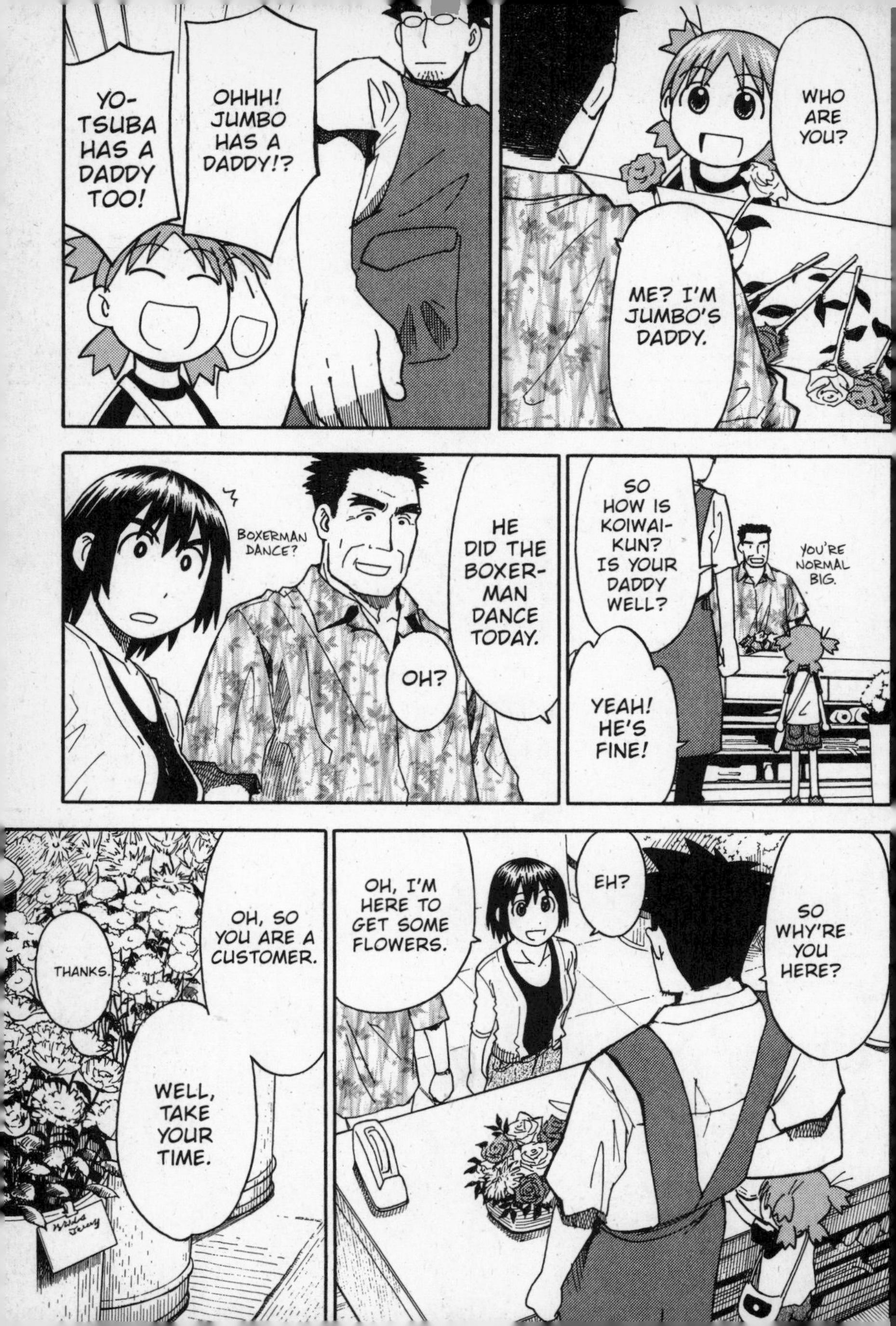
WHO ARE YOU?
ME? I'M JUMBO'S DADDY.
OHHH! JUMBO HAS A DADDY!?
YO-TSUBA HAS A DADDY TOO!
SO HOW IS KOIWAI-KUN? IS YOUR DADDY WELL?
YOU'RE NORMAL BIG.
YEAH! HE'S FINE!
HE DID THE BOXER-MAN DANCE TODAY.
OH?
BOXERMAN DANCE?
SO WHY'RE YOU HERE?
EH?
OH, I'M HERE TO GET SOME FLOWERS.
OH, SO YOU ARE A CUSTOMER.
WELL, TAKE YOUR TIME.
THANKS.

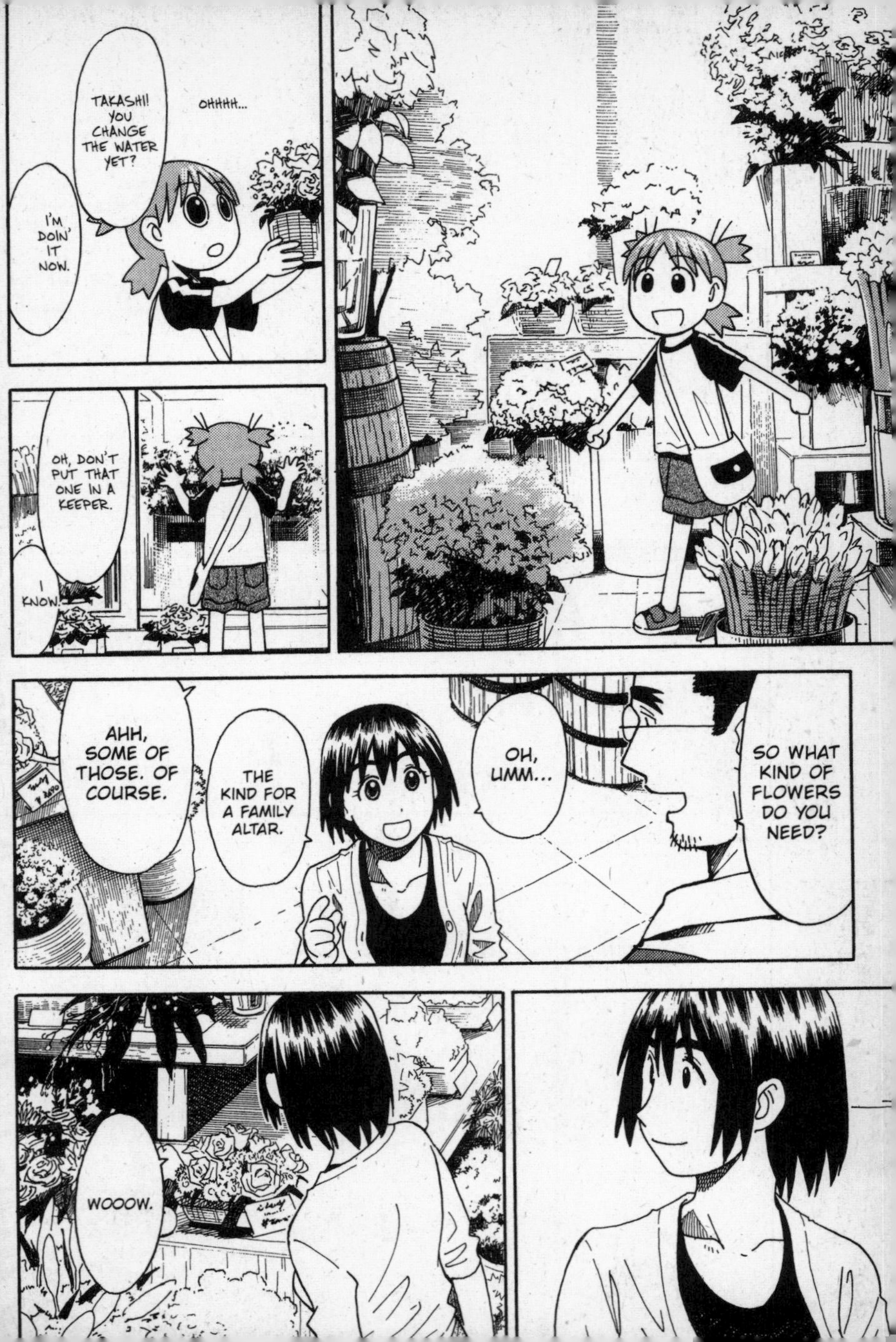
OHHHH...
TAKASHI! YOU CHANGE THE WATER YET?
I'M DOIN' IT NOW.
OH, DON'T PUT THAT ONE IN A KEEPER.
I KNOW.
SO WHAT KIND OF FLOWERS DO YOU NEED?
OH, UMM...
THE KIND FOR A FAMILY ALTAR.
AHH, SOME OF THOSE. OF COURSE.
WOOOW.

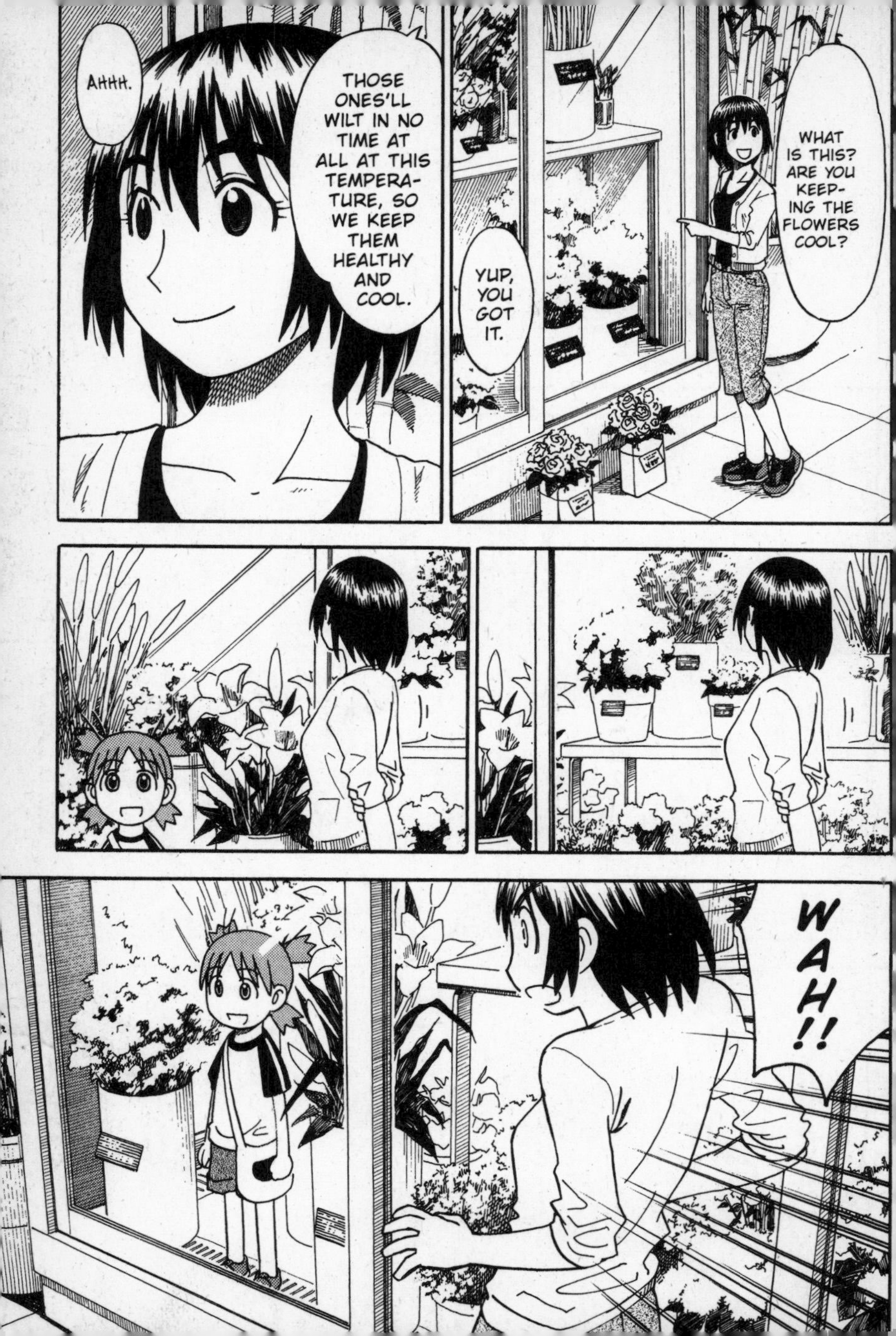
WHAT IS THIS? ARE YOU KEEPING THE FLOWERS COOL?
YUP, YOU GOT IT.
THOSE ONES'LL WILT IN NO TIME AT ALL AT THIS TEMPERATURE, SO WE KEEP THEM HEALTHY AND COOL.
AHHH.
WAH!!

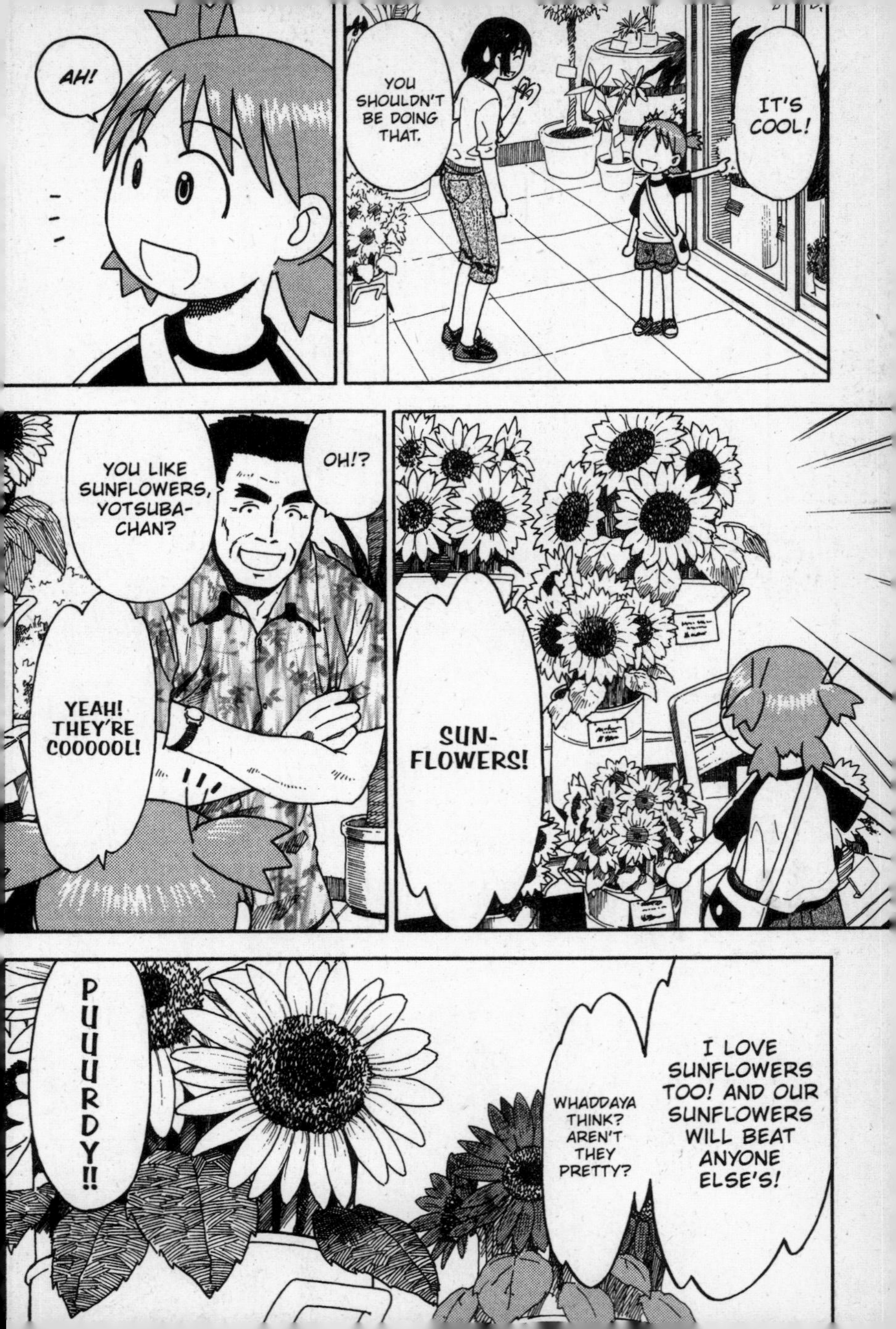
IT'S COOL!
YOU SHOULDN'T BE DOING THAT.
AH!
SUN-FLOWERS!
OH!?
YOU LIKE SUNFLOWERS, YOTSUBA-CHAN?
YEAH! THEY'RE COOOOOL!
I LOVE SUNFLOWERS TOO! AND OUR SUNFLOWERS WILL BEAT ANYONE ELSE'S!
WHADDAYA THINK? AREN'T THEY PRETTY?
PUUURDY!!

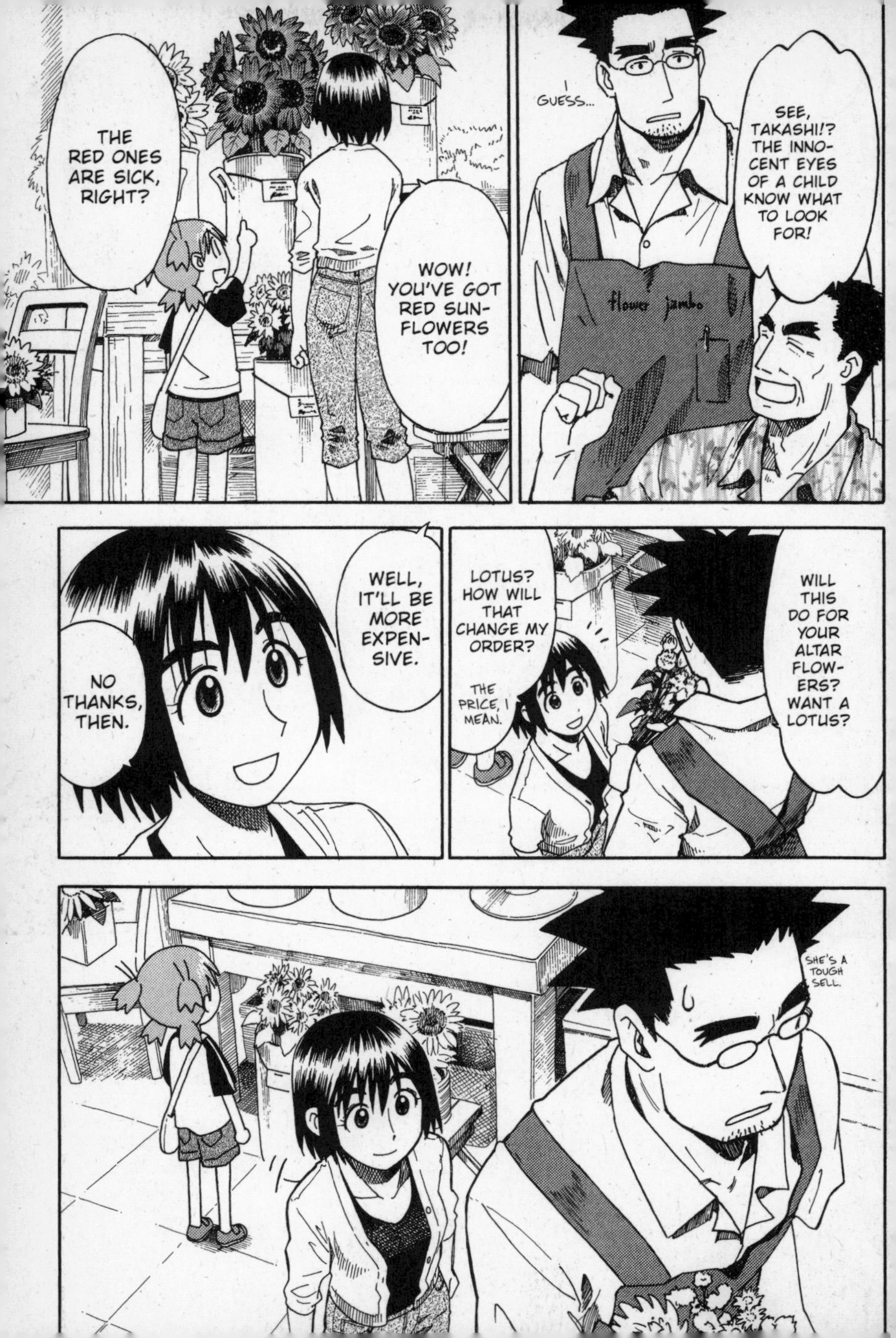
SEE, TAKASHI!? THE INNOCENT EYES OF A CHILD KNOW WHAT TO LOOK FOR!
I GUESS...
WOW! YOU'VE GOT RED SUNFLOWERS TOO!
THE RED ONES ARE SICK, RIGHT?
WILL THIS DO FOR YOUR ALTAR FLOWERS? WANT A LOTUS?
LOTUS? HOW WILL THAT CHANGE MY ORDER?
THE PRICE, I MEAN.
WELL, IT'LL BE MORE EXPENSIVE.
NO THANKS, THEN.
SHE'S A TOUGH SELL.

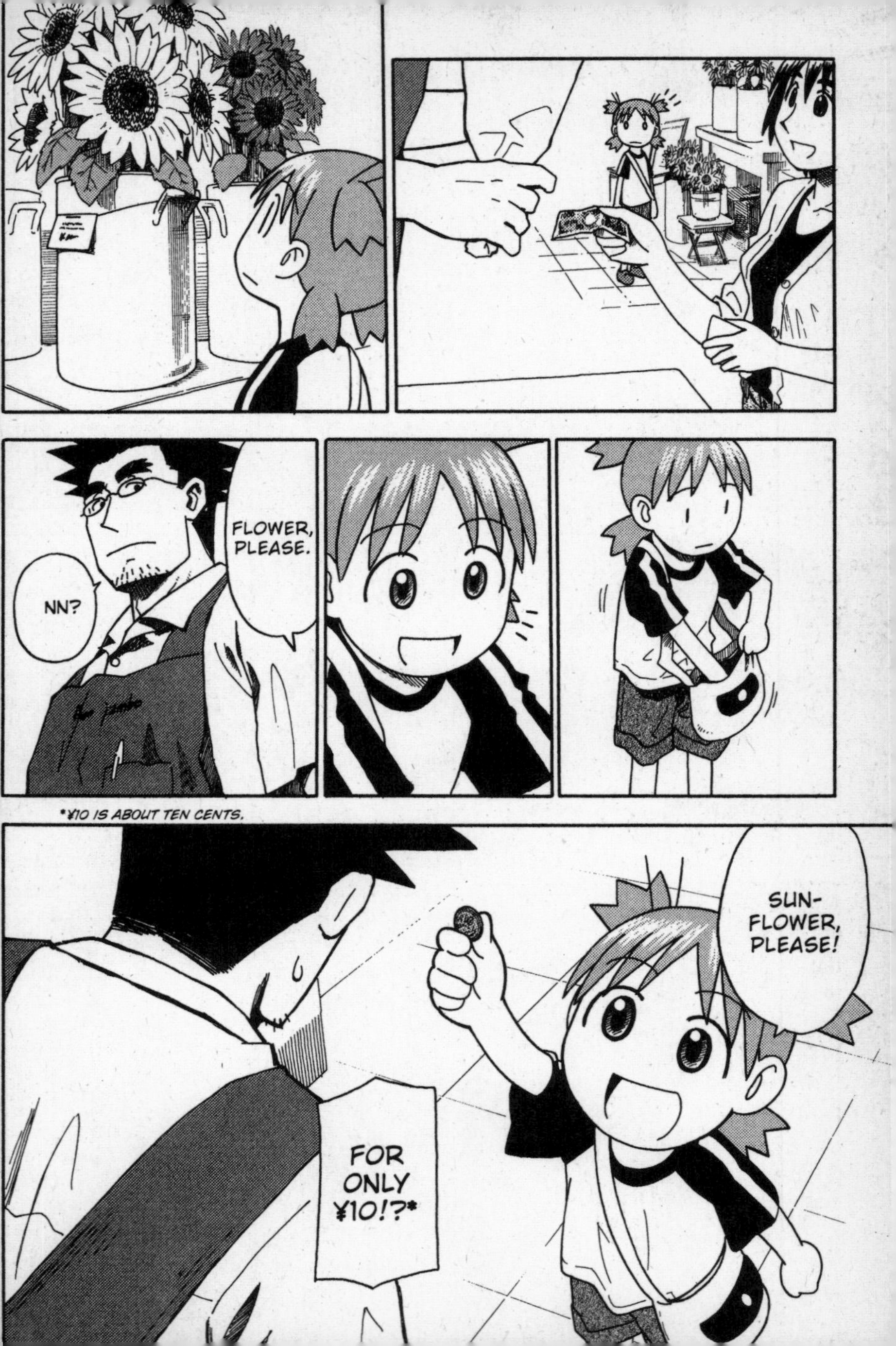
FLOWER, PLEASE.
NN?
SUN-FLOWER, PLEASE!
FOR ONLY ¥10!?*
*¥10 IS ABOUT TEN CENTS.

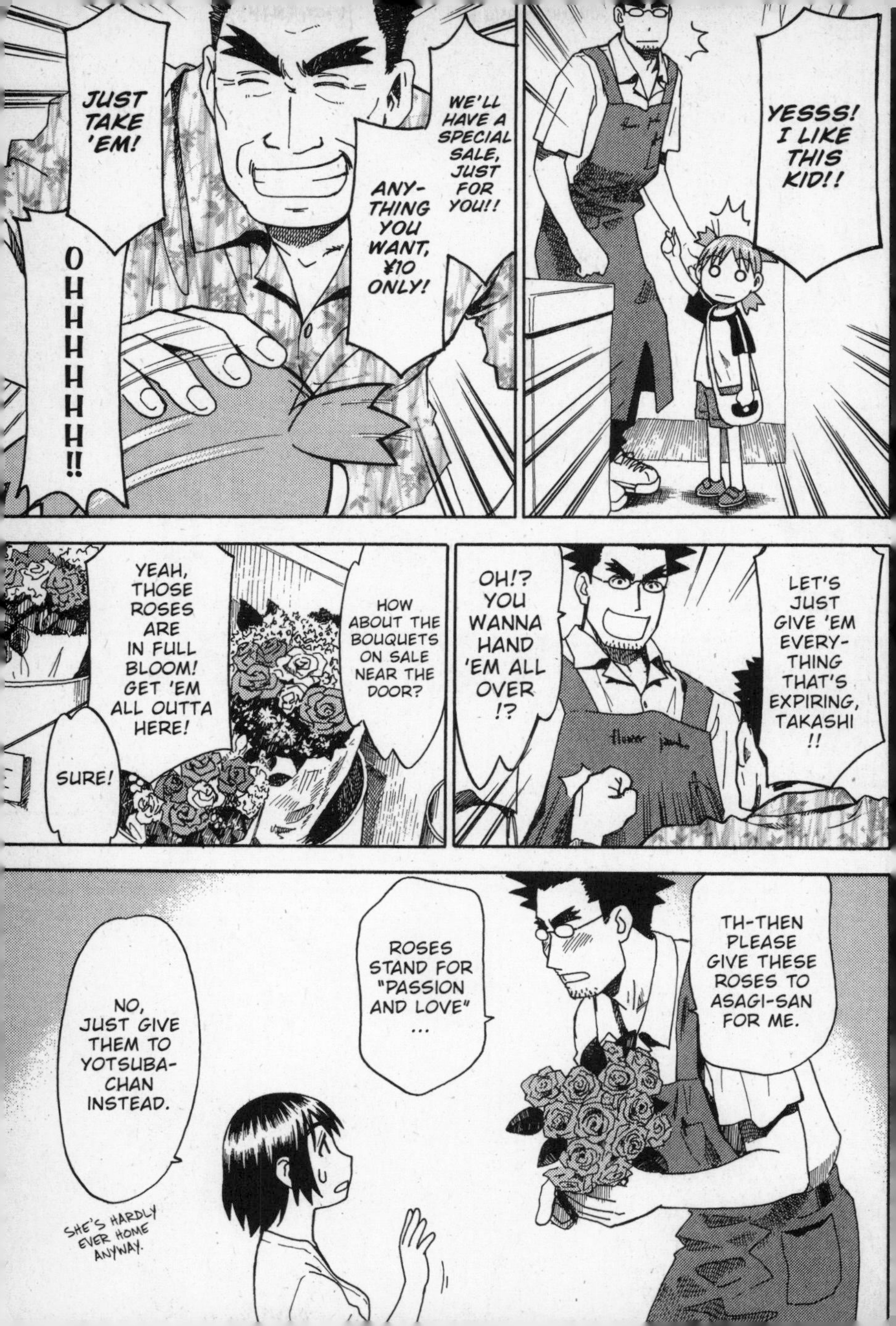
YESSS! I LIKE THIS KID!!
WE'LL HAVE A SPECIAL SALE, JUST FOR YOU!!
ANYTHING YOU WANT, ¥10 ONLY!
JUST TAKE 'EM!
OHHHHHHH!!
LET'S JUST GIVE 'EM EVERYTHING THAT'S EXPIRING, TAKASHI!!
OH!? YOU WANNA HAND 'EM ALL OVER!?
HOW ABOUT THE BOUQUETS ON SALE NEAR THE DOOR?
YEAH, THOSE ROSES ARE IN FULL BLOOM! GET 'EM ALL OUTTA HERE!
SURE!
TH-THEN PLEASE GIVE THESE ROSES TO ASAGI-SAN FOR ME.
ROSES STAND FOR "PASSION AND LOVE"...
NO, JUST GIVE THEM TO YOTSUBA-CHAN INSTEAD.
SHE'S HARDLY EVER HOME ANYWAY.

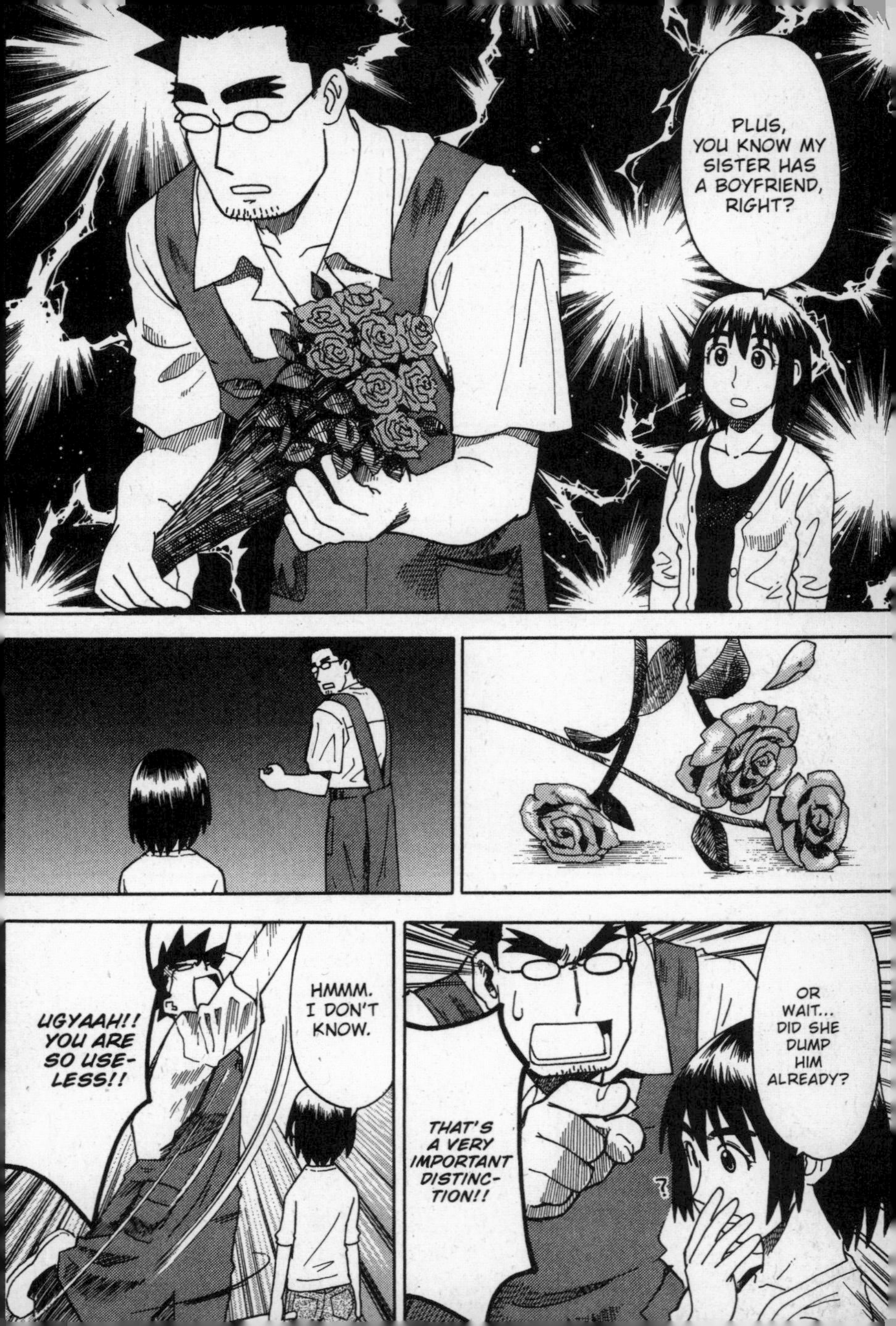
PLUS, YOU KNOW MY SISTER HAS A BOYFRIEND, RIGHT?
OR WAIT... DID SHE DUMP HIM ALREADY?
THAT'S A VERY IMPORTANT DISTINC-TION!!
HMMM. I DON'T KNOW.
UGYAAH!! YOU ARE SO USE-LESS!!

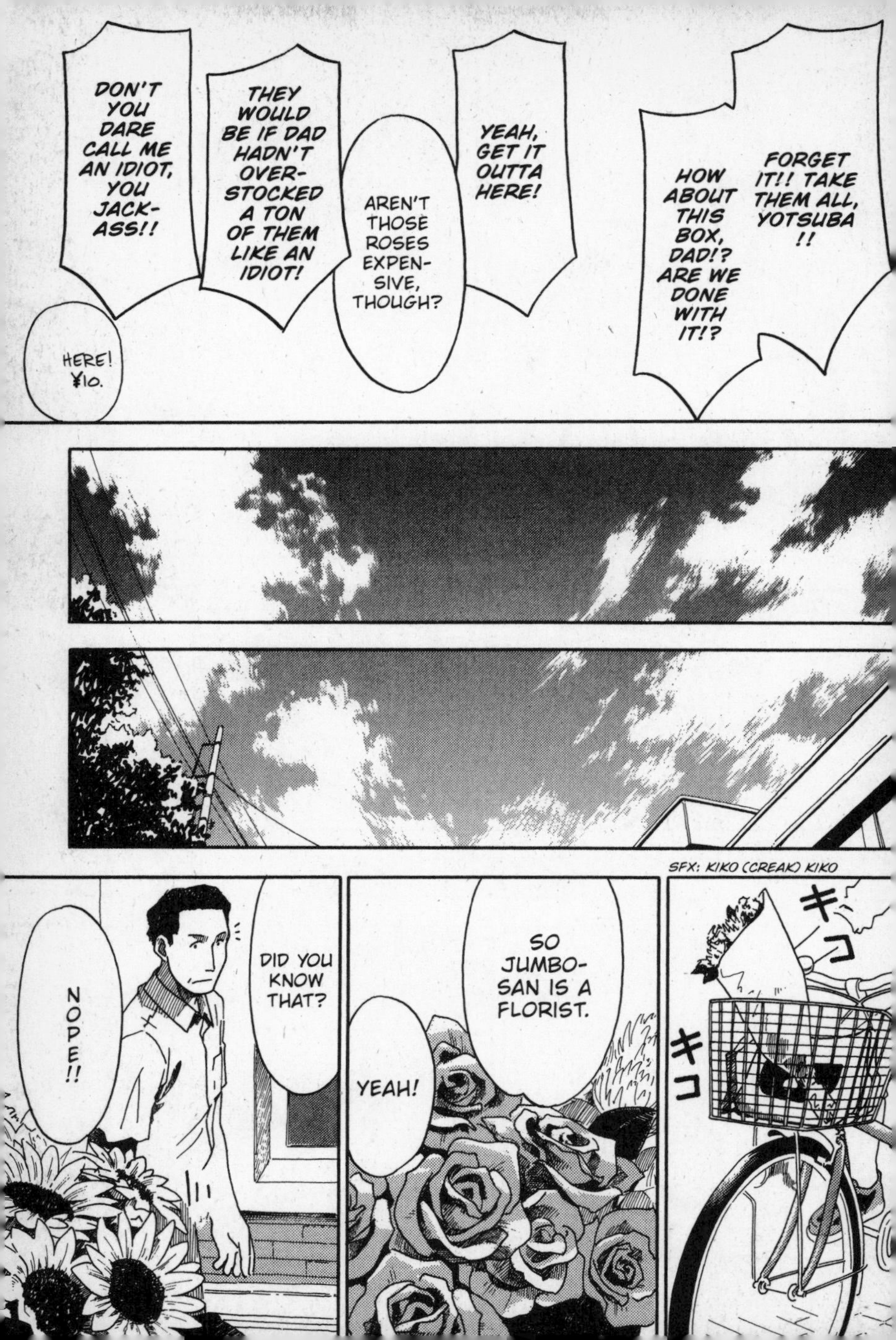
FORGET IT!! TAKE THEM ALL, YOTSUBA!!
HOW ABOUT THIS BOX, DAD!? ARE WE DONE WITH IT!?
YEAH, GET IT OUTTA HERE!
AREN'T THOSE ROSES EXPENSIVE, THOUGH?
THEY WOULD BE IF DAD HADN'T OVER-STOCKED A TON OF THEM LIKE AN IDIOT!
DON'T YOU DARE CALL ME AN IDIOT, YOU JACKASS!!
HERE! ¥10.
SFX: KIKO (CREAK) KIKO
キコ
キコ
SO JUMBO-SAN IS A FLORIST.
YEAH!
DID YOU KNOW THAT?
NOPE!!

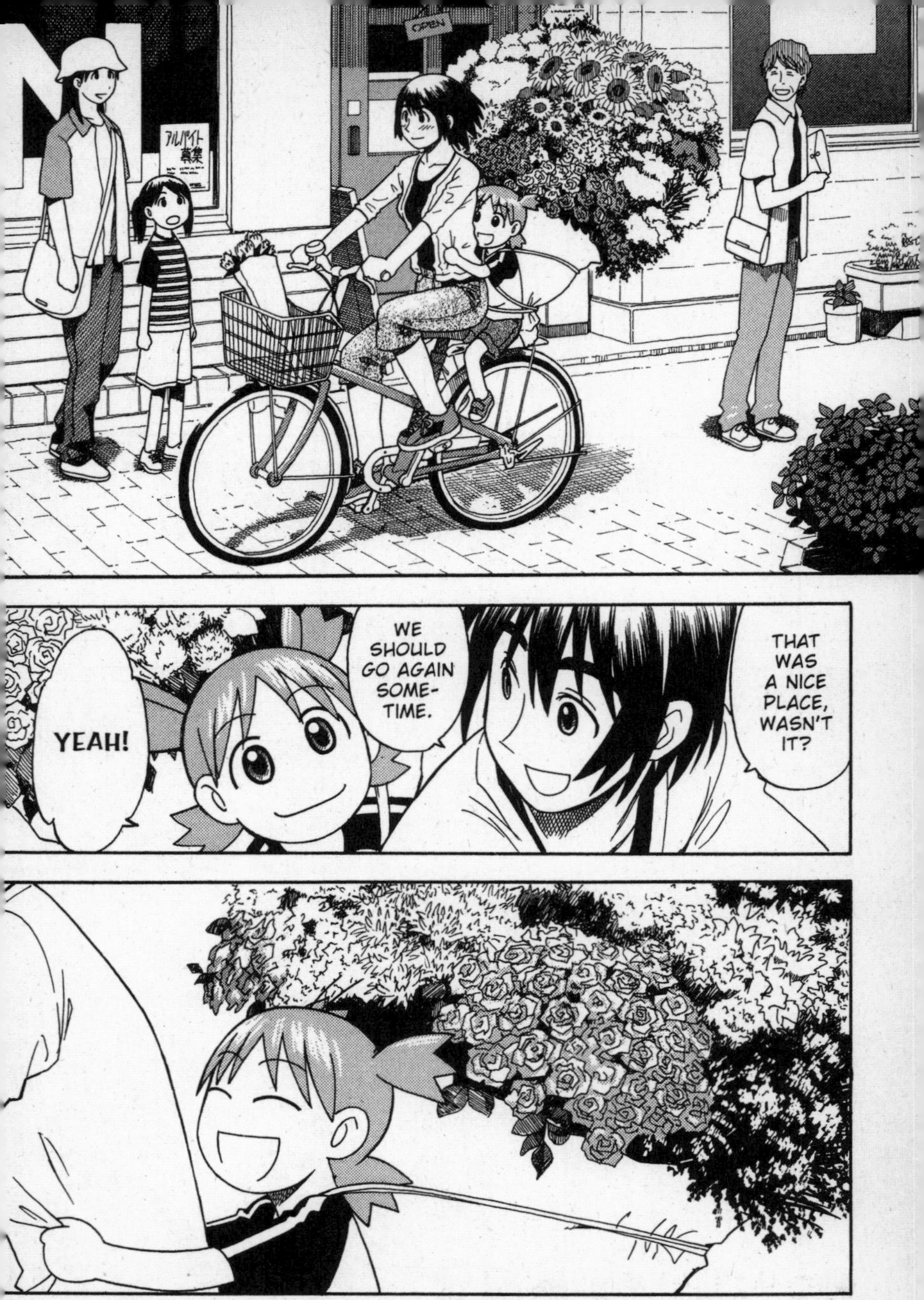
OPEN
アルバイト募集
THAT WAS A NICE PLACE, WASN'T IT?
WE SHOULD GO AGAIN SOME-TIME.
YEAH!

YOTSUBA&!

YOTSUBA& OBON!

#18

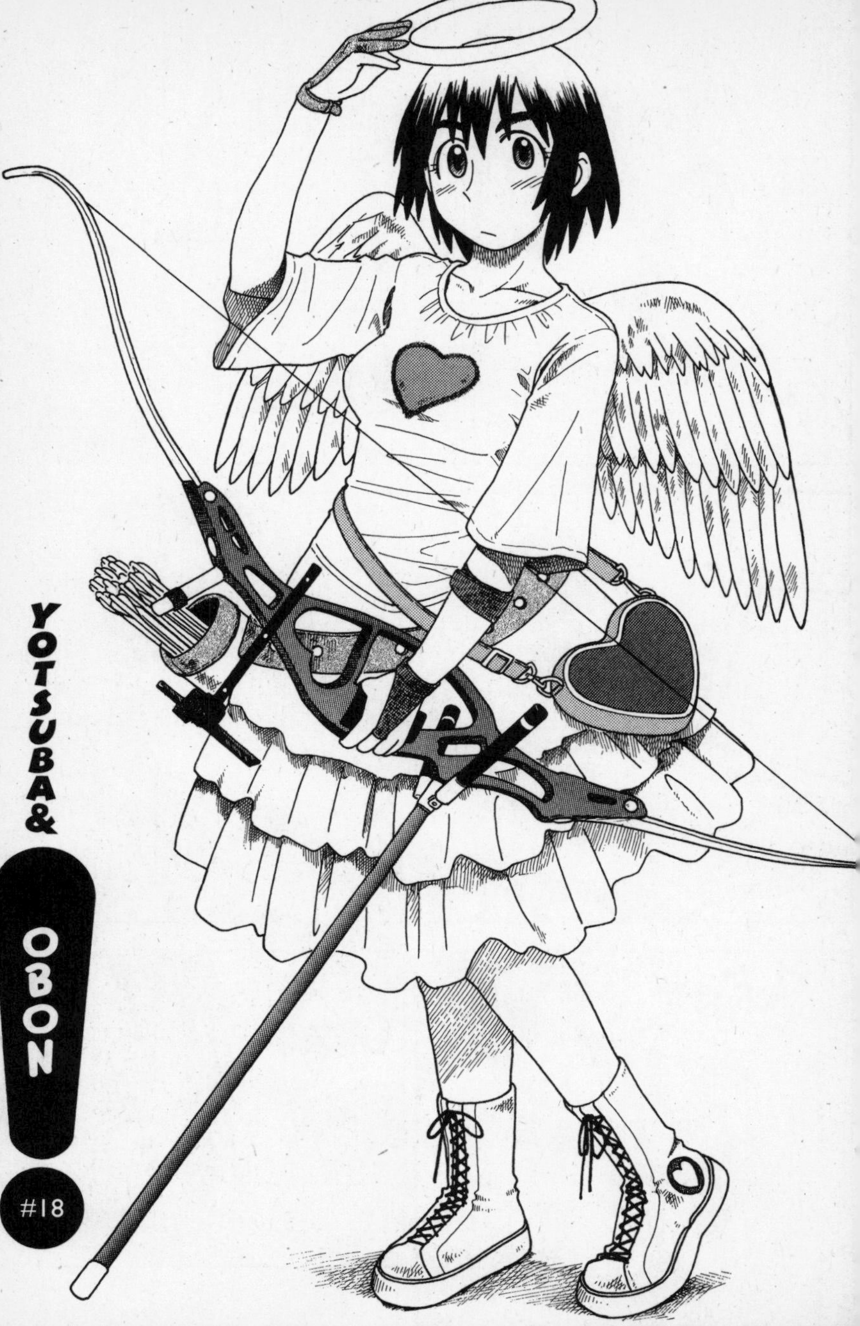

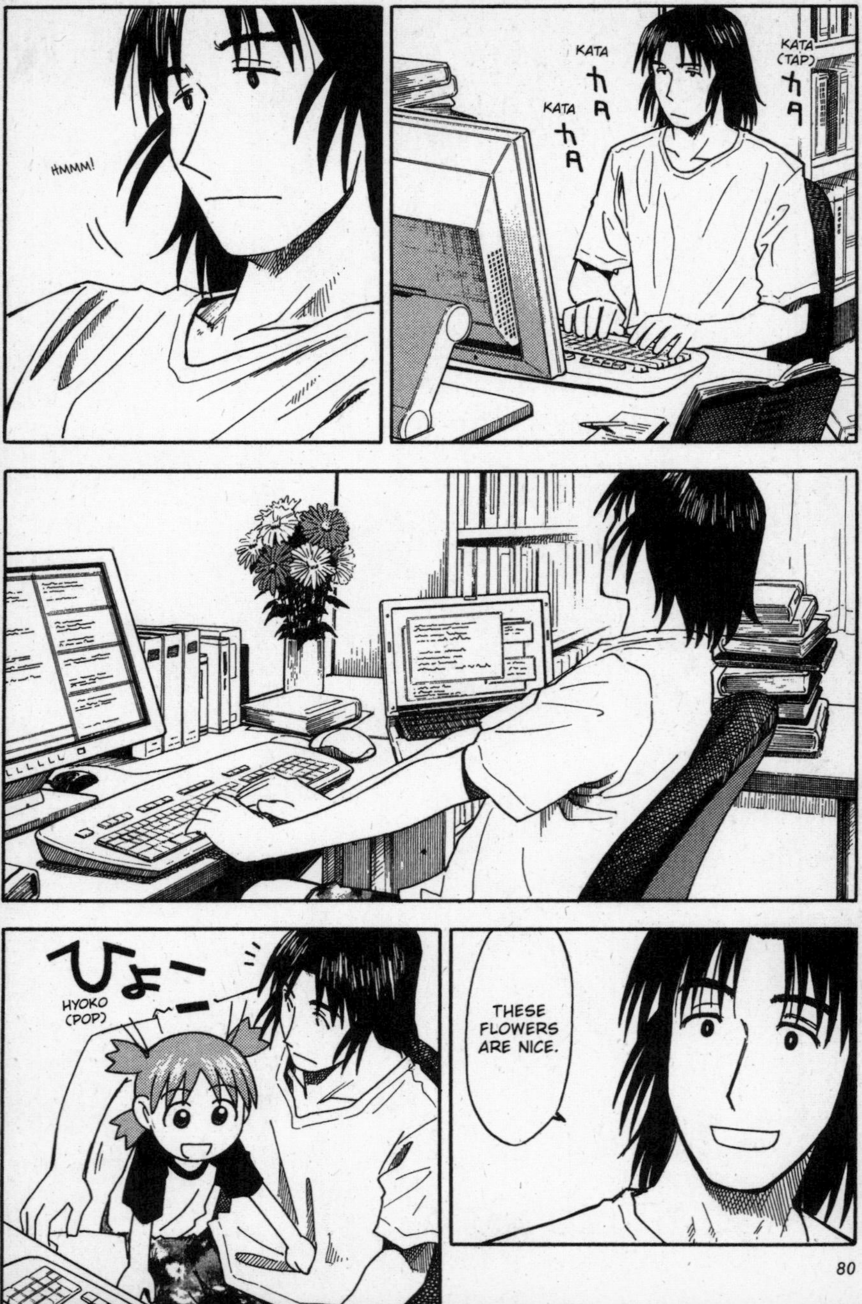
KATA (TAP)
カタ
KATA
カタ
KATA
カタ
HMMM!
THESE FLOWERS ARE NICE.
ひょー
HYOKO (POP)

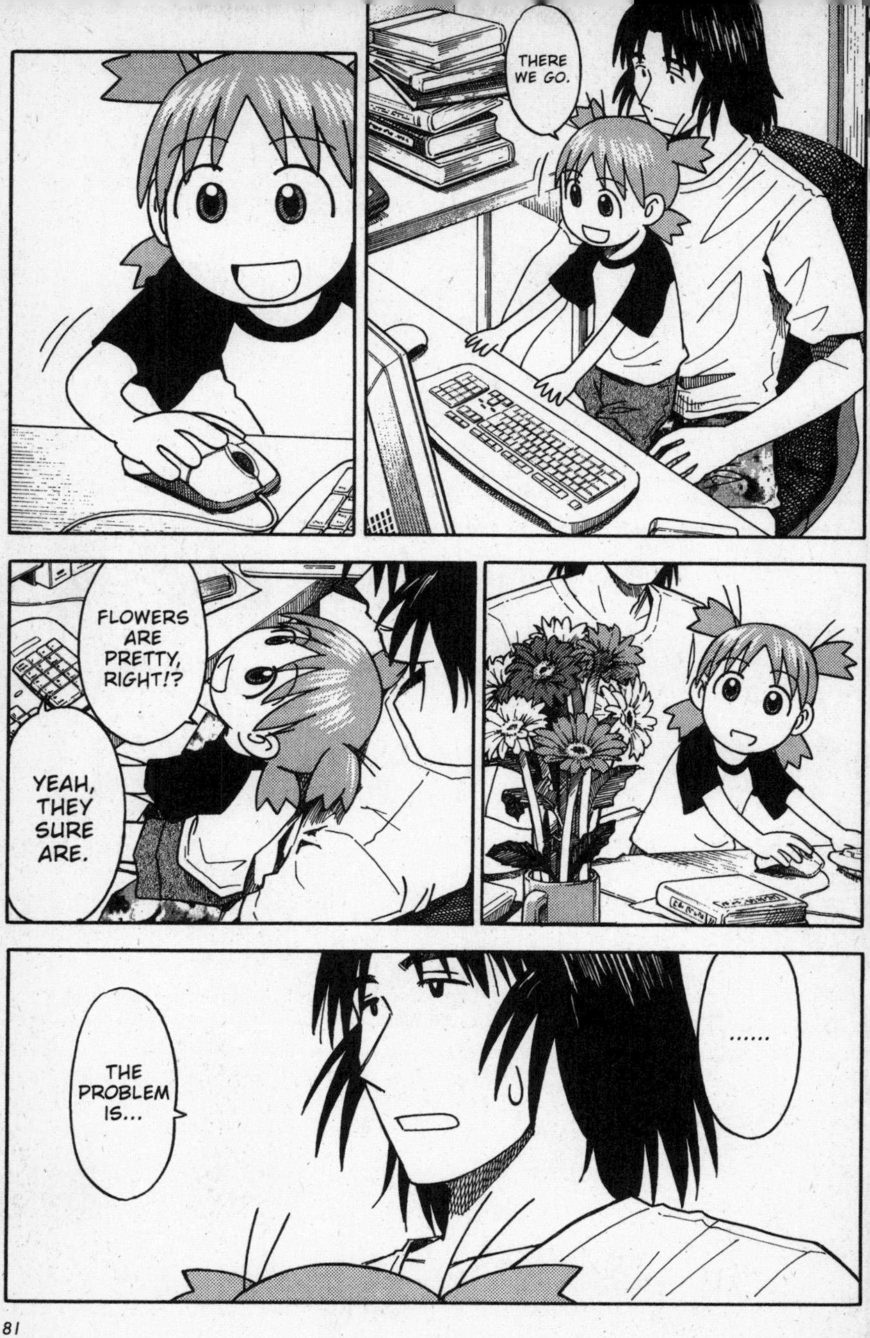
THERE WE GO.
FLOWERS ARE PRETTY, RIGHT!?
YEAH, THEY SURE ARE.
......
THE PROBLEM IS...

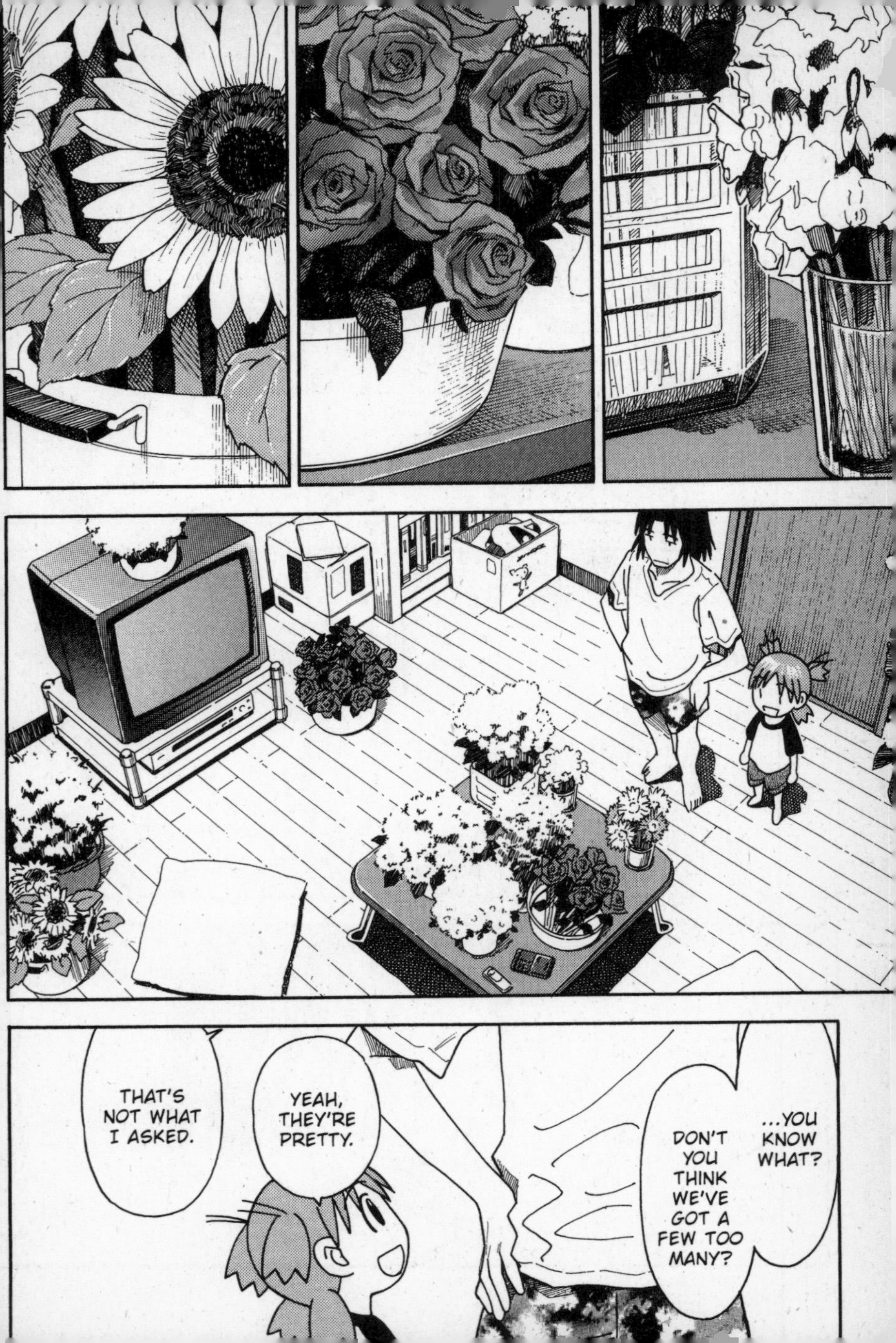
...YOU KNOW WHAT?
DON'T YOU THINK WE'VE GOT A FEW TOO MANY?
YEAH, THEY'RE PRETTY.
THAT'S NOT WHAT I ASKED.

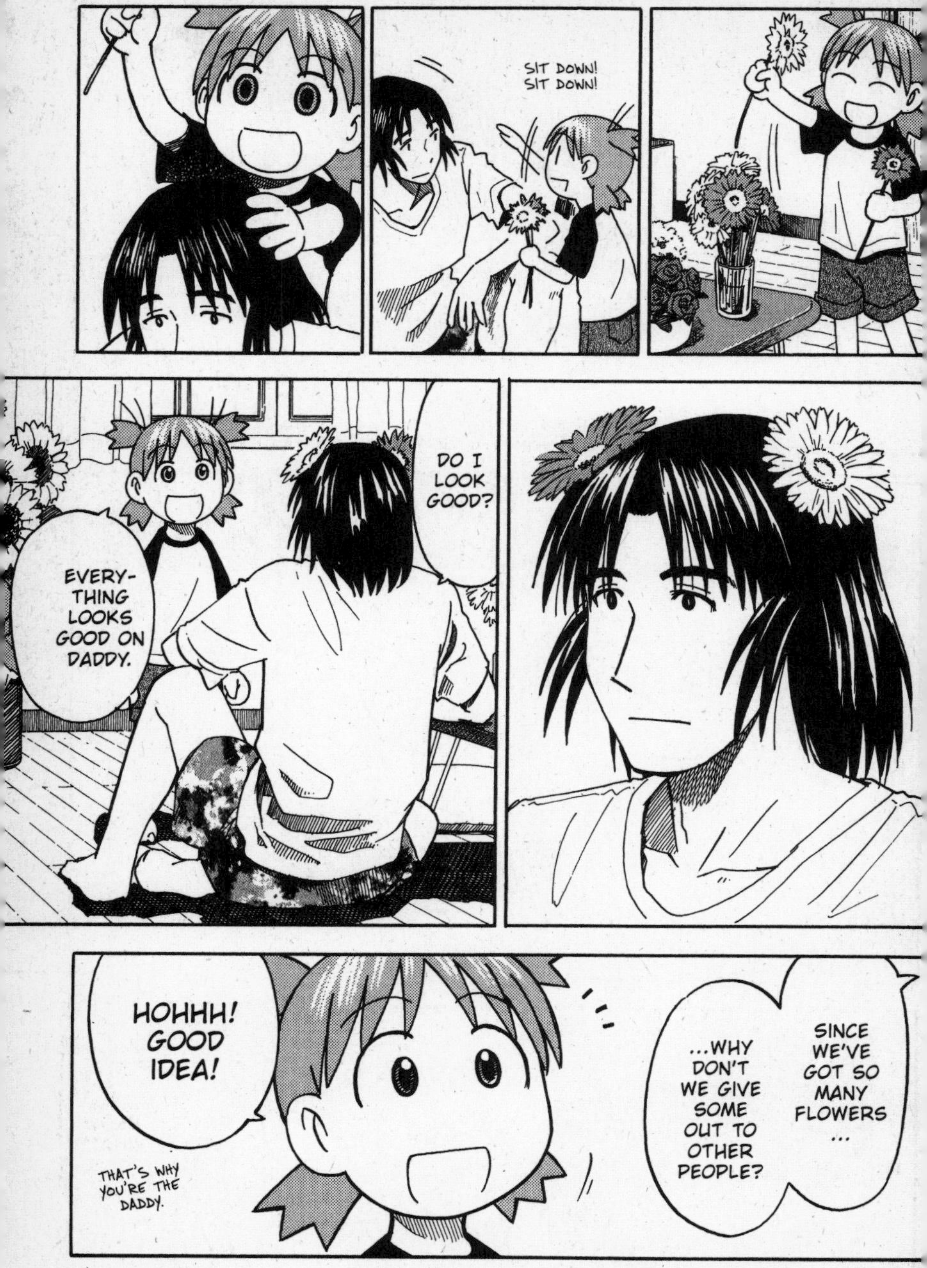
SIT DOWN! SIT DOWN!
DO I LOOK GOOD?
EVERY-THING LOOKS GOOD ON DADDY.
SINCE WE'VE GOT SO MANY FLOWERS...
...WHY DON'T WE GIVE SOME OUT TO OTHER PEOPLE?
HOHHH! GOOD IDEA!
THAT'S WHY YOU'RE THE DADDY.

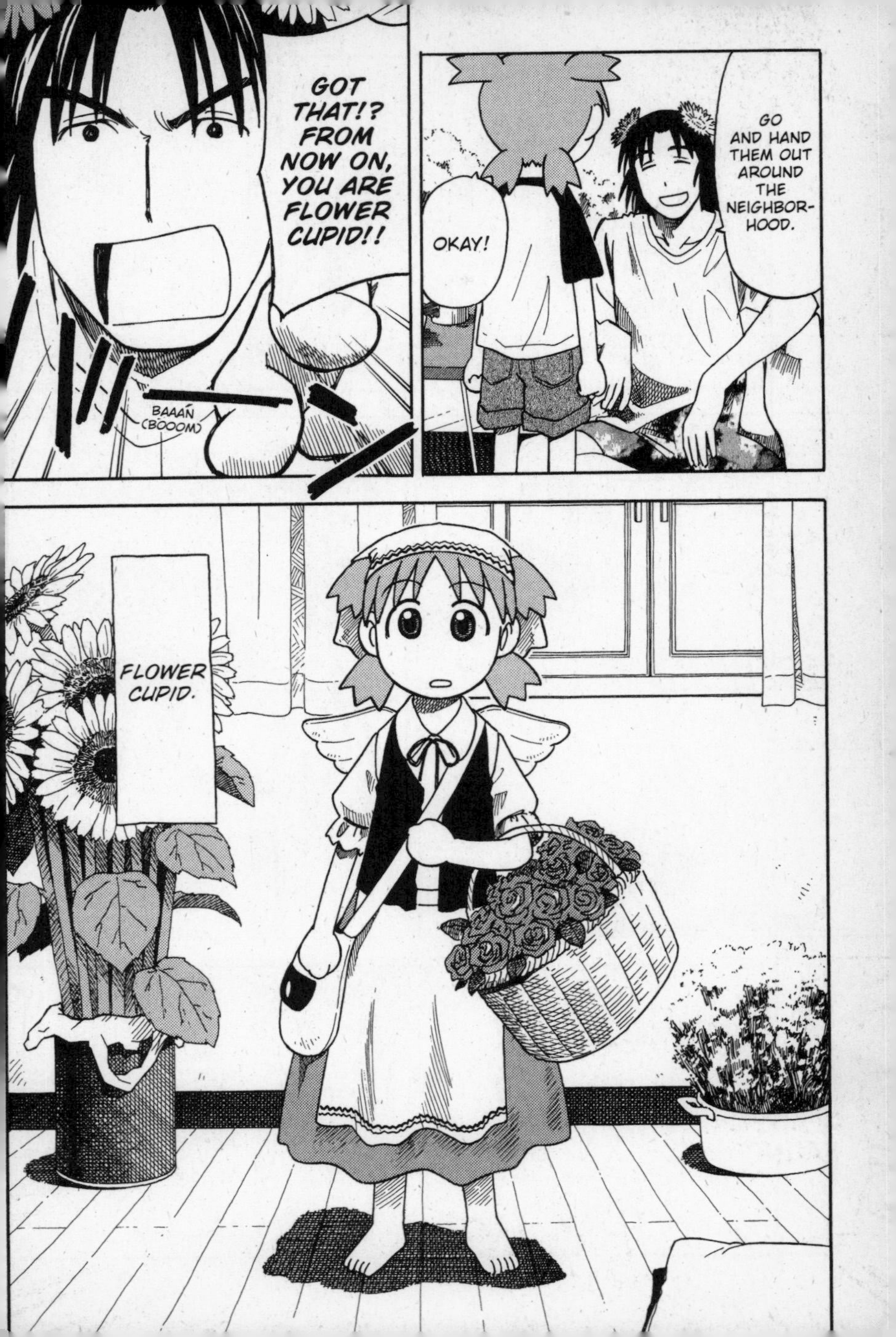
GO AND HAND THEM OUT AROUND THE NEIGHBOR-HOOD.
OKAY!
GOT THAT!? FROM NOW ON, YOU ARE FLOWER CUPID!!
BAAAÑ (BOOOM)
FLOWER CUPID.

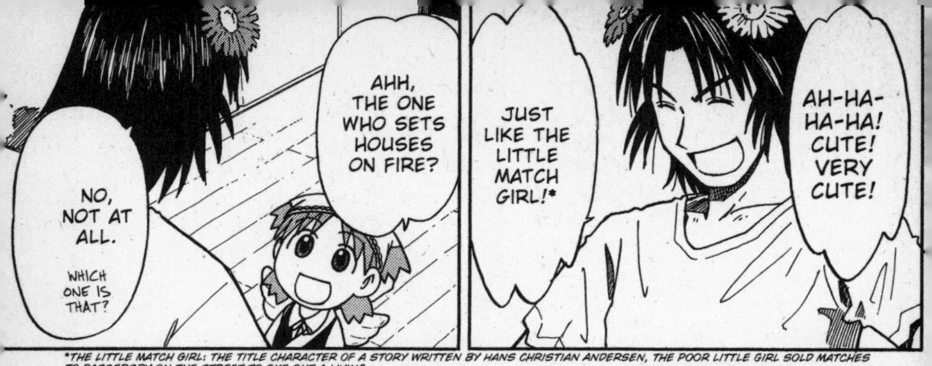
AH-HA-HA-HA! CUTE! VERY CUTE!
JUST LIKE THE LITTLE MATCH GIRL!*
AHH, THE ONE WHO SETS HOUSES ON FIRE?
NO, NOT AT ALL.
WHICH ONE IS THAT?

*THE LITTLE MATCH GIRL: THE TITLE CHARACTER OF A STORY WRITTEN BY HANS CHRISTIAN ANDERSEN, THE POOR LITTLE GIRL SOLD MATCHES TO PASSERSBY ON THE STREET TO EKE OUT A LIVING.

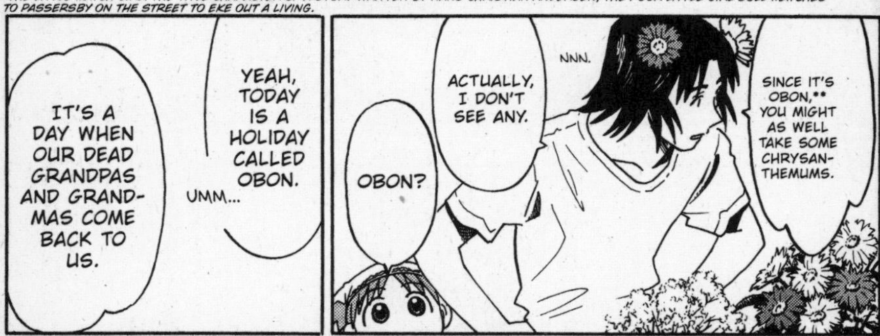
SINCE IT'S OBON,** YOU MIGHT AS WELL TAKE SOME CHRYSANTHEMUMS.
NNN.
ACTUALLY, I DON'T SEE ANY.
OBON?
YEAH, TODAY IS A HOLIDAY CALLED OBON.
UMM...
IT'S A DAY WHEN OUR DEAD GRANDPAS AND GRANDMAS COME BACK TO US.

**OBON: A JAPANESE SUMMER HOLIDAY IN WHICH ONE'S ANCESTORS ARE HONORED. BECAUSE OF THE FAMILIAL NATURE OF THE HOLIDAY, IT IS COMMON TO REUNITE WITH EXTENDED FAMILY MEMBERS.

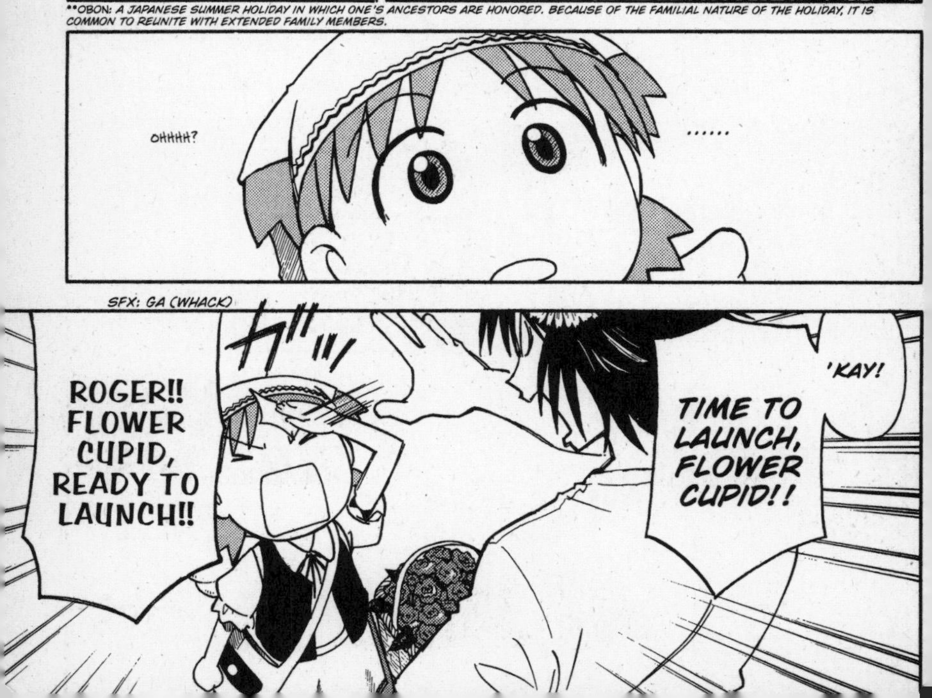
......
OHHHH?
'KAY!
TIME TO LAUNCH, FLOWER CUPID!!
SFX: GA (WHACK)
ROGER!! FLOWER CUPID, READY TO LAUNCH!!

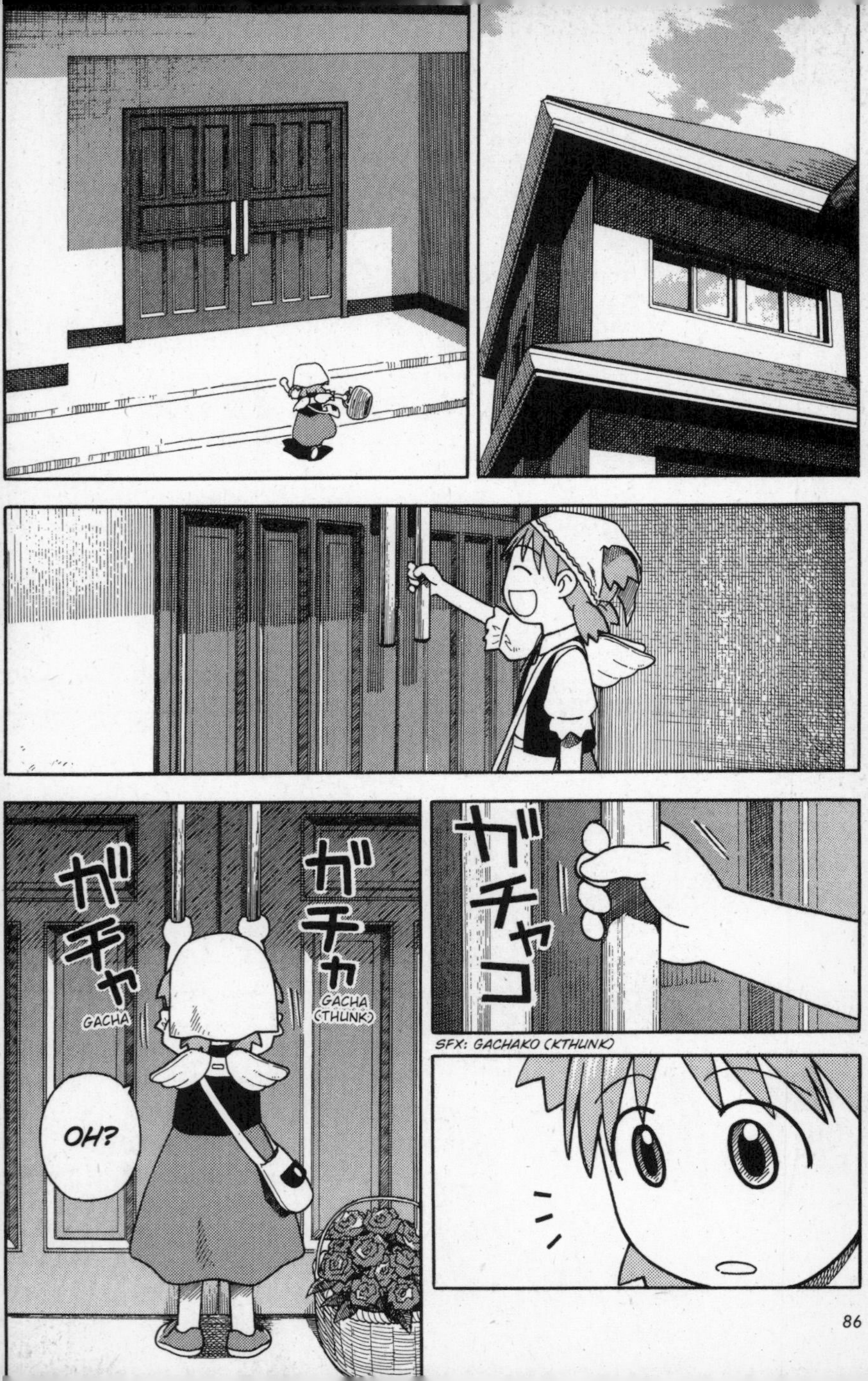
ガチャコ
SFX: GACHAKO (KTHUNK)
ガチャ
GACHA (THUNK)
ガチャ
GACHA
OH?

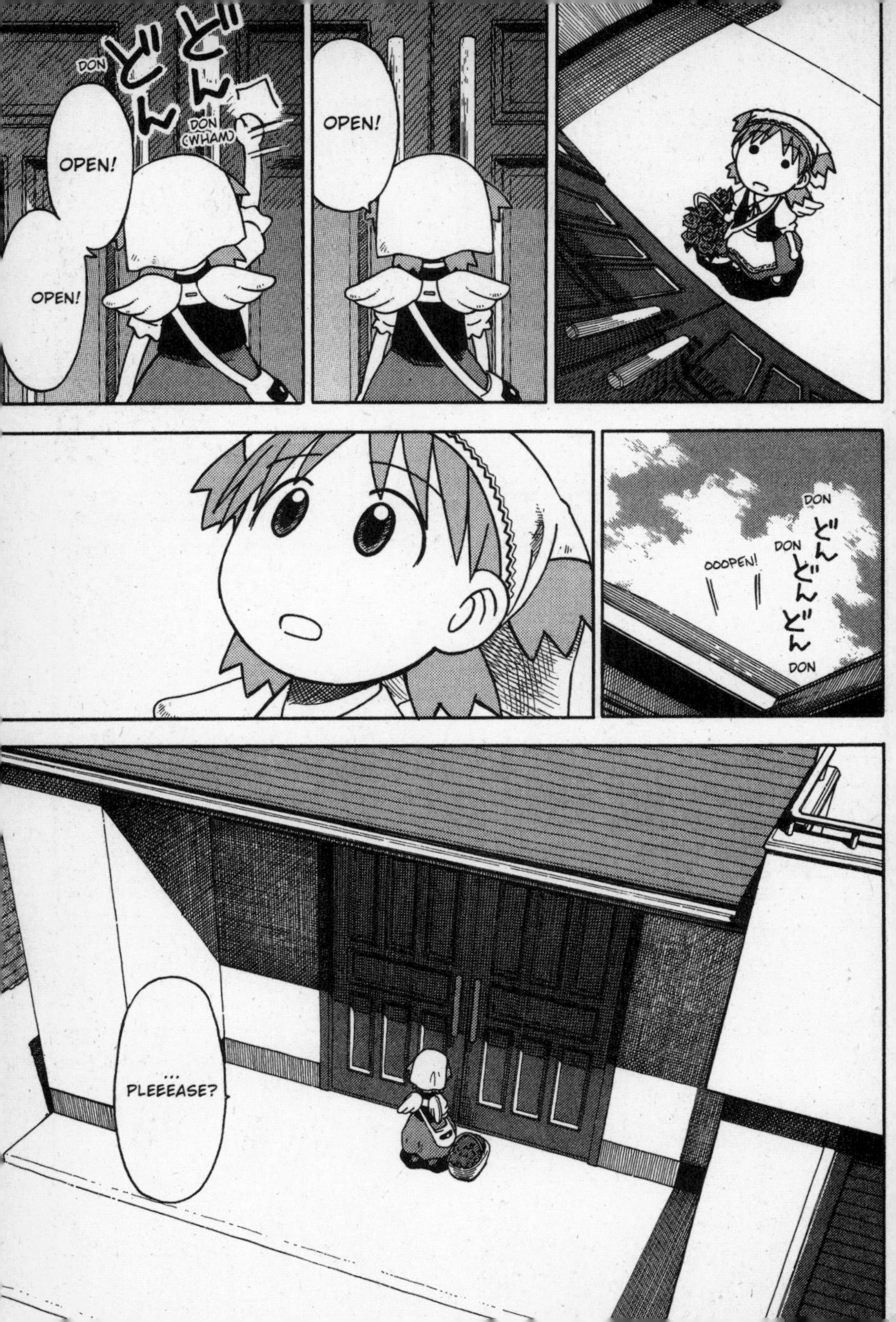
OPEN!
DON
どん
DON
(WHAM)
どん
OPEN!
OPEN!
DON
どん
DON
どん
どん
DON
OOOPEN!
...
PLEEEASE?

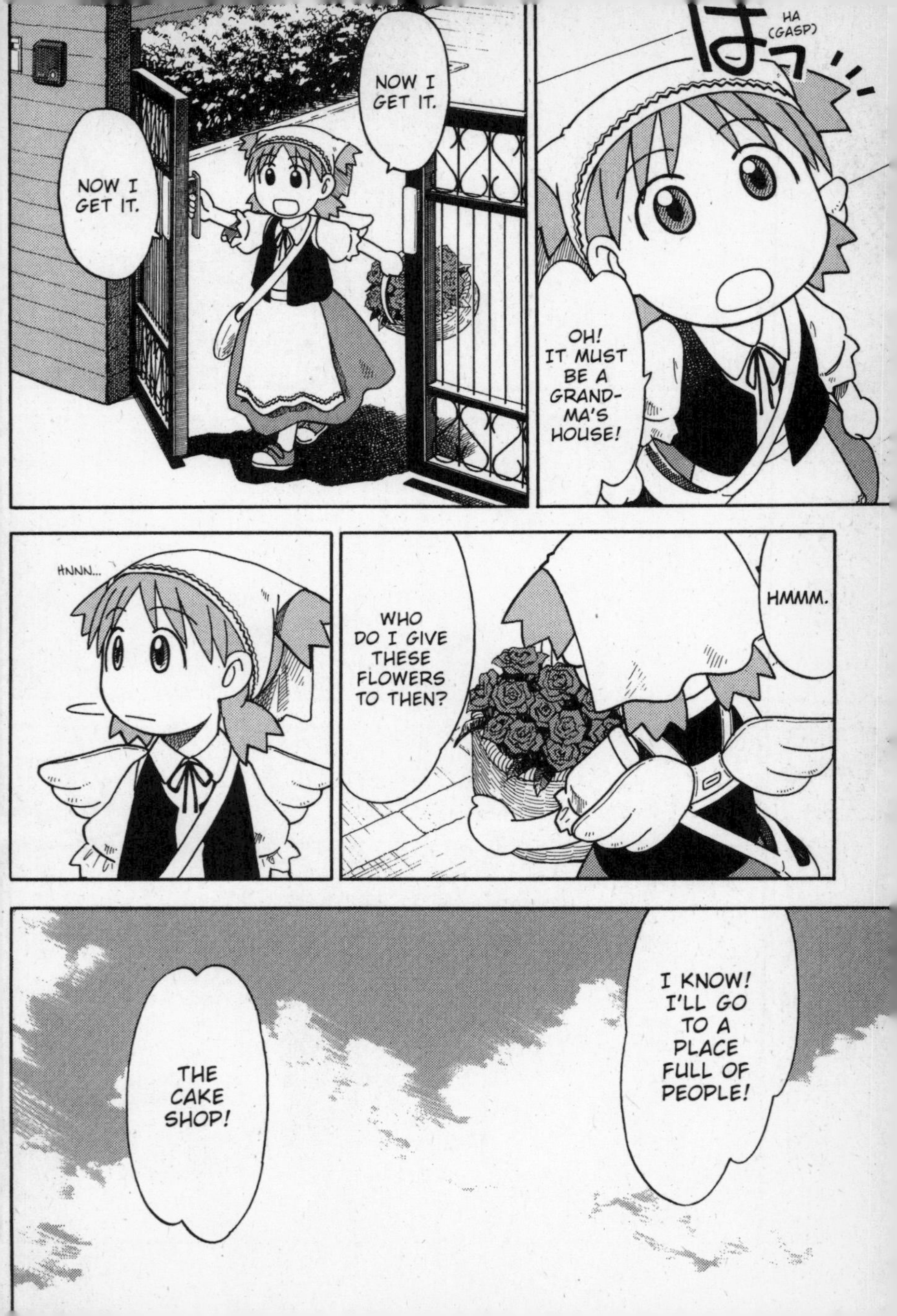
はっ
HA (GASP)
OH! IT MUST BE A GRAND-MA'S HOUSE!
NOW I GET IT.
NOW I GET IT.
HMMM.
WHO DO I GIVE THESE FLOWERS TO THEN?
HNNN...
I KNOW! I'LL GO TO A PLACE FULL OF PEOPLE!
THE CAKE SHOP!

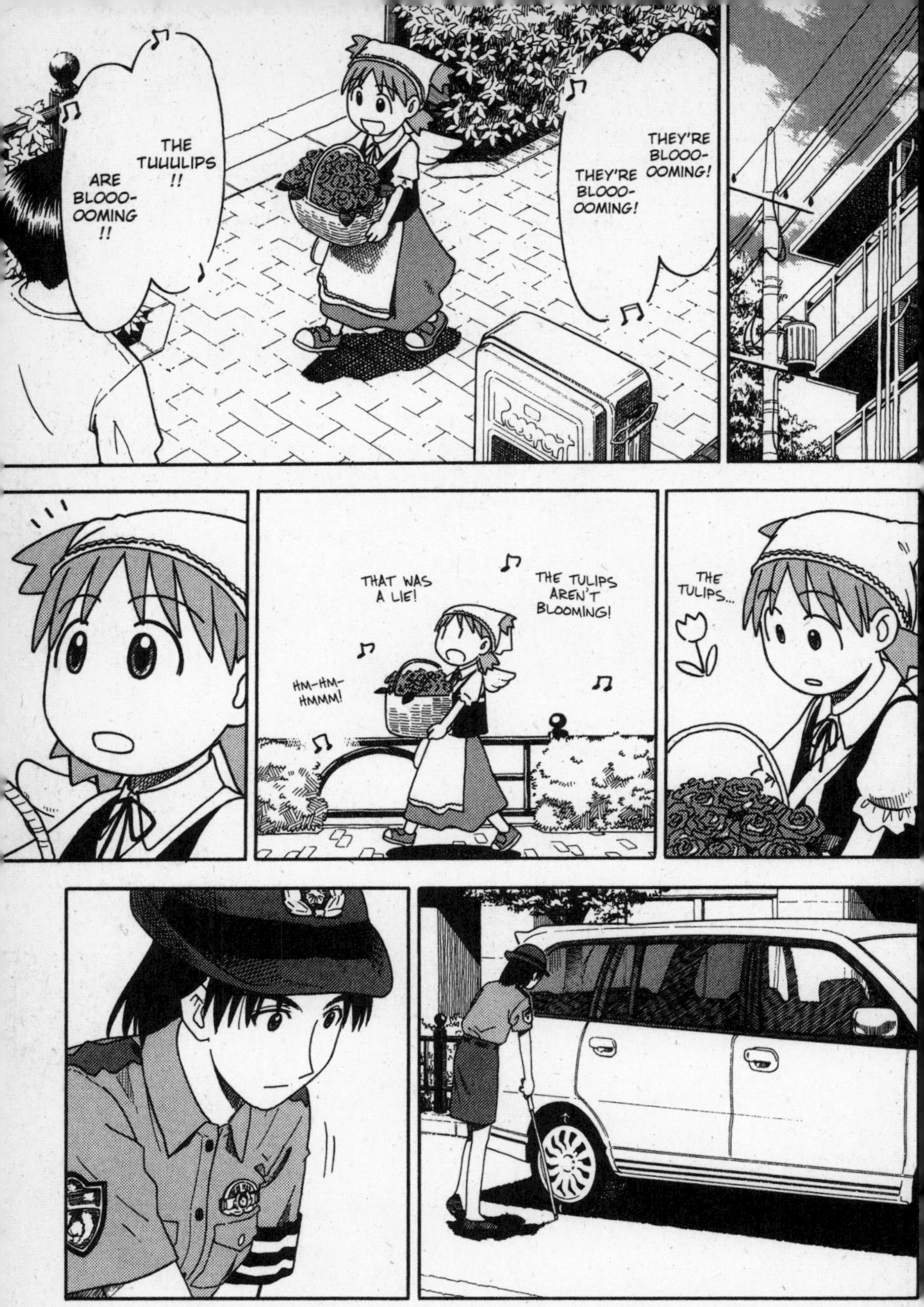
THEY'RE BLOOO-OOMING! THEY'RE BLOOOO-OOMING!
THE TUUULIPS !! ARE BLOOOO-OOMING !!
THE TULIPS...
THE TULIPS AREN'T BLOOMING!
THAT WAS A LIE!
HM-HM-HMMM!

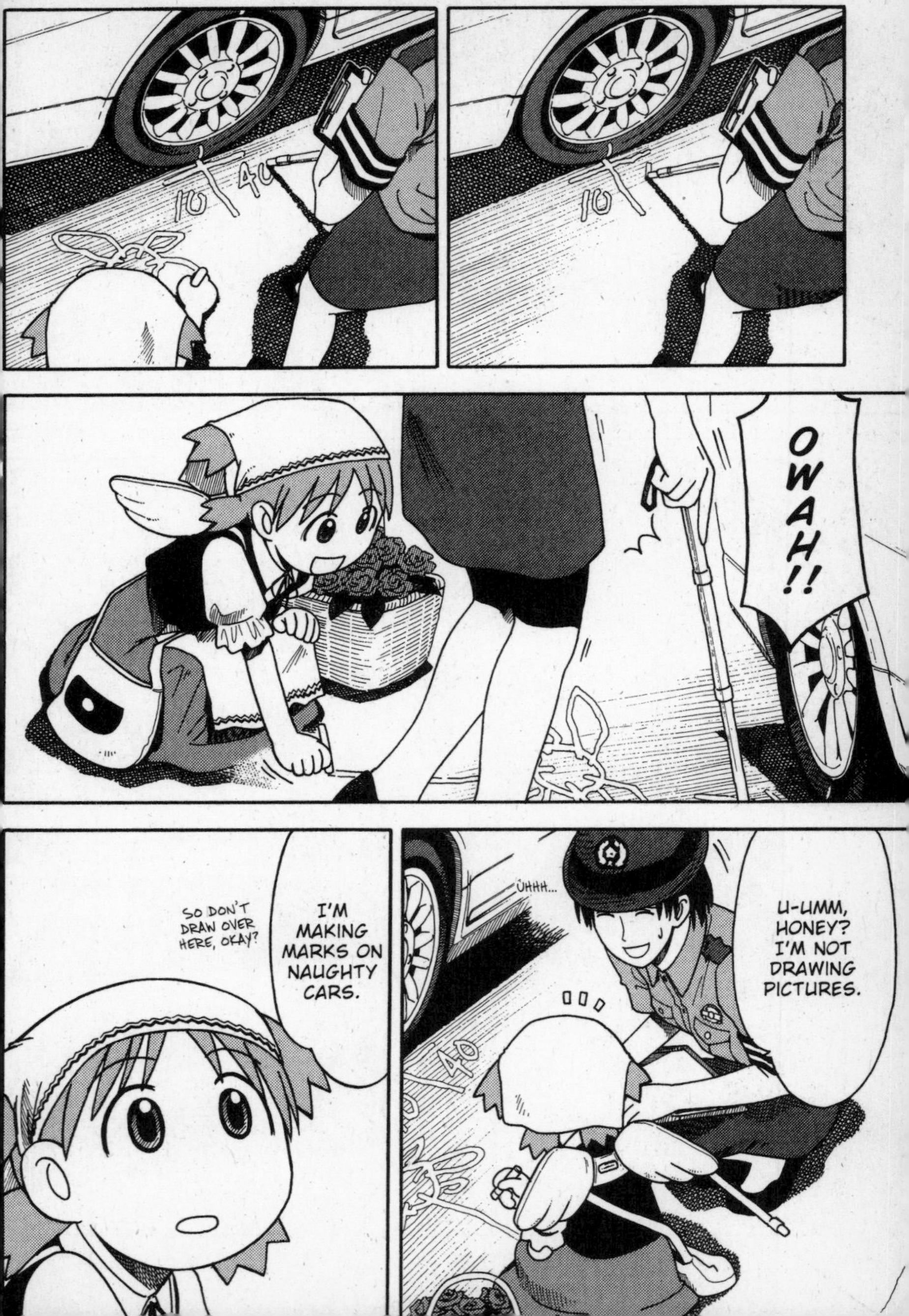
OWAH!!
U-UMM, HONEY? I'M NOT DRAWING PICTURES.
UHHH...
I'M MAKING MARKS ON NAUGHTY CARS.
SO DON'T DRAW OVER HERE, OKAY?

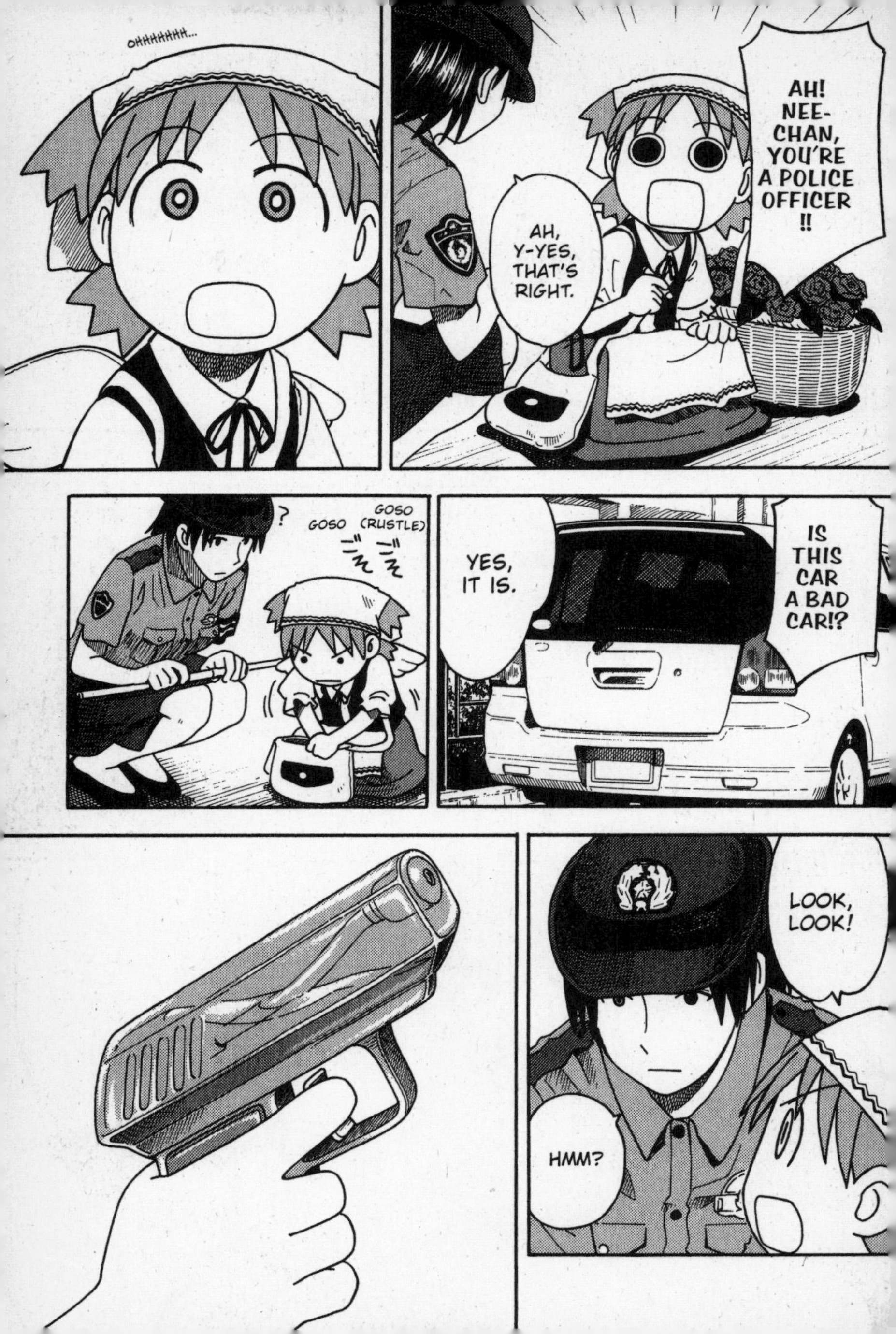
AH! NEE-CHAN, YOU'RE A POLICE OFFICER!!
AH, Y-YES, THAT'S RIGHT.
OHHHHHHH...
IS THIS CAR A BAD CAR!?
YES, IT IS.
GOSO (RUSTLE)
GOSO
?
LOOK, LOOK!
HMM?

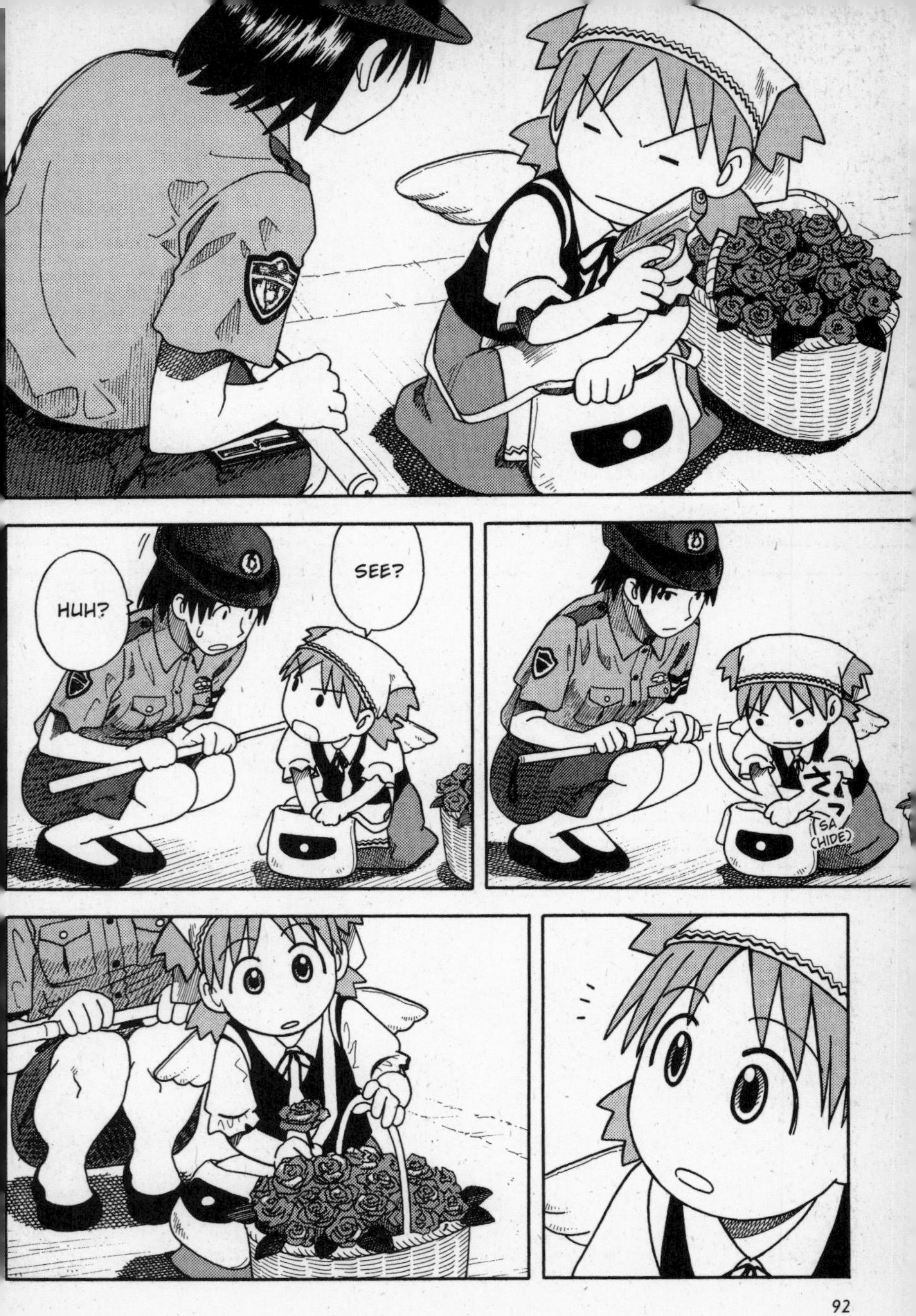
さっ
(SA HIDE)
SEE?
HUH?

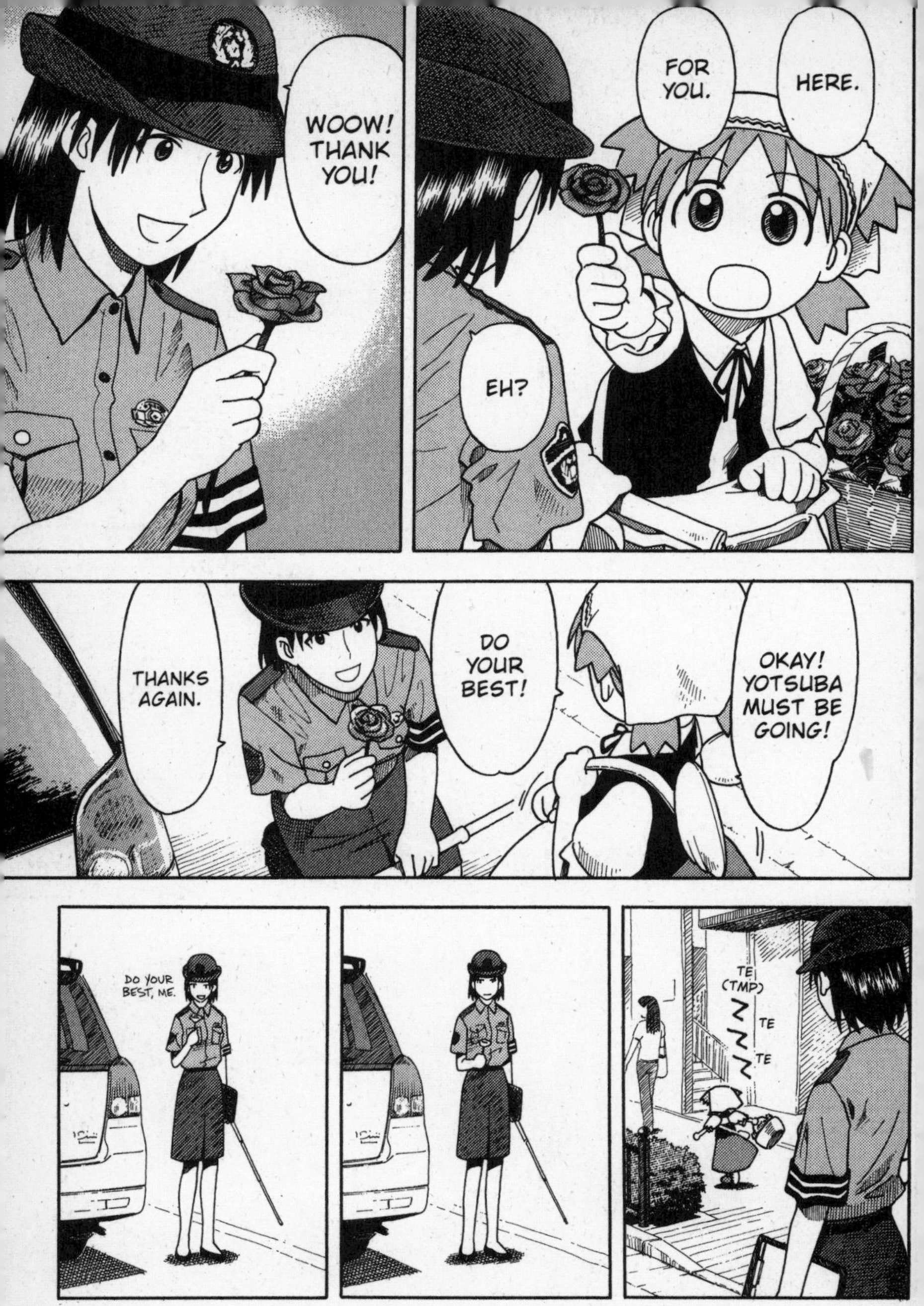
HERE.
FOR YOU.
EH?
WOOW! THANK YOU!
OKAY! YOTSUBA MUST BE GOING!
DO YOUR BEST!
THANKS AGAIN.
TE (TMP)
TE
TE
DO YOUR BEST, ME.

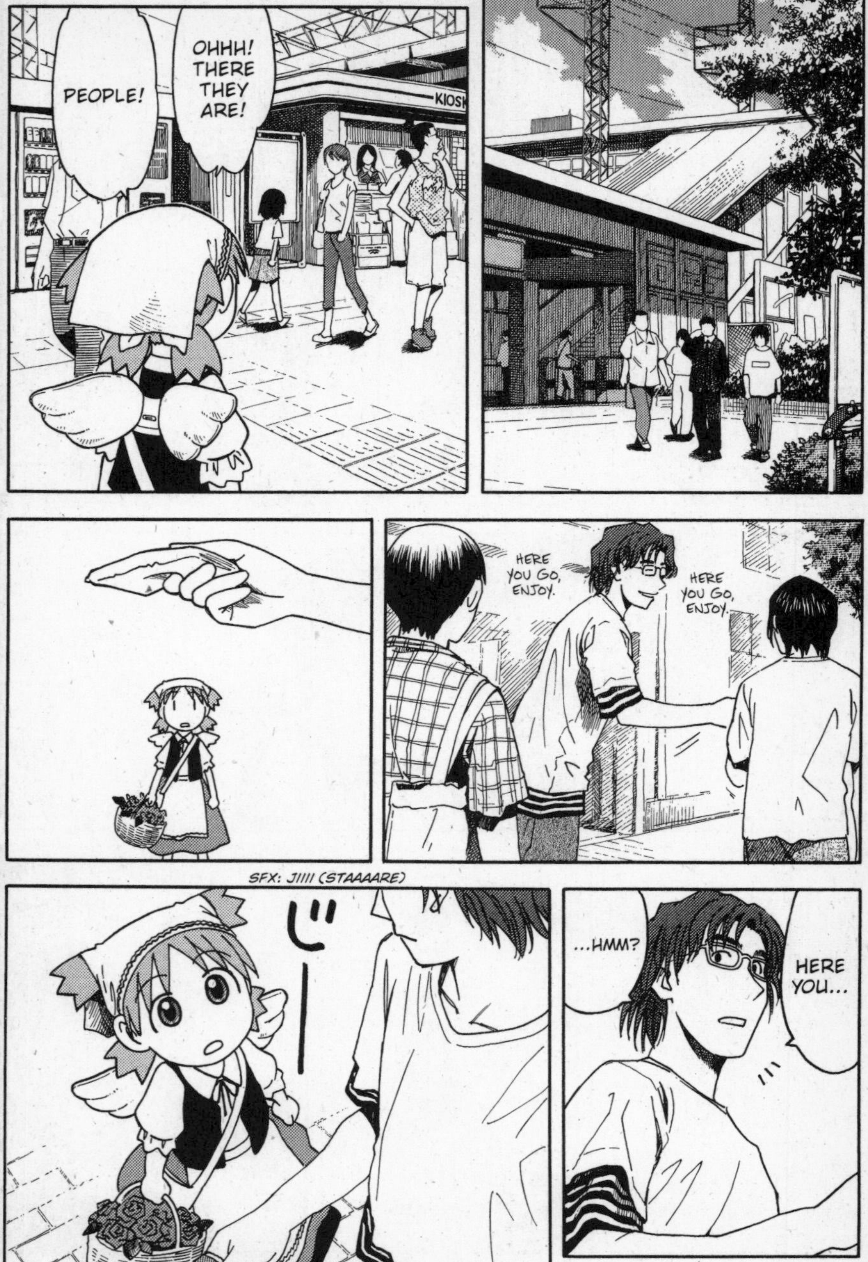
OHHH! THERE THEY ARE!
PEOPLE!
HERE YOU GO, ENJOY.
HERE YOU GO, ENJOY.
SFX: JIIII (STAAAARE)
HERE YOU...
...HMM?
じー

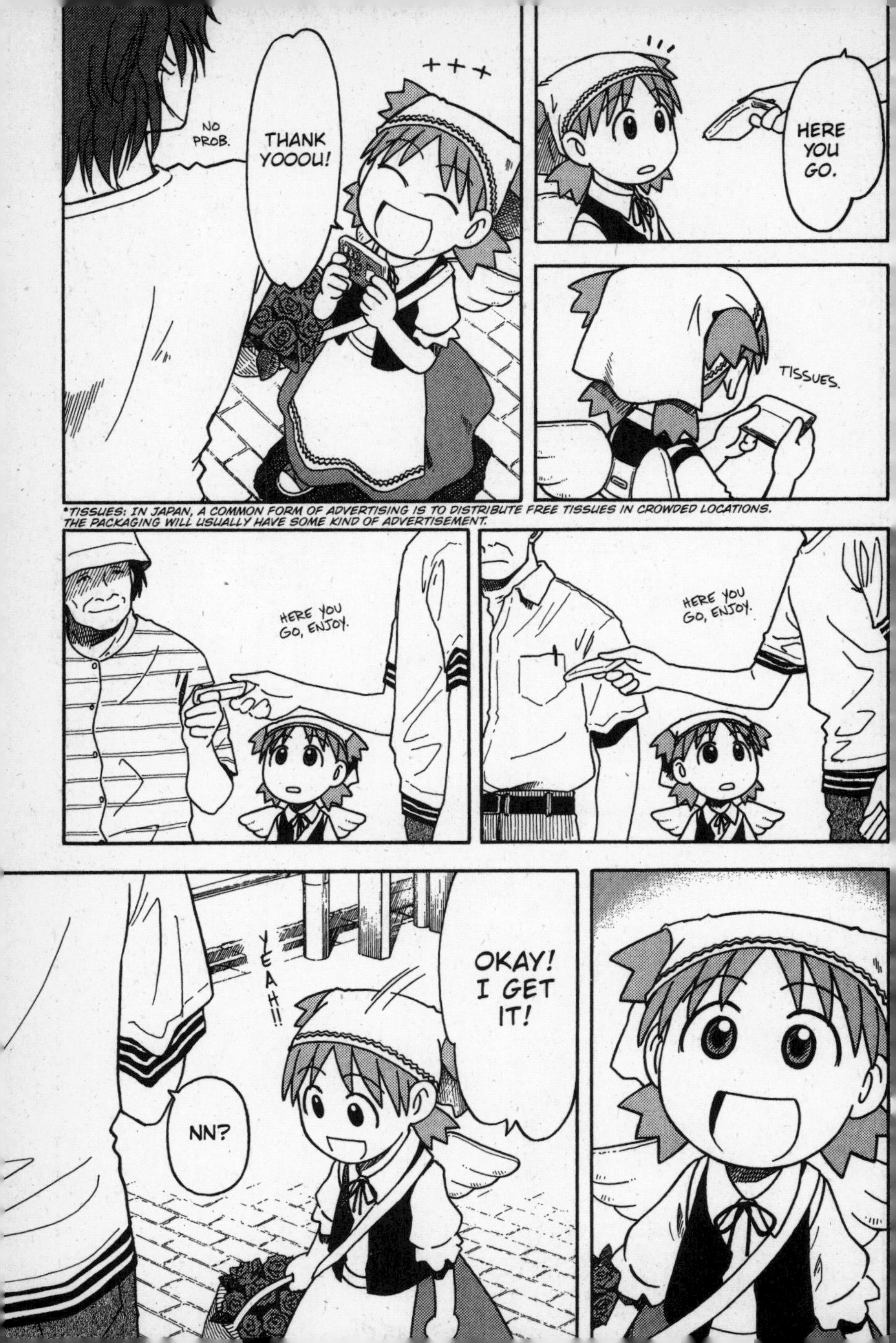
HERE YOU GO.
TISSUES.
THANK YOOOU!
NO PROB.
HERE YOU GO, ENJOY.
HERE YOU GO, ENJOY.
OKAY! I GET IT!
YEAH!!
NN?

*TISSUES: IN JAPAN, A COMMON FORM OF ADVERTISING IS TO DISTRIBUTE FREE TISSUES IN CROWDED LOCATIONS. THE PACKAGING WILL USUALLY HAVE SOME KIND OF ADVERTISEMENT.

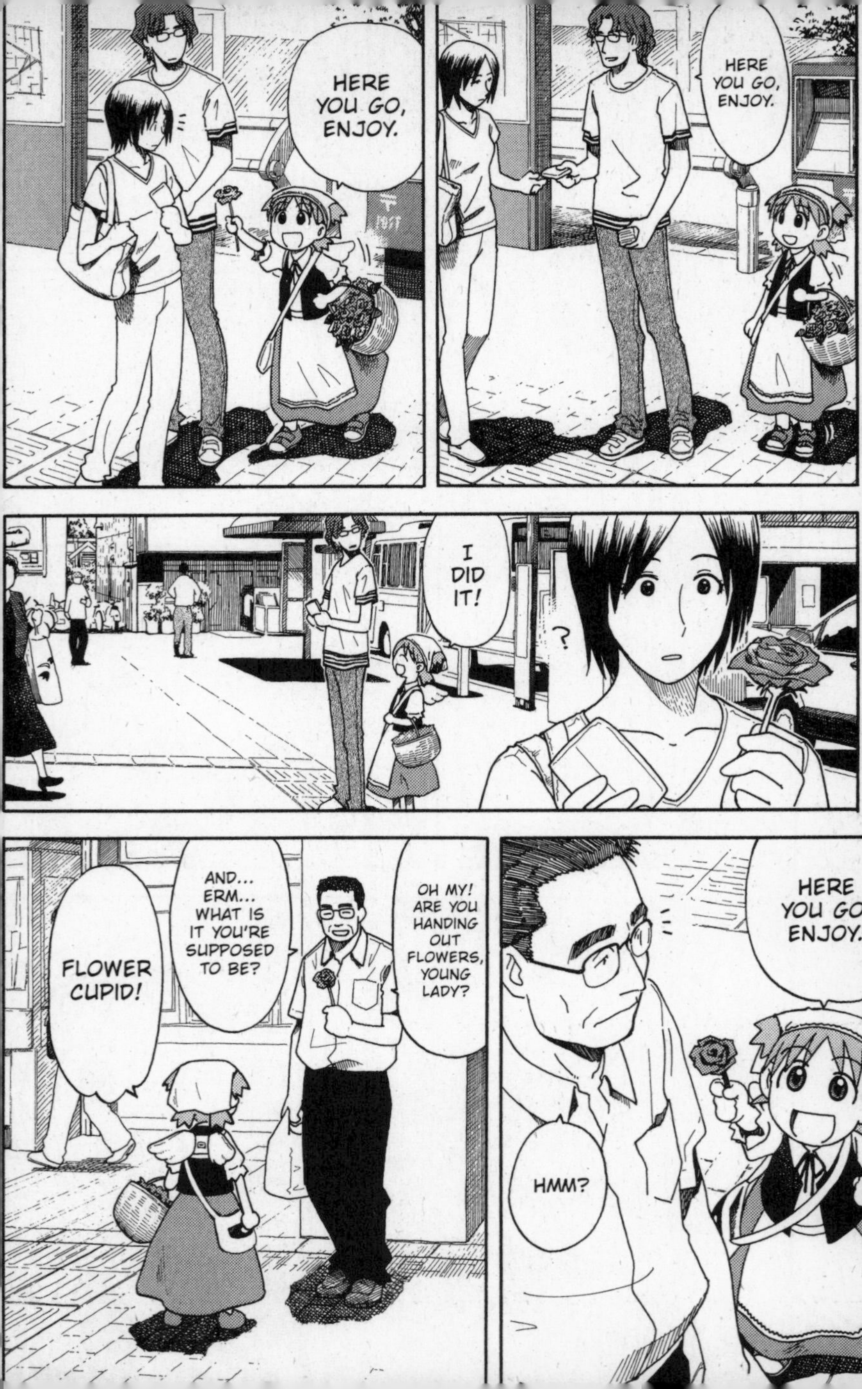
HERE YOU GO, ENJOY.
HERE YOU GO, ENJOY.
I DID IT!
?
HERE YOU GO, ENJOY.
HMM?
OH MY! ARE YOU HANDING OUT FLOWERS, YOUNG LADY?
AND... ERM... WHAT IS IT YOU'RE SUPPOSED TO BE?
FLOWER CUPID!

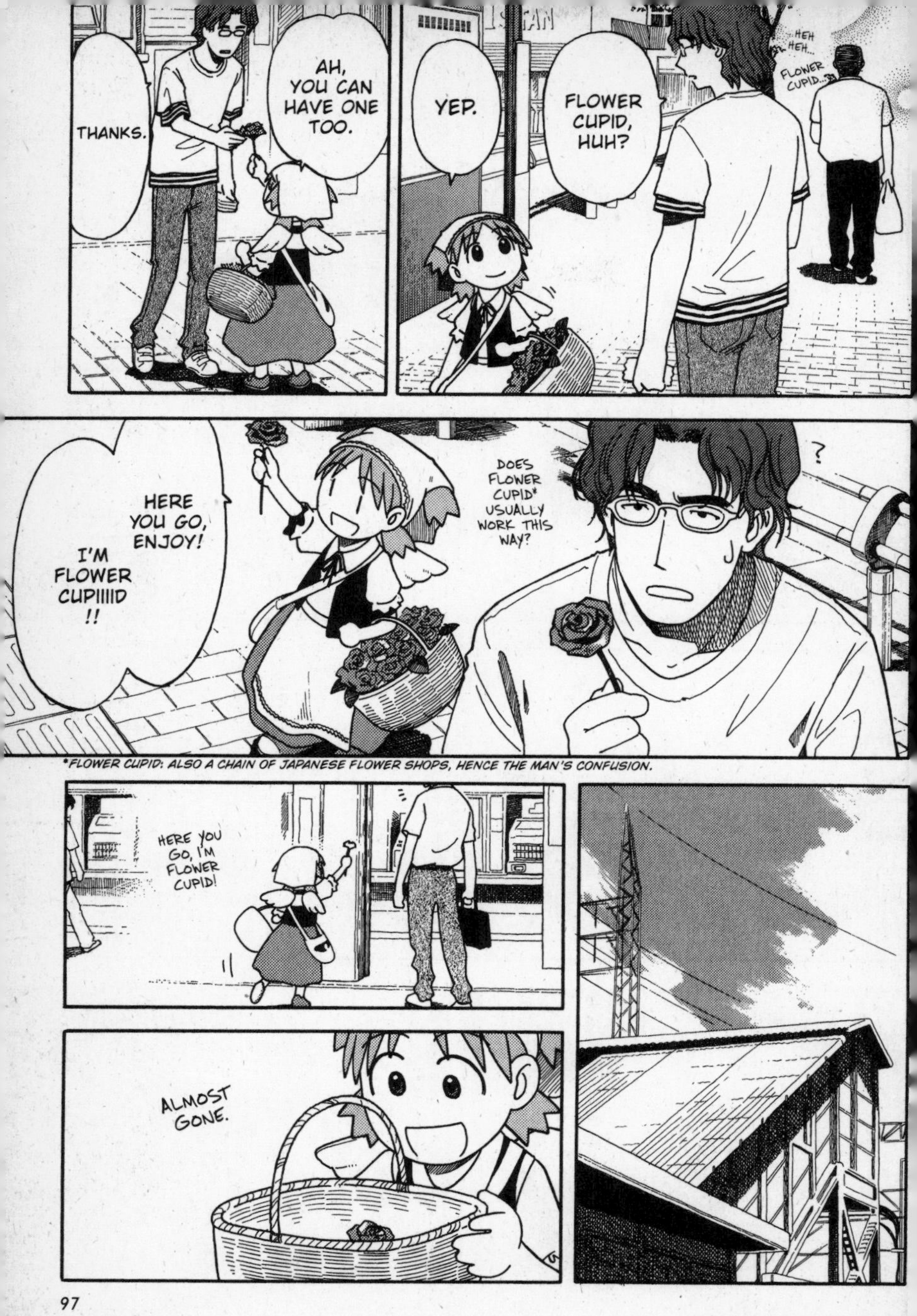
HEH HEH... FLOWER CUPID...
FLOWER CUPID, HUH?
YEP.
AH, YOU CAN HAVE ONE TOO.
THANKS.
?
DOES FLOWER CUPID* USUALLY WORK THIS WAY?
HERE YOU GO, ENJOY!
I'M FLOWER CUPIIIIID!!
HERE YOU GO, I'M FLOWER CUPID!
ALMOST GONE.

*FLOWER CUPID: ALSO A CHAIN OF JAPANESE FLOWER SHOPS, HENCE THE MAN'S CONFUSION.

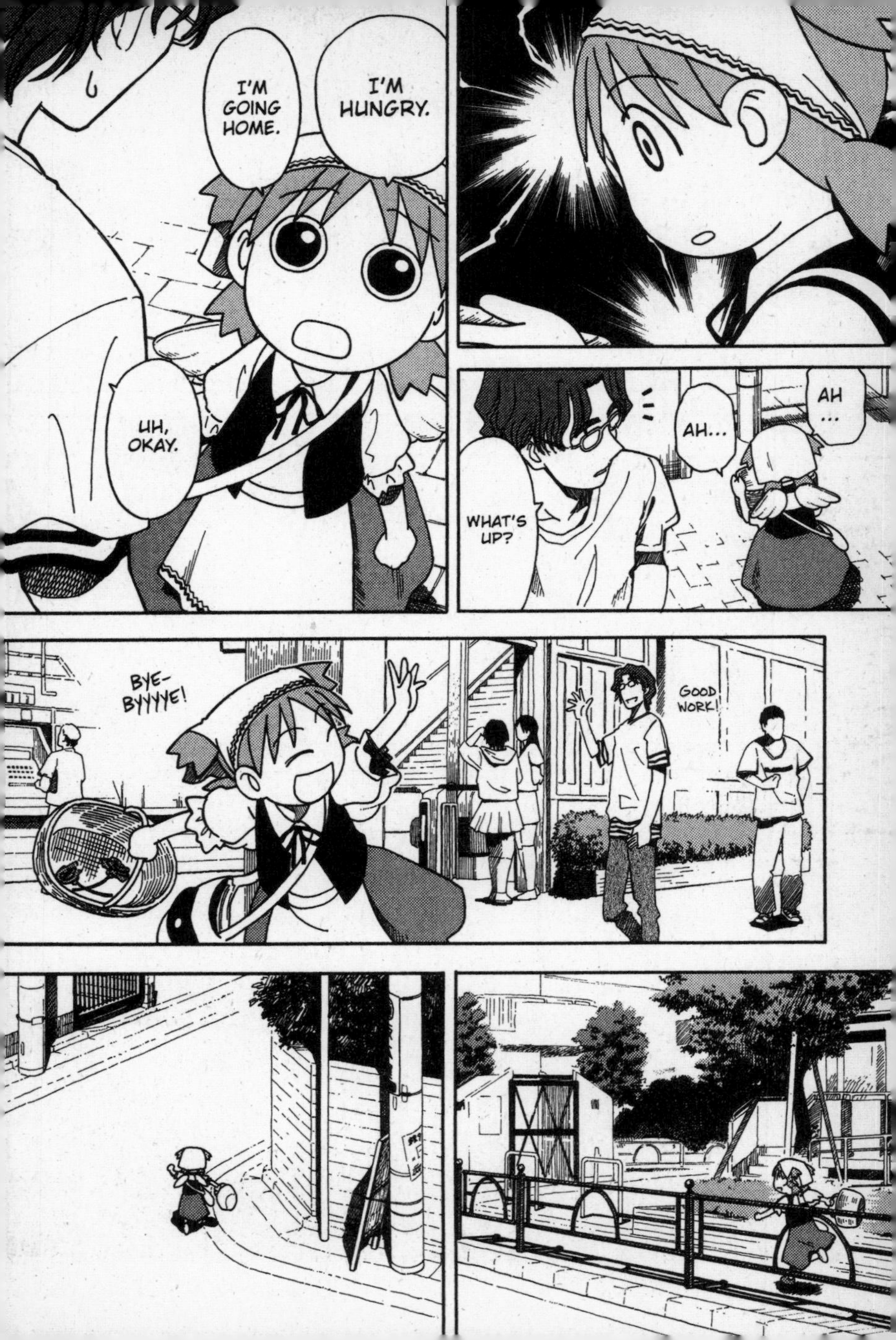
AH ...
AH...
WHAT'S UP?
I'M HUNGRY.
I'M GOING HOME.
UH, OKAY.
GOOD WORK!
BYE-BYYYYE!

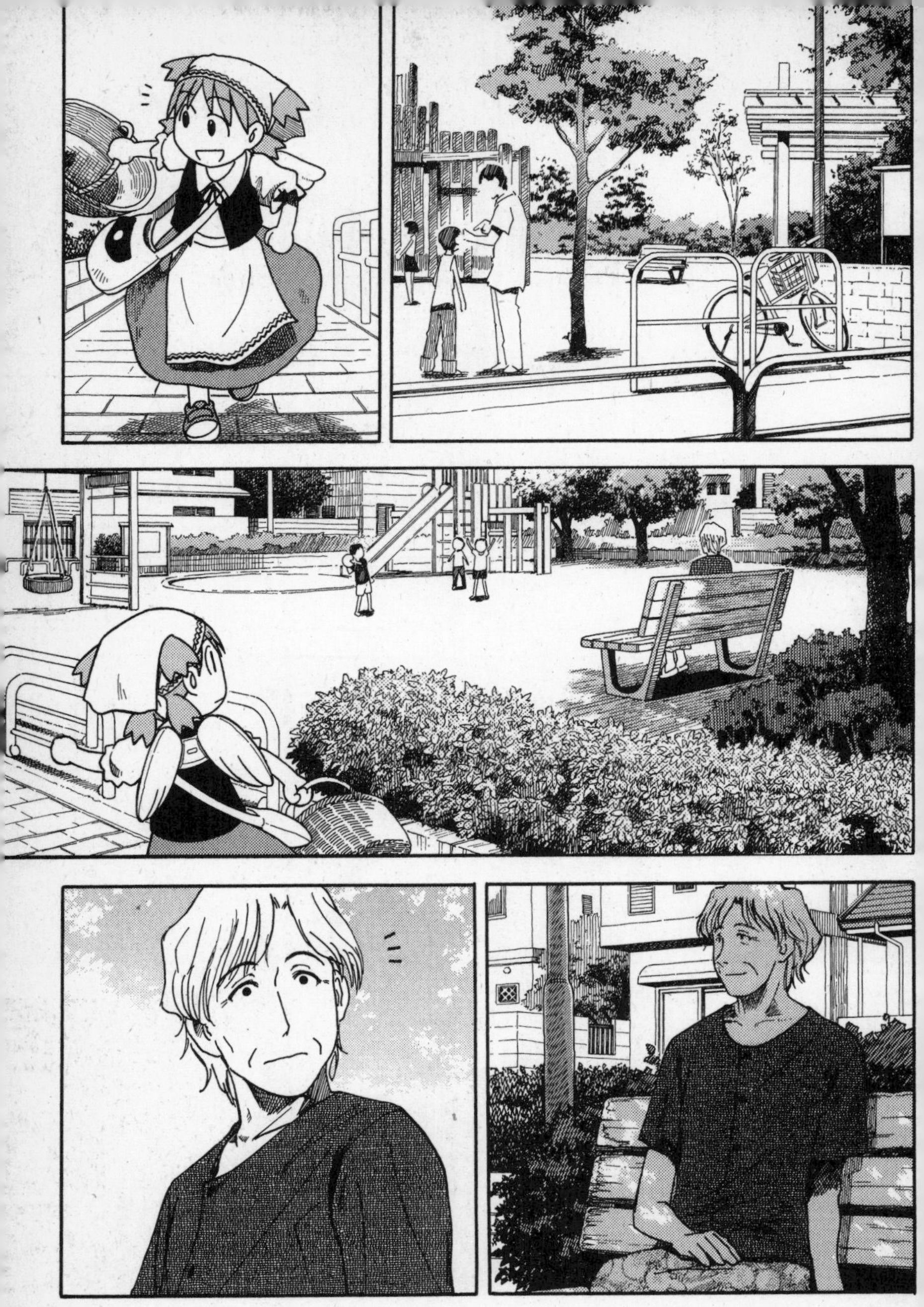

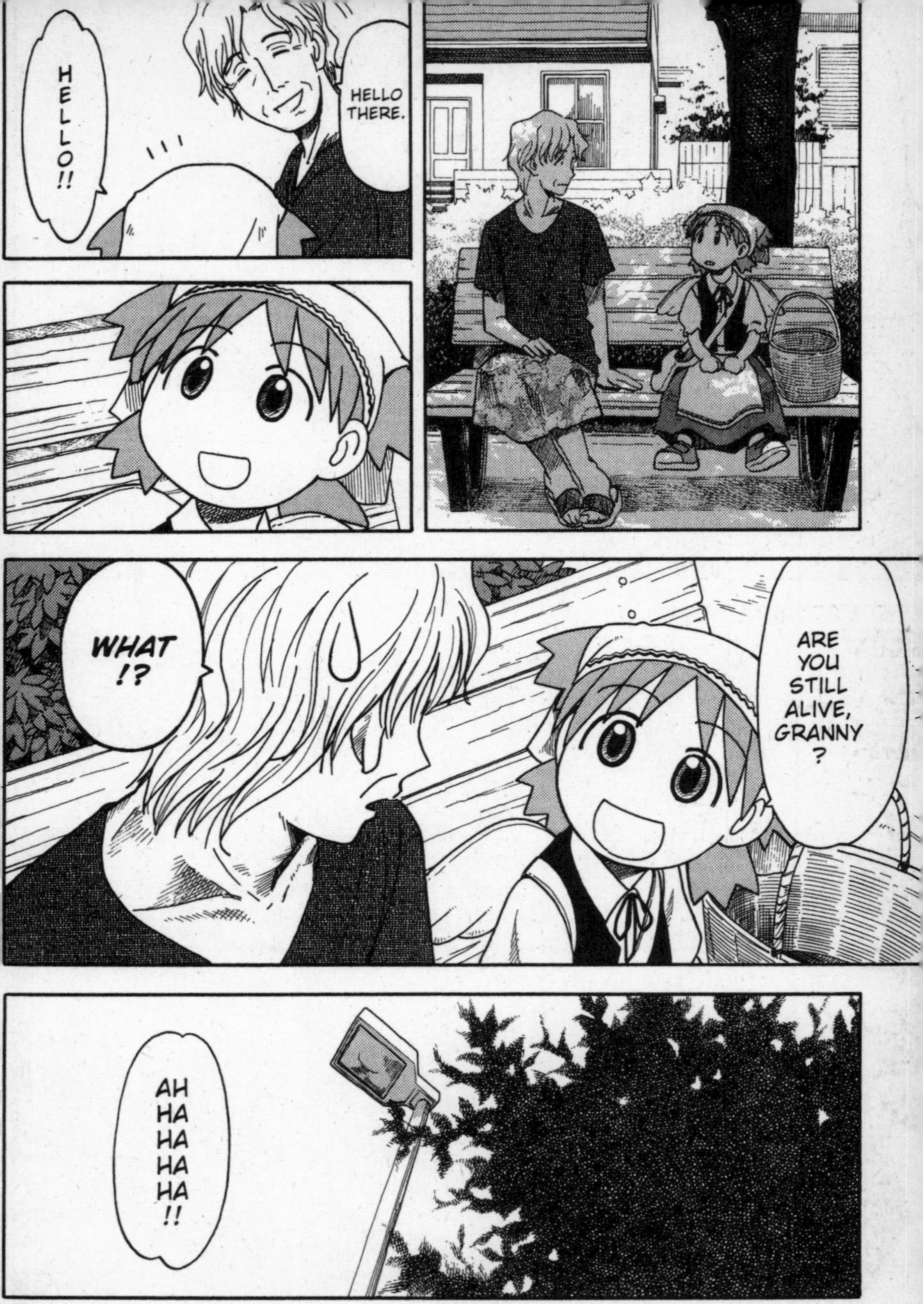
HELLO THERE.
HELLO!!
ARE YOU STILL ALIVE, GRANNY?
WHAT!?
AH HA HA HA HA!!

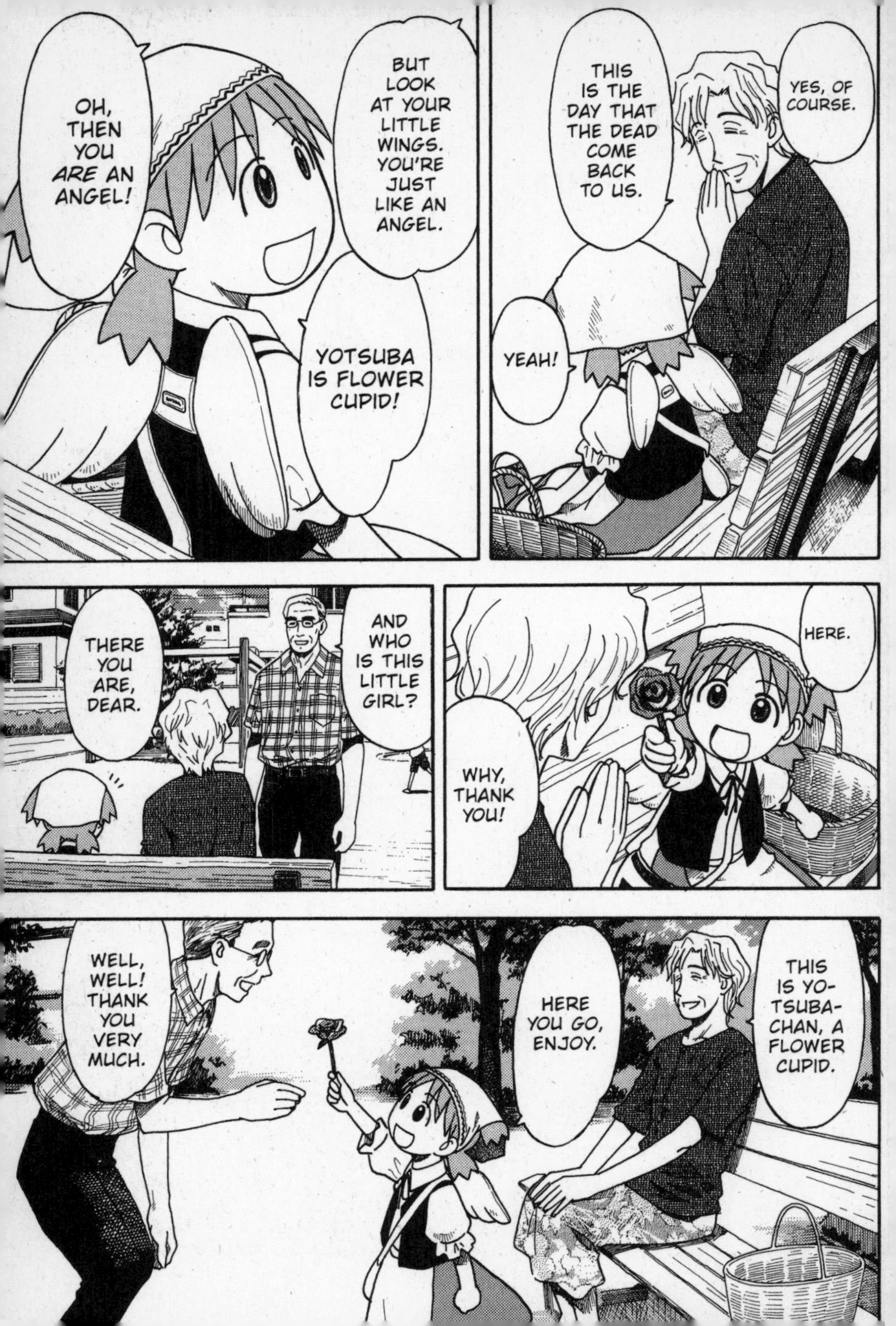
YES, OF COURSE.
THIS IS THE DAY THAT THE DEAD COME BACK TO US.
YEAH!
BUT LOOK AT YOUR LITTLE WINGS. YOU'RE JUST LIKE AN ANGEL.
YOTSUBA IS FLOWER CUPID!
OH, THEN YOU ARE AN ANGEL!
HERE.
WHY, THANK YOU!
AND WHO IS THIS LITTLE GIRL?
THERE YOU ARE, DEAR.
THIS IS YO-TSUBA-CHAN, A FLOWER CUPID.
HERE YOU GO, ENJOY.
WELL, WELL! THANK YOU VERY MUCH.

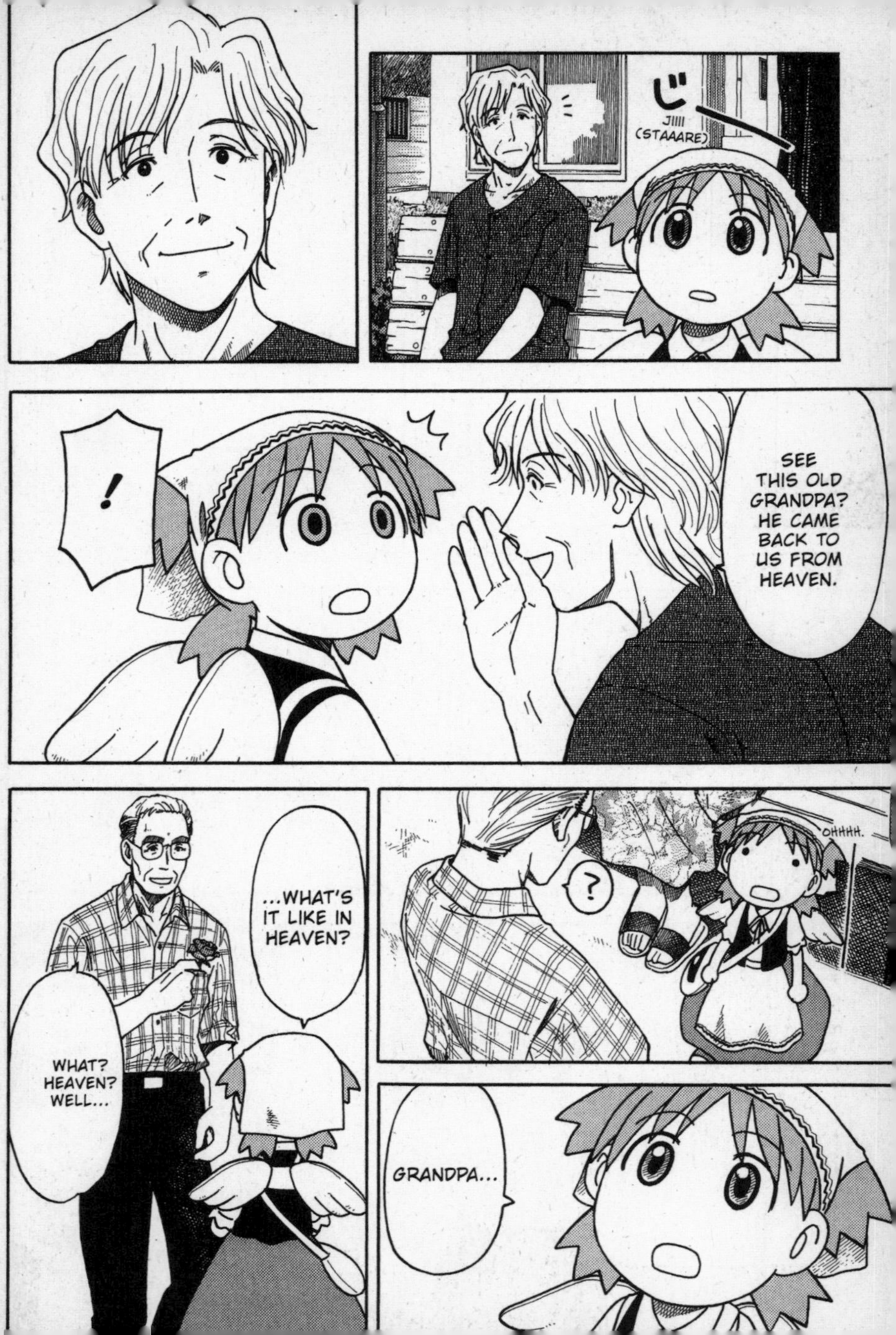
じ
JIIII
(STAAARE)
SEE THIS OLD GRANDPA? HE CAME BACK TO US FROM HEAVEN.
!
OHHHH.
?
GRANDPA...
...WHAT'S IT LIKE IN HEAVEN?
WHAT? HEAVEN? WELL...

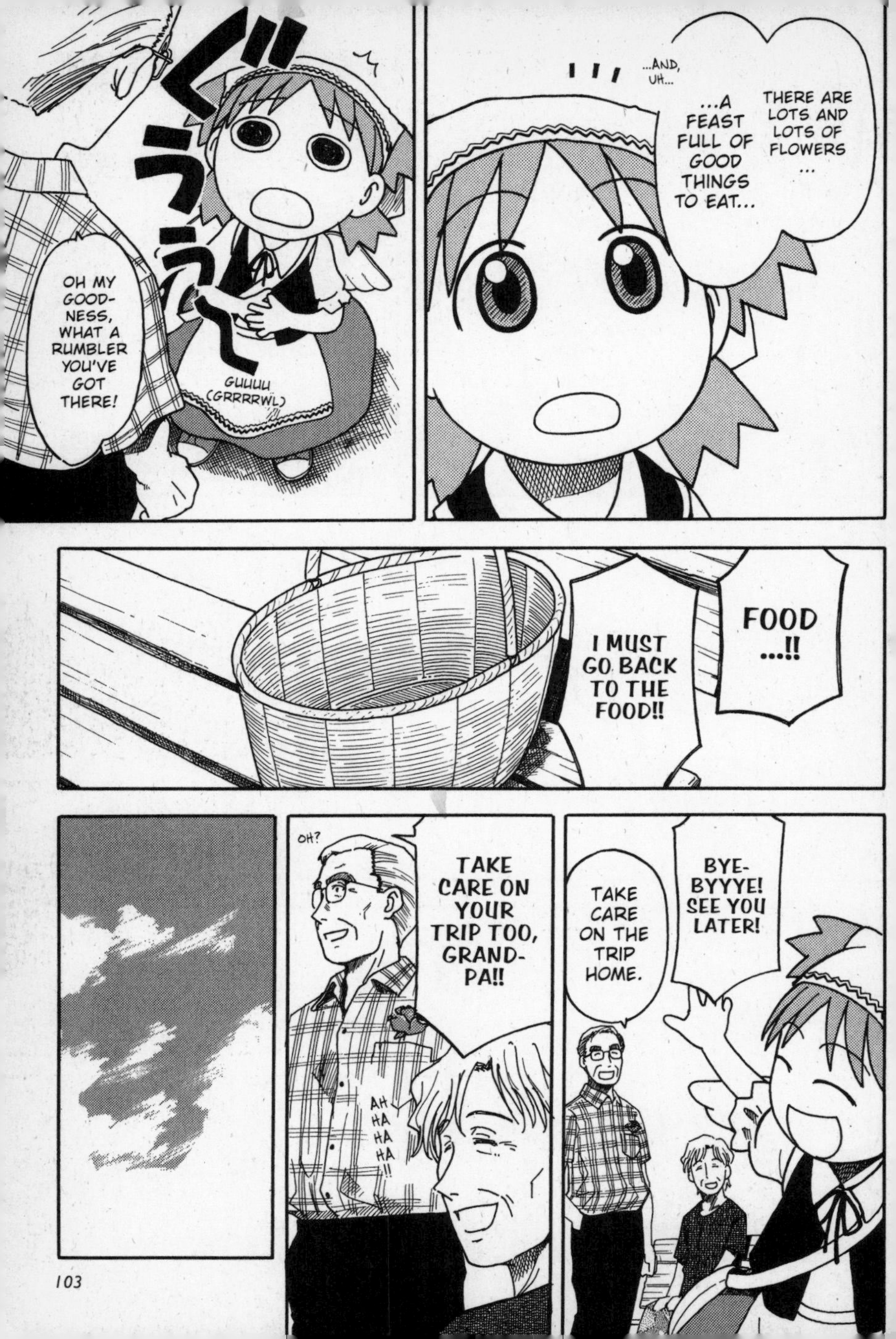
THERE ARE LOTS AND LOTS OF FLOWERS ...
...A FEAST FULL OF GOOD THINGS TO EAT...
...AND, UH...
GUUUU (GRRRRWL)
OH MY GOODNESS, WHAT A RUMBLER YOU'VE GOT THERE!
FOOD ...!!
I MUST GO BACK TO THE FOOD!!
BYE-BYYYE! SEE YOU LATER!
TAKE CARE ON THE TRIP HOME.
OH?
TAKE CARE ON YOUR TRIP TOO, GRAND-PA!!
AH HA HA HA HA!!

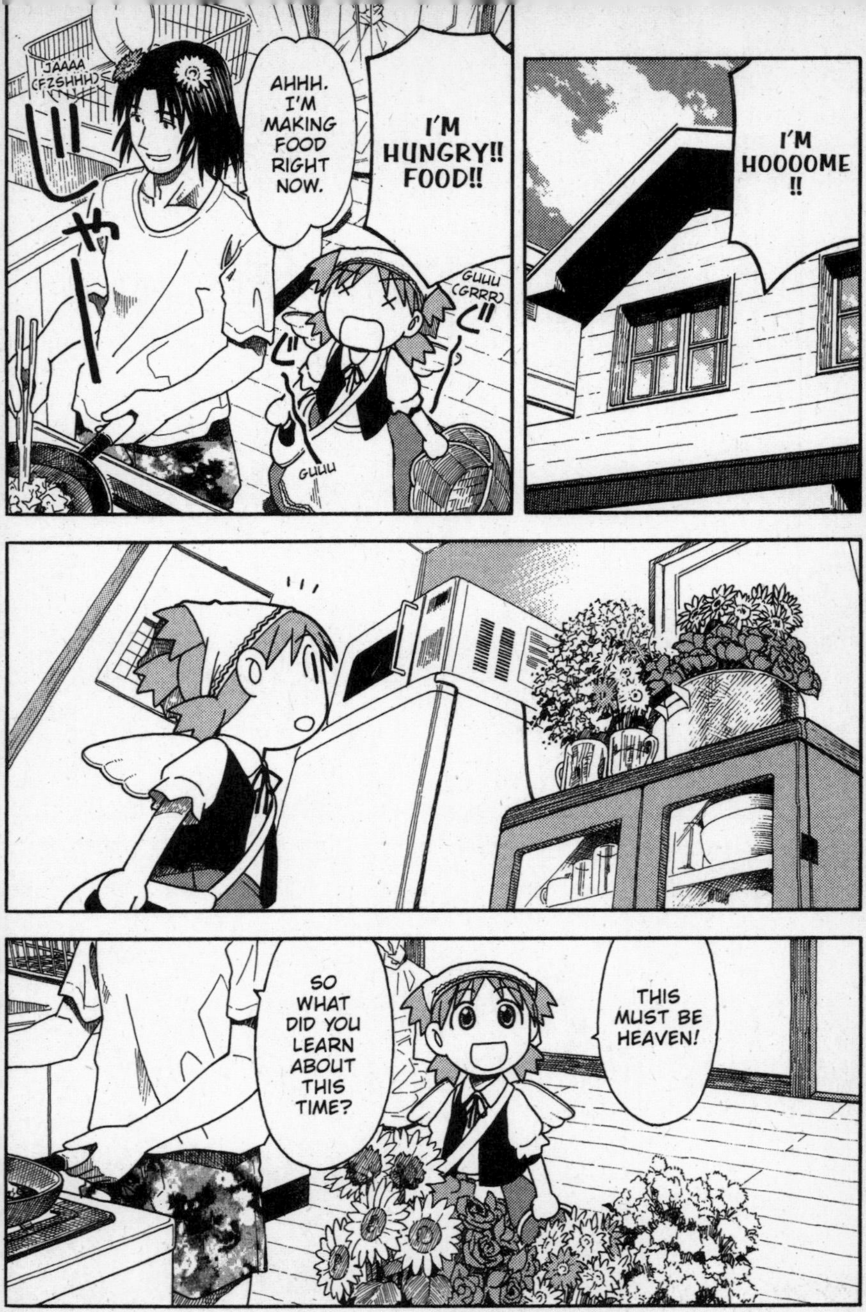
I'M HOOOOME !!
I'M HUNGRY!! FOOD!!
GUUU (GRRR)
GUUU
AHHH. I'M MAKING FOOD RIGHT NOW.
JAAAA (FZSHHH)
THIS MUST BE HEAVEN!
SO WHAT DID YOU LEARN ABOUT THIS TIME?

YOTSUBA&!

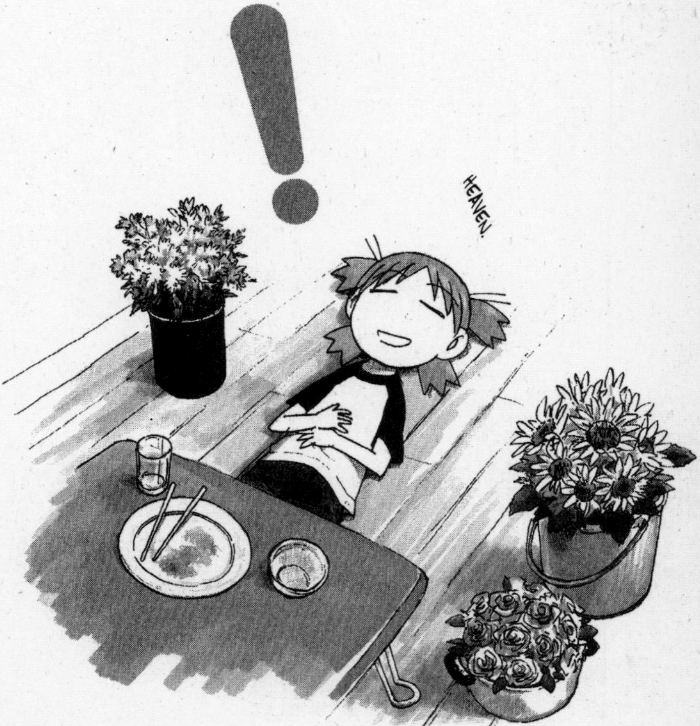
HEAVEN.

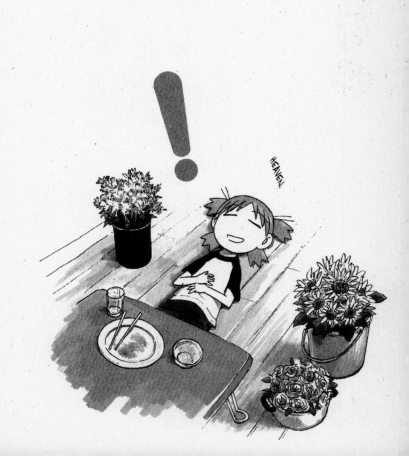

YOTSUBA& THE ELEPHANT

#19

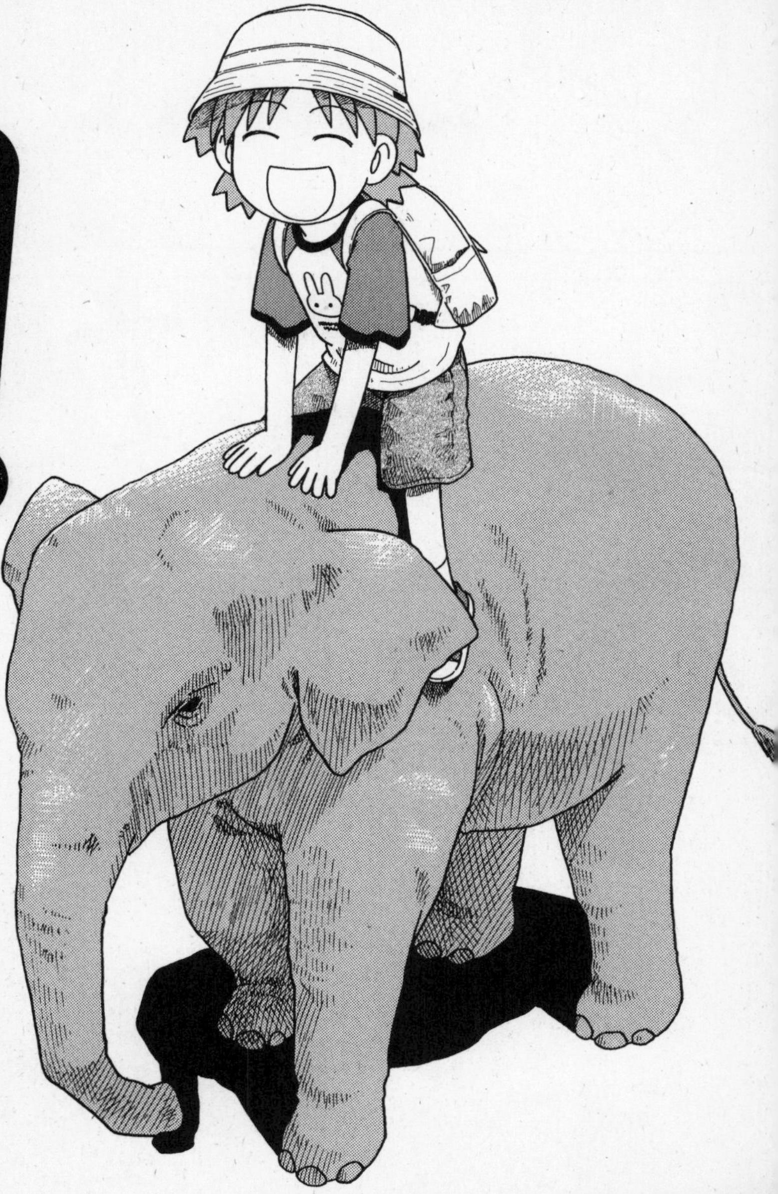

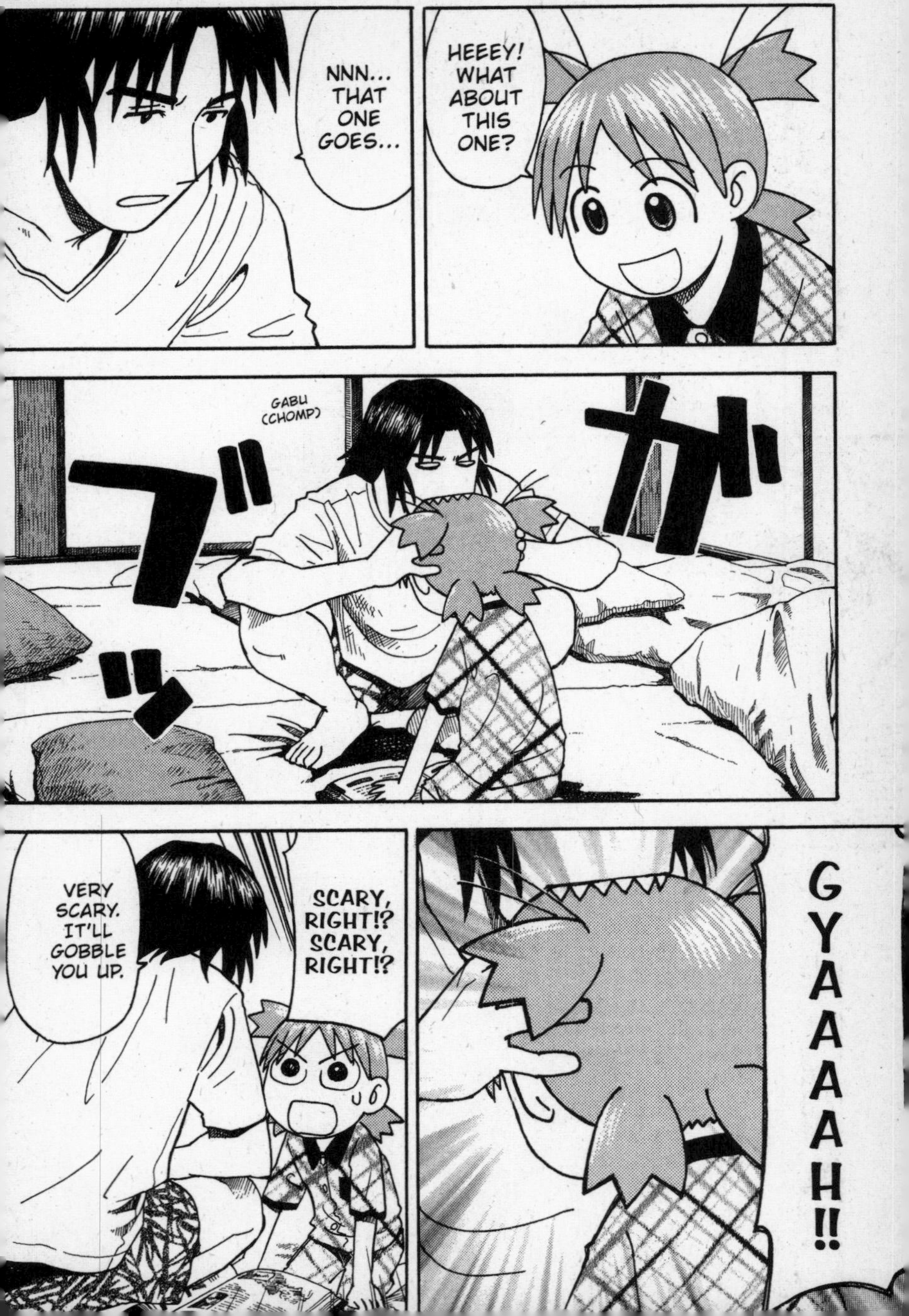
HEEEY! WHAT ABOUT THIS ONE?
NNN... THAT ONE GOES...
ガブッ
GABU (CHOMP)
GYAAAAH!!
SCARY, RIGHT!? SCARY, RIGHT!?
VERY SCARY. IT'LL GOBBLE YOU UP.

OHHHHH...

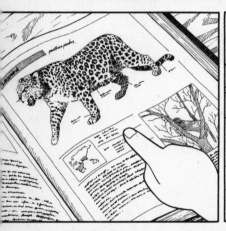

HMM?

AND THIS ONE!? WHAT ABOUT THIS ONE!?

GYAAAAH!!

GARI
(CRUNCH)

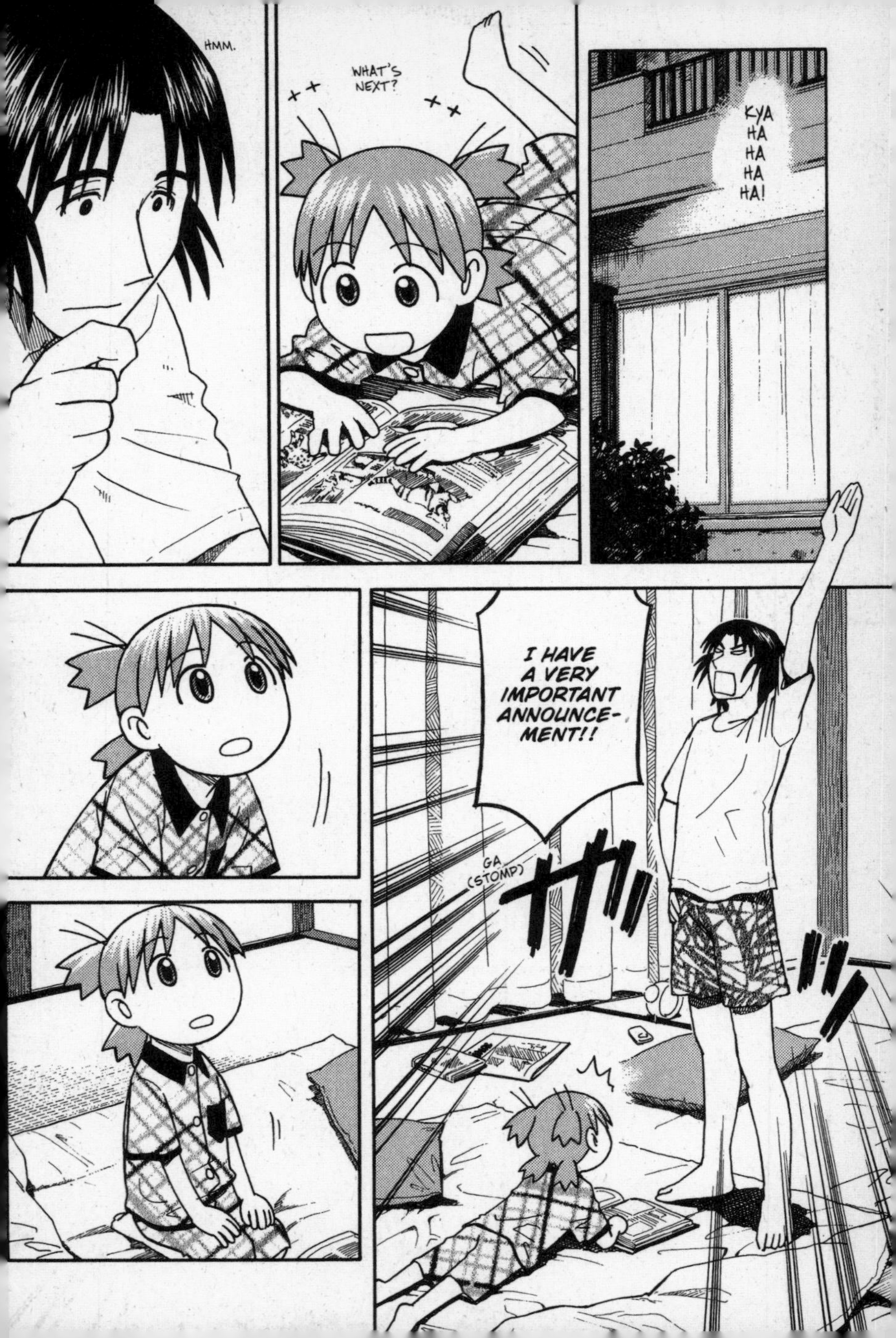
KYA HA HA HA HA!
WHAT'S NEXT?
HMM.
I HAVE A VERY IMPORTANT ANNOUNCEMENT!!
GA (STOMP)

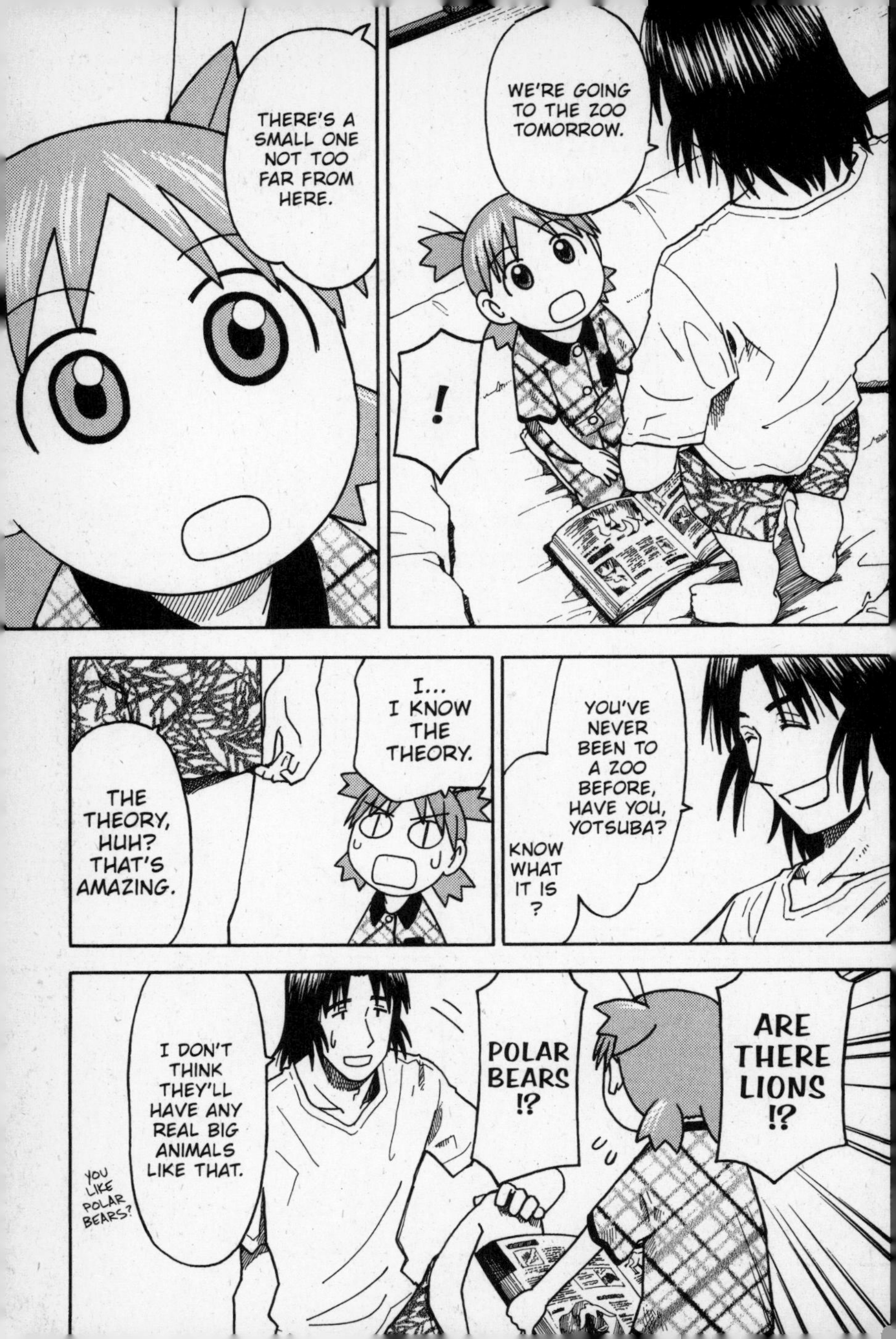
WE'RE GOING TO THE ZOO TOMORROW.
!
THERE'S A SMALL ONE NOT TOO FAR FROM HERE.
YOU'VE NEVER BEEN TO A ZOO BEFORE, HAVE YOU, YOTSUBA?
KNOW WHAT IT IS ?
I... I KNOW THE THEORY.
THE THEORY, HUH? THAT'S AMAZING.
ARE THERE LIONS !?
POLAR BEARS !?
I DON'T THINK THEY'LL HAVE ANY REAL BIG ANIMALS LIKE THAT.
YOU LIKE POLAR BEARS?

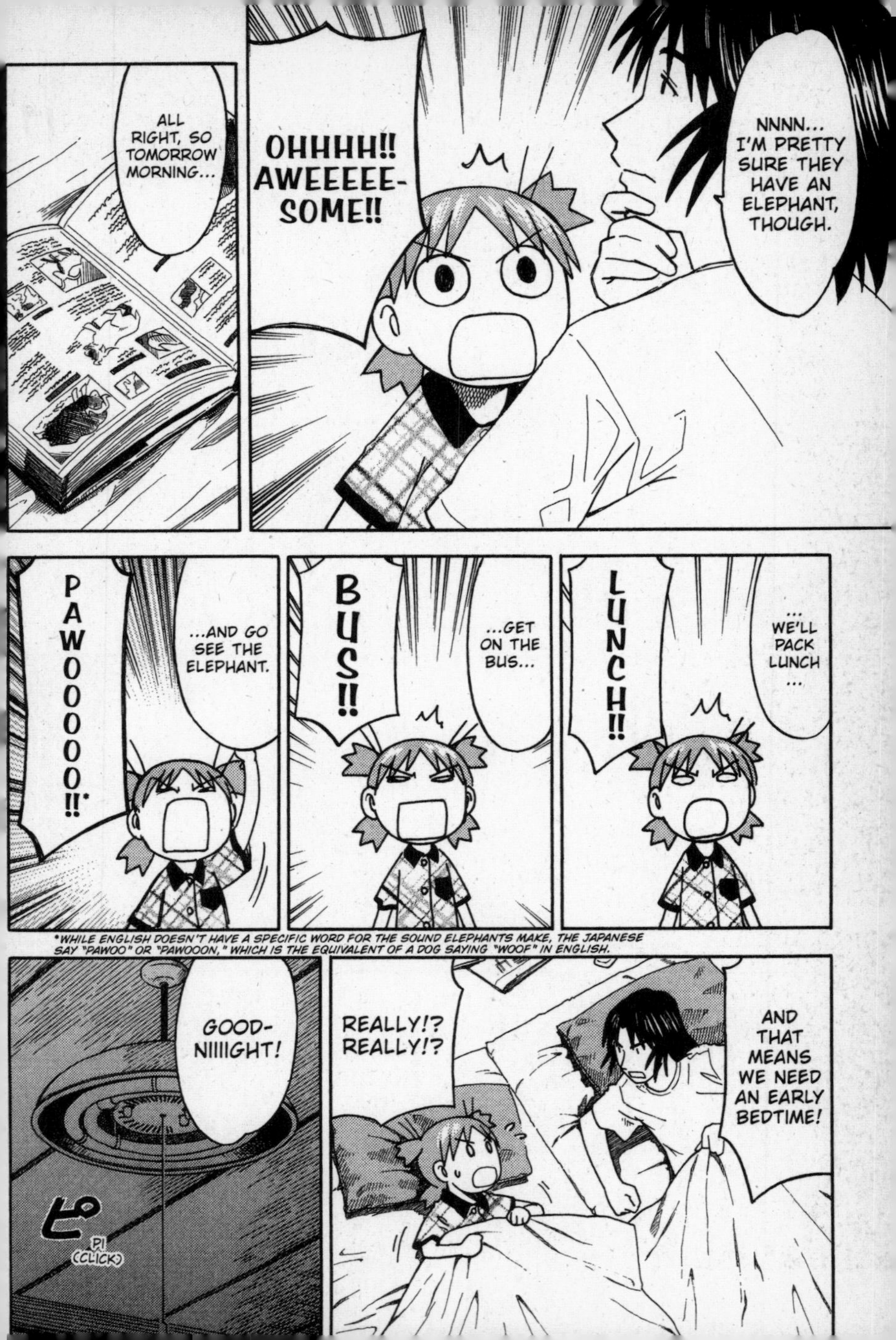
NNNN... I'M PRETTY SURE THEY HAVE AN ELEPHANT, THOUGH.
OHHHH!! AWEEEEE-SOME!!
ALL RIGHT, SO TOMORROW MORNING...
...WE'LL PACK LUNCH...
LUNCH!!
...GET ON THE BUS...
BUS!!
...AND GO SEE THE ELEPHANT.
PAWOOOOOOO!!*
AND THAT MEANS WE NEED AN EARLY BEDTIME!
REALLY!? REALLY!?
GOOD-NIIIIGHT!
ピ
PI (CLICK)

*WHILE ENGLISH DOESN'T HAVE A SPECIFIC WORD FOR THE SOUND ELEPHANTS MAKE, THE JAPANESE SAY "PAWOO" OR "PAWOOON," WHICH IS THE EQUIVALENT OF A DOG SAYING "WOOF" IN ENGLISH.

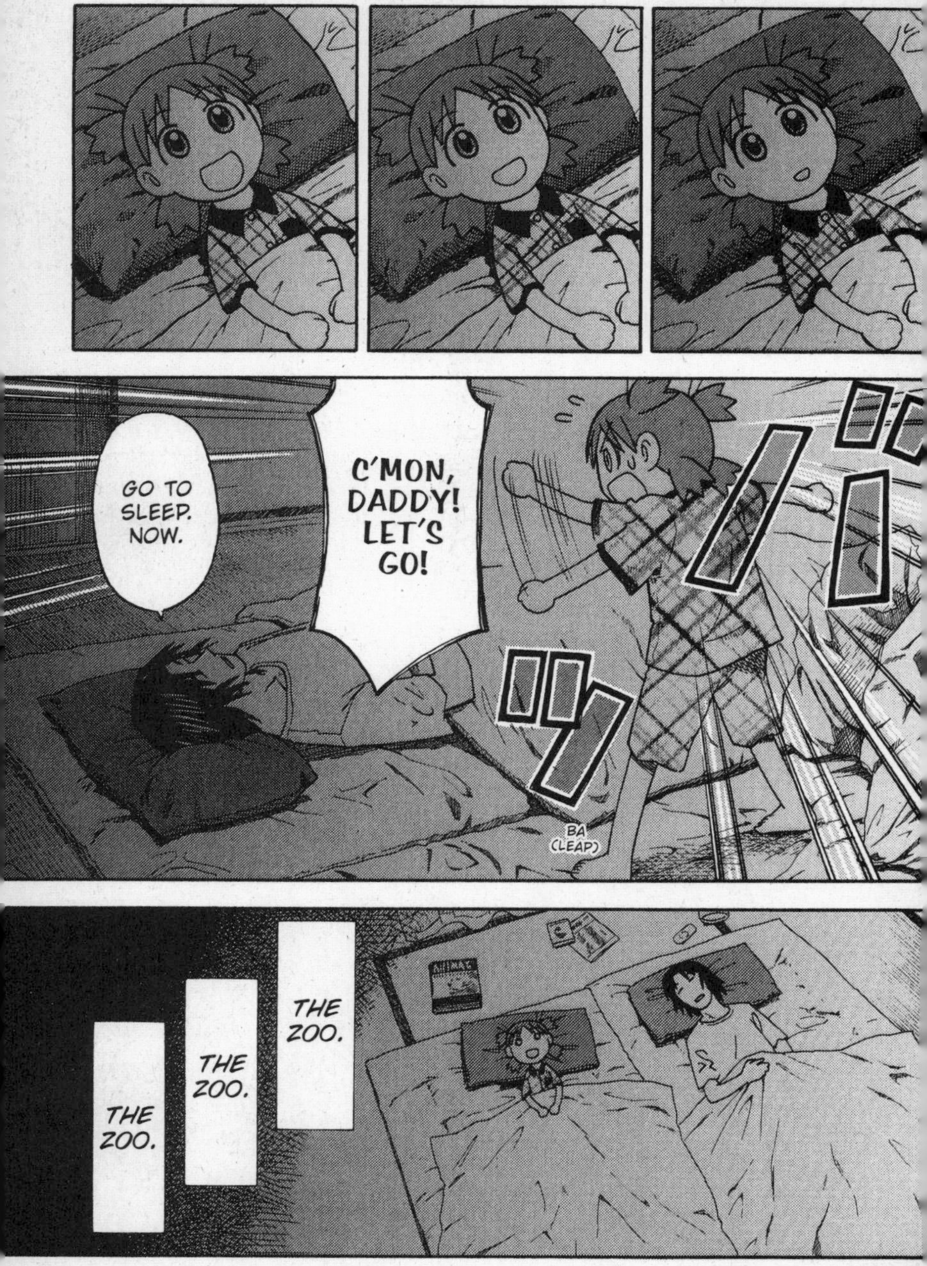
C'MON, DADDY! LET'S GO!
BA (LEAP)
GO TO SLEEP. NOW.
THE ZOO.
THE ZOO.
THE ZOO.

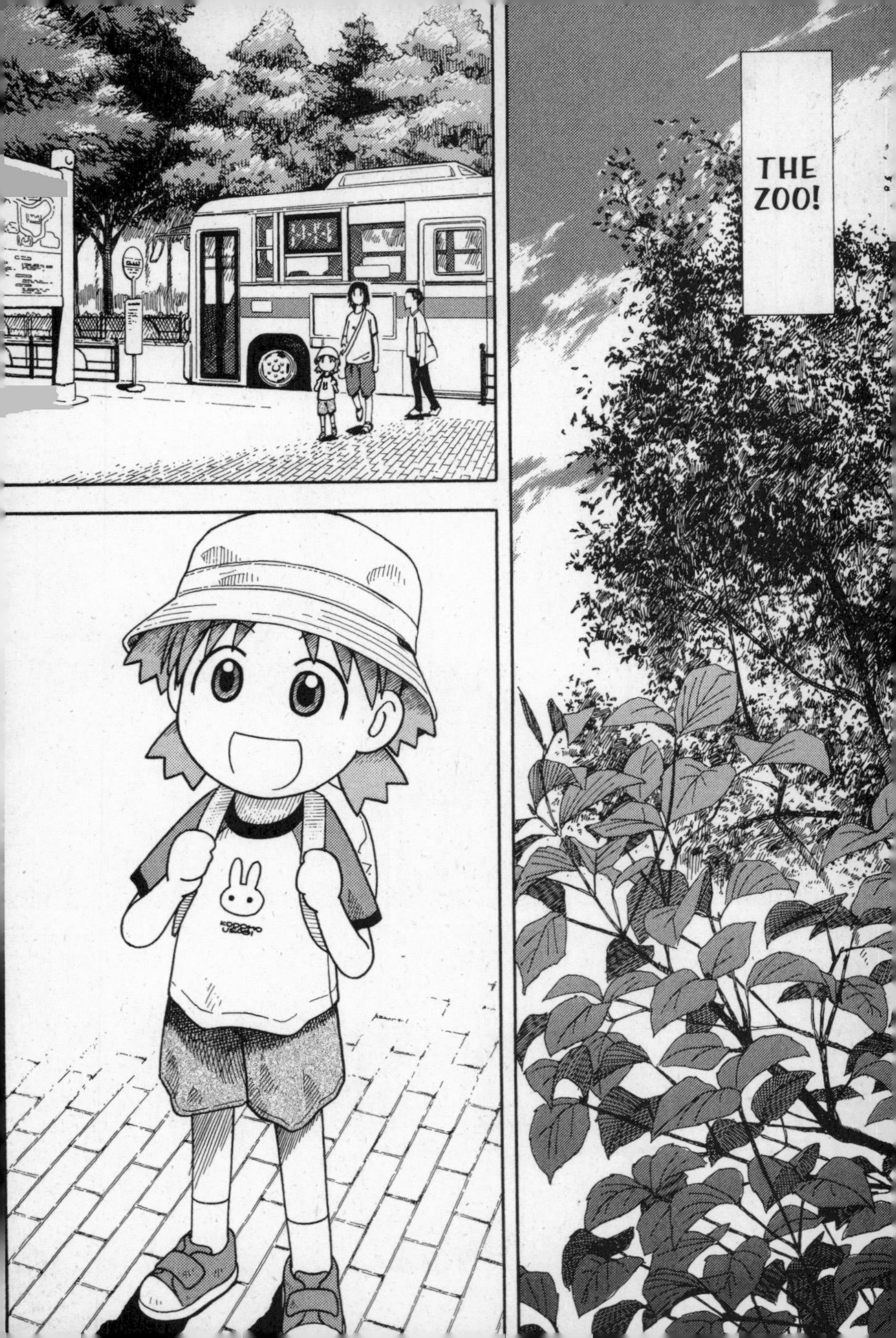
THE ZOO!

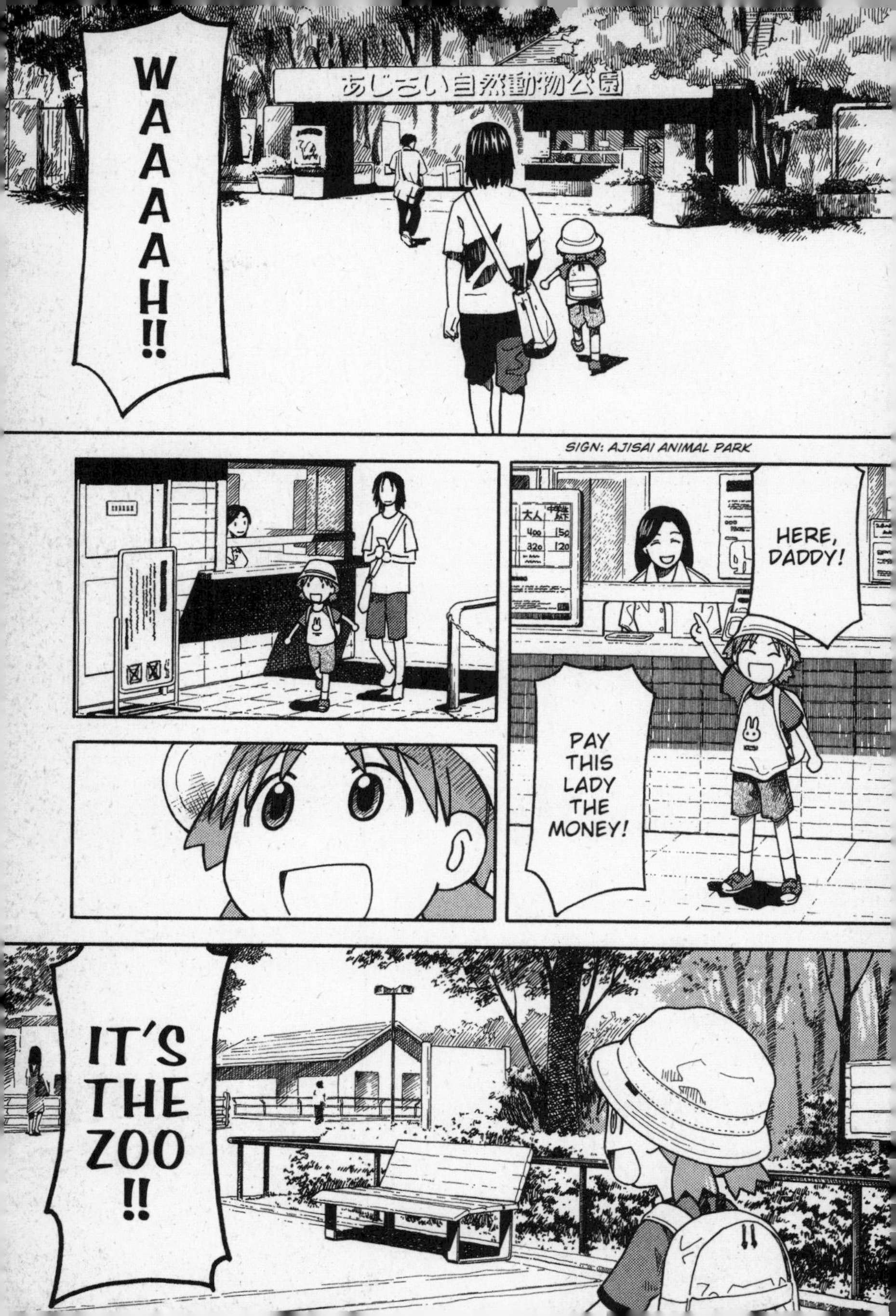
WAAAAAH!!
あじさい自然動物公園
SIGN: AJISAI ANIMAL PARK
HERE, DADDY!
PAY THIS LADY THE MONEY!
IT'S THE ZOO!!

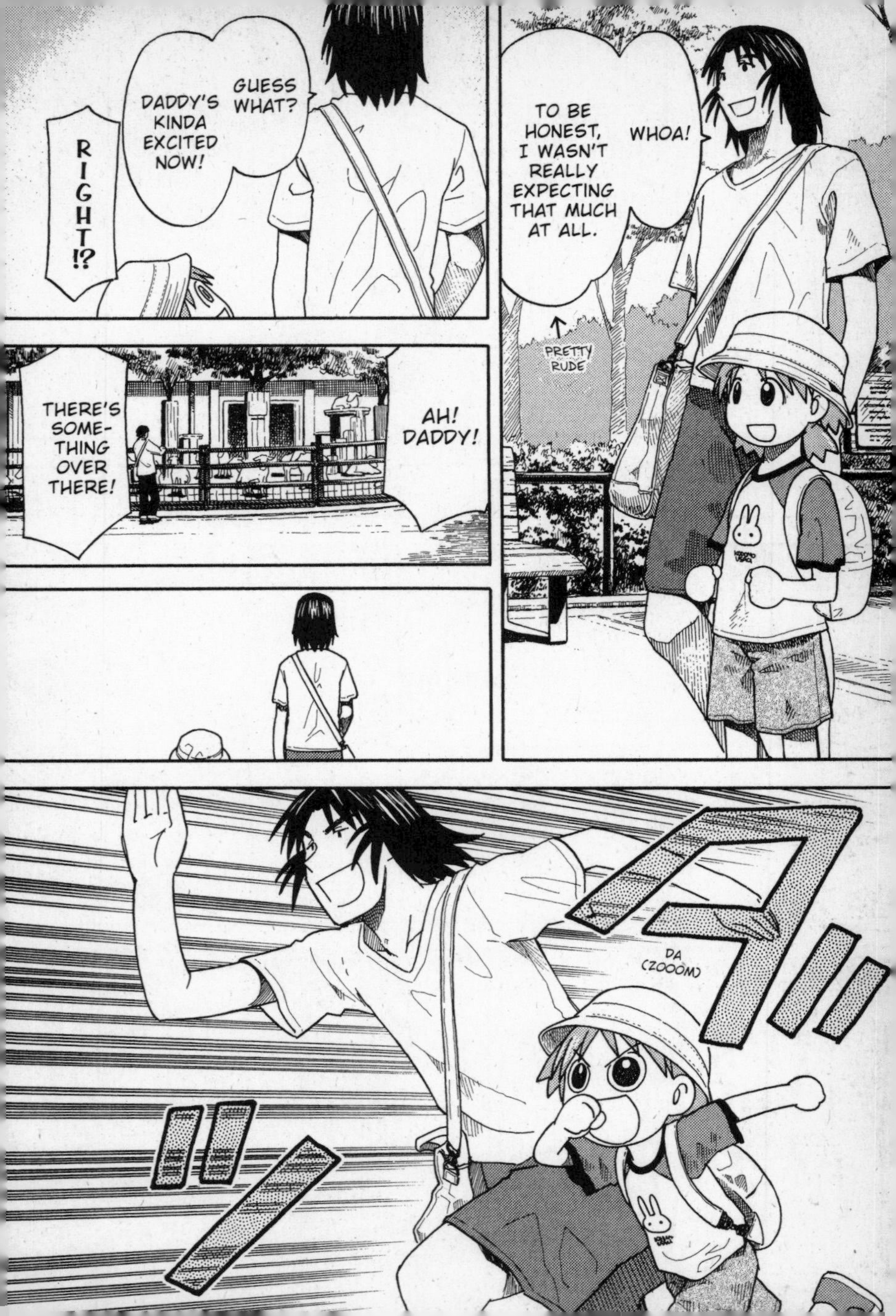
WHOA!
TO BE HONEST, I WASN'T REALLY EXPECTING THAT MUCH AT ALL.
PRETTY RUDE
GUESS WHAT?
DADDY'S KINDA EXCITED NOW!
RIGHT!?
AH! DADDY!
THERE'S SOME-THING OVER THERE!
DA (ZOOOM)

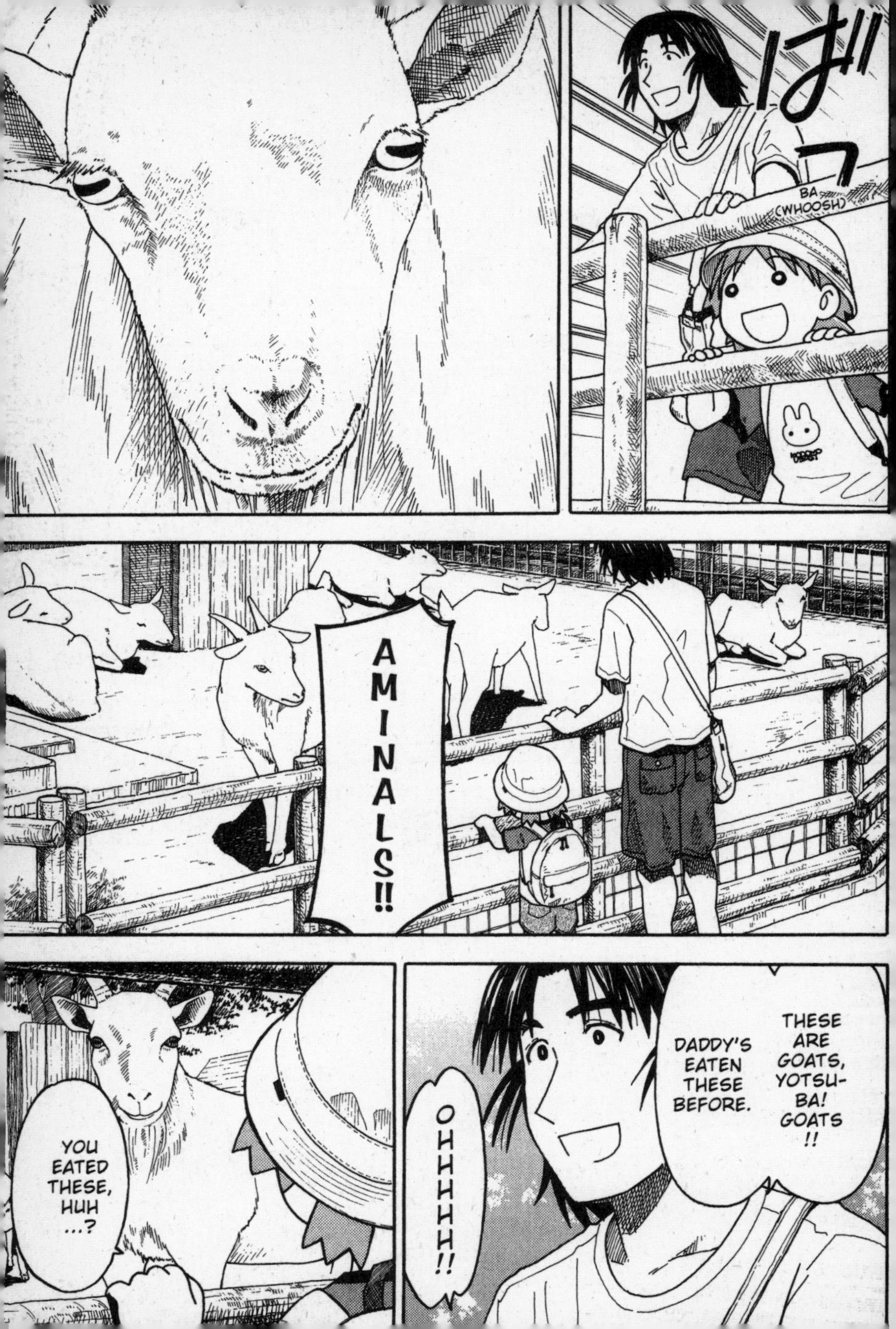
ばッ
BA (WHOOSH)
AMINALS!!
THESE ARE GOATS, YOTSUBA! GOATS!!
DADDY'S EATEN THESE BEFORE.
OHHHHH!!
YOU EATED THESE, HUH ...?

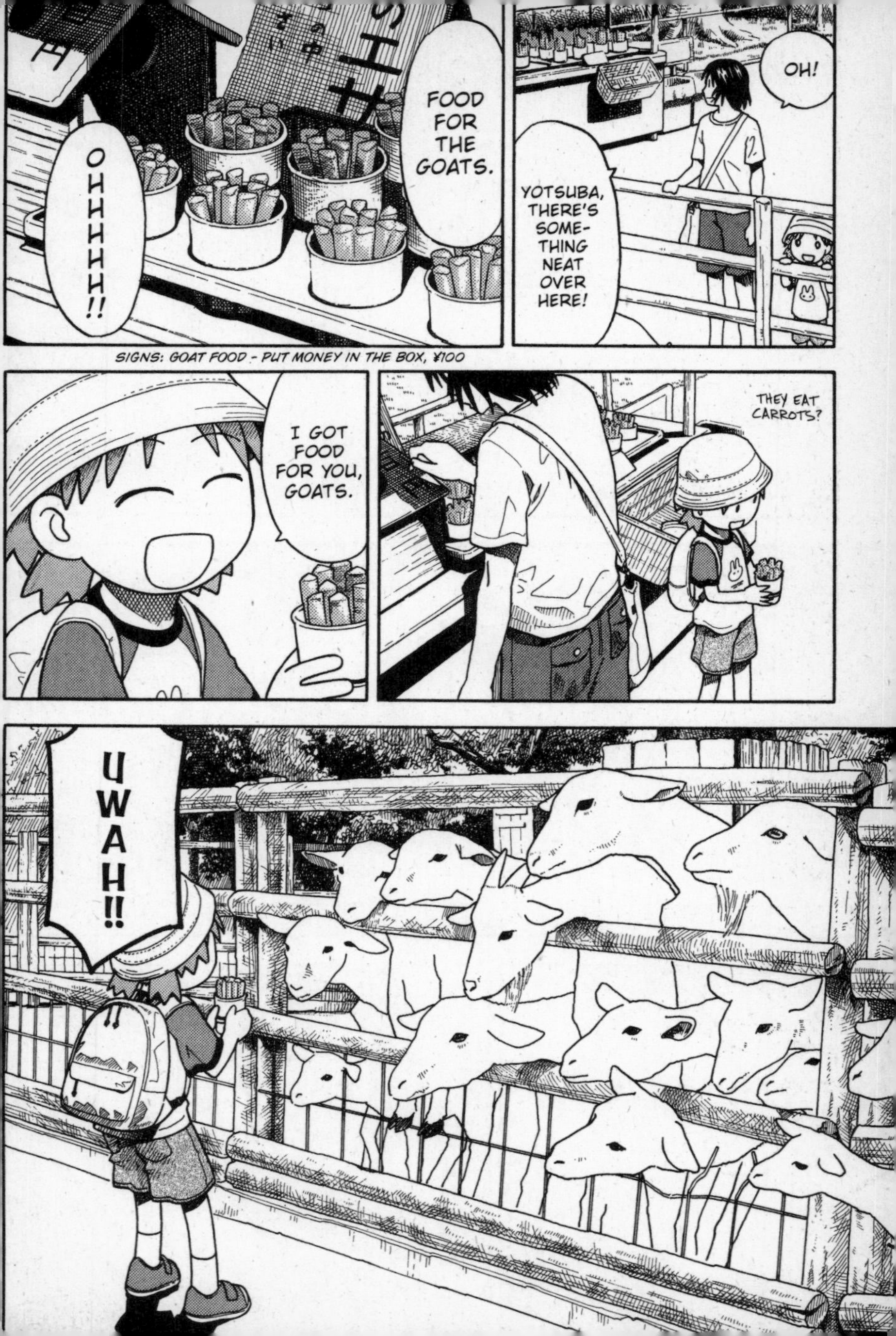
OH!
YOTSUBA, THERE'S SOMETHING NEAT OVER HERE!
FOOD FOR THE GOATS.
OHHHHH!!
SIGNS: GOAT FOOD - PUT MONEY IN THE BOX, ¥100
THEY EAT CARROTS?
I GOT FOOD FOR YOU, GOATS.
UWAH!!

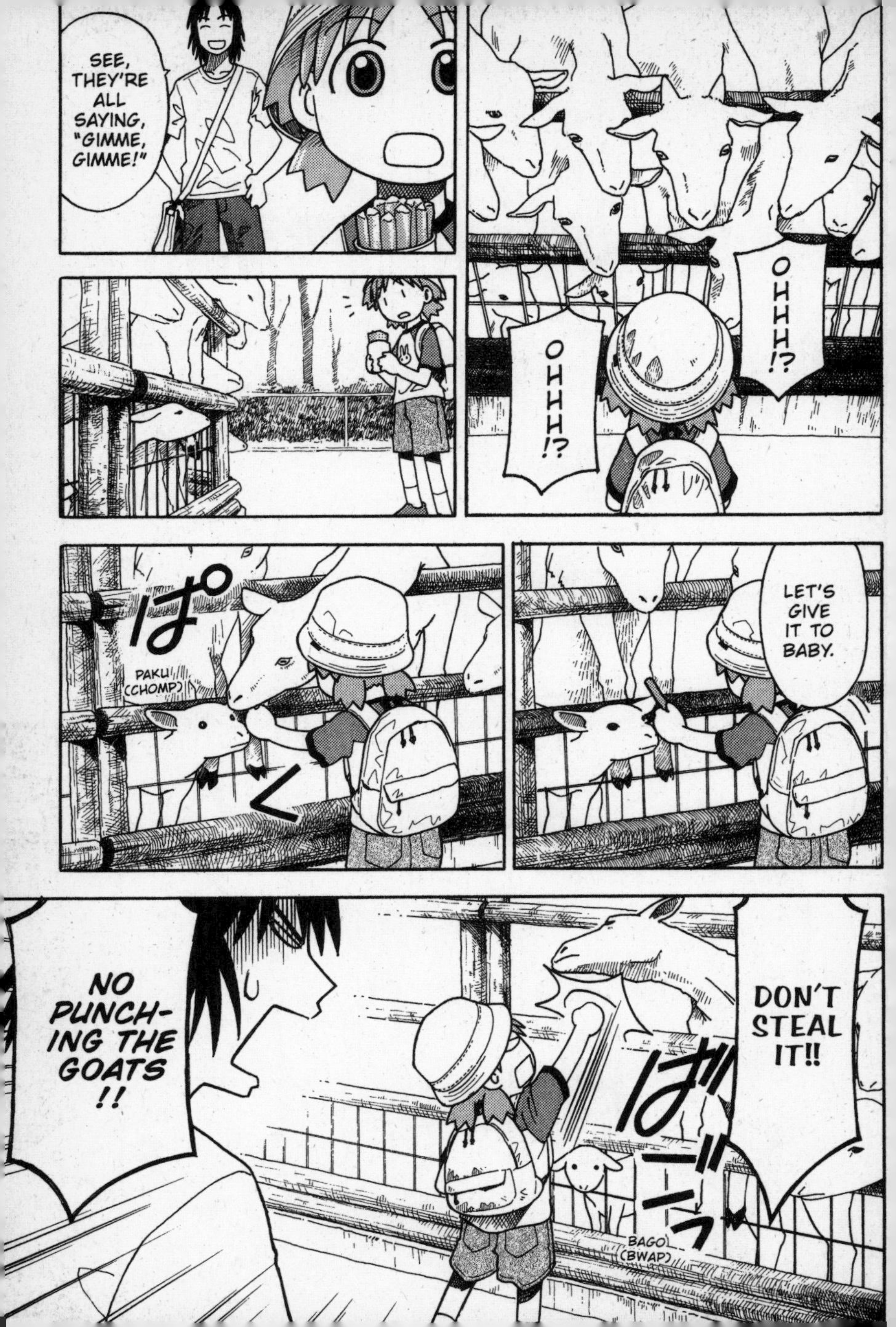
OHHH!?
OHHH!?
SEE, THEY'RE ALL SAYING, "GIMME, GIMME!"
LET'S GIVE IT TO BABY.
ぱく
PAKU (CHOMP)
DON'T STEAL IT!!
BAGO (BWAP)
NO PUNCH-ING THE GOATS!!

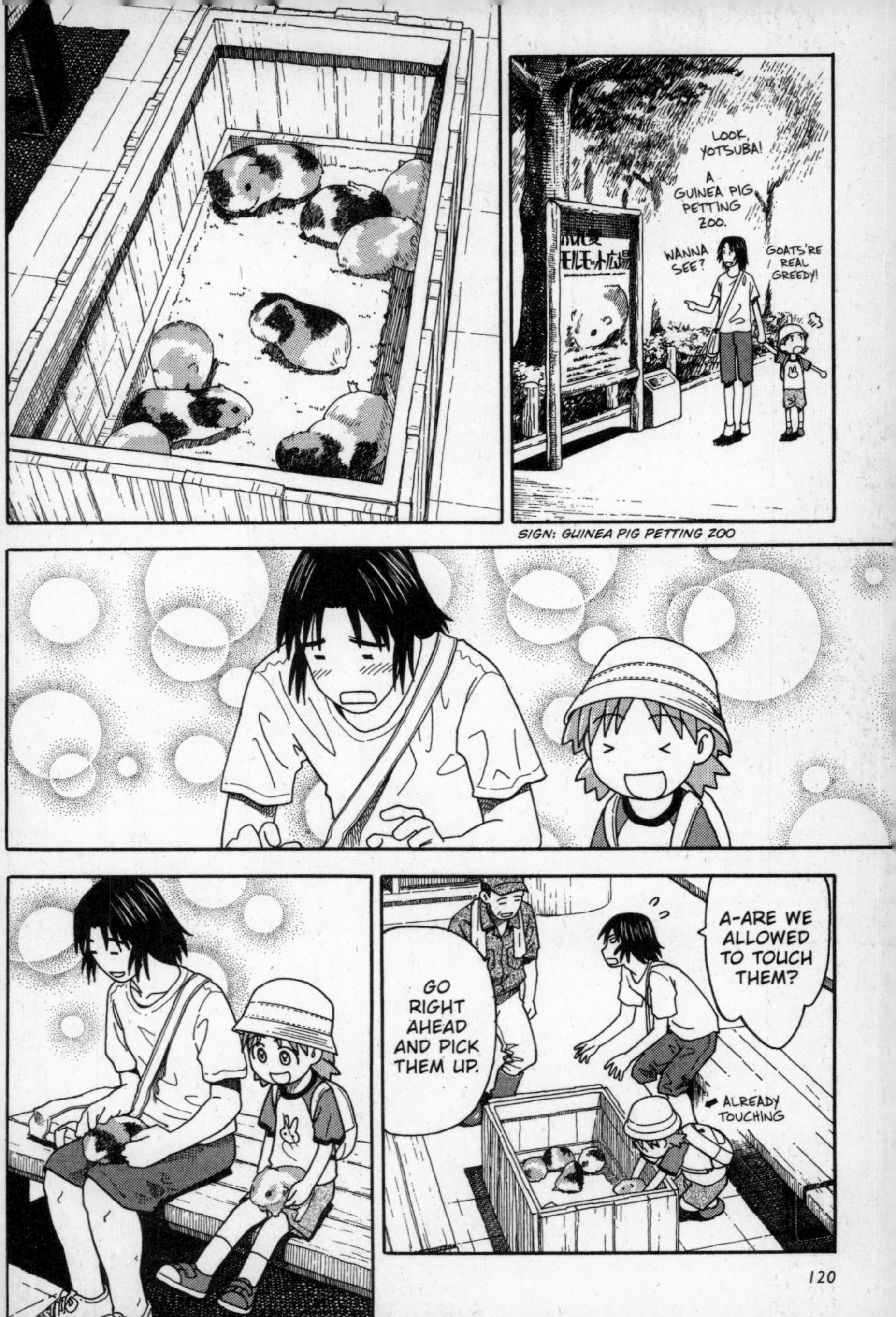
LOOK, YOTSUBA!
A GUINEA PIG PETTING ZOO.
WANNA SEE?
GOATS'RE REAL GREEDY!
SIGN: GUINEA PIG PETTING ZOO
A-ARE WE ALLOWED TO TOUCH THEM?
GO RIGHT AHEAD AND PICK THEM UP.
ALREADY TOUCHING

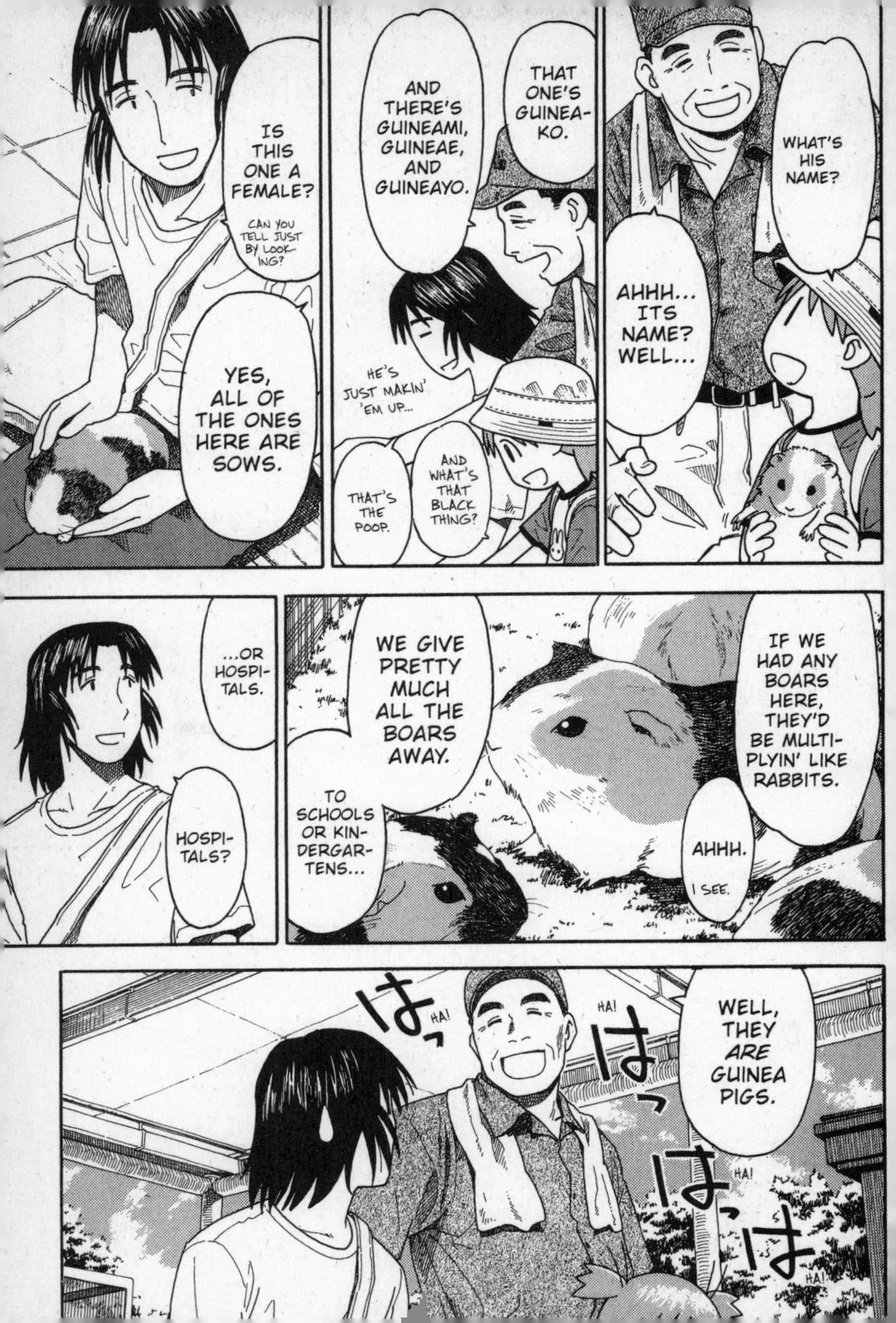
WHAT'S HIS NAME?
AHHH... ITS NAME? WELL...
THAT ONE'S GUINEA-KO.
AND THERE'S GUINEAMI, GUINEAE, AND GUINEAYO.
HE'S JUST MAKIN' 'EM UP...
AND WHAT'S THAT BLACK THING?
THAT'S THE POOP.
IS THIS ONE A FEMALE?
CAN YOU TELL JUST BY LOOKING?
YES, ALL OF THE ONES HERE ARE SOWS.
IF WE HAD ANY BOARS HERE, THEY'D BE MULTIPLYIN' LIKE RABBITS.
AHHH.
I SEE.
WE GIVE PRETTY MUCH ALL THE BOARS AWAY.
TO SCHOOLS OR KINDERGARTENS...
...OR HOSPITALS.
HOSPITALS?
WELL, THEY *ARE* GUINEA PIGS.
はっ HA!
はっ HA!
はっ HA!
は HA!

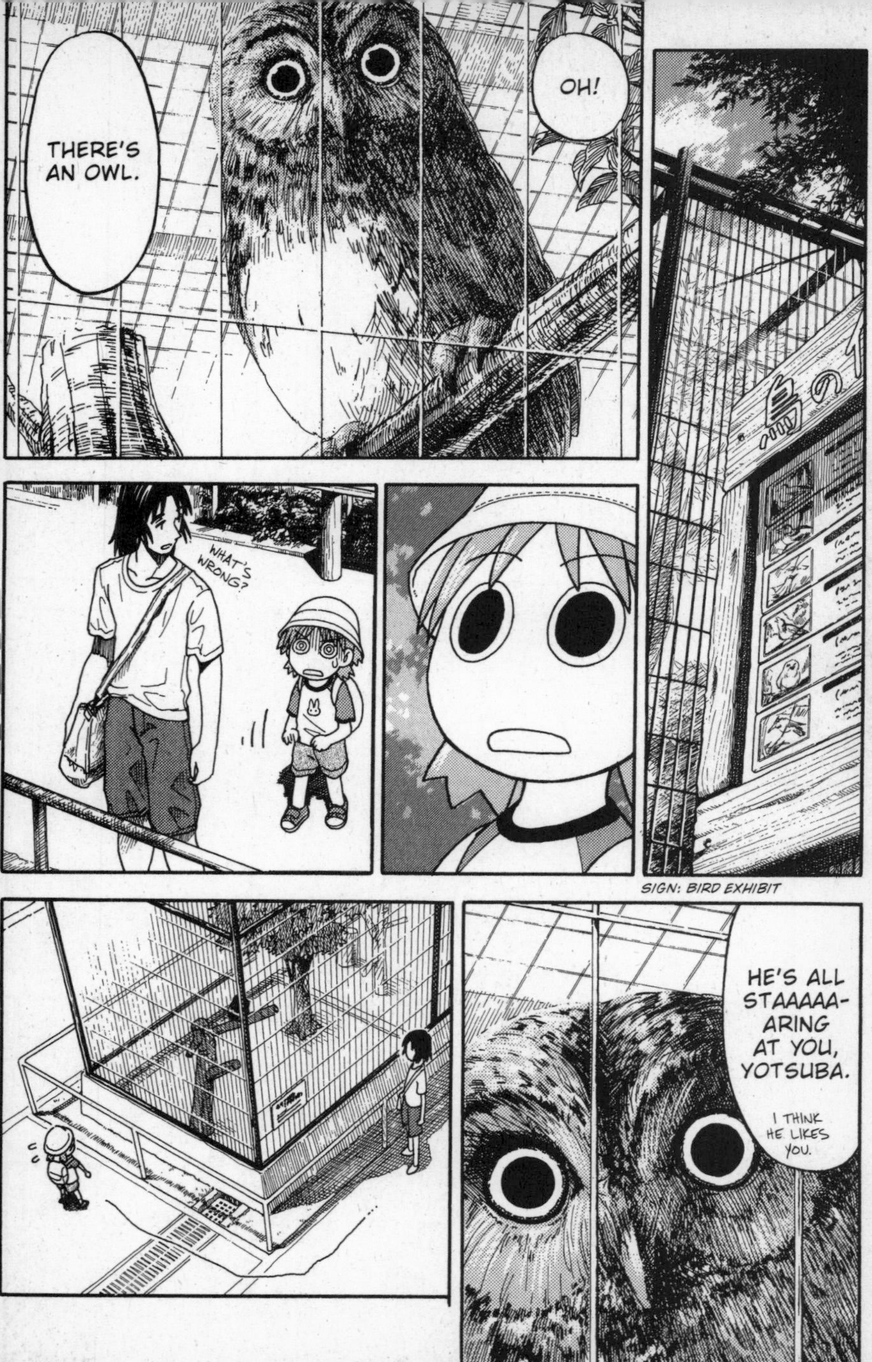
SIGN: BIRD EXHIBIT
OH!
THERE'S AN OWL.
WHAT'S WRONG?
HE'S ALL STAAAAAA-ARING AT YOU, YOTSUBA.
I THINK HE LIKES YOU.

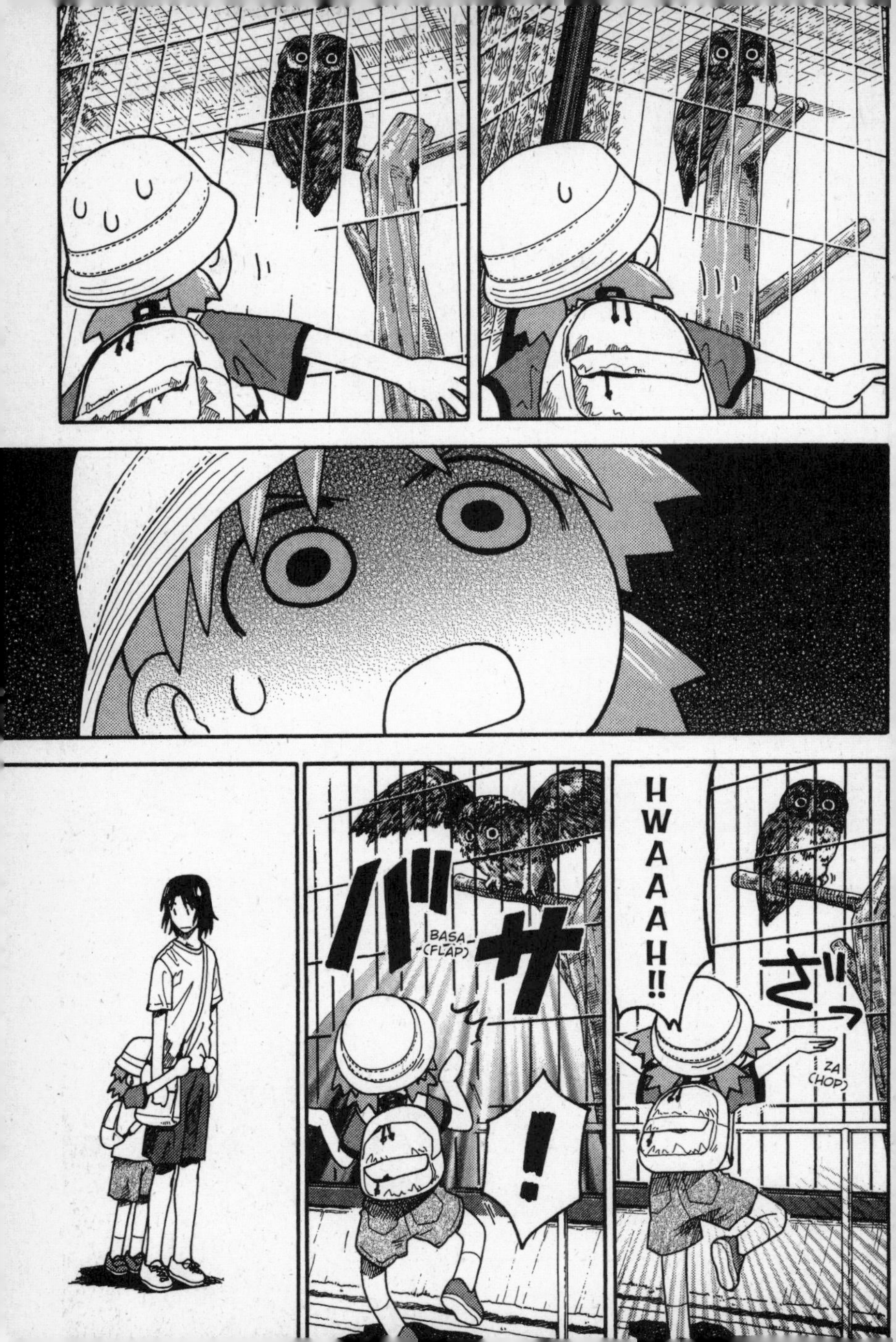
HWAAAAH!!
ざっ
ZA (HOP)
バサ
BASA (FLAP)
!

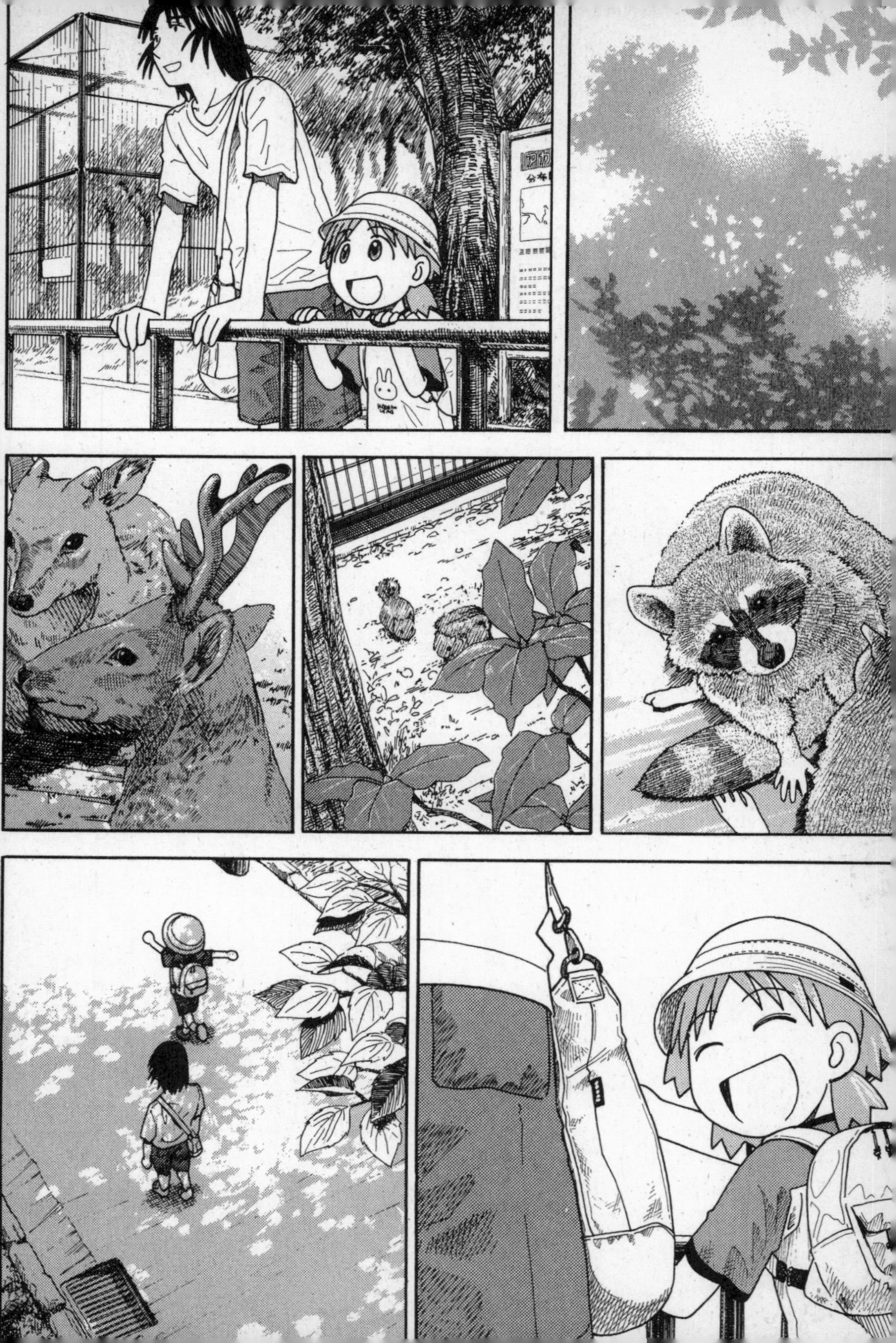

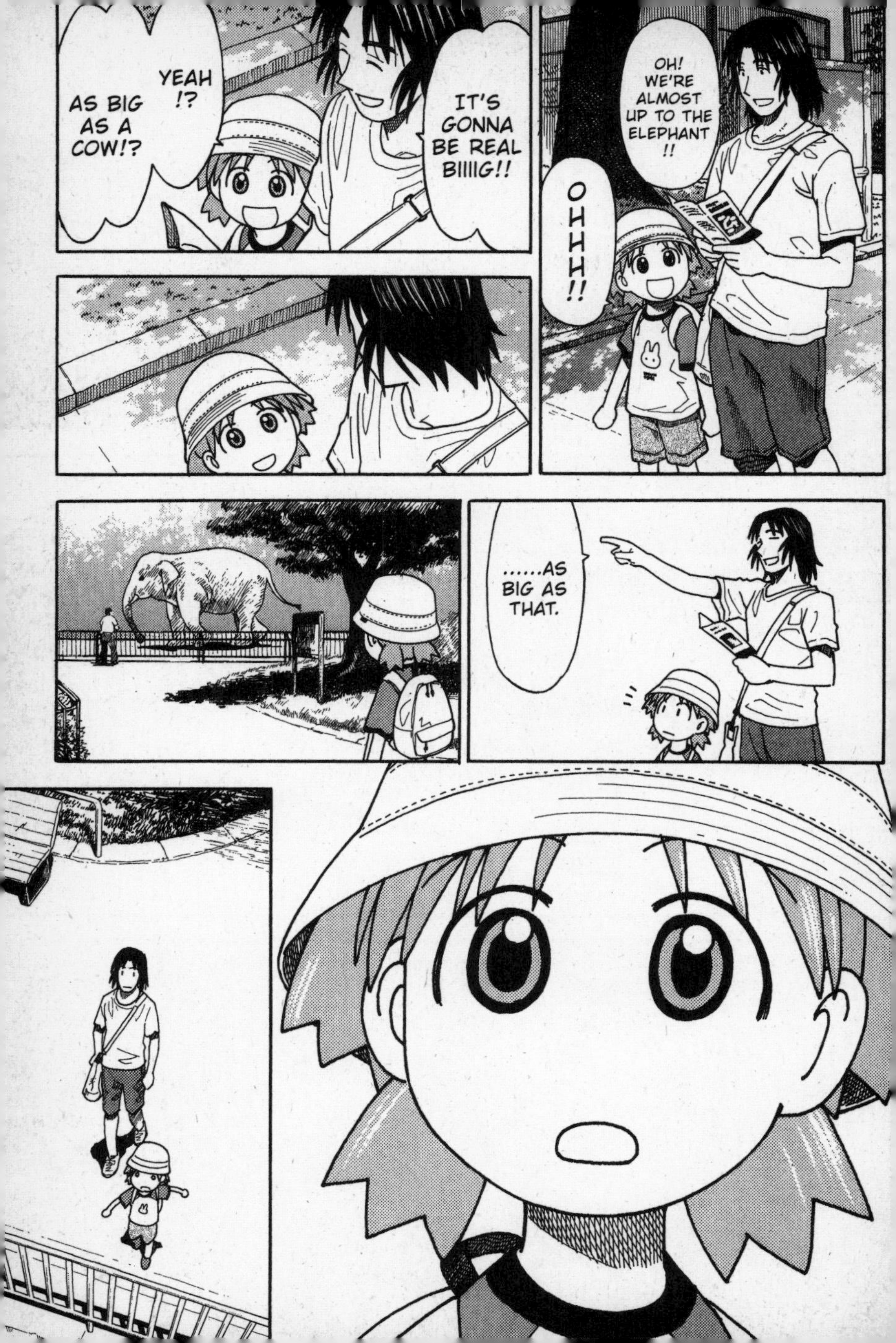
OH! WE'RE ALMOST UP TO THE ELEPHANT!!
OHHHH!!
IT'S GONNA BE REAL BIIIIG!!
YEAH!? AS BIG AS A COW!?
......AS BIG AS THAT.

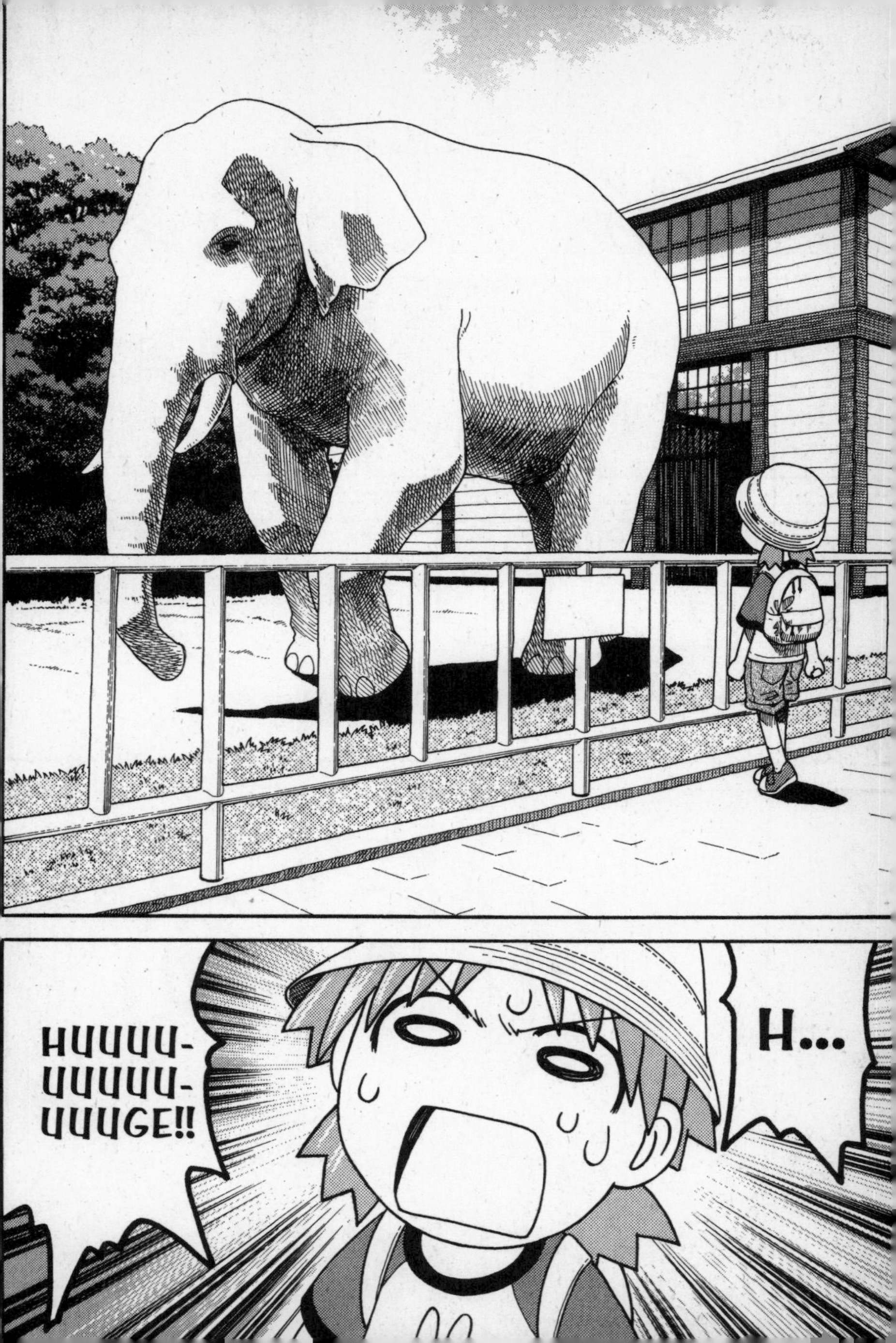
H...
HUUUU-UUUUU-UUUGE!!

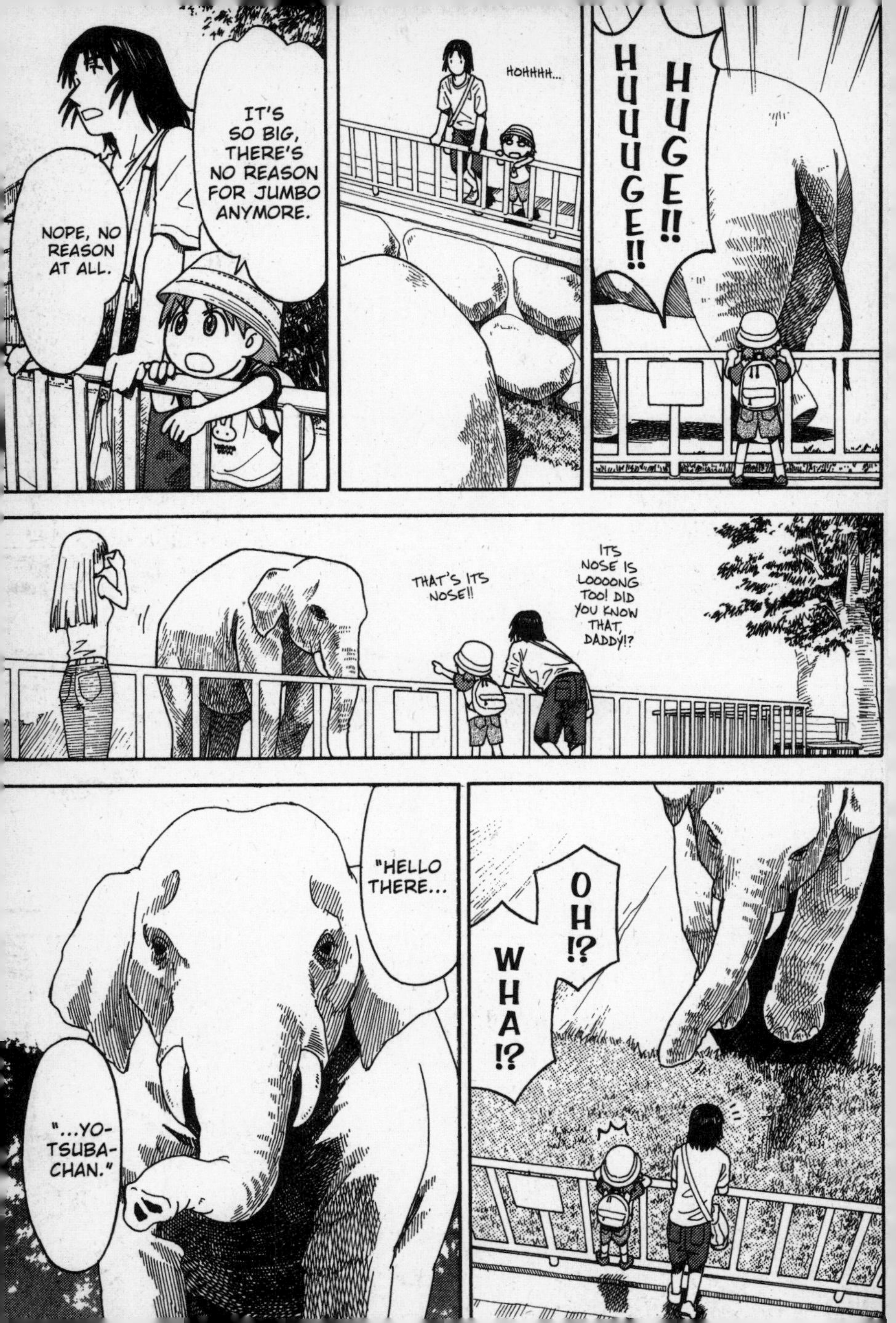
HUGE!!
HUUUGE!!
HOHHHH...
IT'S SO BIG, THERE'S NO REASON FOR JUMBO ANYMORE.
NOPE, NO REASON AT ALL.
ITS NOSE IS LOOOONG TOO! DID YOU KNOW THAT, DADDY!?
THAT'S ITS NOSE!!
OH!?
WHA!?
"HELLO THERE...
"...YO-TSUBA-CHAN."

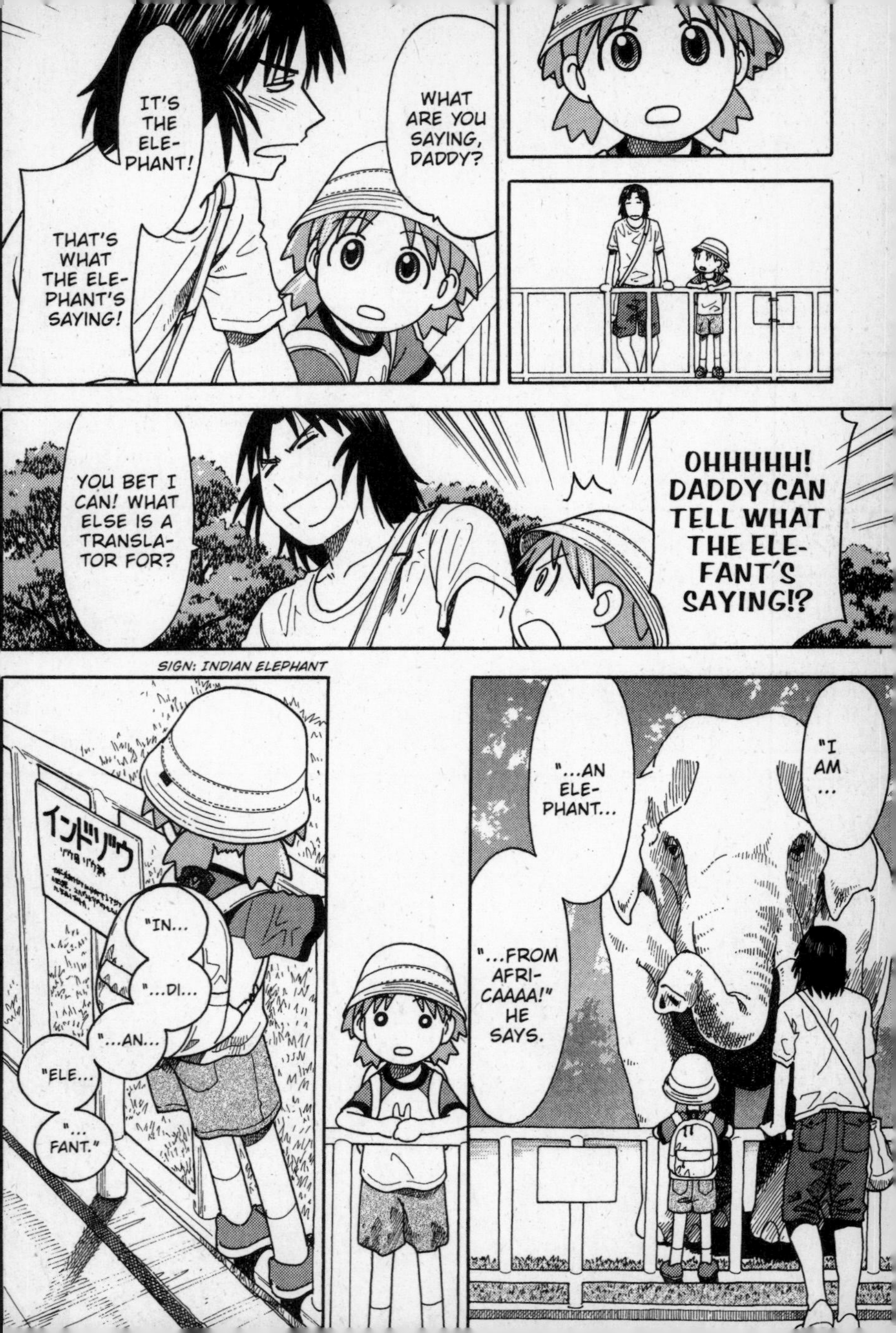
WHAT ARE YOU SAYING, DADDY?
IT'S THE ELE-PHANT!
THAT'S WHAT THE ELE-PHANT'S SAYING!
OHHHHH! DADDY CAN TELL WHAT THE ELE-FANT'S SAYING!?
YOU BET I CAN! WHAT ELSE IS A TRANSLA-TOR FOR?
"I AM ...
"...AN ELE-PHANT...
"...FROM AFRI-CAAAA!" HE SAYS.
SIGN: INDIAN ELEPHANT
インドゾウ
"IN...
"...DI...
"...AN...
"ELE...
"...FANT."

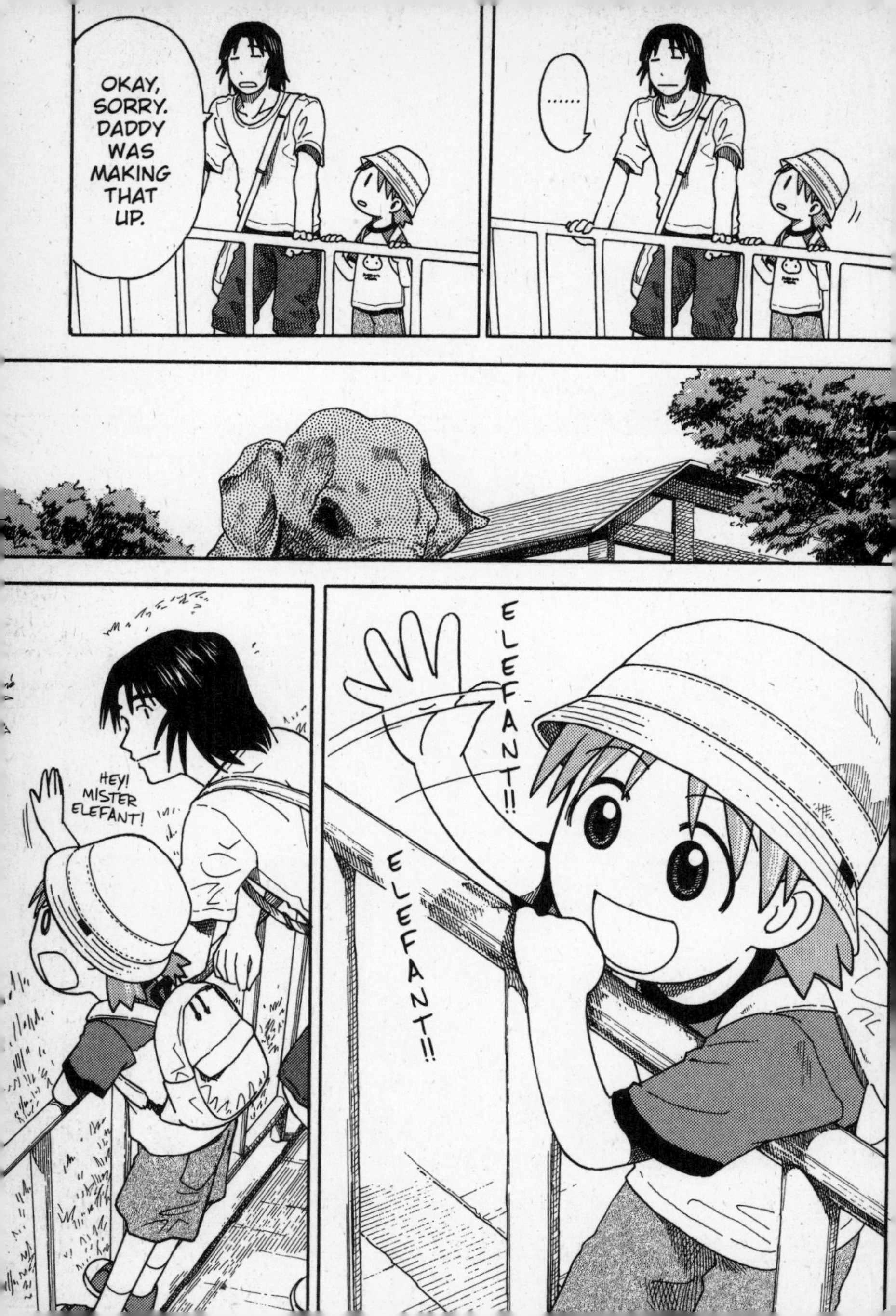
......
OKAY, SORRY. DADDY WAS MAKING THAT UP.
ELEFANT!!
ELEFANT!!
HEY! MISTER ELEFANT!

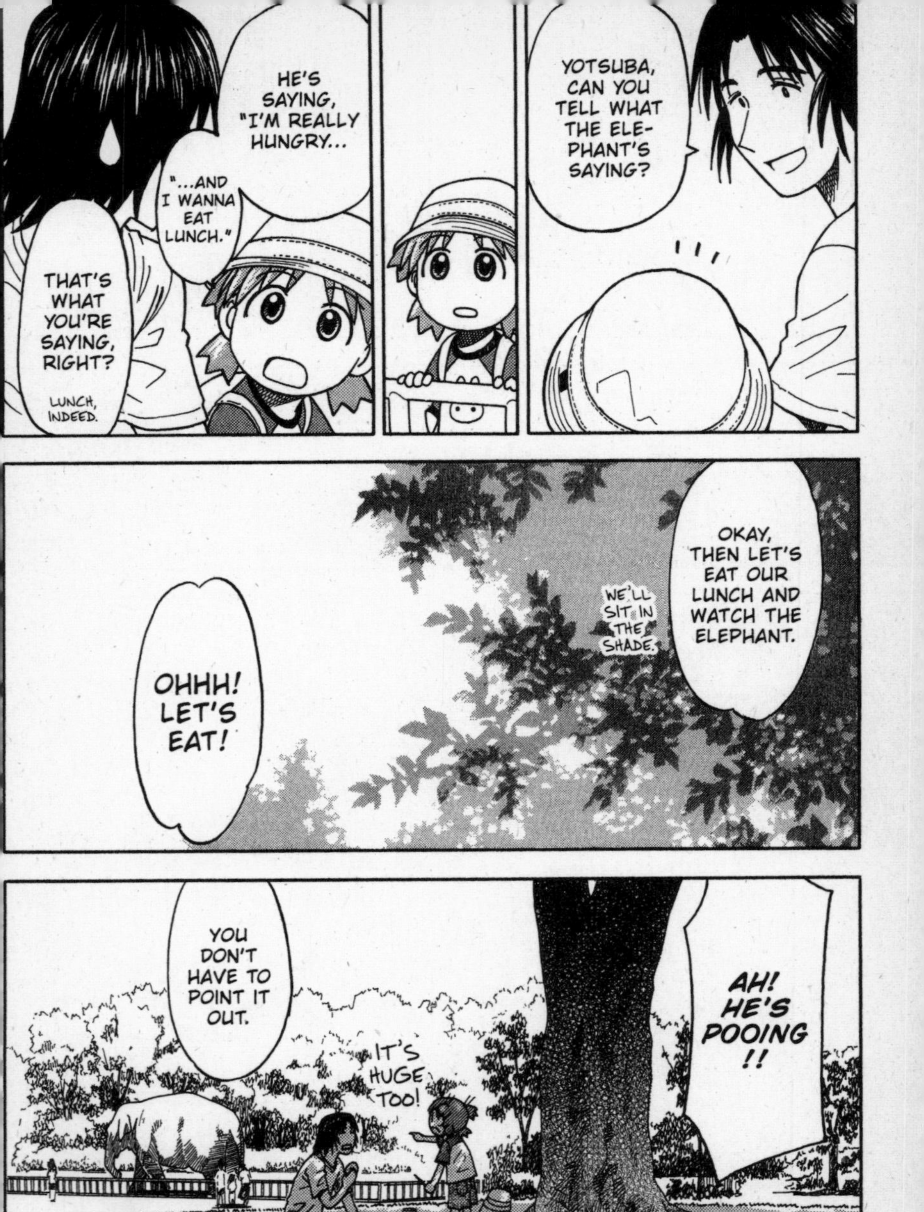
YOTSUBA, CAN YOU TELL WHAT THE ELE-PHANT'S SAYING?
HE'S SAYING, "I'M REALLY HUNGRY...
"...AND I WANNA EAT LUNCH."
THAT'S WHAT YOU'RE SAYING, RIGHT?
LUNCH, INDEED.
OKAY, THEN LET'S EAT OUR LUNCH AND WATCH THE ELEPHANT.
WE'LL SIT IN THE SHADE.
OHHH! LET'S EAT!
AH! HE'S POOING!!
IT'S HUGE TOO!
YOU DON'T HAVE TO POINT IT OUT.

YOTSUBA&!

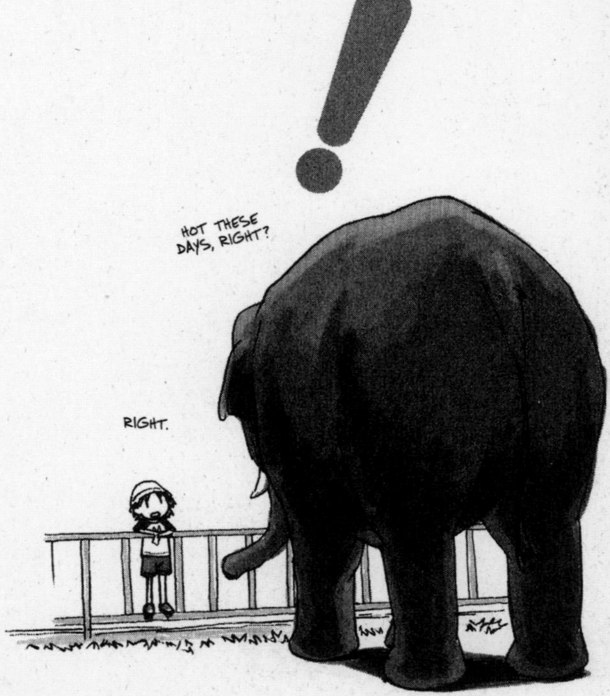
!
HOT THESE DAYS, RIGHT?
RIGHT.

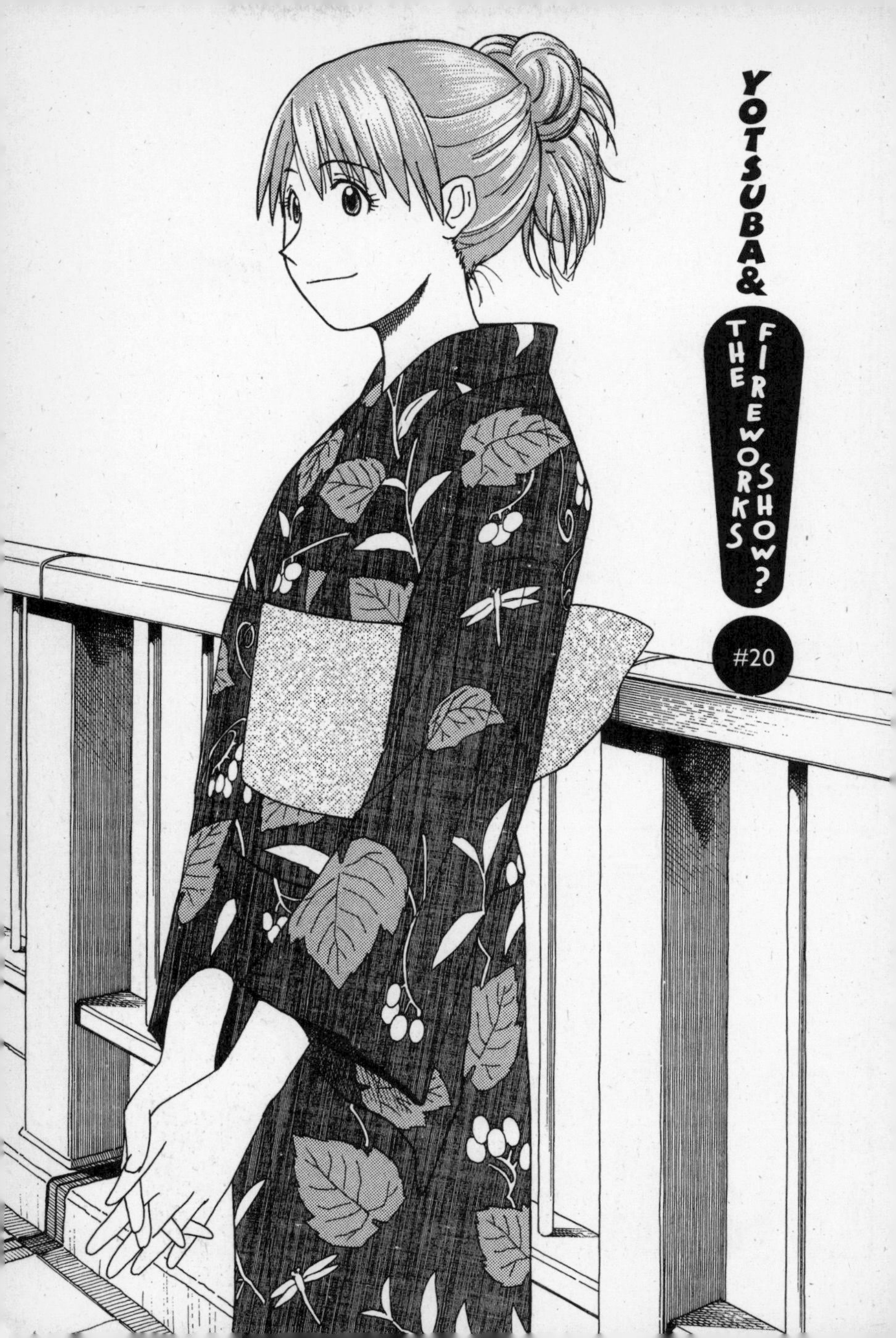
YOTSUBA&
THE FIREWORKS SHOW?
#20

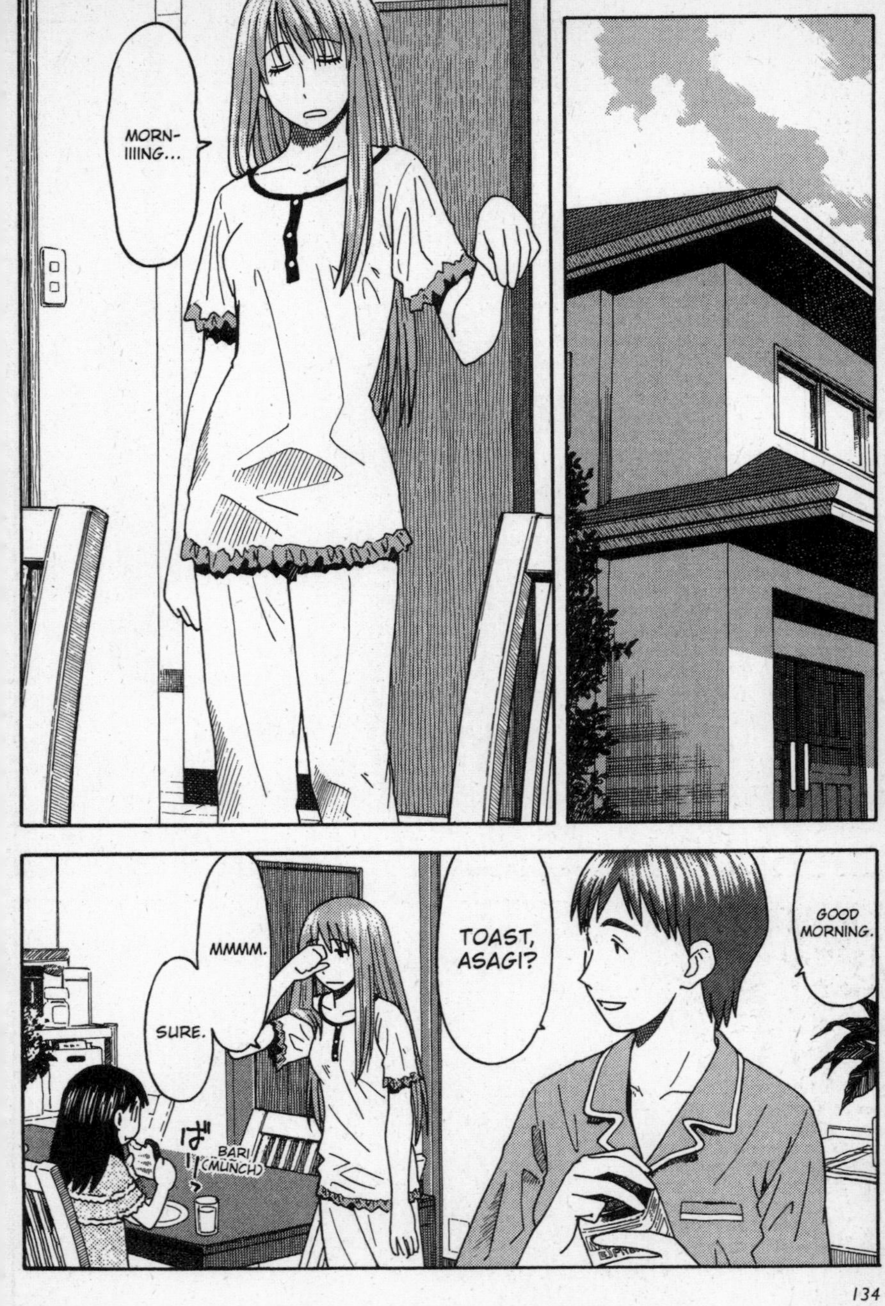
MORN-
IIIING...
GOOD MORNING.
TOAST, ASAGI?
MMMM.
SURE.
ばり
BARI (MUNCH)

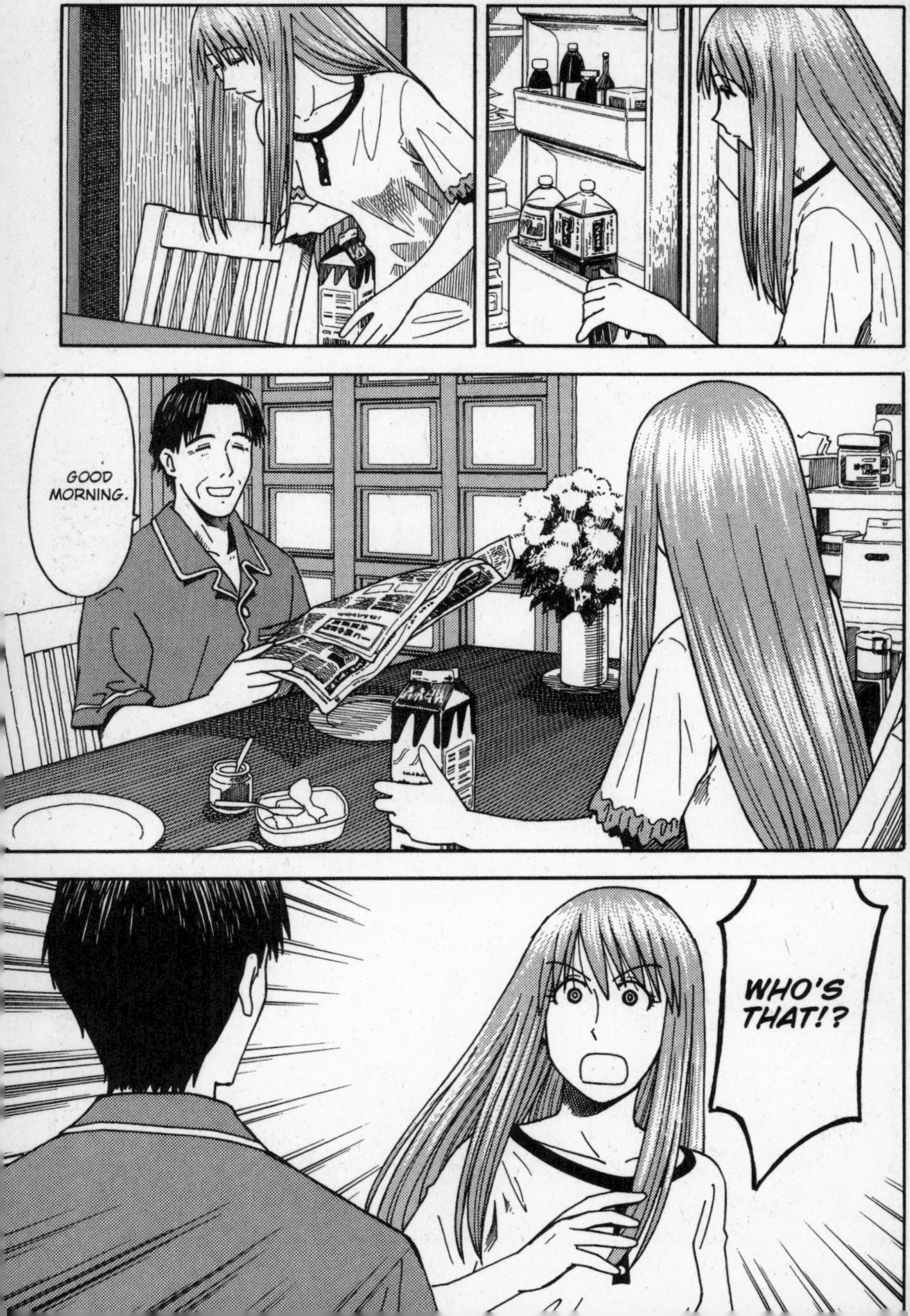
GOOD MORNING.
WHO'S THAT!?

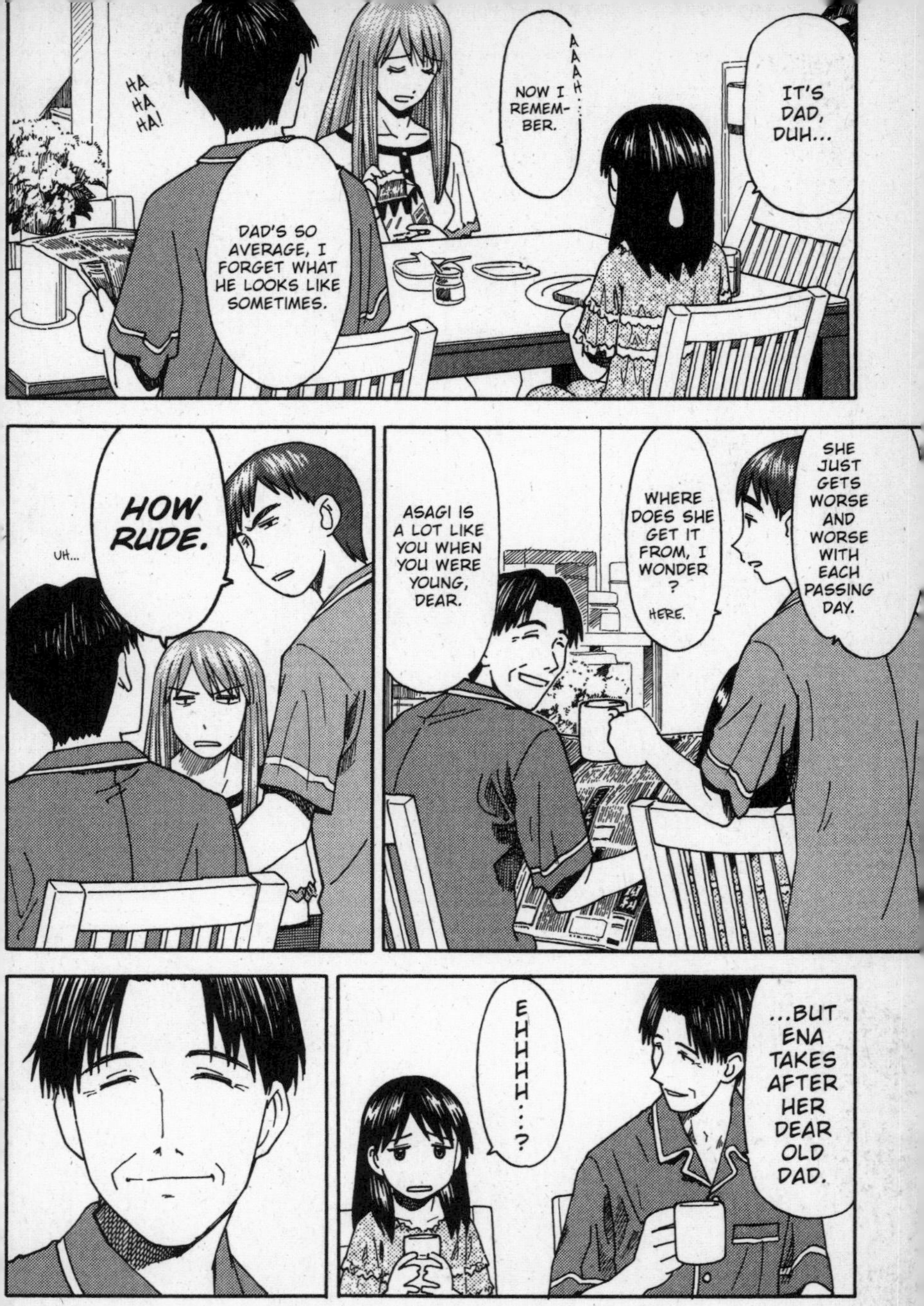
IT'S DAD, DUH...
AAAH...
NOW I REMEMBER.
HA HA HA!
DAD'S SO AVERAGE, I FORGET WHAT HE LOOKS LIKE SOMETIMES.
SHE JUST GETS WORSE AND WORSE WITH EACH PASSING DAY.
WHERE DOES SHE GET IT FROM, I WONDER?
HERE.
ASAGI IS A LOT LIKE YOU WHEN YOU WERE YOUNG, DEAR.
HOW RUDE.
UH...
...BUT ENA TAKES AFTER HER DEAR OLD DAD.
EHHHH...?

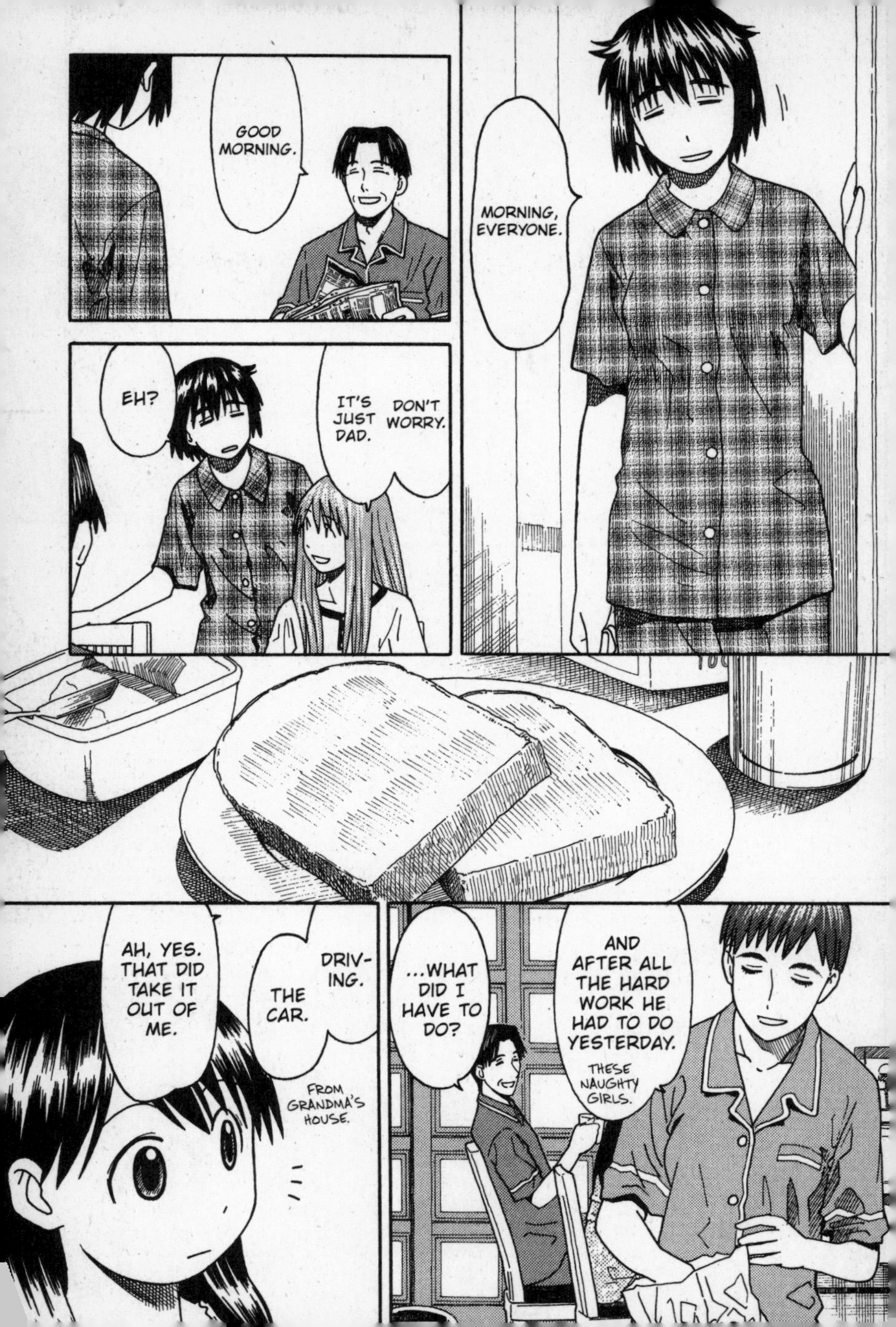
MORNING, EVERYONE.
GOOD MORNING.
IT'S JUST DAD. DON'T WORRY.
EH?
AND AFTER ALL THE HARD WORK HE HAD TO DO YESTERDAY.
THESE NAUGHTY GIRLS.
...WHAT DID I HAVE TO DO?
DRIV-ING. THE CAR.
FROM GRANDMA'S HOUSE.
AH, YES. THAT DID TAKE IT OUT OF ME.

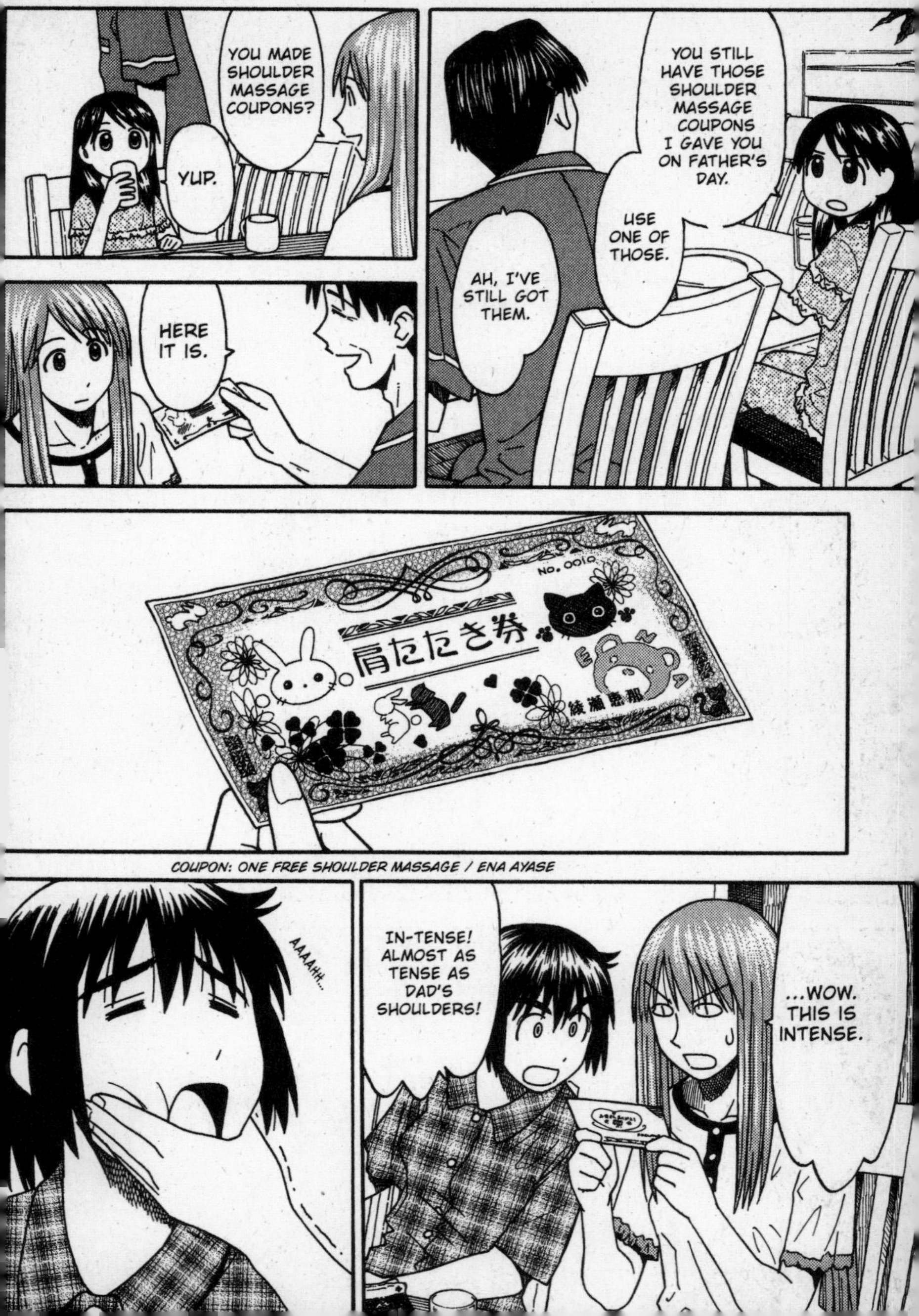
YOU STILL HAVE THOSE SHOULDER MASSAGE COUPONS I GAVE YOU ON FATHER'S DAY.
USE ONE OF THOSE.
AH, I'VE STILL GOT THEM.
YOU MADE SHOULDER MASSAGE COUPONS?
YUP.
HERE IT IS.
NO. 0010
肩たたき券
綾瀬恵那
COUPON: ONE FREE SHOULDER MASSAGE / ENA AYASE
...WOW. THIS IS INTENSE.
IN-TENSE! ALMOST AS TENSE AS DAD'S SHOULDERS!
AAAAHH...

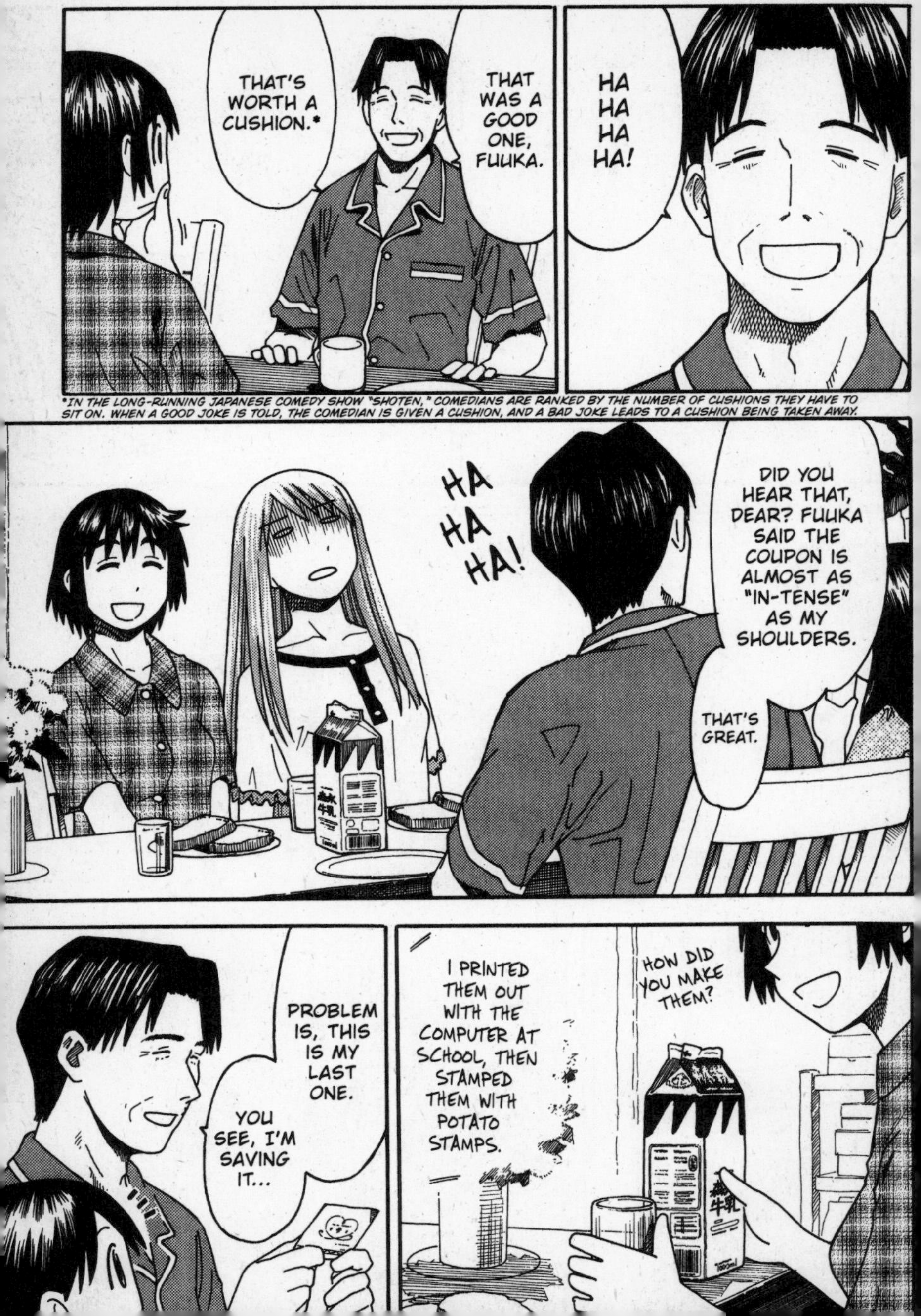
HA HA HA HA!
THAT WAS A GOOD ONE, FUUKA.
THAT'S WORTH A CUSHION.*
*IN THE LONG-RUNNING JAPANESE COMEDY SHOW "SHOTEN," COMEDIANS ARE RANKED BY THE NUMBER OF CUSHIONS THEY HAVE TO SIT ON. WHEN A GOOD JOKE IS TOLD, THE COMEDIAN IS GIVEN A CUSHION, AND A BAD JOKE LEADS TO A CUSHION BEING TAKEN AWAY.
DID YOU HEAR THAT, DEAR? FUUKA SAID THE COUPON IS ALMOST AS "IN-TENSE" AS MY SHOULDERS.
THAT'S GREAT.
HA HA HA!
HOW DID YOU MAKE THEM?
I PRINTED THEM OUT WITH THE COMPUTER AT SCHOOL, THEN STAMPED THEM WITH POTATO STAMPS.
PROBLEM IS, THIS IS MY LAST ONE.
YOU SEE, I'M SAVING IT...

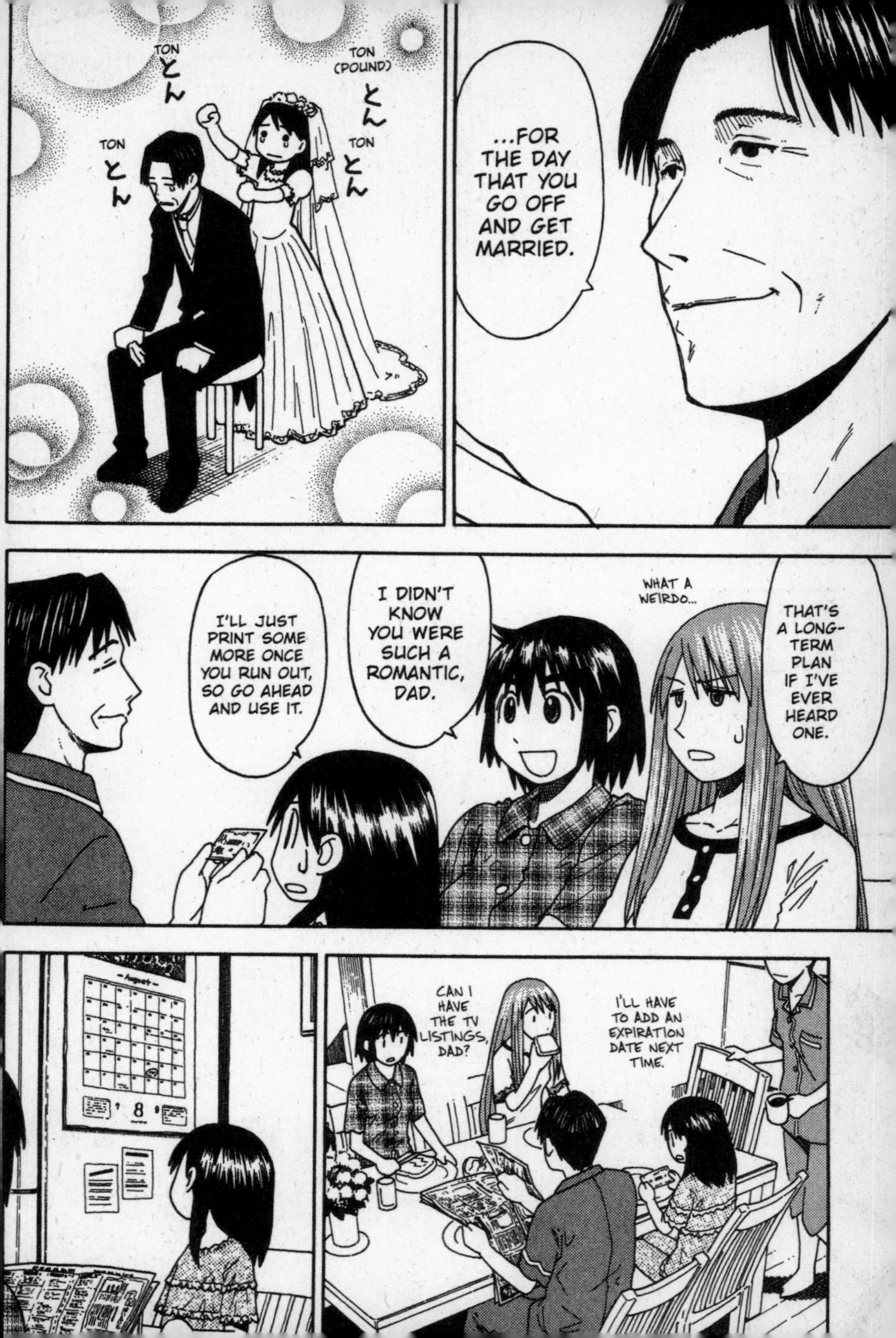
...FOR THE DAY THAT YOU GO OFF AND GET MARRIED.
TON (POUND) とん
TON とん
TON とん
TON とん
THAT'S A LONG-TERM PLAN IF I'VE EVER HEARD ONE.
WHAT A WEIRDO...
I DIDN'T KNOW YOU WERE SUCH A ROMANTIC, DAD.
I'LL JUST PRINT SOME MORE ONCE YOU RUN OUT, SO GO AHEAD AND USE IT.
I'LL HAVE TO ADD AN EXPIRATION DATE NEXT TIME.
CAN I HAVE THE TV LISTINGS, DAD?
August
8

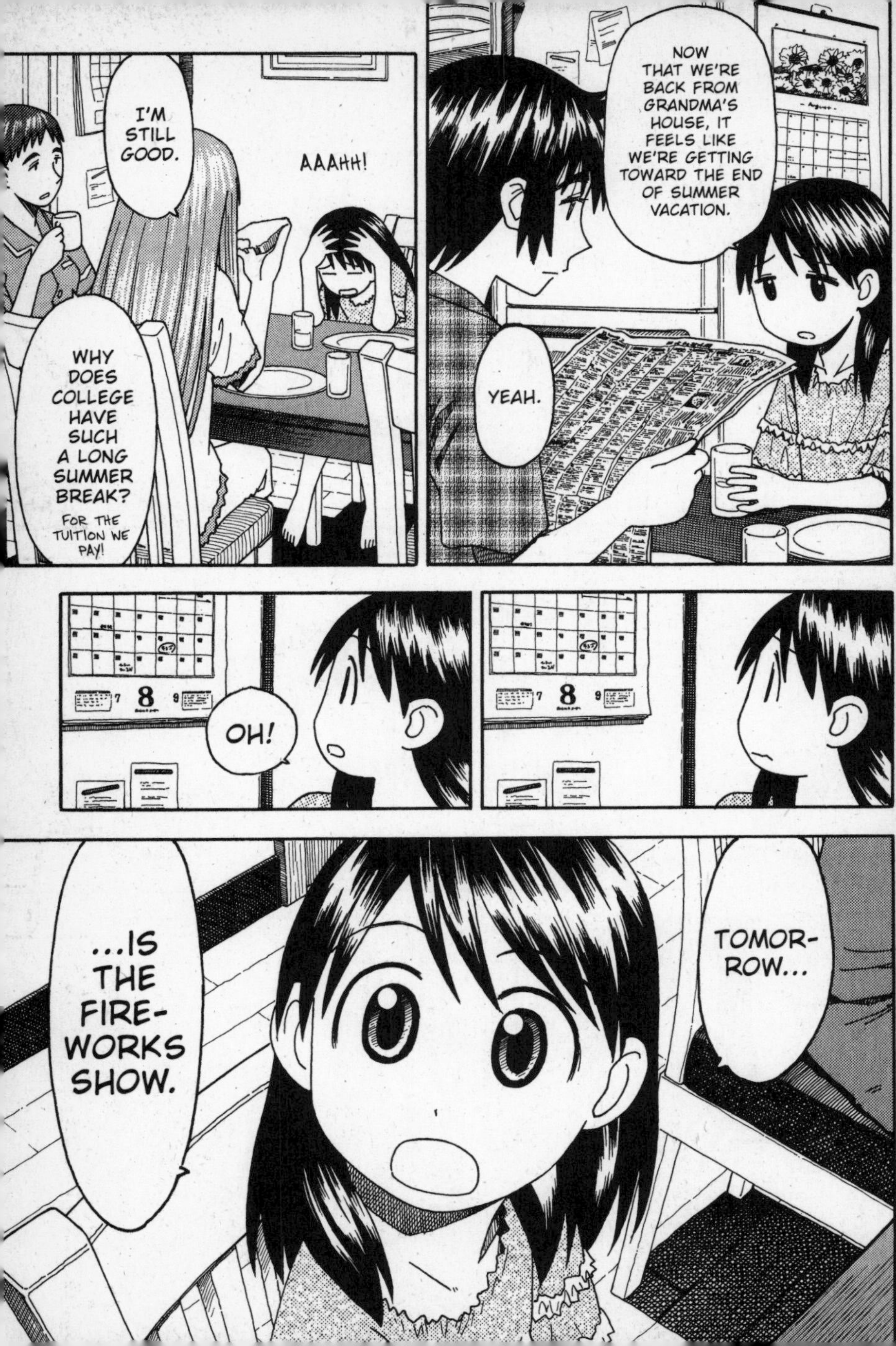
NOW THAT WE'RE BACK FROM GRANDMA'S HOUSE, IT FEELS LIKE WE'RE GETTING TOWARD THE END OF SUMMER VACATION.
YEAH.
I'M STILL GOOD.
AAAHH!
WHY DOES COLLEGE HAVE SUCH A LONG SUMMER BREAK?
FOR THE TUITION WE PAY!
OH!
TOMOR-ROW...
...IS THE FIRE-WORKS SHOW.

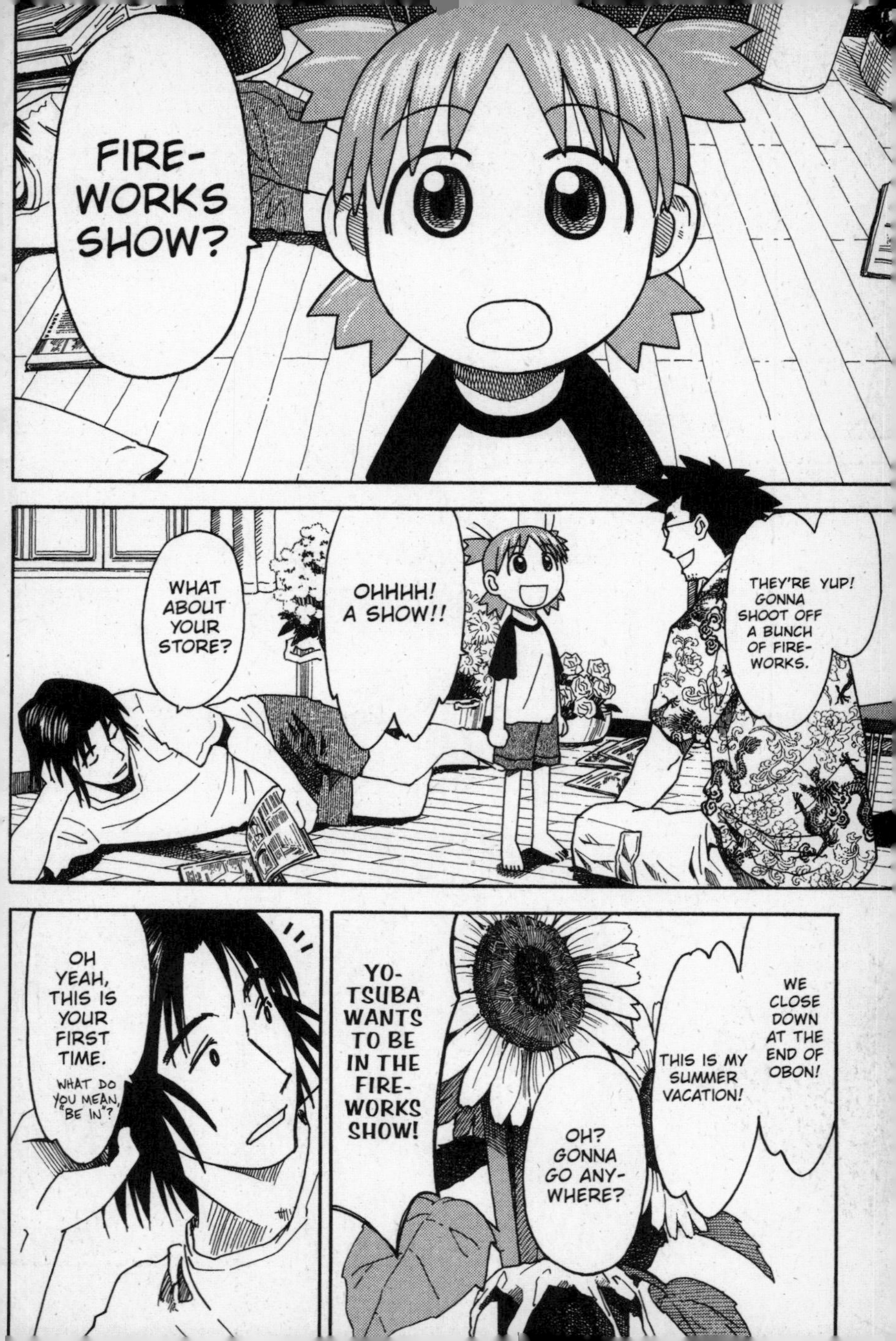
FIRE-WORKS SHOW?
YUP!
THEY'RE GONNA SHOOT OFF A BUNCH OF FIRE-WORKS.
OHHHH! A SHOW!!
WHAT ABOUT YOUR STORE?
WE CLOSE DOWN AT THE END OF OBON!
THIS IS MY SUMMER VACATION!
OH? GONNA GO ANY-WHERE?
YO-TSUBA WANTS TO BE IN THE FIRE-WORKS SHOW!
OH YEAH, THIS IS YOUR FIRST TIME.
WHAT DO YOU MEAN, "BE IN"?

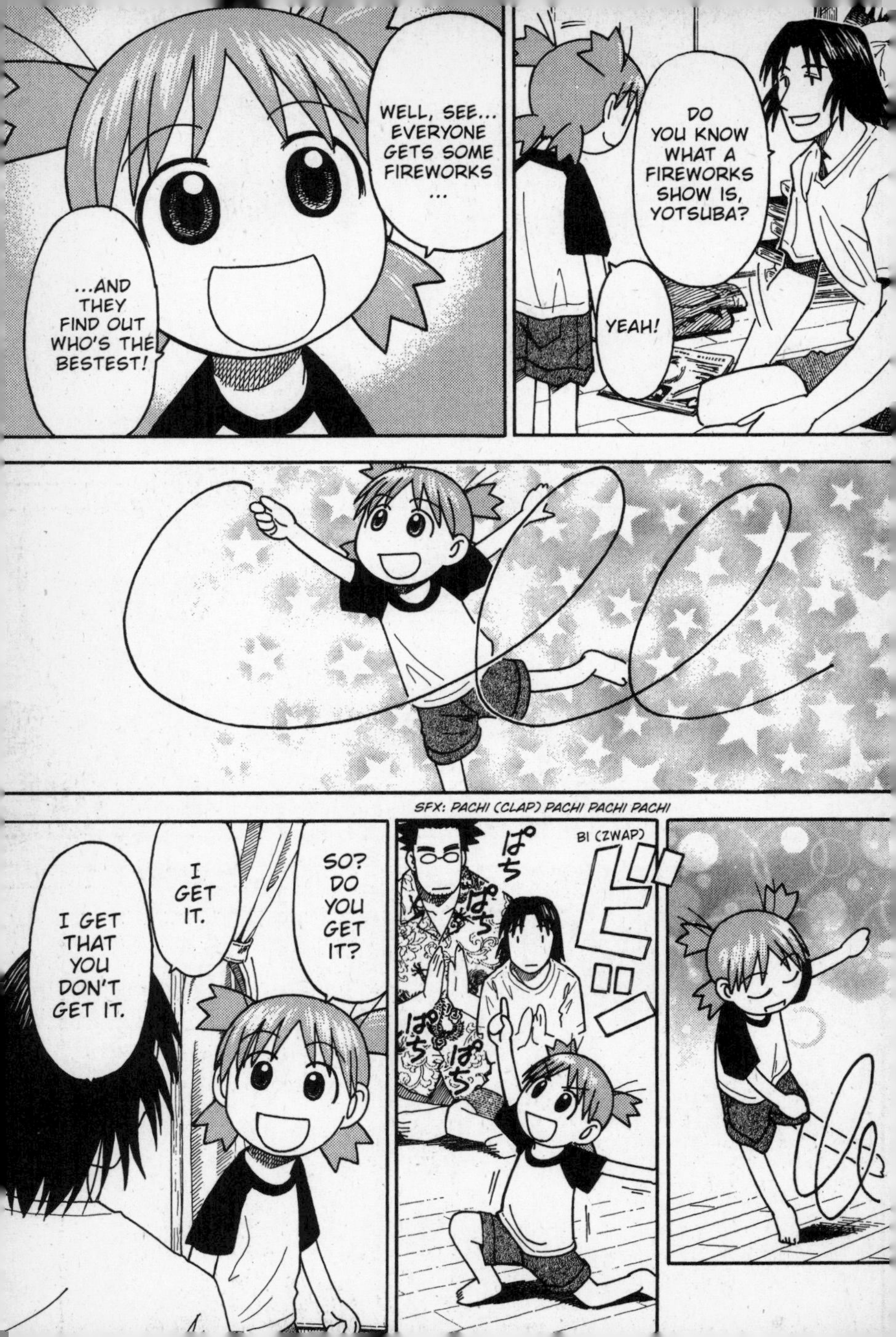
DO YOU KNOW WHAT A FIREWORKS SHOW IS, YOTSUBA?
YEAH!
WELL, SEE... EVERYONE GETS SOME FIREWORKS ...
...AND THEY FIND OUT WHO'S THE BESTEST!
SFX: PACHI (CLAP) PACHI PACHI PACHI
ぱち ぱち ぱち ぱち
BI (ZWAP)
SO? DO YOU GET IT?
I GET IT.
I GET THAT YOU DON'T GET IT.

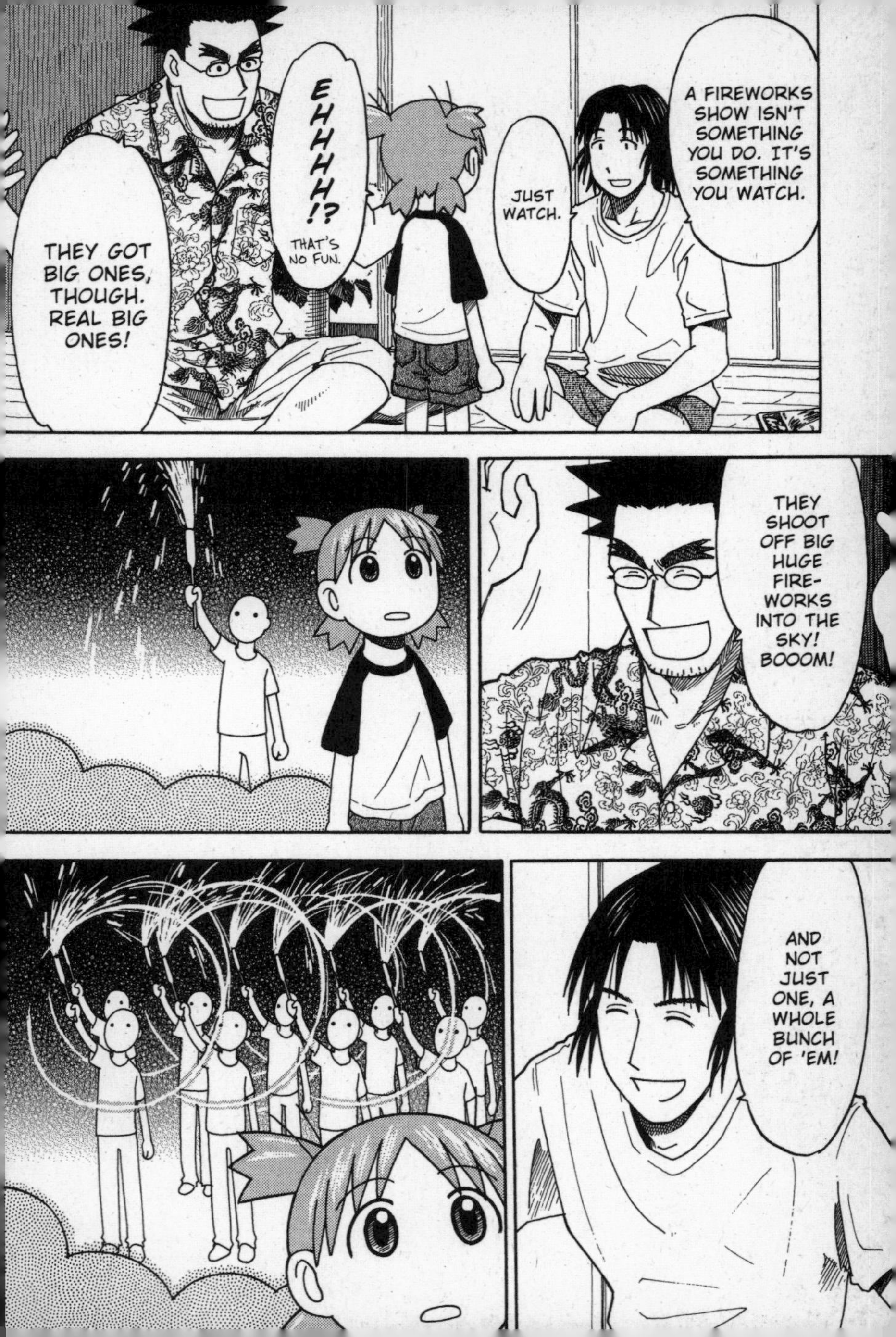
A FIREWORKS SHOW ISN'T SOMETHING YOU DO. IT'S SOMETHING YOU WATCH.
JUST WATCH.
EHHHH!?
THAT'S NO FUN.
THEY GOT BIG ONES, THOUGH. REAL BIG ONES!
THEY SHOOT OFF BIG HUGE FIRE-WORKS INTO THE SKY! BOOOM!
AND NOT JUST ONE, A WHOLE BUNCH OF 'EM!

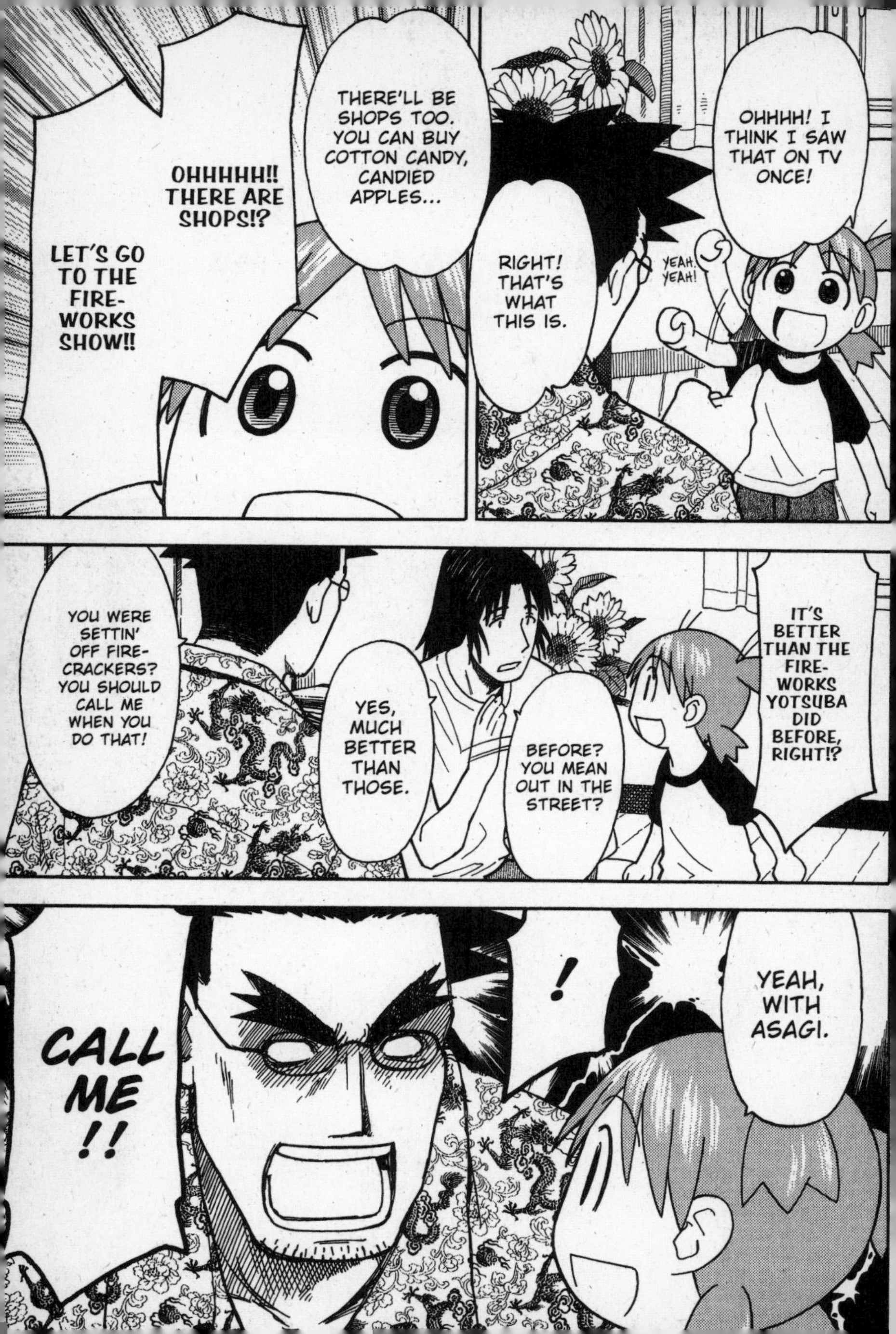
OHHHH! I THINK I SAW THAT ON TV ONCE!
YEAH, YEAH!
RIGHT! THAT'S WHAT THIS IS.
THERE'LL BE SHOPS TOO. YOU CAN BUY COTTON CANDY, CANDIED APPLES...
OHHHHH!! THERE ARE SHOPS!?
LET'S GO TO THE FIRE-WORKS SHOW!!
IT'S BETTER THAN THE FIRE-WORKS YOTSUBA DID BEFORE, RIGHT!?
BEFORE? YOU MEAN OUT IN THE STREET?
YES, MUCH BETTER THAN THOSE.
YOU WERE SETTIN' OFF FIRE-CRACKERS? YOU SHOULD CALL ME WHEN YOU DO THAT!
YEAH, WITH ASAGI.
!
CALL ME !!

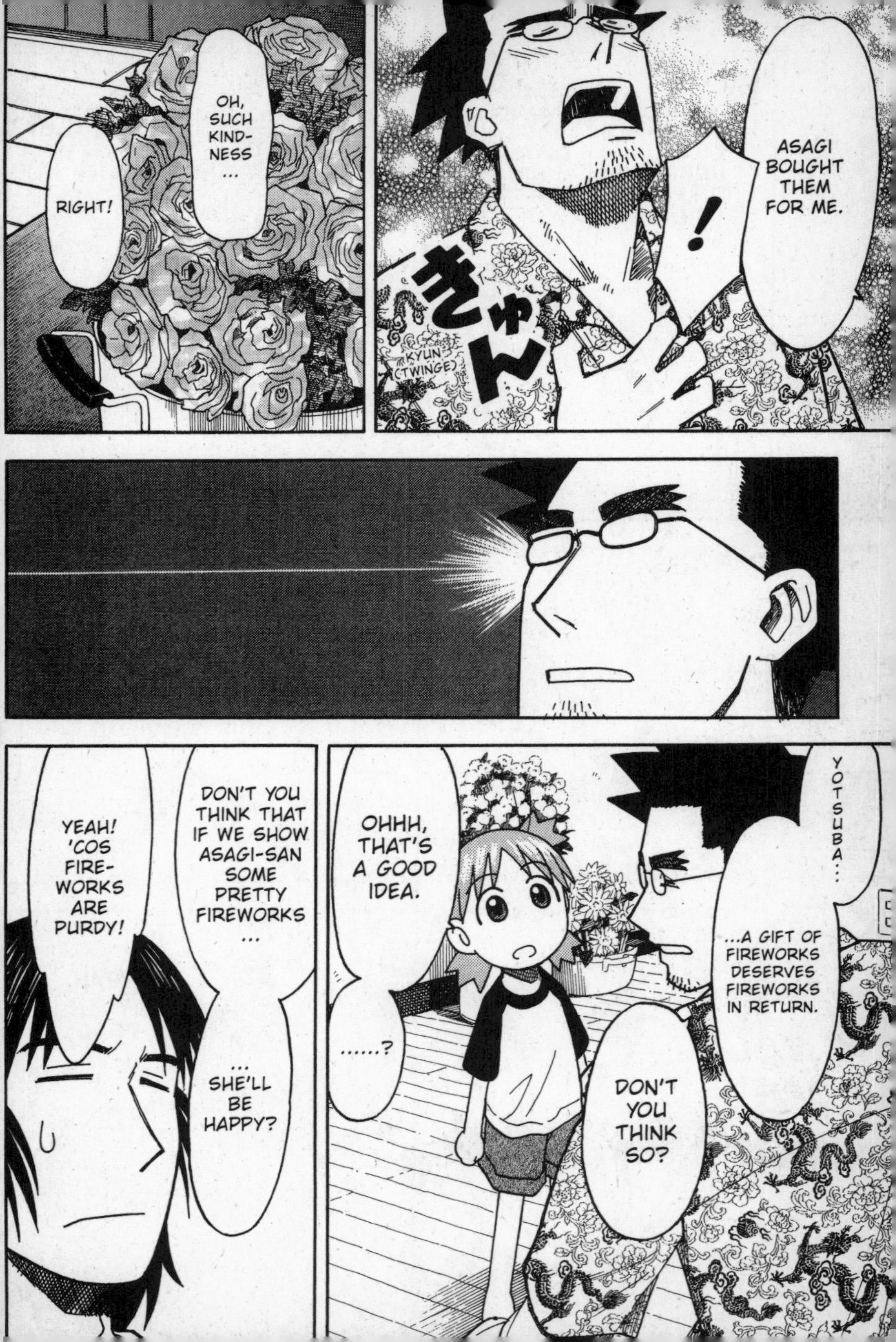
ASAGI BOUGHT THEM FOR ME.
!
きゅん
KYUN (TWINGE)
OH, SUCH KINDNESS ...
RIGHT!
YOTSUBA...
...A GIFT OF FIREWORKS DESERVES FIREWORKS IN RETURN.
OHHH, THAT'S A GOOD IDEA.
DON'T YOU THINK SO?
......?
DON'T YOU THINK THAT IF WE SHOW ASAGI-SAN SOME PRETTY FIREWORKS ...
... SHE'LL BE HAPPY?
YEAH! 'COS FIREWORKS ARE PURDY!

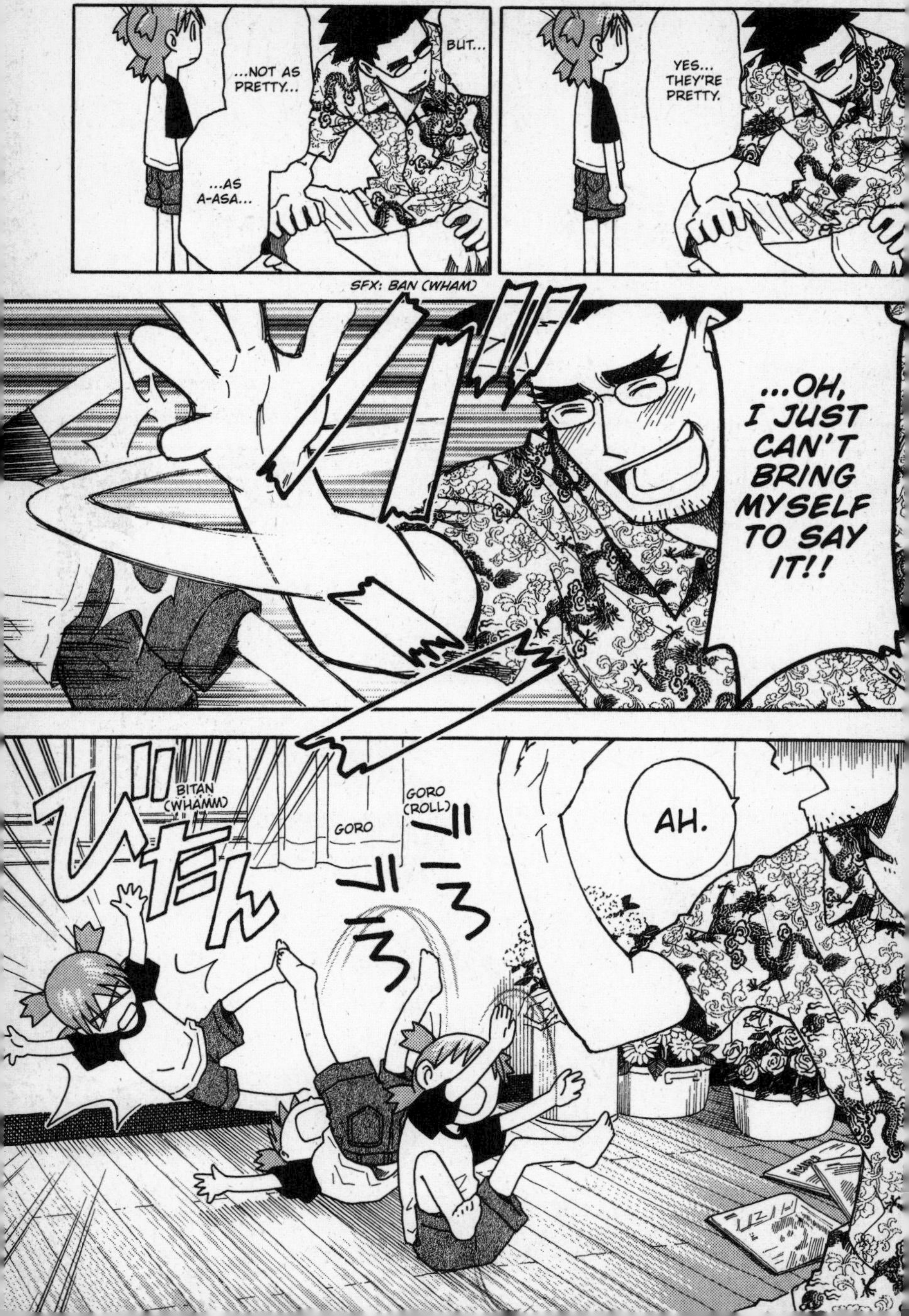
YES... THEY'RE PRETTY.
BUT...
...NOT AS PRETTY...
...AS A-ASA...
SFX: BAN (WHAM)
...OH, I JUST CAN'T BRING MYSELF TO SAY IT!!
AH.
GORO (ROLL)
GORO
BITAN (WHAMM)

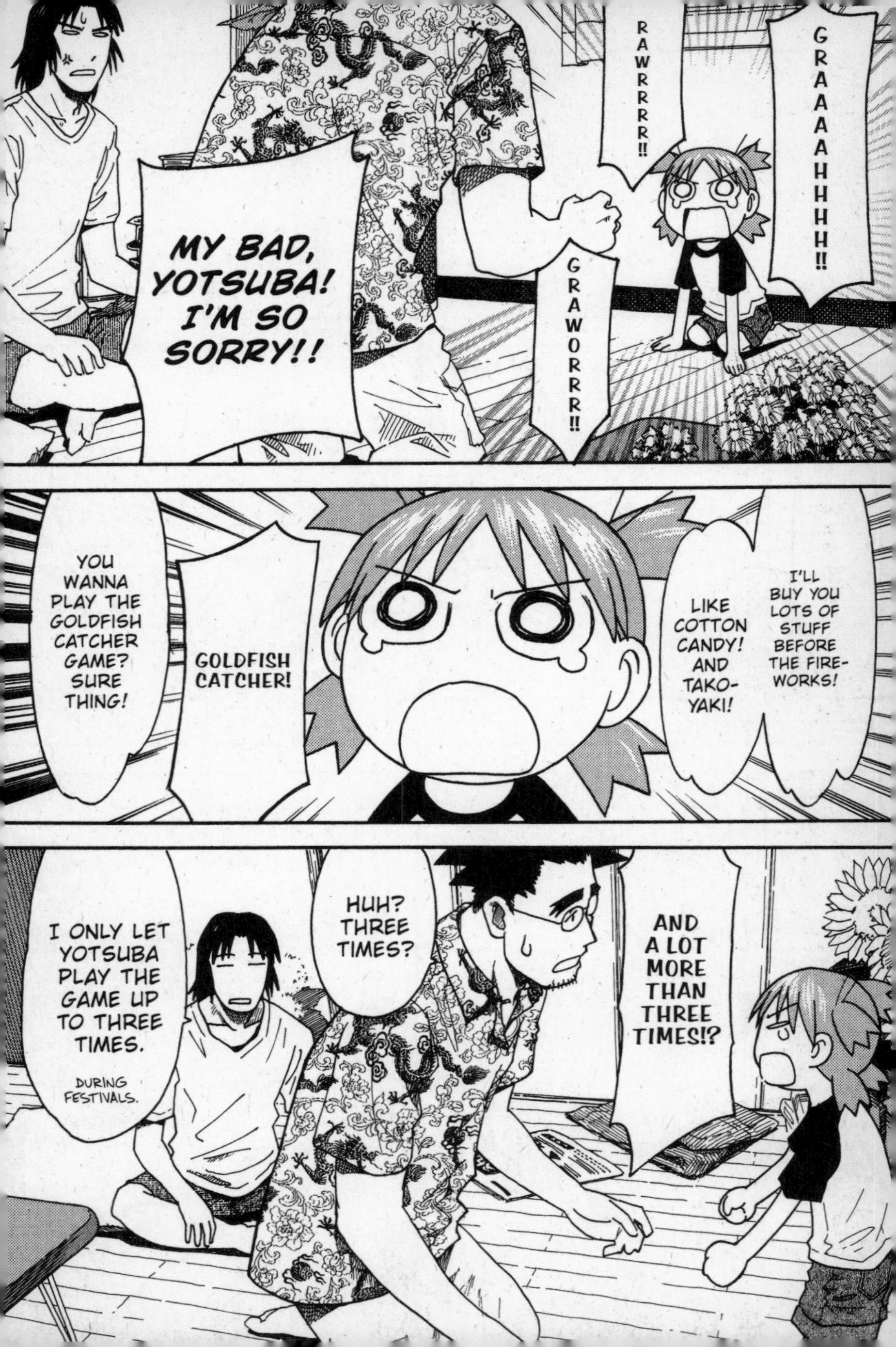
GRAAAAHHHHH!!
RAWRRRR!!
GRAWORRRR!!
MY BAD, YOTSUBA! I'M SO SORRY!!
I'LL BUY YOU LOTS OF STUFF BEFORE THE FIRE-WORKS!
LIKE COTTON CANDY! AND TAKO-YAKI!
GOLDFISH CATCHER!
YOU WANNA PLAY THE GOLDFISH CATCHER GAME? SURE THING!
AND A LOT MORE THAN THREE TIMES!?
HUH? THREE TIMES?
I ONLY LET YOTSUBA PLAY THE GAME UP TO THREE TIMES.
DURING FESTIVALS.

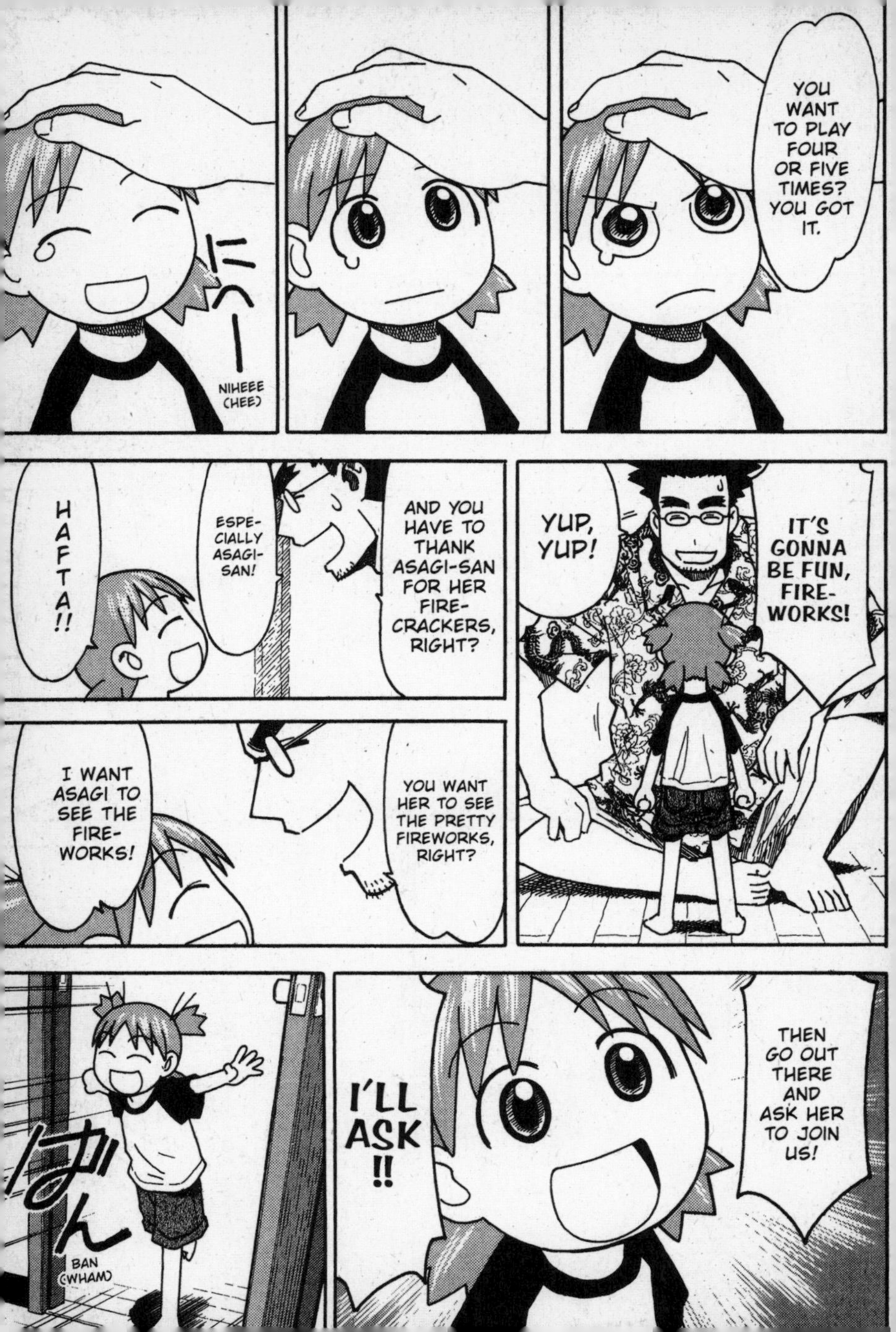
YOU WANT TO PLAY FOUR OR FIVE TIMES? YOU GOT IT.
NIHEEE (HEE)
IT'S GONNA BE FUN, FIRE-WORKS!
YUP, YUP!
AND YOU HAVE TO THANK ASAGI-SAN FOR HER FIRE-CRACKERS, RIGHT?
ESPE-CIALLY ASAGI-SAN!
HAFTA!!
YOU WANT HER TO SEE THE PRETTY FIREWORKS, RIGHT?
I WANT ASAGI TO SEE THE FIRE-WORKS!
THEN GO OUT THERE AND ASK HER TO JOIN US!
I'LL ASK!!
BAN (WHAM)

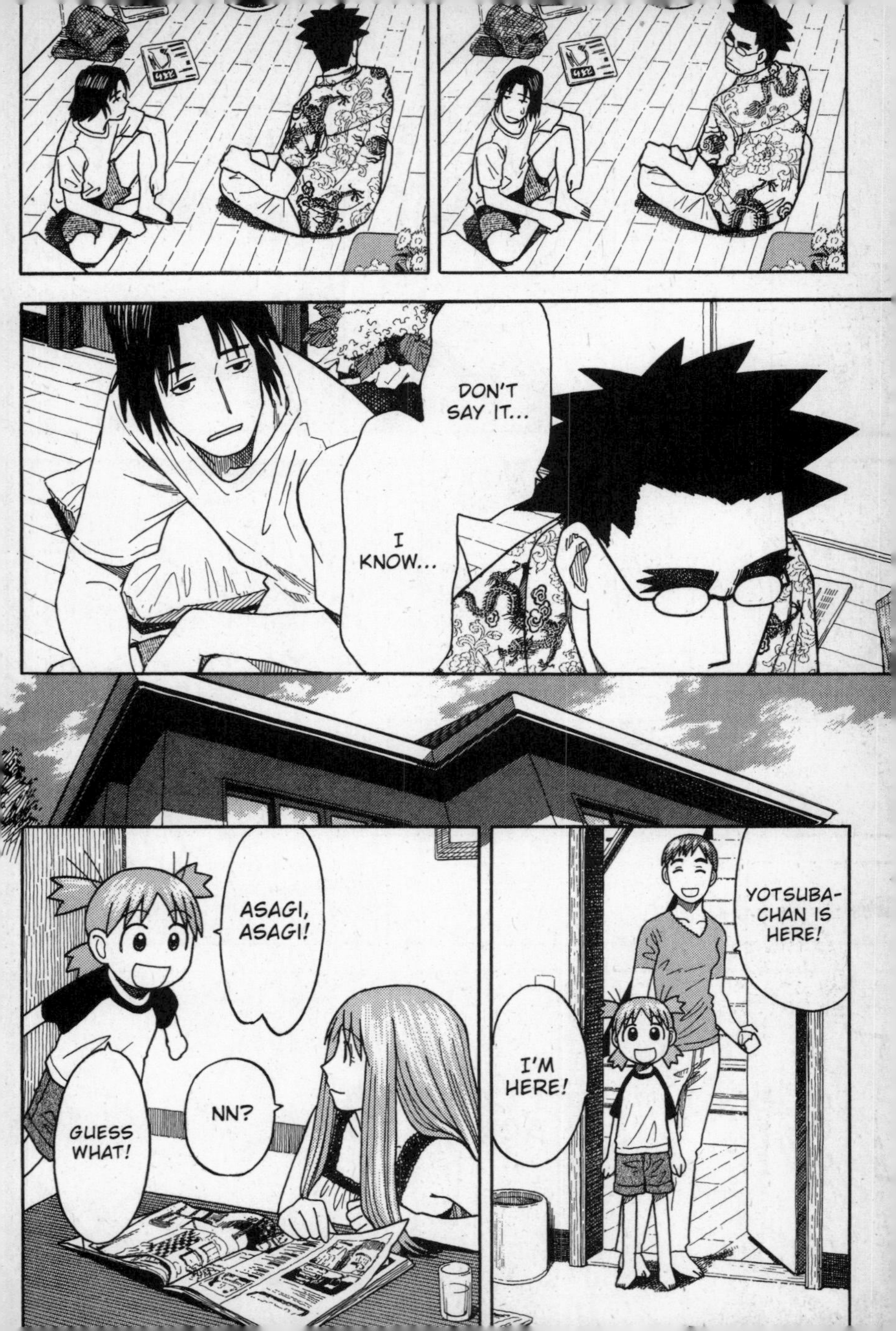
DON'T SAY IT...
I KNOW...
YOTSUBA-CHAN IS HERE!
I'M HERE!
ASAGI, ASAGI!
NN?
GUESS WHAT!

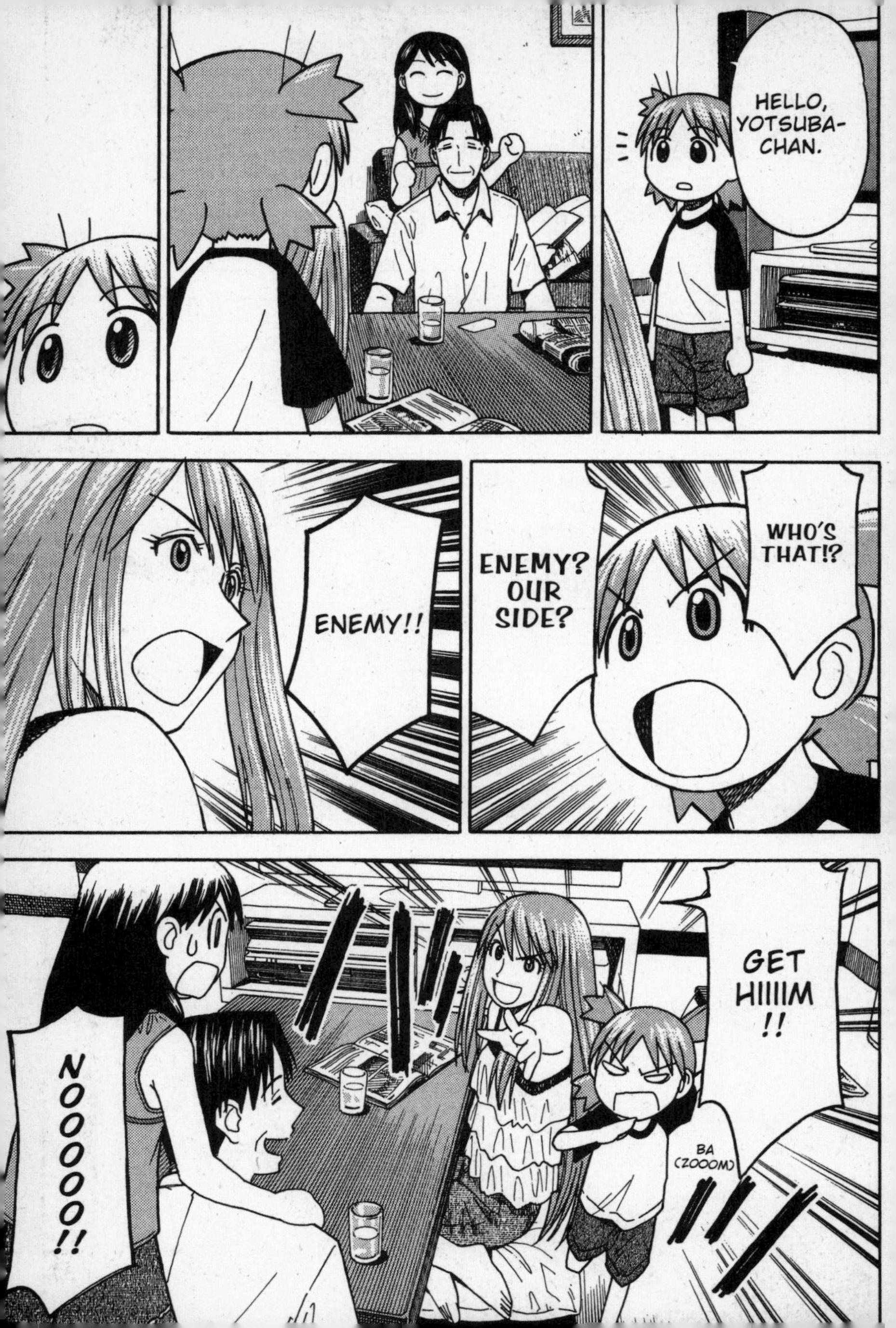
HELLO, YOTSUBA-CHAN.
WHO'S THAT!?
ENEMY? OUR SIDE?
ENEMY!!
GET HIIIIM !!
BA (ZOOOM)
NOOOOOO!!

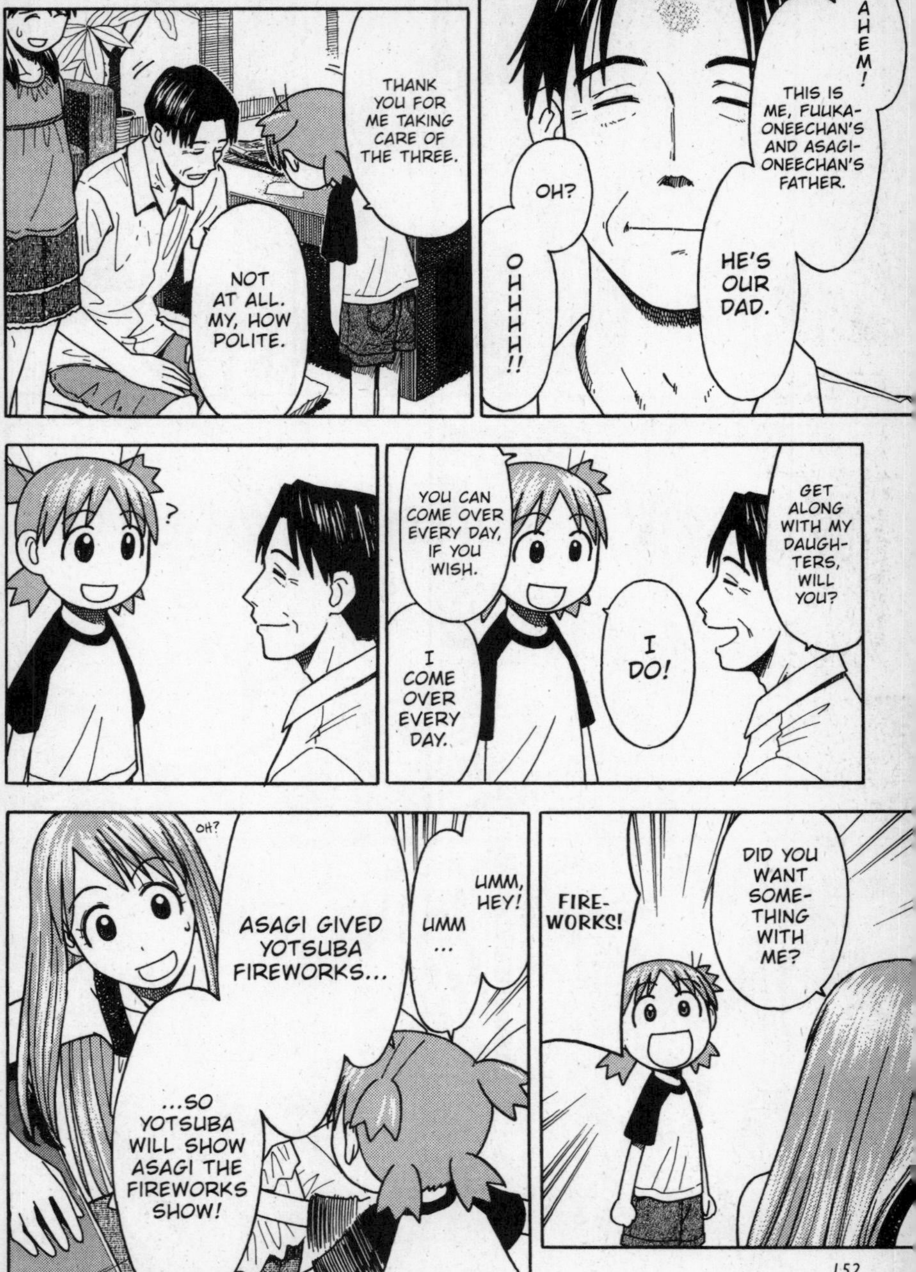
AHEM!
THIS IS ME, FUUKA-ONEECHAN'S AND ASAGI-ONEECHAN'S FATHER.
HE'S OUR DAD.
OH?
OHHHHH!!
THANK YOU FOR ME TAKING CARE OF THE THREE.
NOT AT ALL. MY, HOW POLITE.
GET ALONG WITH MY DAUGH-TERS, WILL YOU?
I DO!
YOU CAN COME OVER EVERY DAY, IF YOU WISH.
I COME OVER EVERY DAY.
?
DID YOU WANT SOME-THING WITH ME?
FIRE-WORKS!
UMM, HEY!
UMM ...
OH?
ASAGI GIVED YOTSUBA FIREWORKS...
...SO YOTSUBA WILL SHOW ASAGI THE FIREWORKS SHOW!

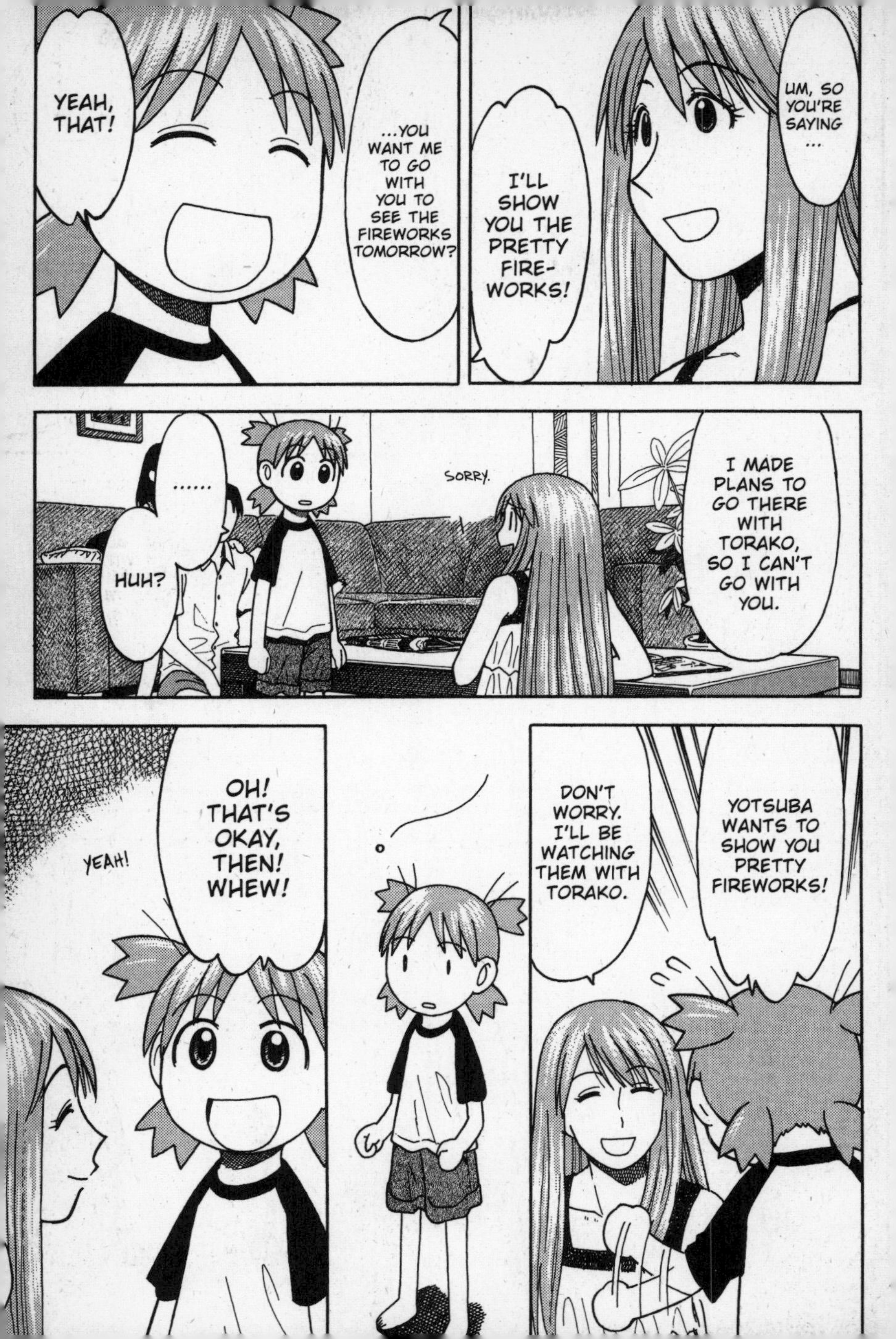
UM, SO YOU'RE SAYING ...
I'LL SHOW YOU THE PRETTY FIRE-WORKS!
...YOU WANT ME TO GO WITH YOU TO SEE THE FIREWORKS TOMORROW?
YEAH, THAT!
I MADE PLANS TO GO THERE WITH TORAKO, SO I CAN'T GO WITH YOU.
SORRY.
......
HUH?
YOTSUBA WANTS TO SHOW YOU PRETTY FIREWORKS!
DON'T WORRY. I'LL BE WATCHING THEM WITH TORAKO.
OH! THAT'S OKAY, THEN! WHEW!
YEAH!

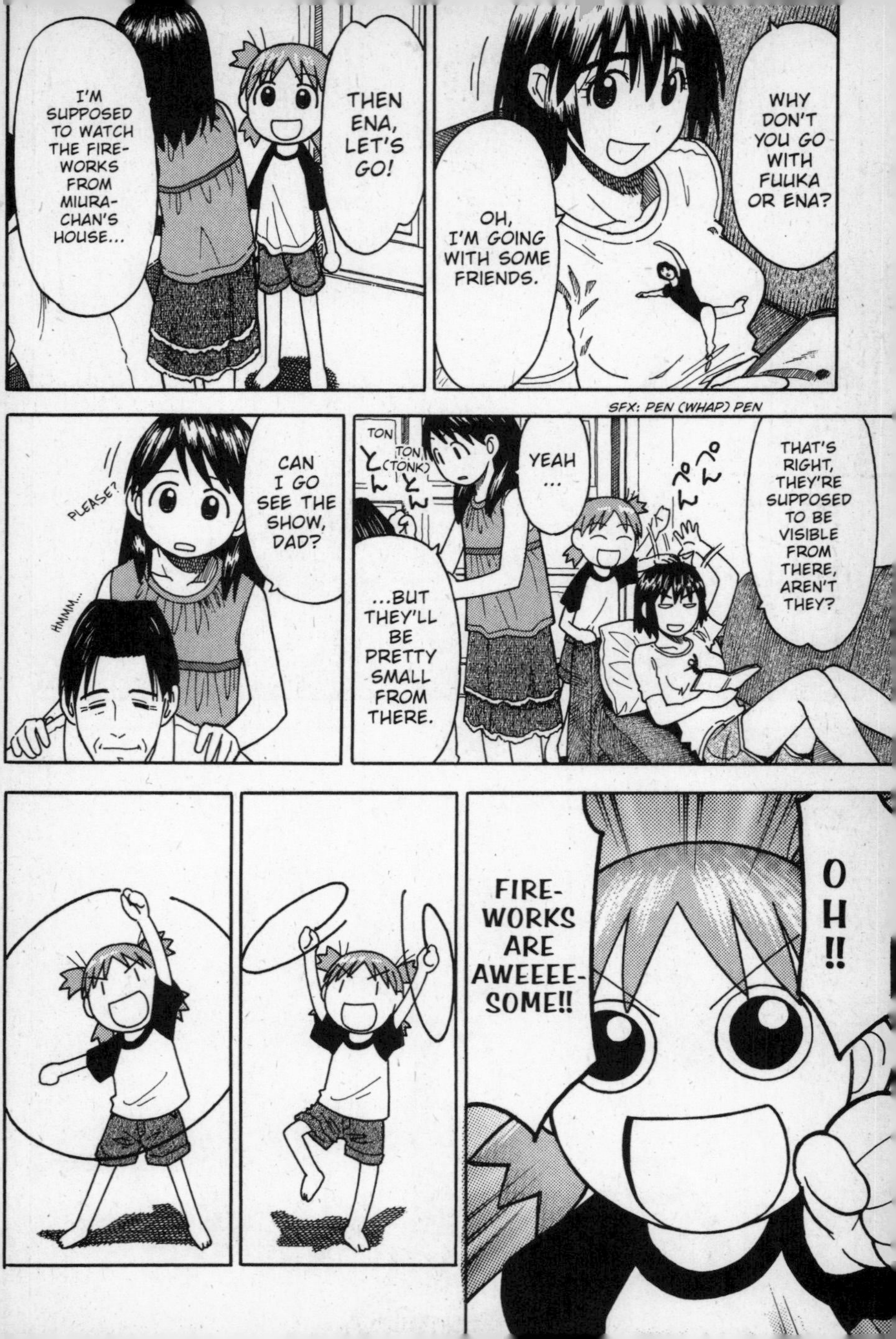

WHY DON'T YOU GO WITH FUUKA OR ENA?
OH, I'M GOING WITH SOME FRIENDS.
SFX: PEN (WHAP) PEN
THEN ENA, LET'S GO!
I'M SUPPOSED TO WATCH THE FIRE-WORKS FROM MIURA-CHAN'S HOUSE...
THAT'S RIGHT, THEY'RE SUPPOSED TO BE VISIBLE FROM THERE, AREN'T THEY?
ぺんぺん
YEAH ...
TON
とん
TON (TONK)
とん
...BUT THEY'LL BE PRETTY SMALL FROM THERE.
CAN I GO SEE THE SHOW, DAD?
PLEASE?
HMMM...
OH!!
FIRE-WORKS ARE AWEEEE-SOME!!

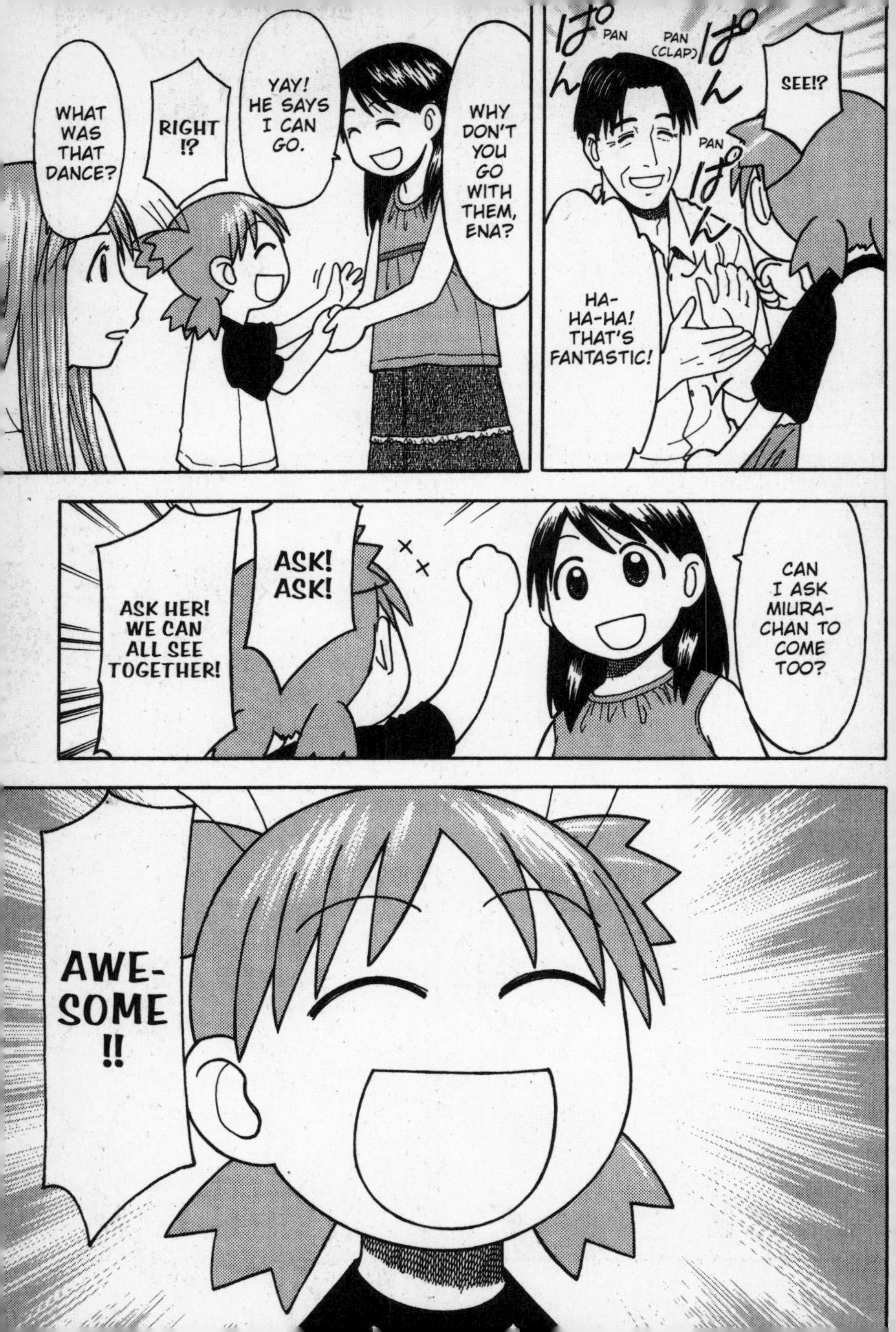
SEE!?
ぱん PAN (CLAP)
ぱん PAN
ぱん PAN
HA-HA-HA! THAT'S FANTASTIC!
WHY DON'T YOU GO WITH THEM, ENA?
YAY! HE SAYS I CAN GO.
RIGHT!?
WHAT WAS THAT DANCE?
CAN I ASK MIURA-CHAN TO COME TOO?
ASK! ASK!
ASK HER! WE CAN ALL SEE TOGETHER!
AWE-SOME!!

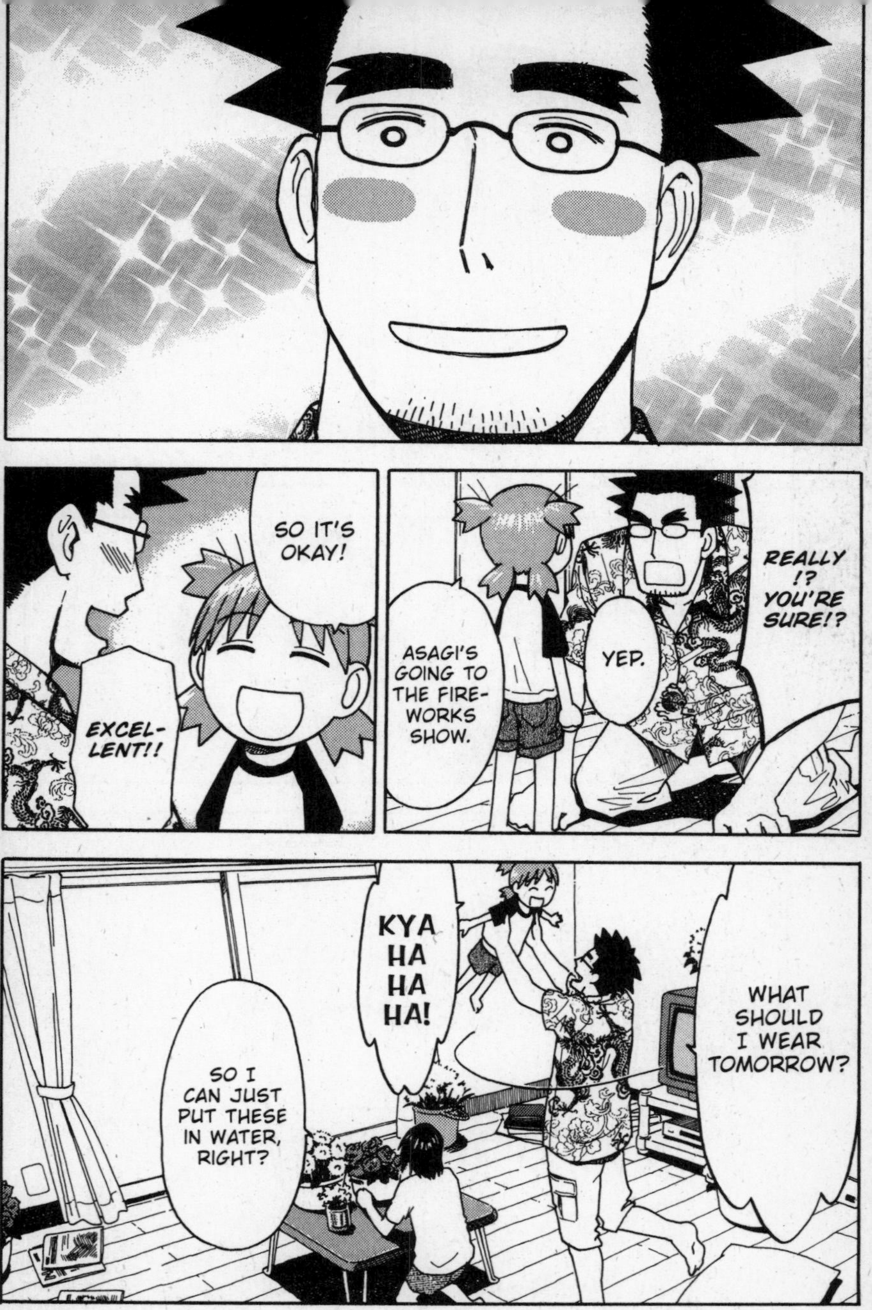
REALLY!? YOU'RE SURE!?
YEP.
ASAGI'S GOING TO THE FIRE-WORKS SHOW.
SO IT'S OKAY!
EXCEL-LENT!!
WHAT SHOULD I WEAR TOMORROW?
KYA HA HA HA!
SO I CAN JUST PUT THESE IN WATER, RIGHT?

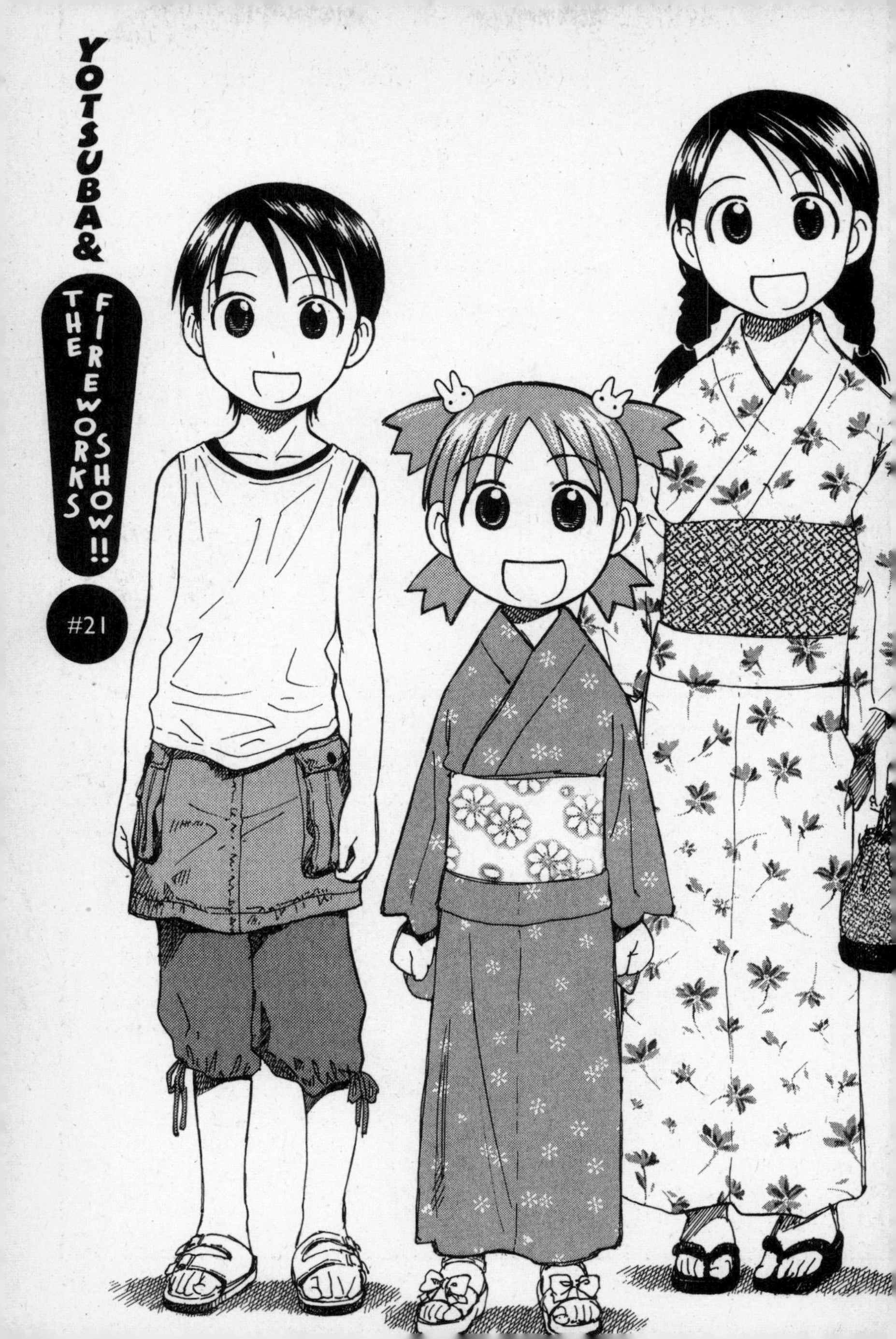
YOTSUBA&
THE FIREWORKS SHOW!!
#21

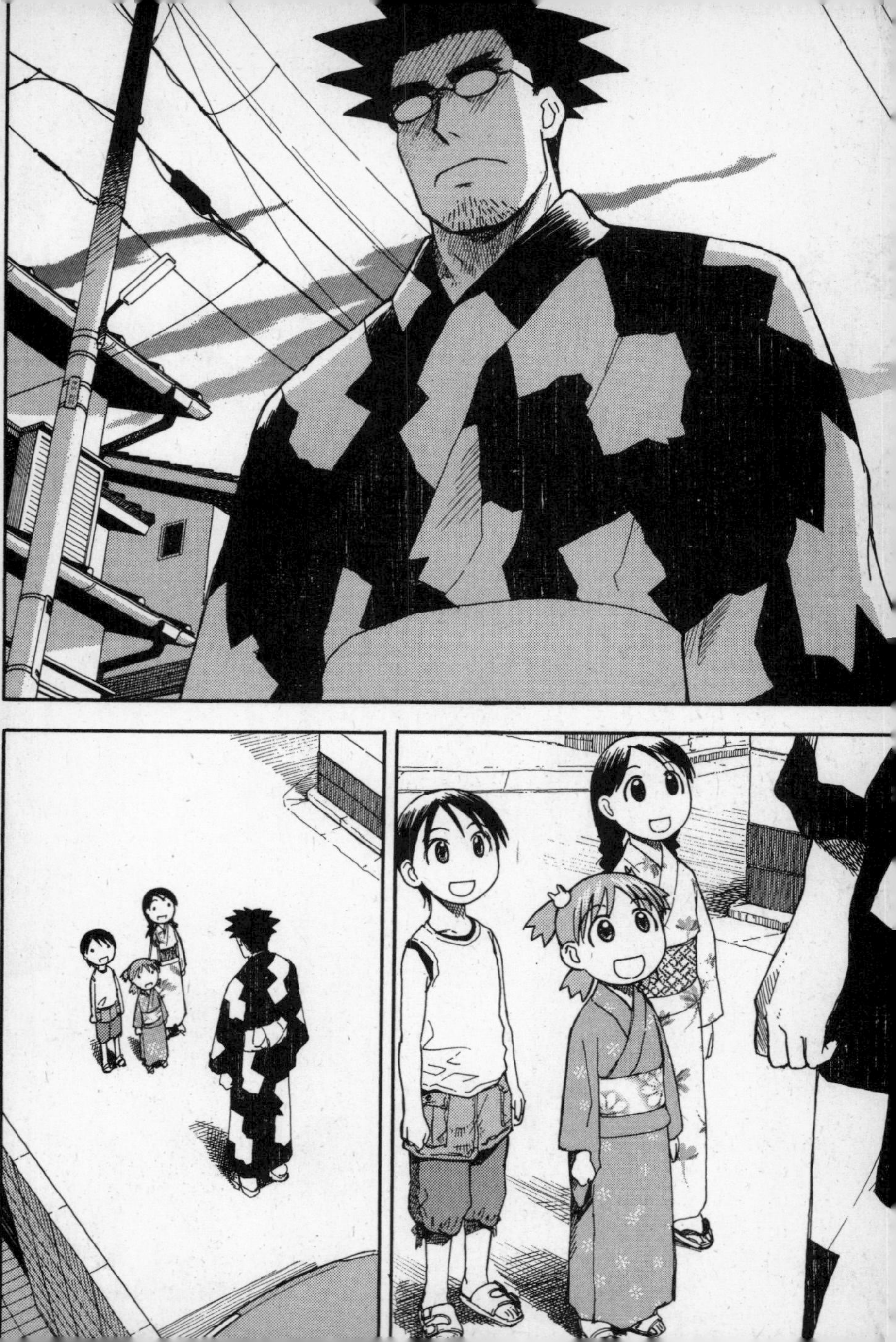

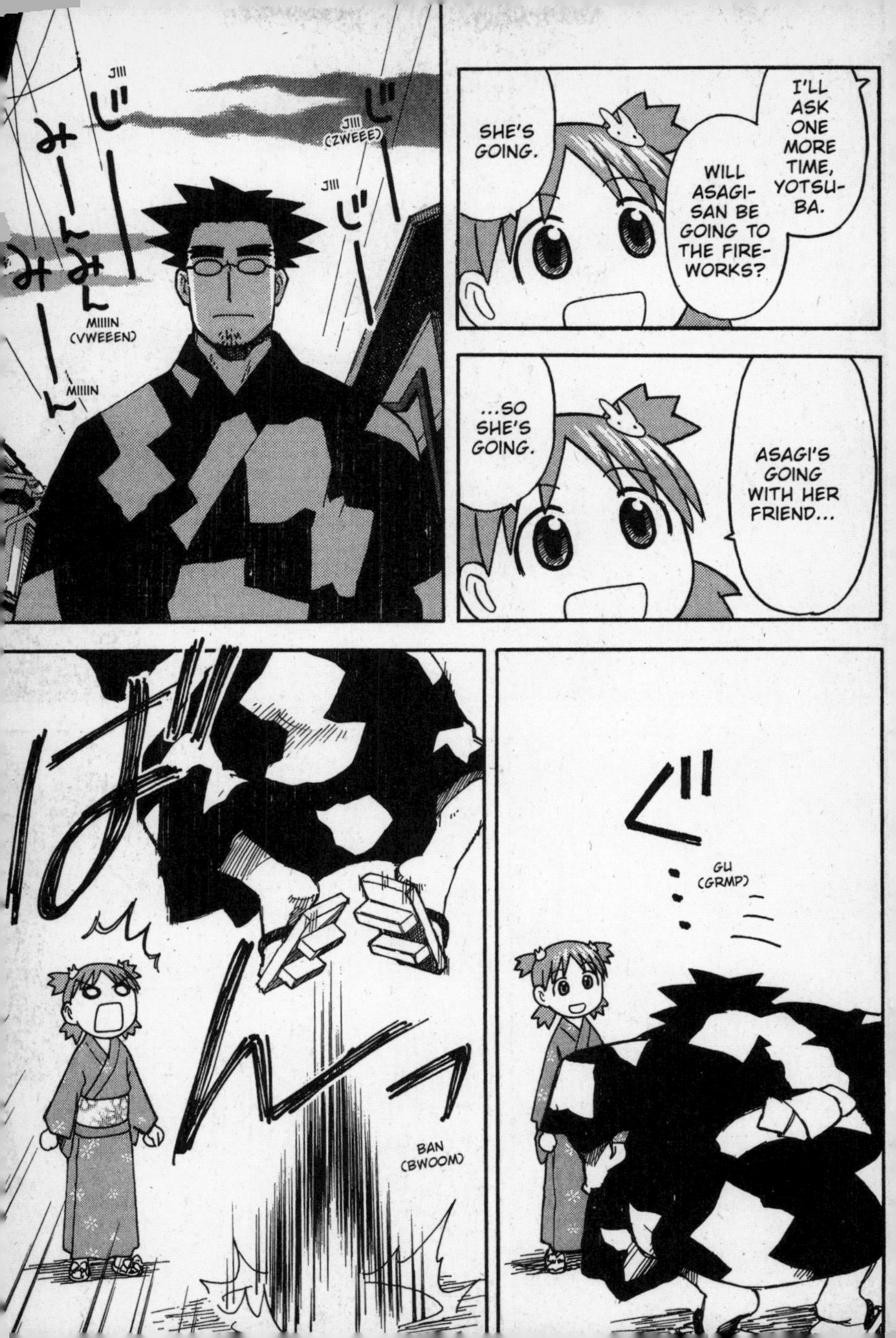
I'LL ASK ONE MORE TIME, YOTSUBA.
WILL ASAGI-SAN BE GOING TO THE FIREWORKS?
SHE'S GOING.
ASAGI'S GOING WITH HER FRIEND...
...SO SHE'S GOING.
JIII (ZWEEE)
JIII
JIII
MIIIN (VWEEEN)
MIIIN
ぐ
GU (GRMP)
BAN (BWOOM)

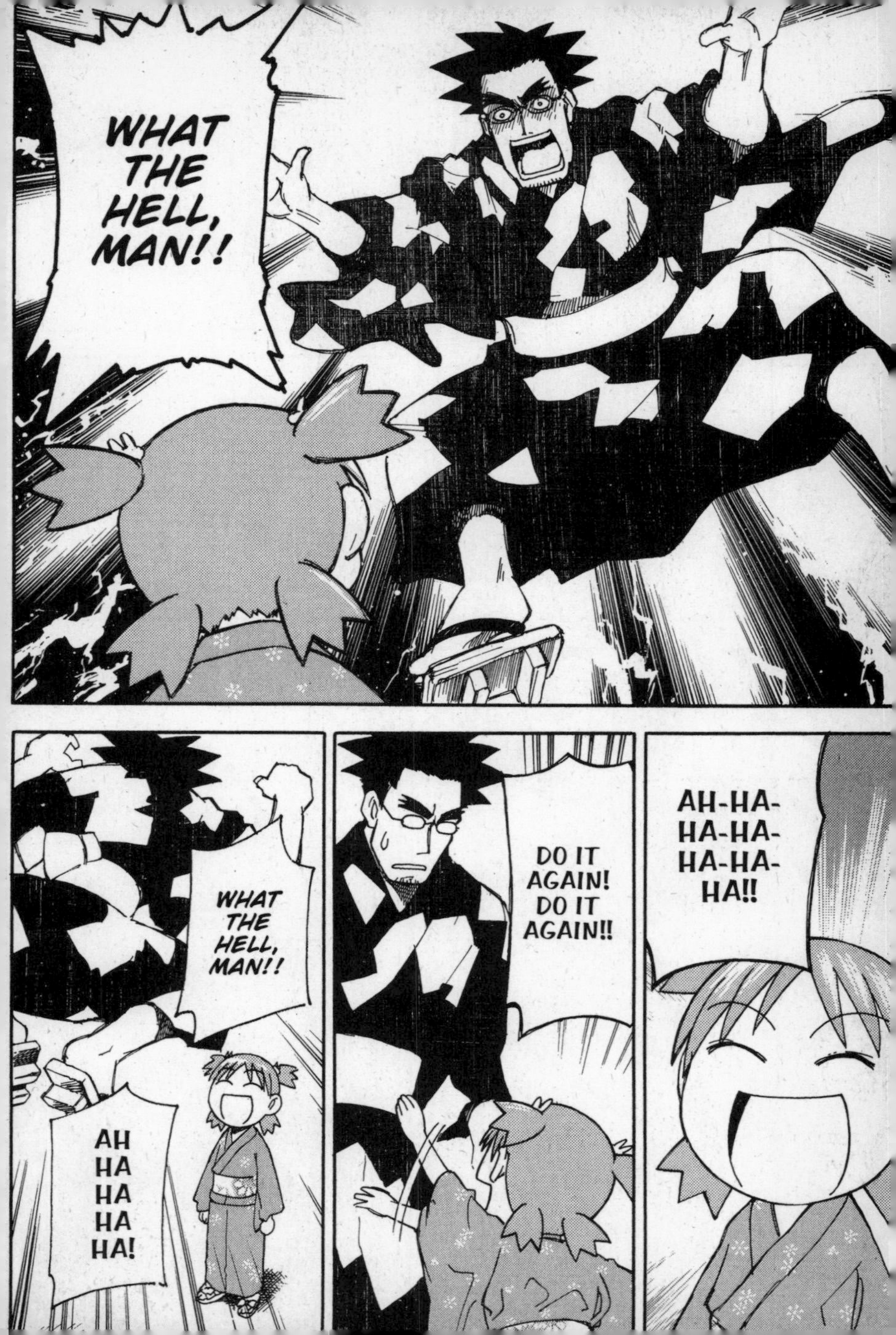
WHAT THE HELL, MAN!!
AH-HA-HA-HA-HA-HA-HA!!
DO IT AGAIN! DO IT AGAIN!!
WHAT THE HELL, MAN!!
AH HA HA HA HA!

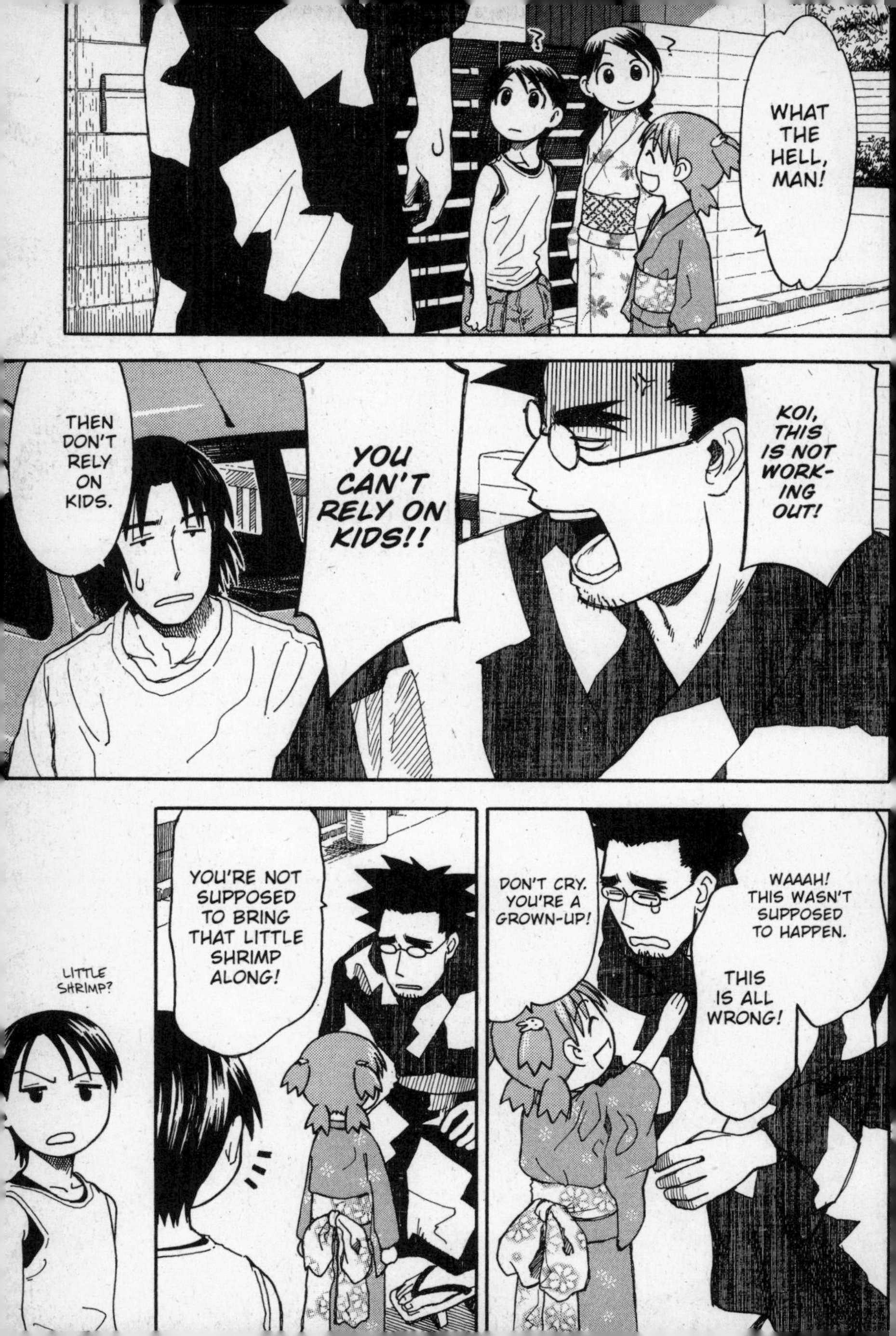
WHAT THE HELL, MAN!
KOI, THIS IS NOT WORK-ING OUT!
YOU CAN'T RELY ON KIDS!!
THEN DON'T RELY ON KIDS.
WAAAH! THIS WASN'T SUPPOSED TO HAPPEN.
THIS IS ALL WRONG!
DON'T CRY. YOU'RE A GROWN-UP!
YOU'RE NOT SUPPOSED TO BRING THAT LITTLE SHRIMP ALONG!
LITTLE SHRIMP?

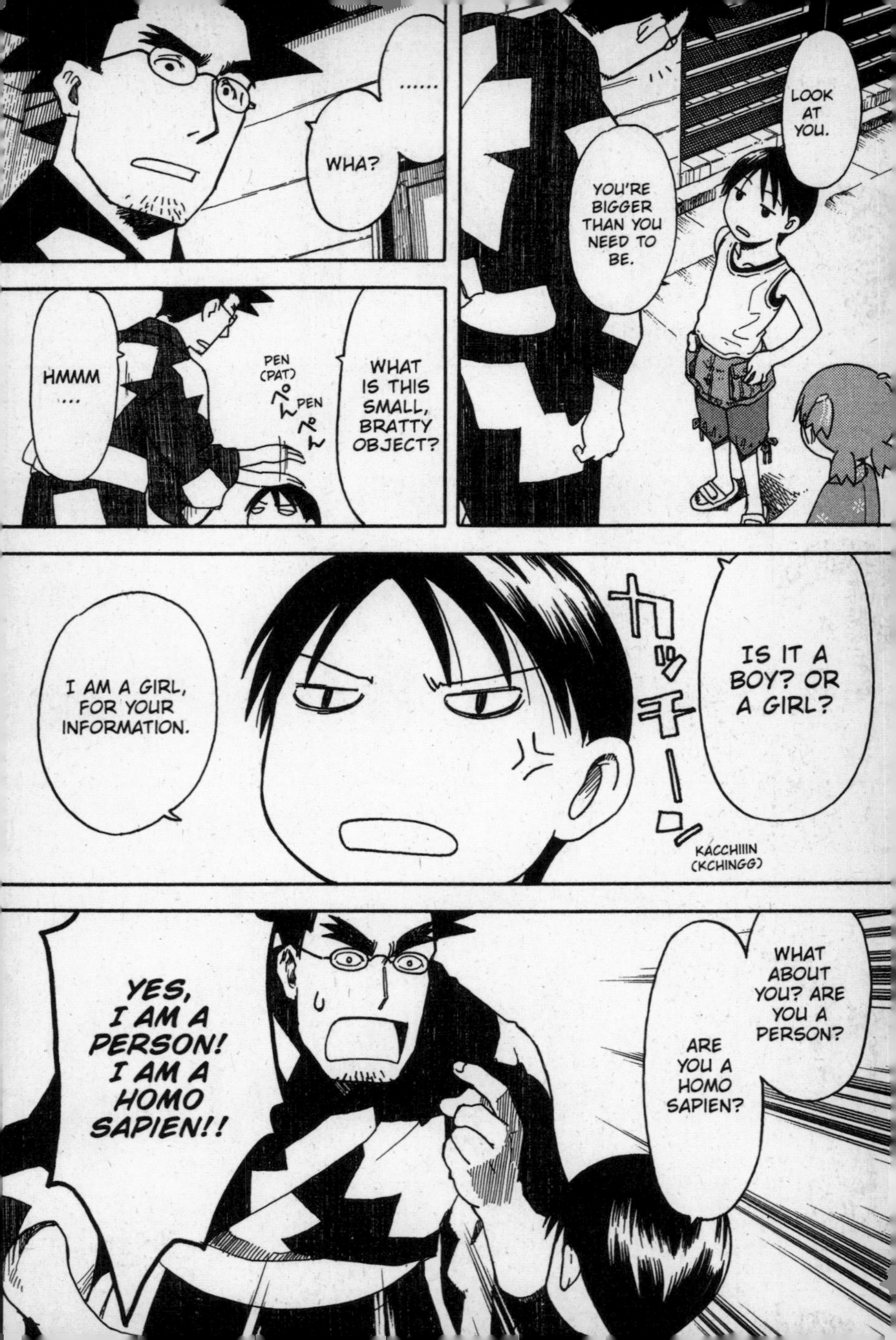
LOOK AT YOU.
YOU'RE BIGGER THAN YOU NEED TO BE.
......
WHA?
WHAT IS THIS SMALL, BRATTY OBJECT?
ぺん ぺん
PEN (PAT) PEN
HMMM ....
IS IT A BOY? OR A GIRL?
カッチーン
KACCHIIIN (KCHINGG)
I AM A GIRL, FOR YOUR INFORMATION.
WHAT ABOUT YOU? ARE YOU A PERSON?
ARE YOU A HOMO SAPIEN?
YES, I AM A PERSON! I AM A HOMO SAPIEN!!

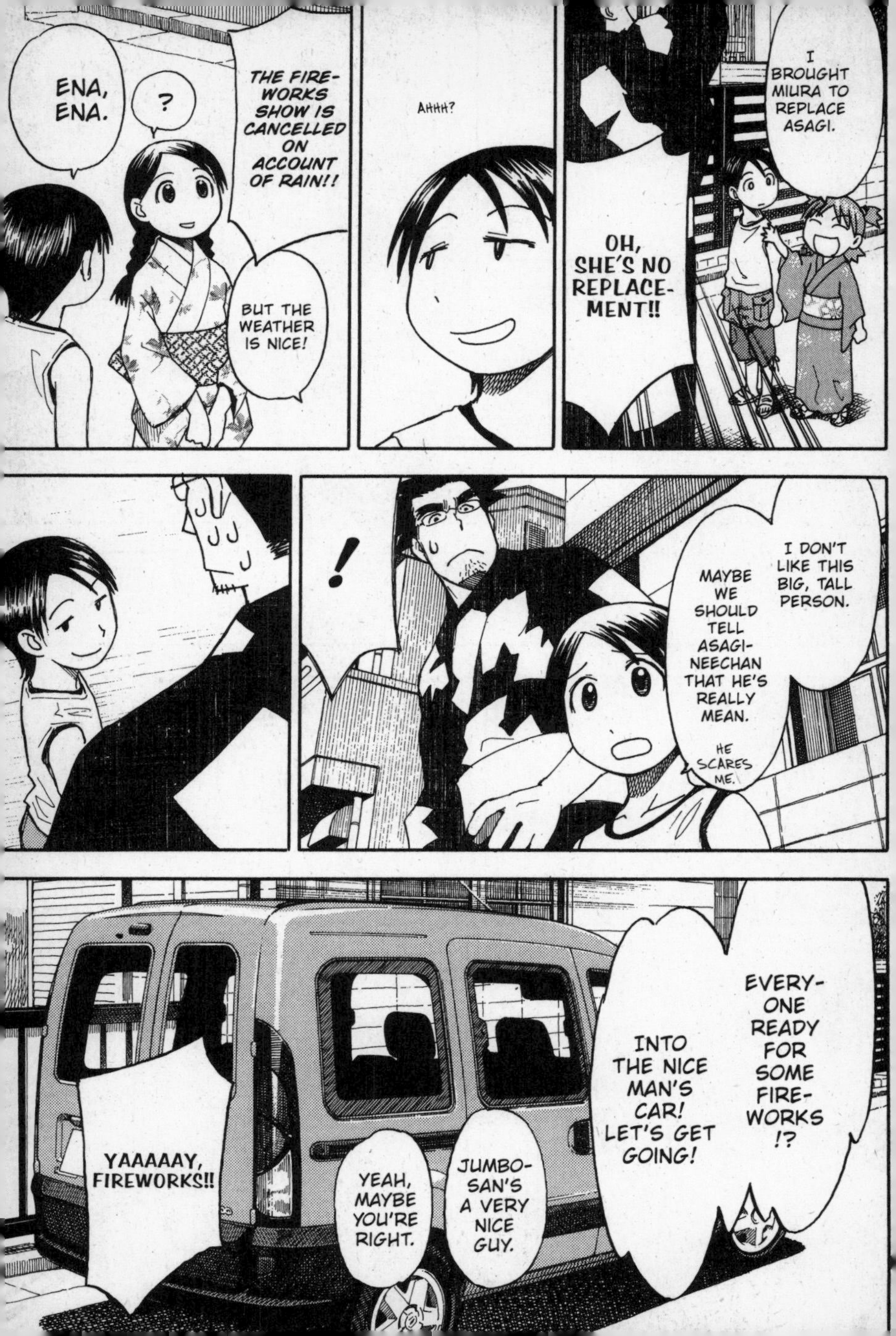
I BROUGHT MIURA TO REPLACE ASAGI.
OH, SHE'S NO REPLACEMENT!!
AHHH?
ENA, ENA.
?
THE FIREWORKS SHOW IS CANCELLED ON ACCOUNT OF RAIN!!
BUT THE WEATHER IS NICE!
I DON'T LIKE THIS BIG, TALL PERSON.
MAYBE WE SHOULD TELL ASAGI-NEECHAN THAT HE'S REALLY MEAN.
HE SCARES ME.
!
EVERYONE READY FOR SOME FIREWORKS!?
INTO THE NICE MAN'S CAR! LET'S GET GOING!
JUMBO-SAN'S A VERY NICE GUY.
YEAH, MAYBE YOU'RE RIGHT.
YAAAAAY, FIREWORKS!!

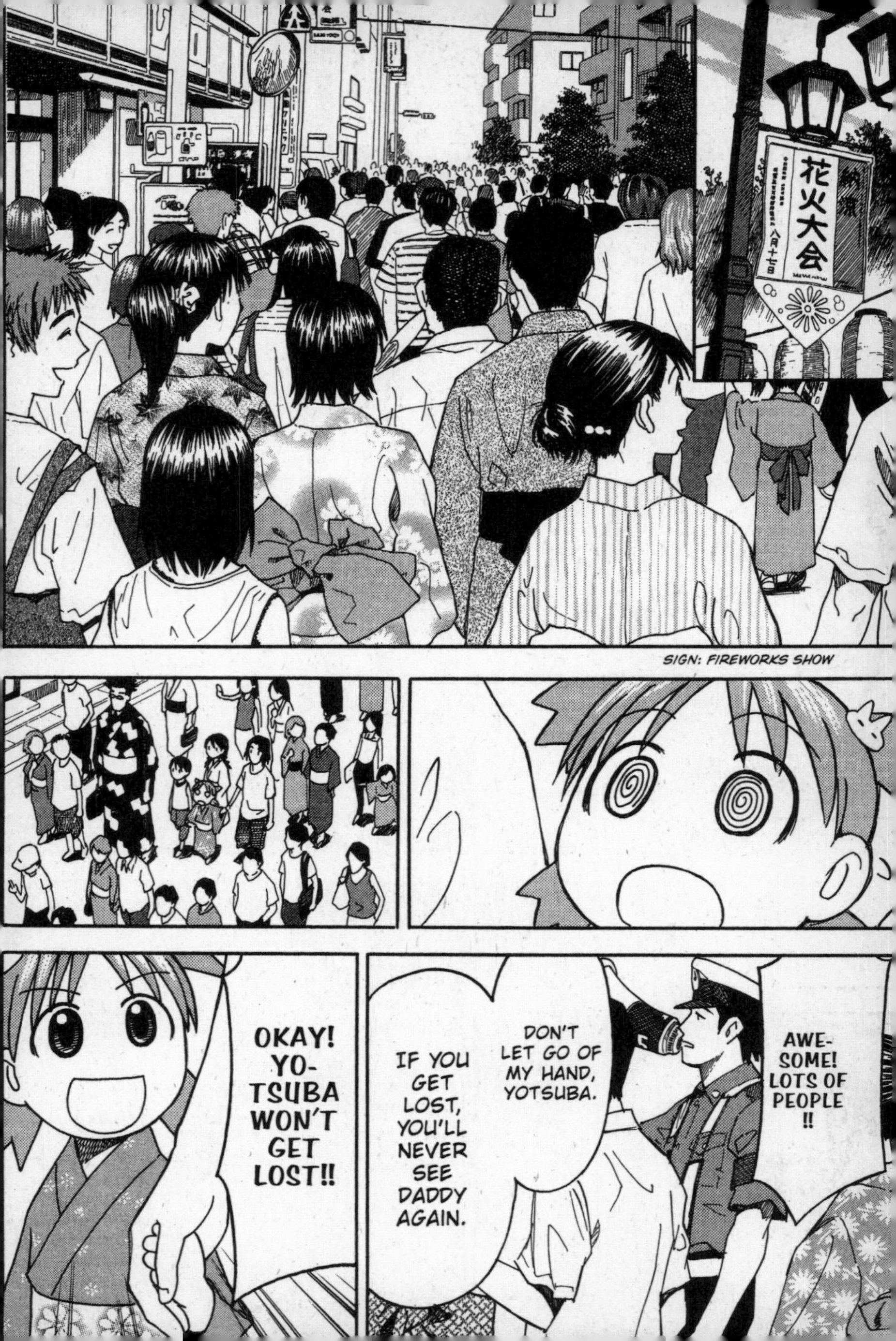
納涼
花火大会
八月十七日
SIGN: FIREWORKS SHOW
AWE-SOME! LOTS OF PEOPLE !!
DON'T LET GO OF MY HAND, YOTSUBA.
IF YOU GET LOST, YOU'LL NEVER SEE DADDY AGAIN.
OKAY! YO-TSUBA WON'T GET LOST!!

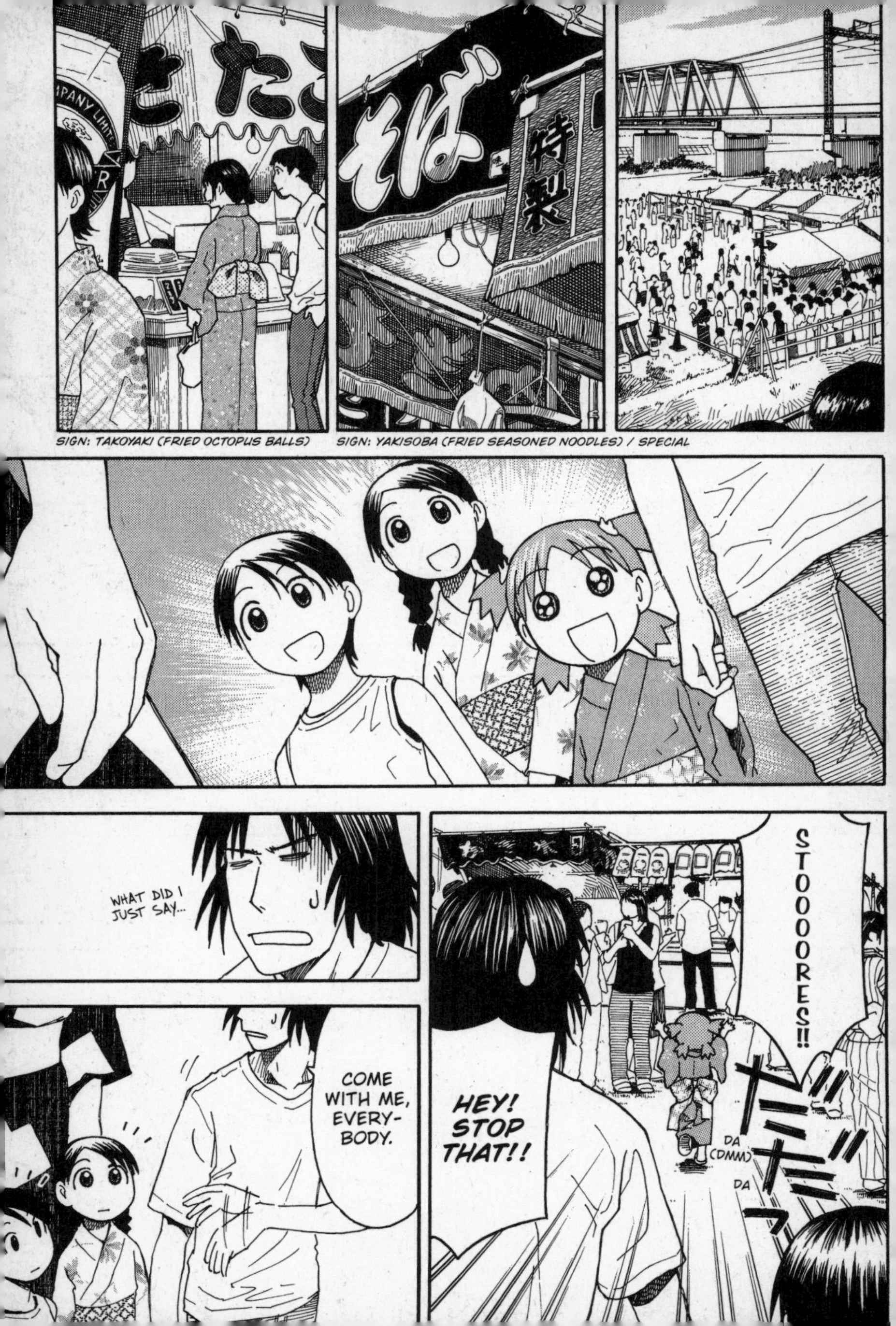
SIGN: YAKISOBA (FRIED SEASONED NOODLES) / SPECIAL
SIGN: TAKOYAKI (FRIED OCTOPUS BALLS)
STOOOORES!!
HEY! STOP THAT!!
DA (DMM) DA
WHAT DID I JUST SAY...
COME WITH ME, EVERY-BODY.

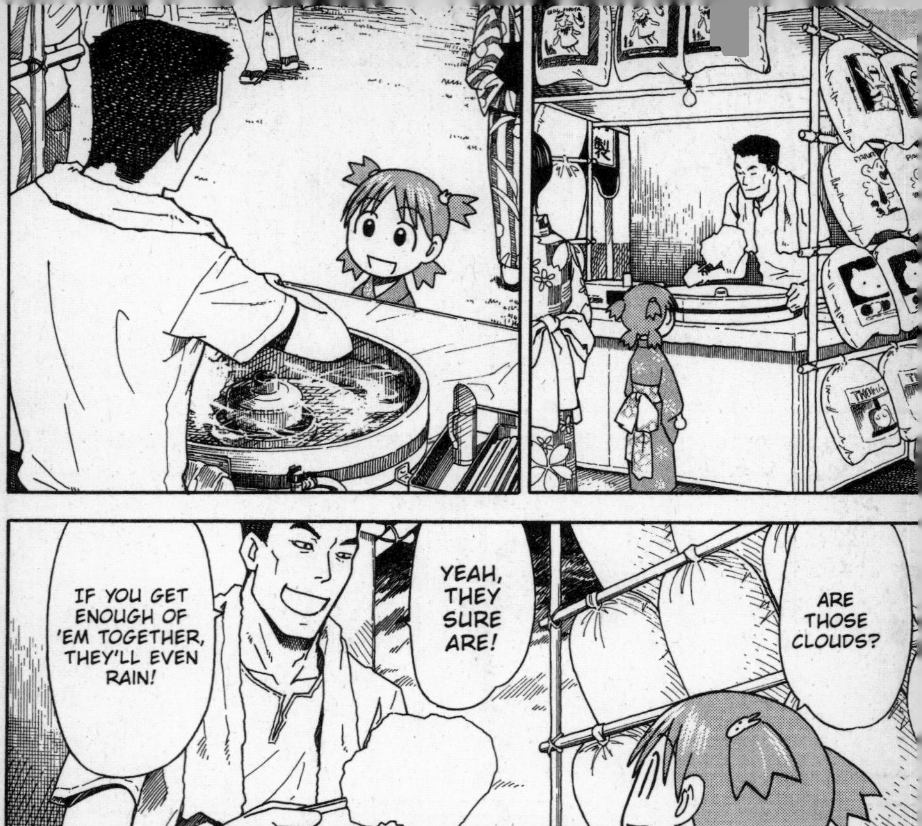
ARE THOSE CLOUDS?
YEAH, THEY SURE ARE!
IF YOU GET ENOUGH OF 'EM TOGETHER, THEY'LL EVEN RAIN!

*COTTON CANDY: THE JAPANESE WORD FOR "COTTON CANDY" IS WATA-AME, A LITERAL TRANSLATION OF THE ENGLISH. HOWEVER, AME, THE WORD FOR "CANDY," SOUNDS IDENTICAL TO THE WORD FOR "RAIN," WHICH LEADS TO YOTSUBA'S MISTAKEN ASSUMPTION.

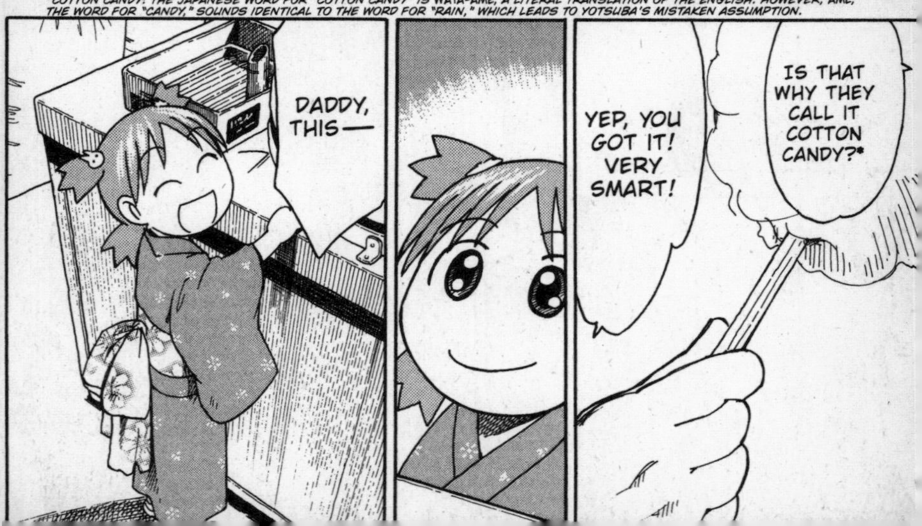
IS THAT WHY THEY CALL IT COTTON CANDY?*
YEP, YOU GOT IT! VERY SMART!
DADDY, THIS—

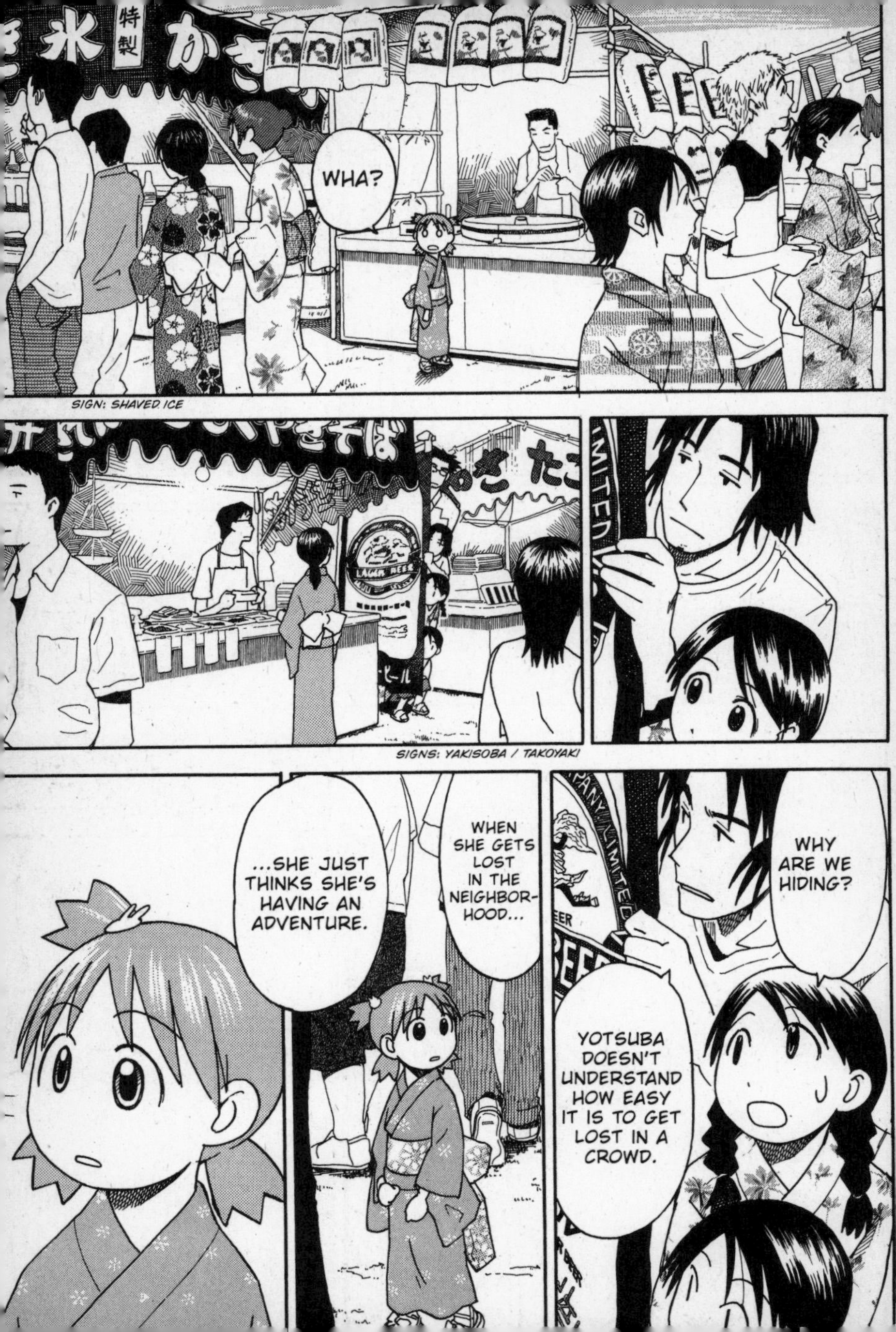
WHA?
SIGN: SHAVED ICE
SIGNS: YAKISOBA / TAKOYAKI
WHY ARE WE HIDING?
YOTSUBA DOESN'T UNDERSTAND HOW EASY IT IS TO GET LOST IN A CROWD.
WHEN SHE GETS LOST IN THE NEIGHBOR-HOOD...
...SHE JUST THINKS SHE'S HAVING AN ADVENTURE.

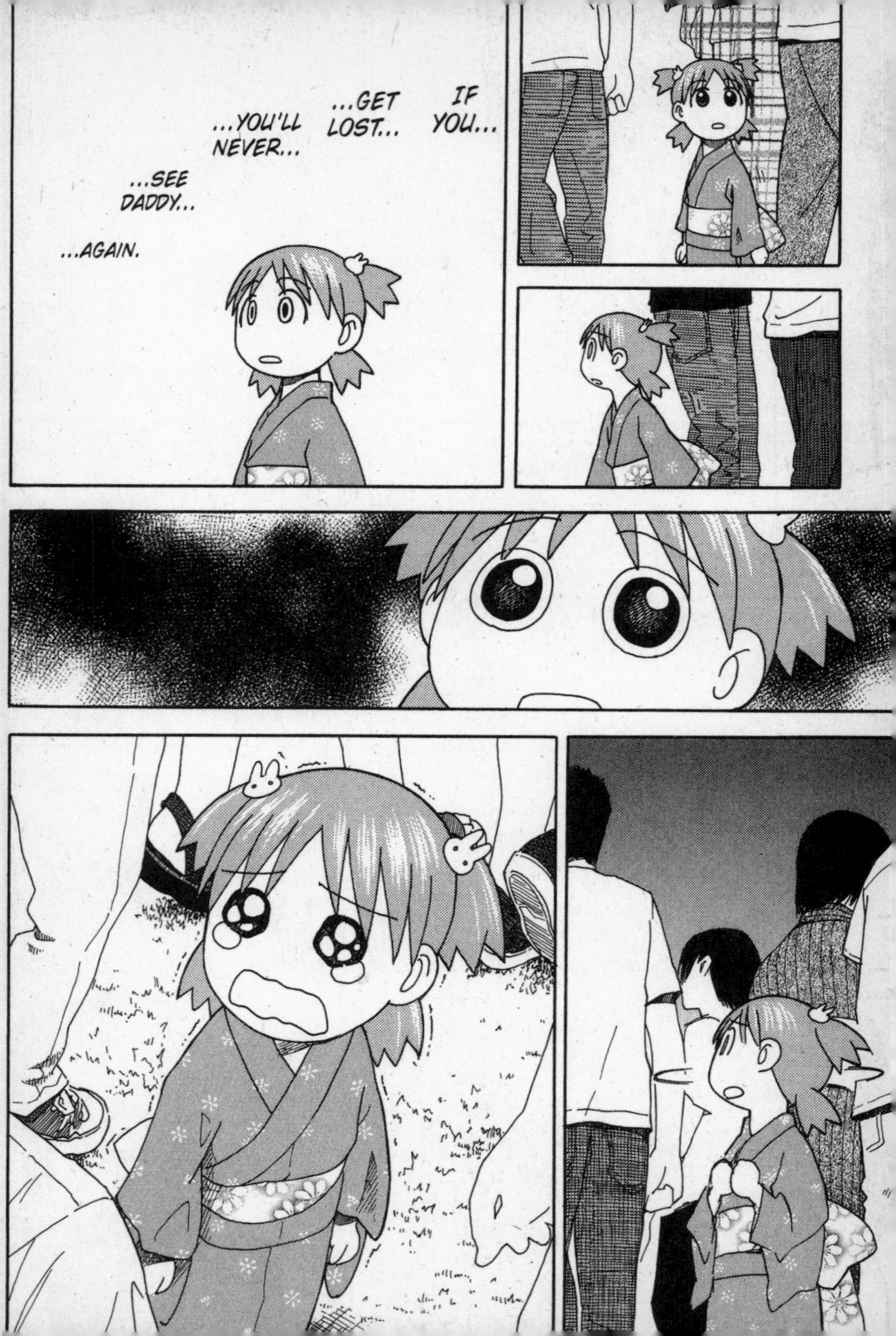
IF YOU...
...GET LOST...
...YOU'LL NEVER...
...SEE DADDY...
...AGAIN.

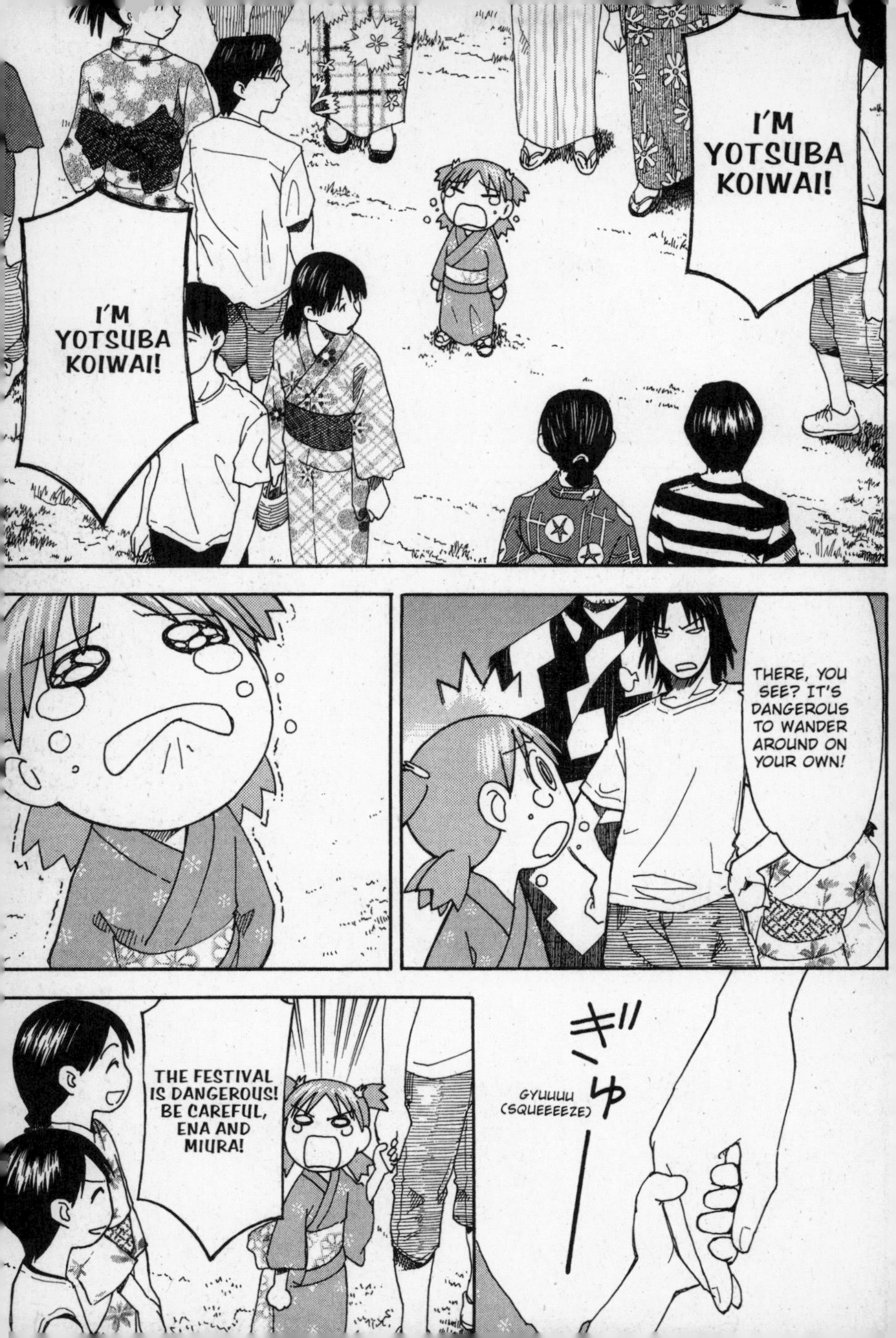
I'M YOTSUBA KOIWAI!
I'M YOTSUBA KOIWAI!
THERE, YOU SEE? IT'S DANGEROUS TO WANDER AROUND ON YOUR OWN!
ぎゅー
GYUUUU (SQUEEEEZE)
THE FESTIVAL IS DANGEROUS! BE CAREFUL, ENA AND MIURA!

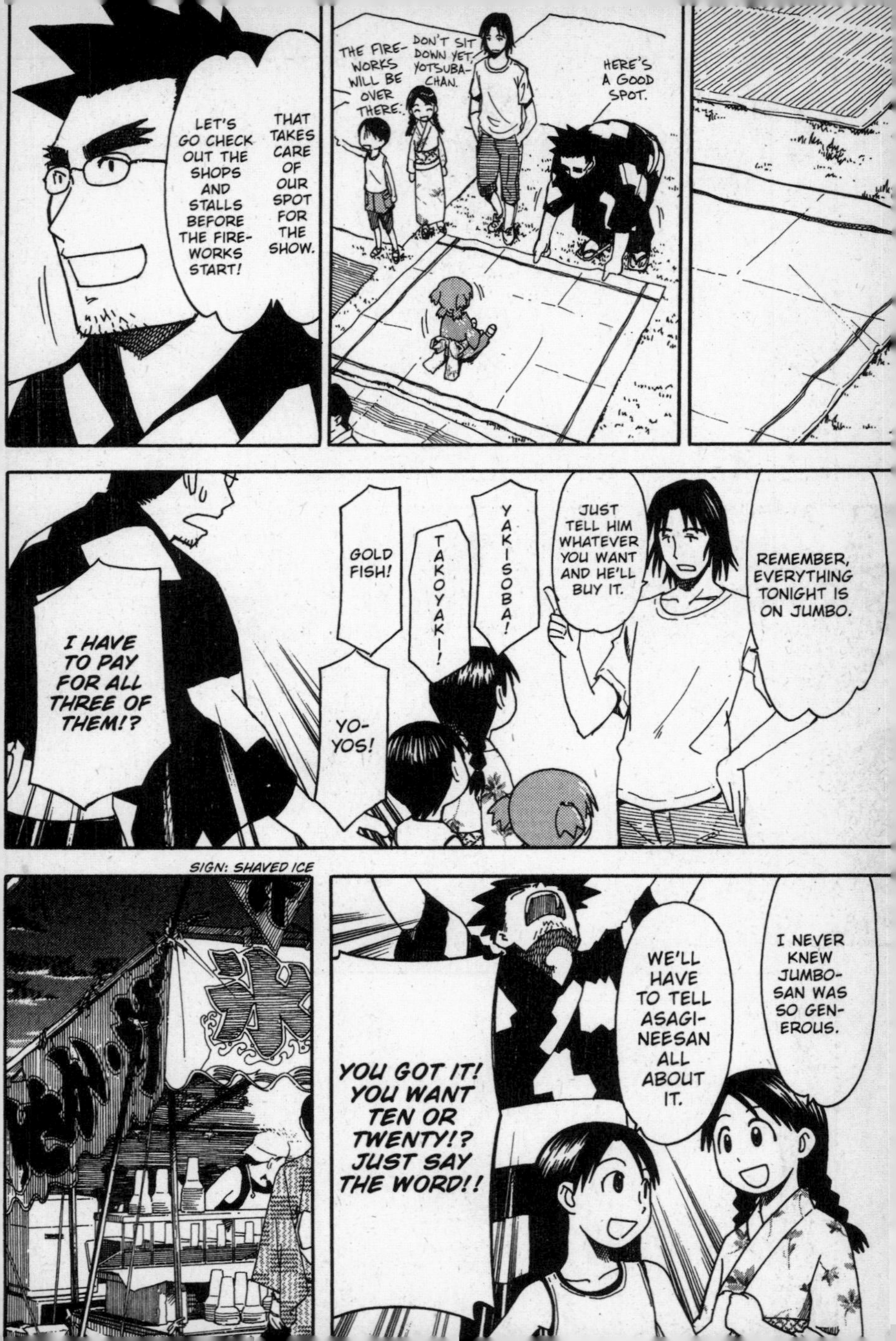
HERE'S A GOOD SPOT.
DON'T SIT DOWN YET, YOTSUBA-CHAN.
THE FIRE-WORKS WILL BE OVER THERE.
THAT TAKES CARE OF OUR SPOT FOR THE SHOW.
LET'S GO CHECK OUT THE SHOPS AND STALLS BEFORE THE FIRE-WORKS START!
REMEMBER, EVERYTHING TONIGHT IS ON JUMBO.
JUST TELL HIM WHATEVER YOU WANT AND HE'LL BUY IT.
YAKISOBA!
TAKOYAKI!
GOLD FISH!
YO-YOS!
I HAVE TO PAY FOR ALL THREE OF THEM!?
I NEVER KNEW JUMBO-SAN WAS SO GEN-EROUS.
WE'LL HAVE TO TELL ASAGI-NEESAN ALL ABOUT IT.
YOU GOT IT! YOU WANT TEN OR TWENTY!? JUST SAY THE WORD!!
SIGN: SHAVED ICE

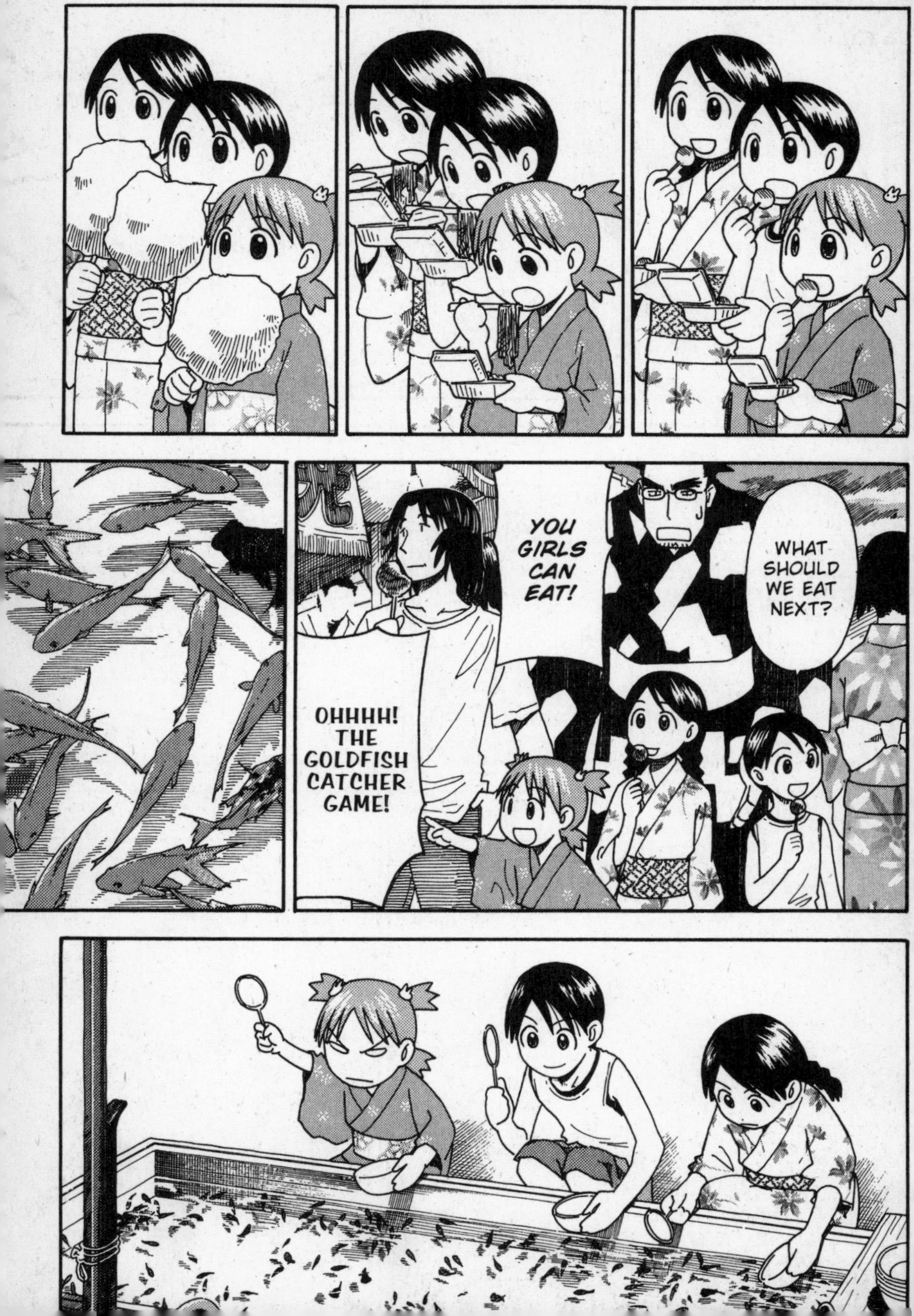
WHAT SHOULD WE EAT NEXT?
YOU GIRLS CAN EAT!
OHHHH! THE GOLDFISH CATCHER GAME!

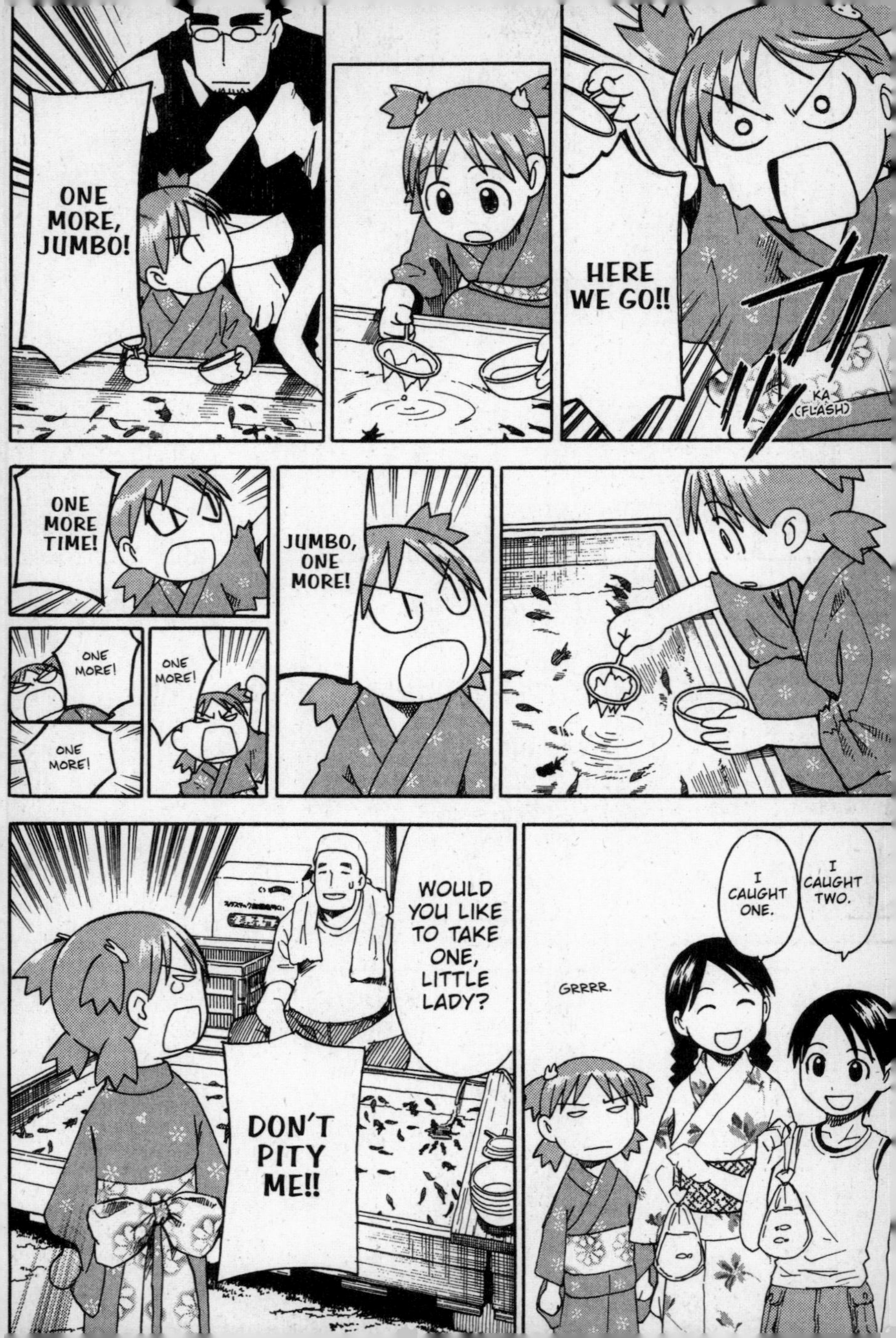
HERE WE GO!!
KA (FLASH)
ONE MORE, JUMBO!
JUMBO, ONE MORE!
ONE MORE TIME!
ONE MORE!
ONE MORE!
ONE MORE!
I CAUGHT TWO.
I CAUGHT ONE.
GRRRR.
WOULD YOU LIKE TO TAKE ONE, LITTLE LADY?
DON'T PITY ME!!

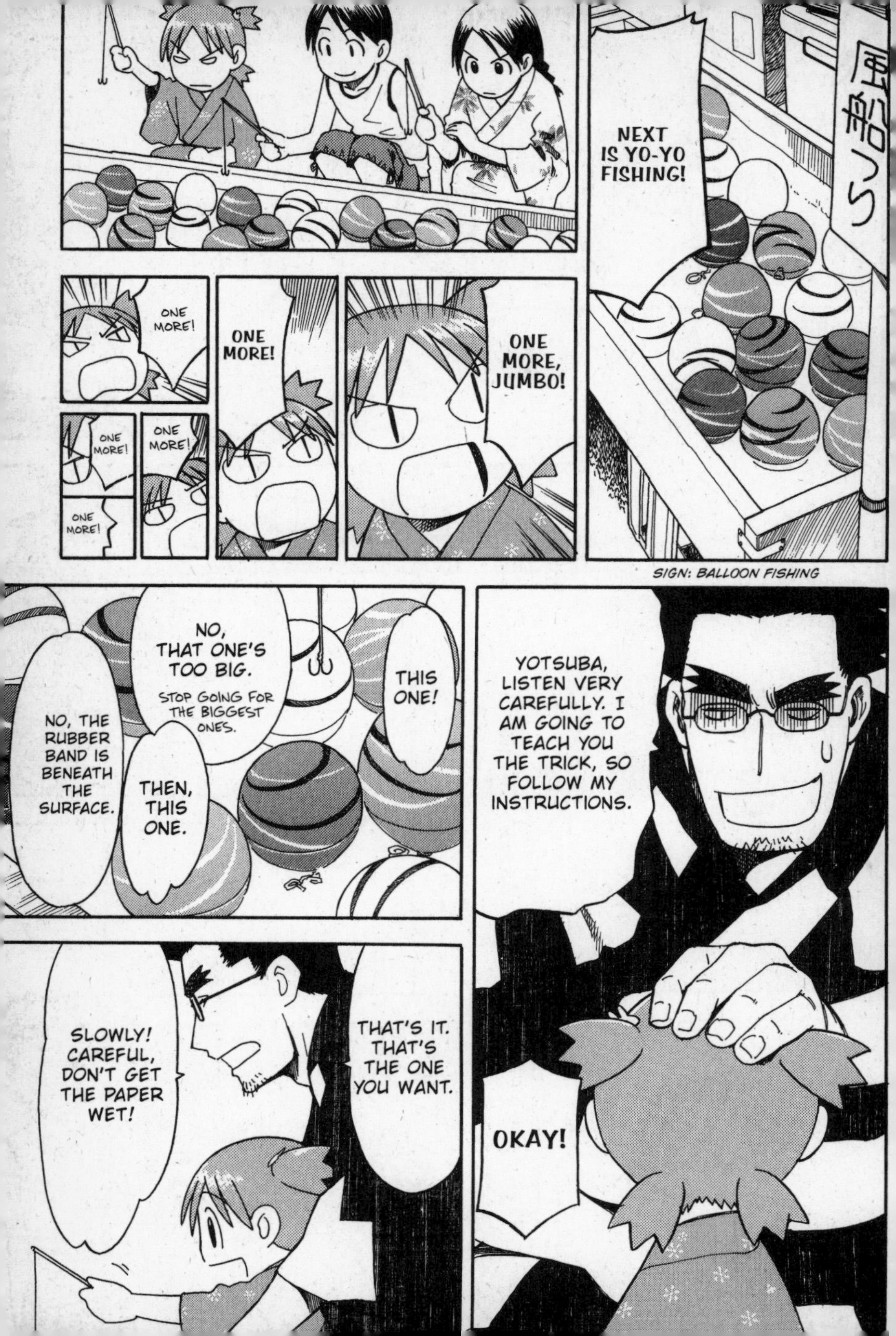
風船つり
NEXT IS YO-YO FISHING!
SIGN: BALLOON FISHING
ONE MORE, JUMBO!
ONE MORE!
ONE MORE!
ONE MORE!
ONE MORE!
ONE MORE!
YOTSUBA, LISTEN VERY CAREFULLY. I AM GOING TO TEACH YOU THE TRICK, SO FOLLOW MY INSTRUCTIONS.
OKAY!
THIS ONE!
NO, THAT ONE'S TOO BIG.
STOP GOING FOR THE BIGGEST ONES.
THEN, THIS ONE.
NO, THE RUBBER BAND IS BENEATH THE SURFACE.
THAT'S IT. THAT'S THE ONE YOU WANT.
SLOWLY! CAREFUL, DON'T GET THE PAPER WET!

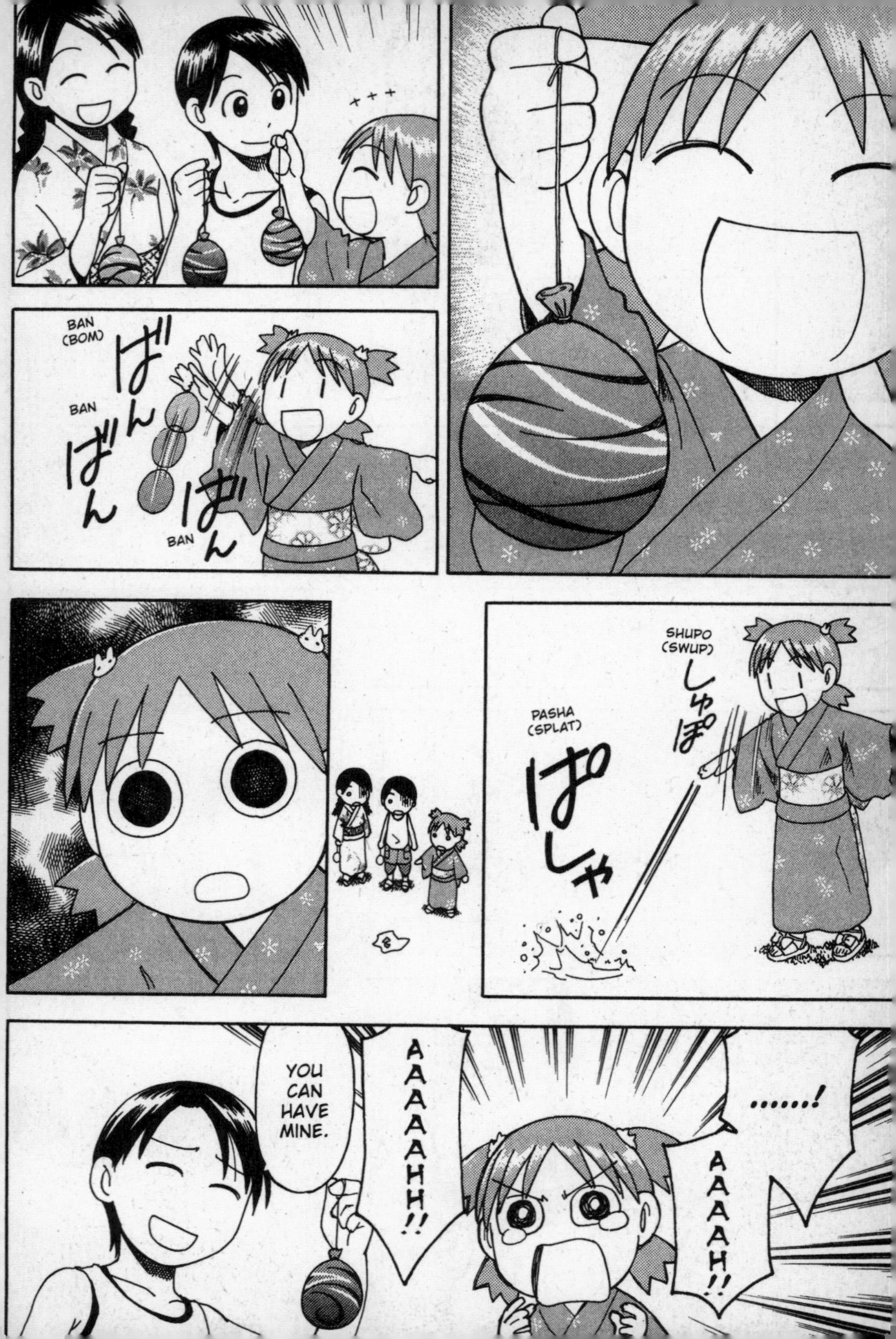
BAN (BOM)
ばん
BAN
ばん
BAN
ばん
SHUPO (SWUP)
しゅぽ
PASHA (SPLAT)
ぱしゃ
......!
AAAAAH!!
AAAAAAHH!!
YOU CAN HAVE MINE.

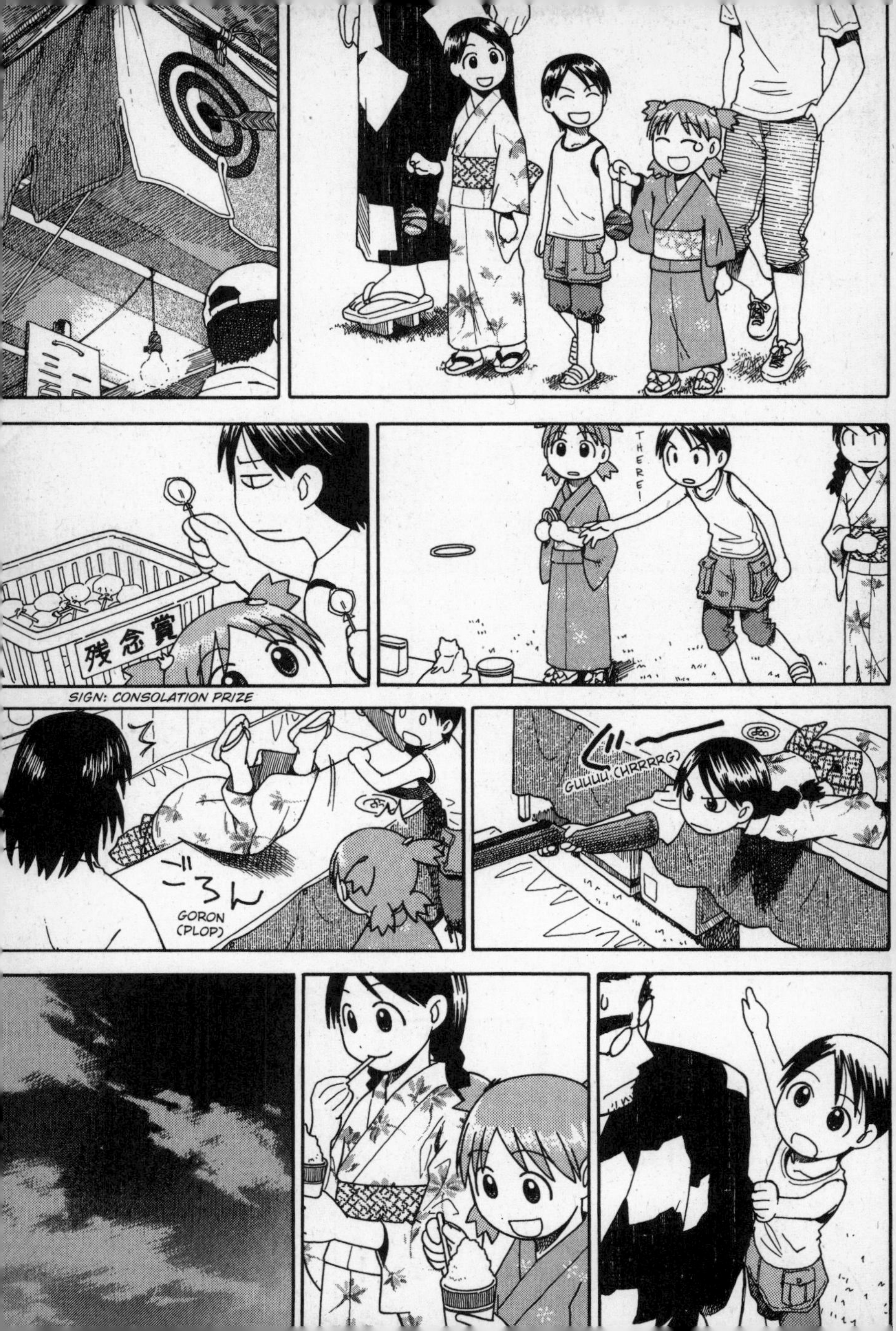
THERE!
残念賞
SIGN: CONSOLATION PRIZE
GUUUU (HRRRRG)
ごろん
GORON (PLOP)

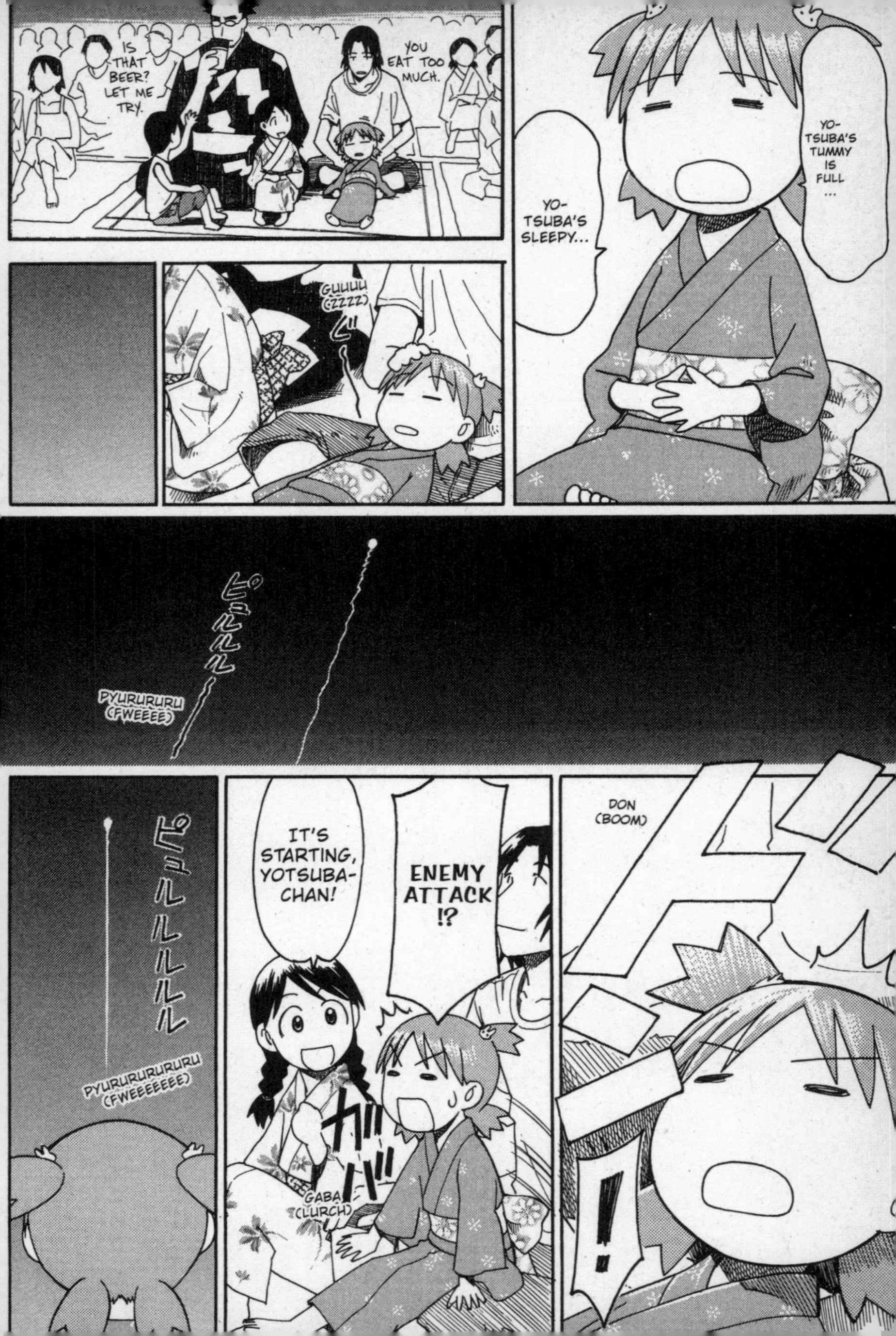
YO-TSUBA'S TUMMY IS FULL ...
YO-TSUBA'S SLEEPY...
YOU EAT TOO MUCH.
IS THAT BEER? LET ME TRY.
GUUUU (ZZZZ)
PYURURURU (FWEEEE)
DON (BOOM)
IT'S STARTING, YOTSUBA-CHAN!
ENEMY ATTACK !?
GABA (LURCH)
PYURURURURURU (FWEEEEEEE)

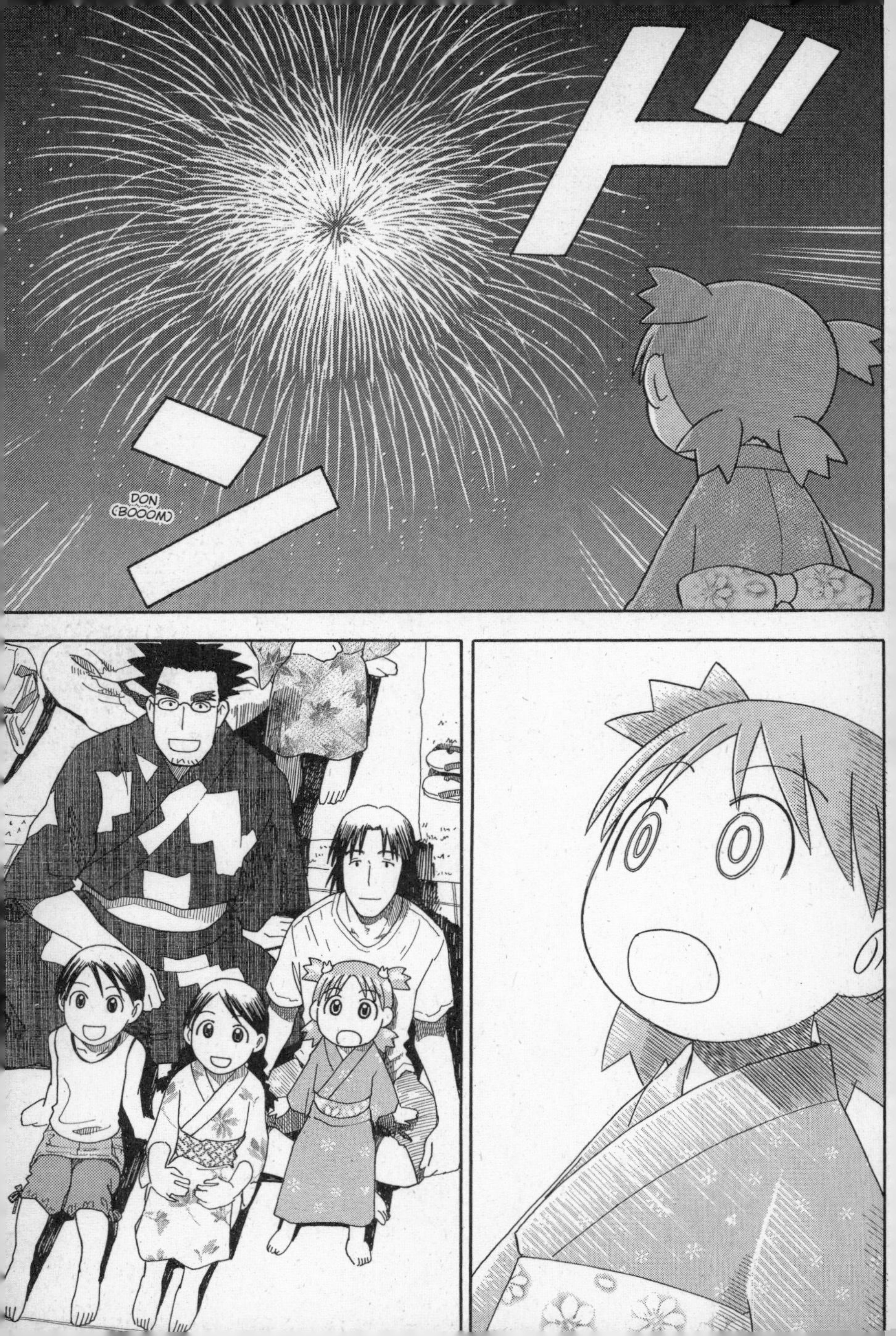
DON (BOOOM)

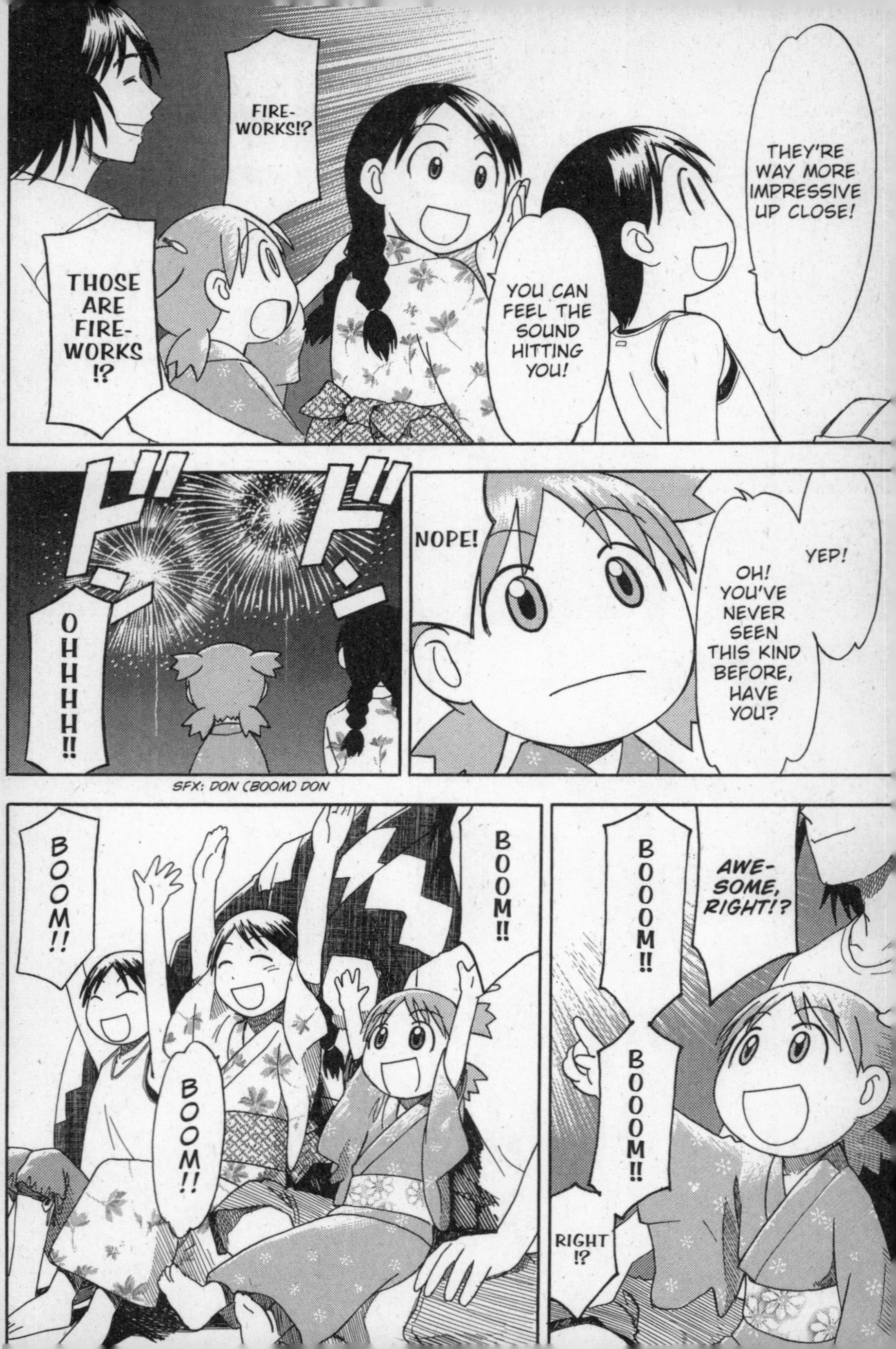
THEY'RE WAY MORE IMPRESSIVE UP CLOSE!
YOU CAN FEEL THE SOUND HITTING YOU!
FIRE-WORKS!?
THOSE ARE FIRE-WORKS !?
YEP!
OH! YOU'VE NEVER SEEN THIS KIND BEFORE, HAVE YOU?
NOPE!
OHHHHH!!
SFX: DON (BOOM) DON
AWE-SOME, RIGHT!?
BOOOOM!!
BOOOOM!!
RIGHT !?
BOOOM!!
BOOOM!!
BOOOM!!

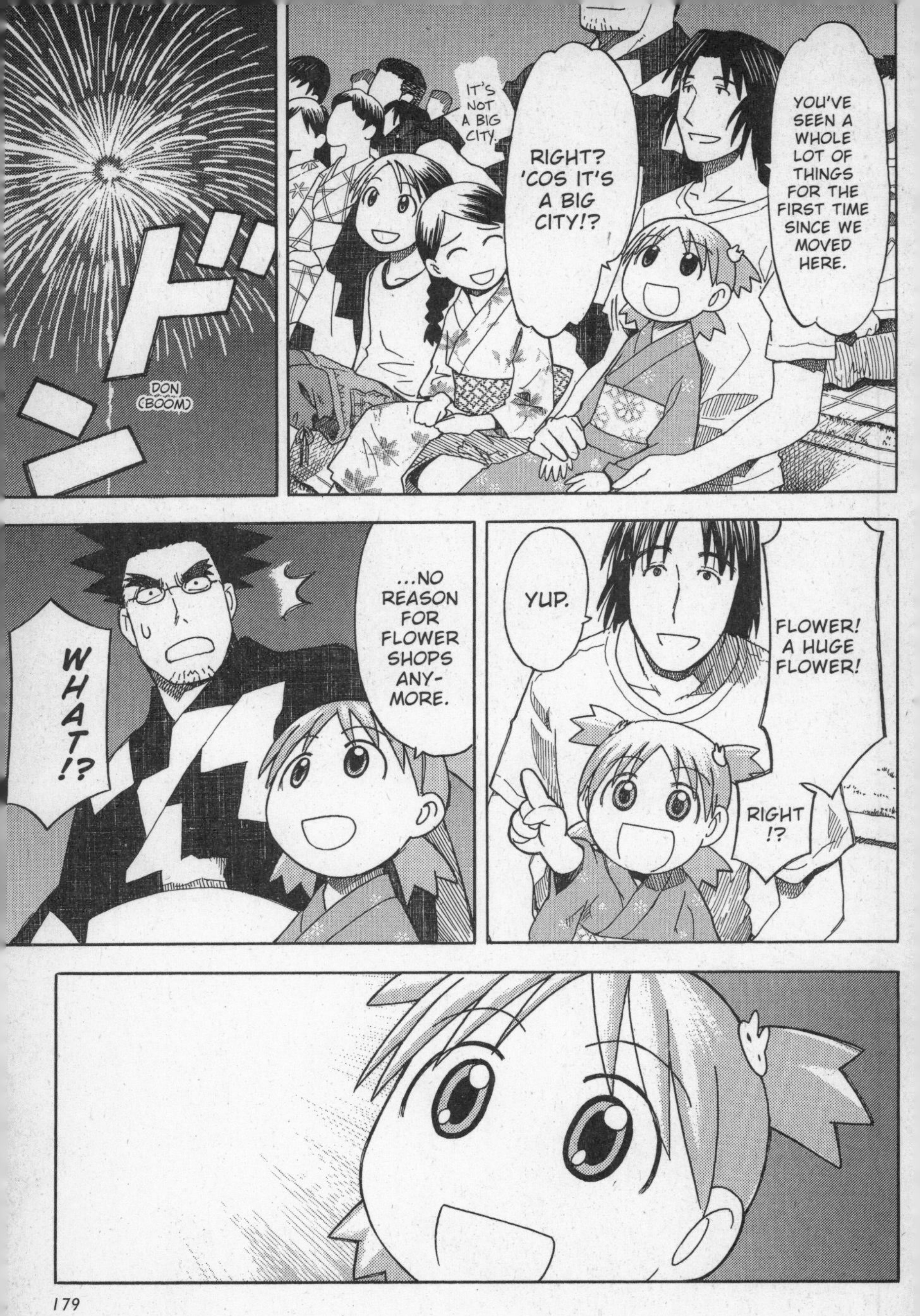
YOU'VE SEEN A WHOLE LOT OF THINGS FOR THE FIRST TIME SINCE WE MOVED HERE.
RIGHT? 'COS IT'S A BIG CITY!?
IT'S NOT A BIG CITY.
ドン
DON (BOOM)
FLOWER! A HUGE FLOWER!
RIGHT!?
YUP.
...NO REASON FOR FLOWER SHOPS ANYMORE.
WHAT!?

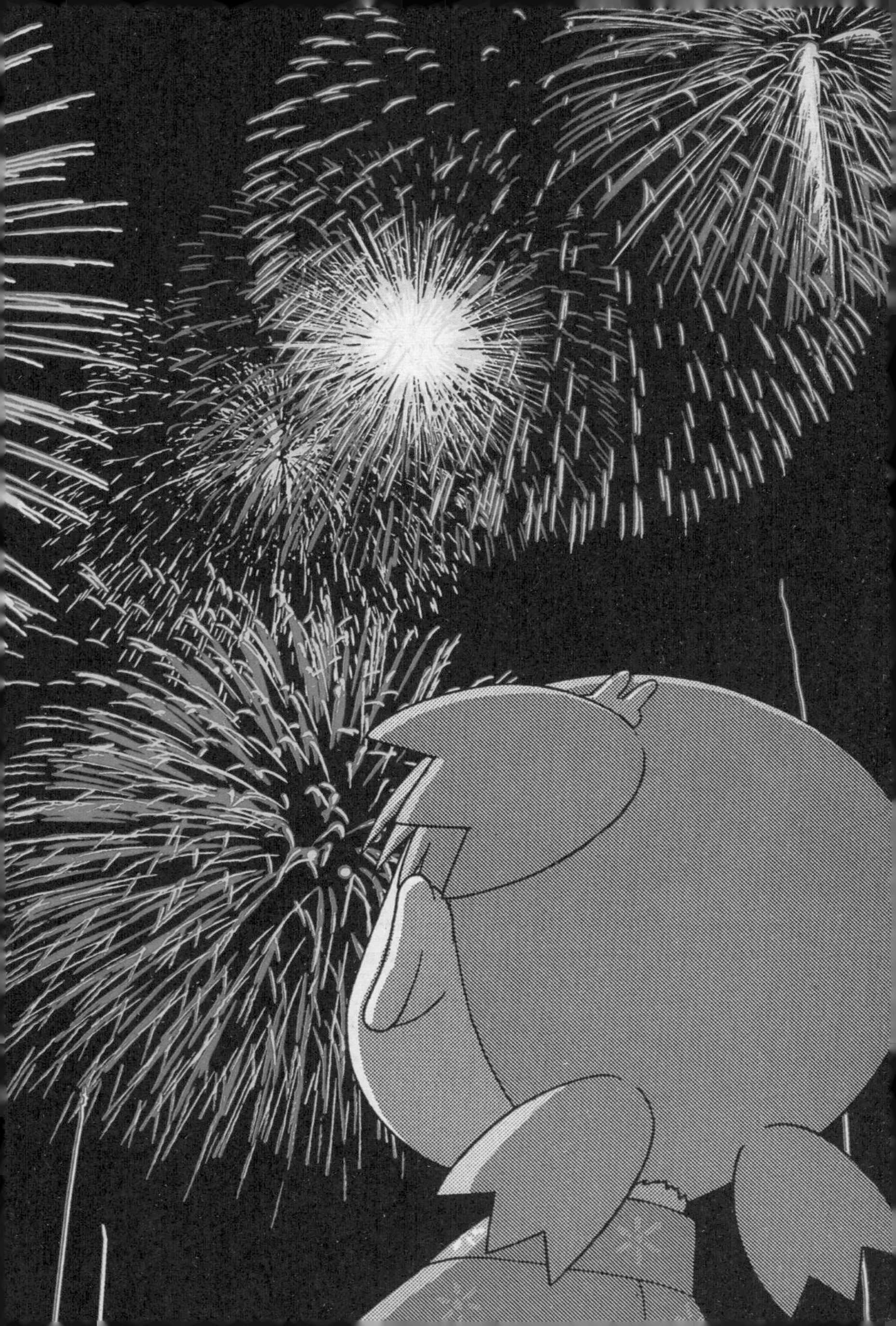

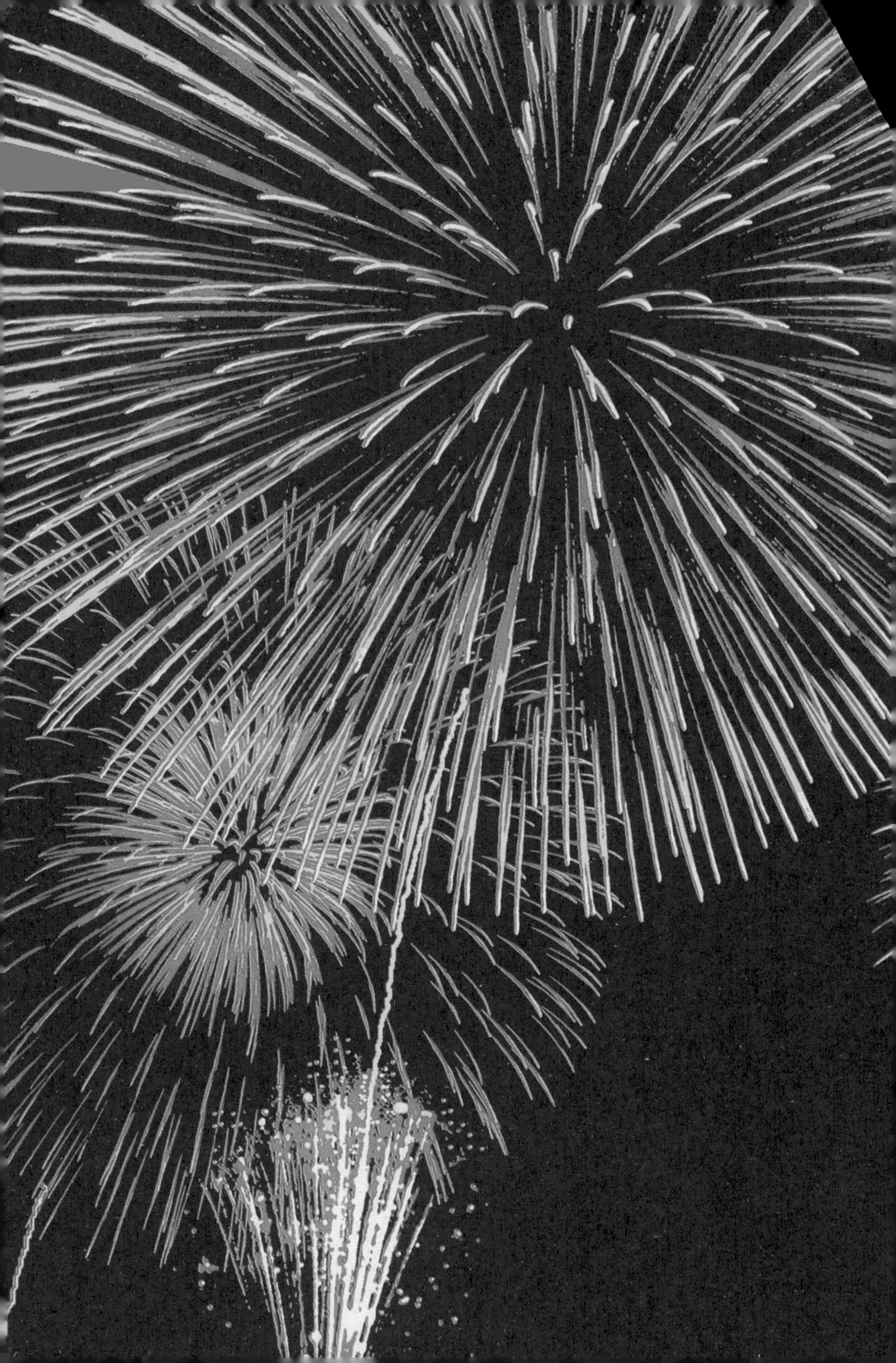

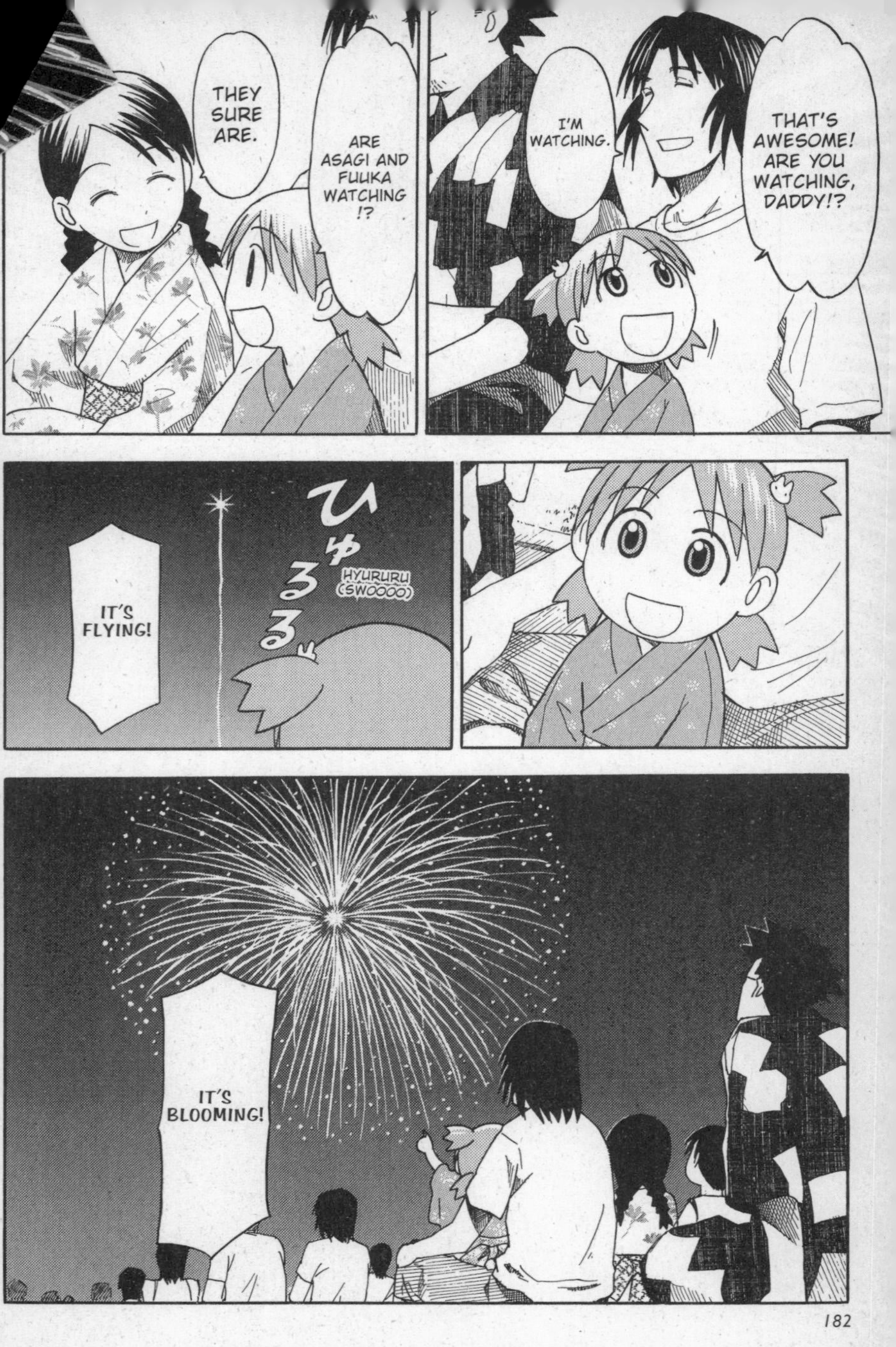
THAT'S AWESOME! ARE YOU WATCHING, DADDY!?
I'M WATCHING.
ARE ASAGI AND FUUKA WATCHING!?
THEY SURE ARE.
ひゅるる
HYURURU (SWOOOO)
IT'S FLYING!
IT'S BLOOMING!

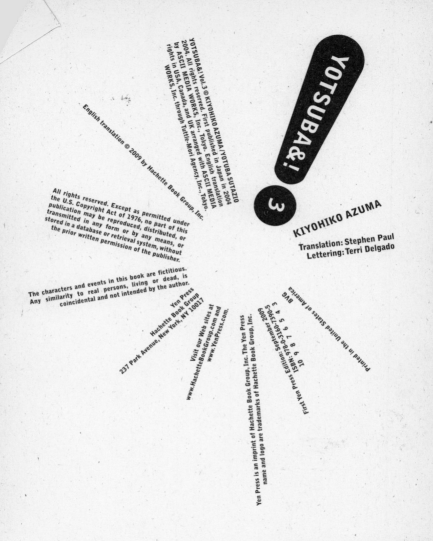

YOTSUBA&!

3

KIYOHIKO AZUMA

Translation: Stephen Paul
Lettering: Terri Delgado

YOTSUBA&!Vol.3 ©KIYOHIKO AZUMA/YOTSUBA SUTAZIO 2004. All rights reserved. First published in Japan in 2004 by ASCII MEDIA WORKS, Inc., Tokyo. English translation rights in USA, Canada and UK arranged with ASCII MEDIA WORKS, Inc. through Tuttle-Mori Agency, Inc., Tokyo.

English translation © 2009 by Hachette Book Group, Inc.

Yen Press
Hachette Book Group
237 Park Avenue, New York, NY 10017

Visit our Web sites at
www.HachetteBookGroup.com and
www.YenPress.com.

Yen Press is an imprint of Hachette Book Group, Inc. The Yen Press name and logo are trademarks of Hachette Book Group, Inc.

First Yen Press Edition: September 2009
ISBN: 978-0-316-07390-5

10 9 8 7 6 5 4 3

BVG

Printed in the United States of America

TO BE CONTINUED!